The Guide to James Joyce's *Ulysses*

# THE GUIDE TO
# JAMES JOYCE'S
# ULYSSES

PATRICK HASTINGS

JOHNS HOPKINS UNIVERSITY PRESS
*Baltimore*

© 2022 Patrick Hastings
All rights reserved. Published 2022
Printed in the United States of America on acid-free paper

2 4 6 8 9 7 5 3

Johns Hopkins University Press
2715 North Charles Street
Baltimore, Maryland 21218-4363
www.press.jhu.edu

Library of Congress Cataloging-in-Publication Data

Names: Hastings, Patrick, 1982– author.
Title: The guide to James Joyce's *Ulysses* / Patrick Hastings.
Description: Baltimore : Johns Hopkins University Press, 2022. |
    Includes bibliographical references and index.
Identifiers: LCCN 2021022700 | ISBN 9781421443492 (paperback)
    | ISBN 9781421443508 (ebook)
Subjects: LCSH: Joyce, James, 1882–1941. Ulysses. | Joyce, James,
    1882–1941—Criticism and interpretation.
Classification: LCC PR6019.O9 U65436 2022 | DDC 823/.912—dc23
LC record available at https://lccn.loc.gov/2021022700

A catalog record for this book is available from the British Library.

All photographs are by the author unless otherwise credited. Maps are
by Jade Myers of Matrix Art Services. Sources consulted in the prepara-
tion of the maps are *The "Ulysses" Guide: Tours through Joyce's Dublin*,
by Robert Nicholson; *Joyce's Dublin: A Walking Guide to "Ulysses,"* by
Jack McCarthy and Danis Rose; and *James Joyce's Dublin: A Topographical
Guide to the Dublin of "Ulysses,"* by Ian Gunn and Clive Hart.

*Special discounts are available for bulk purchases of this book.*
*For more information, please contact Special Sales at specialsales@jh.edu.*

*"Something to hand on"* (*U* 6.74–75)
For Pierce, Bradley, and Renwick

# CONTENTS

**✻**

# PREFACE

In May of 1932, an unwieldly object arrived in the New York City Customs office, and a huffy gentleman demanded that the package be seized as contraband. The customs officer looked down at the offending item, a thick book bulging with papers taped inside its covers, and shrugged at what seemed like a mad genius's strange assemblage of hoarded text.[1] The book was called *Ulysses*, and its would-be American publisher, Random House, had intended for it to be confiscated and tried for obscenity. The book had been banned in most of the English-speaking world since 1921, only increasing the allure and value of *Ulysses* to its publishers, who thought that the novel's place in the modern canon warranted a reweighing of its literary merit against its imagined corrupting influence. Buttressed by the scholarly praise taped into the book (and therefore taken into evidence along with the novel itself), Joyce's masterpiece of modernism would soon be released from the confines of censorship, and its labyrinthine systems of style, characterization, and allusion could then be openly read and puzzled over.

If you are reading this, you are at least considering joining the throng of readers who have been baffled and enthralled by James Joyce's *Ulysses*. Do it. Joyce stated that "if *Ulysses* isn't fit to read, life isn't fit to live" (*JJ* 537). Indeed, this reading experience will enrich and inform your life. But Joyce also said that "the demand that I make of my reader is that he should devote his whole life to reading my works" (*JJ* 703). I have acceded to his demand so that you don't have to, and this book is the fruit of that labor of love.

A transcendent cultural phenomenon, James Joyce's *Ulysses* is celebrated each year on Bloomsday (June 16) in bookstores and pubs across the globe. Now in its second century, the novel remains insurgent and capable of provoking lively debates, yet it may be more famous for its intimidating density than for its emotionally resonant story. Most scholars would agree that a first reading of the novel requires some external support to navigate, appreciate, and ultimately finish the book. For example, a reader must go outside the text to discover even the Homeric chapter titles, which Joyce identified in the schema he privately disclosed to friends and early critics; had Joyce not titled the novel *Ulysses*, the intentional correspondences to *The Odyssey* may have remained more obscure than they already are. In this book, I seek to provide comprehensive, accessible, and insightful guidance as you undertake this emphatically worthwhile but unquestionably demanding reading experience.

While reading (and, ultimately, finishing) Joyce's novel requires some measure of dedication, the rewards are well worth the effort. This guidebook aims to mitigate some of the challenges *Ulysses* poses by providing explanation and context without putting a thumb on too many interpretive scales. Ultimately, I hope to ground you securely enough in the text for you to have your own reading experience and to develop your own interpretive opinions. In this way, my book is oriented primarily toward the first-time reader of *Ulysses* and is by no means an exhaustive study of the novel. Yet, I hope to offer a few ideas that even devoted Joyceans might find engaging.

Most first-time readers of *Ulysses* will find the Episode Guides to be the chief resource of this book. Each Episode Guide focuses on one of the novel's eighteen episodes, blending narrative summary, explanations of style, interpretive insight, seminal criticism, and maps of locations in Dublin. You may find it helpful to read the relevant Episode Guide prior to reading the text itself in order to prepare yourself for what happens in the plot and to provide some conceptual framework for the episode's stylistic innovations. Or, you might prefer to read the chapter in the novel first and then check the Episode Guide afterward to clear up confusing bits and to point out details you might have missed. Regardless of how you choose to use this guidebook, I recommend reading at least one episode of the novel per week. You should aim to complete each of the first eight episodes within the same day (if not in one sitting) in order to build the momentum and confidence you need to finish the book. Joyce trains you in how to read his novel, beginning with challenging but rather short chapters, gradually building your reading muscles so that you are prepared to handle "Scylla and Charybdis," "Oxen of the Sun," and "Circe" later.

In terms of the ergonomics of reading this novel, try reading actively with a pen or pencil at a table or desk. If you want to get answers to a few of the novel's many "what on earth?" passages, get a copy of Don Gifford's *"Ulysses" Annotated* and keep it open beside the novel as you read. But you needn't get bogged down in checking each of the allusions. You may find entire paragraphs and even full pages where you say, "Well, there's a lot of stuff in there that I don't understand." That's fine. Keep going. Even after studying the book carefully for nearly two decades, I still encounter many passages like that. Just accept that there's no way of grasping the entire book in one reading (or five . . . or fifteen); indeed, Joyce hoped that *Ulysses* would "keep the professors busy for centuries" (*JJ* 521). Once you finish reading the novel, you'll want to read it again (if not immediately, then later in life). And no book better rewards rereading than *Ulysses*.

My introduction provides an overview of the novel's plot, outlines its correspondences to Homer's *Odyssey*, explains some of its stylistic innovations, and offers brief biographical information on Joyce, including his major works prior to *Ulysses*. The appendixes contain a variety of useful resources, including chronologies for June 16, 1904 (the single day on which *Ulysses* is set), explanations of the old British system of currency (pounds, shillings, and pence) with its monetary values relative to today, and the schema Joyce privately developed as the skeleton key to unlocking the novel's structure and meaning. If you are interested in delving into the enormous body of critical scholarship related to *Ulysses*, I have provided an annotated bibliography of selected major works related to the novel, and I have listed at the end of each Episode Guide a few articles and essays that might direct your further reading and research regarding that particular episode.

In this guidebook, I strive to help you unpack what that customs officer saw back in 1932: a big, strange, and wonderful book.

# ABBREVIATIONS

The text of *Ulysses* used throughout is *Ulysses: The Corrected Text*, edited by Hans Walter Gabler, with Wolfhard Steppe and Claus Melchior (London: Bodley Head, 2008). It is cited in the introduction by *U*, plus episode, followed by line number, and in the rest of the book simply by episode and line number.

The other abbreviations and editions used in the text are the following:

D       *Dubliners*. New York: Vintage, 1993.

JJ      *James Joyce*, by Richard Ellmann. Rev. ed. New York: Oxford University Press, 1983.

Letters *Letters of James Joyce*. Vol. 1. Edited by Stuart Gilbert. New York: Viking, 1966.

P       *A Portrait of the Artist as a Young Man*. New York: Penguin, 2016.

SH      *Stephen Hero*. New York: New Directions, 1959.

SL      *Selected Letters*. Edited by Richard Ellmann. New York: Viking, 1975.

# INTRODUCTION

I celebrated my first Bloomsday in 2003 at Shakespeare and Company Bookstore on the Left Bank of Paris, where I was spending the summer working the night shift and sleeping in a bed tucked beneath the shelves of this wonderland of books. On the final day of a weeklong literary festival, the shop hosted a series of Joyce-related lectures under a grand white tent in a leafy park nearby. There, I joined a community of readers listening to scholars unfurl dazzling arguments about James Joyce's stylistic innovations in *Ulysses* and his influence on the Lost Generation of expatriate writers living in Paris in the 1920s. When the programmed events under the tent concluded, crowds gathered on the cobblestone esplanade in front of the bookstore to hear impromptu readings of *Ulysses*. At one point, a man gave an unscripted yet impassioned speech, explaining with clarity what actually happens in Joyce's novel and why this work of literature resonates so deeply in the lives of its readers. That night, as I lay awake in my little bed under the bookshelves of Shakespeare and Company, I found myself just as charmed by the appeal of the man's rousing speech on the esplanade as I was engrossed by the scholarly insight conveyed under the tent. I had caught the Joyce bug. It seems to be an incurable condition.

After studying and teaching *Ulysses* for the better part of the next fifteen years, I began a website called UlyssesGuide.com, seeking to bring together the academic discourse of the tent with the accessibility and conviviality of the esplanade. As I gradually added content to the site, it climbed the ranks of internet search results and attracted a dedicated readership; my project seemed to be filling a gap within the thousands of existing works on Joyce's *Ulysses*. This guidebook represents an enhanced version of the content of my website, but my intention remains consistent with my initial project: to equip first-time readers with helpful contextual information, to encourage you through the challenges of this novel, to present my best understanding of the book, and to bring good humor to your experience of this unparalleled work of art.

Before getting into the individual chapters of *Ulysses* in the Episode Guides ahead, I'd like to offer some basic information and a few foundational concepts that will be useful to have in mind as you begin your reading of the novel.

## *Ulysses* and *The Odyssey*

One of humanity's great masterpieces, James Joyce's *Ulysses* celebrates the strength of spirit required to endure the trials of everyday life, exploring the patterns of human thought while also fostering an appreciation for differences among people. Famously, not much happens in this book, yet all of life is contained in its pages. In terms of plot, the novel depicts the events of one day (June 16, 1904) in one smallish European city (Dublin, Ireland) through, mostly, the consciousness of two men, twenty-two-year-old Stephen Dedalus and thirty-eight-year-old Leopold Bloom. Nineteen hours pass.

Stephen has breakfast with his roommates, teaches a class, goes for a walk, engages in a conversation about Shakespeare with other intellectuals, gets drunk, goes to a brothel, and gets knocked out in the street by a belligerent British soldier (Ireland is under English rule). Oh, and Stephen is haunted by the recent death of his mother, for whom he refused to pray on account of his rejection of religion.

Mr. Bloom begins his day by making breakfast for himself and his wife, Molly. He runs some errands in town, attends a funeral, does some business (he works as an advertising agent), has lunch, writes a letter, gets into an argument with an Irish nationalist in a pub, watches fireworks on the beach at sunset, visits a maternity hospital where a friend is in the throes of a difficult labor, crosses paths with Stephen, and decides to look after the drunk young man. Oh, and Bloom's wife has sex with another man in the afternoon. And Bloom knows about it.

Equal parts compelling and mundane, the plot of *Ulysses* is infused with correspondences to *The Odyssey*. Joyce titled the episodes/chapters of his novel with names borrowed from *The Odyssey*, and the plot of *Ulysses* roughly follows that of Homer's epic. Most obviously, Stephen is like Telemachus, a son searching for a suitable father, and Mr. Bloom is like Odysseus, a father hoping to return home and find a son. But whereas the journey of *The Odyssey* spans a decade, the wanderings of *Ulysses* last only one day. Also, Joyce often makes fun of these correspondences; for example, Penelope is famous for her faithfulness in rebuffing her suitors, but Molly Bloom makes a cuckhold of Mr. Bloom on this afternoon. In each Episode Guide, I will provide brief explanations of the relevant Homeric correspondences.

## A Few Elements of Joyce's Writing Style

The plot of *Ulysses* is also enhanced by the style in which Joyce presents the story. Through a combination of innovative narrative techniques, we develop intimacy with the minds of Stephen and Mr. Bloom as they go about their day, reacting to the people and places they encounter, recalling memories of past joys and pains, and wrestling with anxieties over uncertain futures. One of these techniques, inner monologue, directly presents the characters' thoughts in first person. Snatches of inner monologue are woven seamlessly into the narration, such as when Mr. Bloom leaves his home for the first time: "On the doorstep he felt in his hip pocket for the latchkey. Not there. In the trousers I left off. Must get it. Potato I have. Creaky wardrobe. No use disturbing her" (*U* 4.72–74). In this passage, the third-person narrator first describes Mr. Bloom feeling for his key, but the text then shifts to inner monologue as Bloom realizes that his key is in another pair of pants. Such abrupt shifts between narration and inner monologue take some getting used to (and it doesn't help that Joyce uses dashes instead of standard quotation marks to indicate dialogue), but you'll catch the rhythm with practice. Direct, unmediated access to inner monologue compels the reader's growing intimacy with the characters and forces us to make inferences as we follow his mental jumps. Why is Mr. Bloom anxious over disturbing his snoozing wife? What does this say about their marriage? Why does he have a potato? From the beginning, we need the deep knowledge of the characters that we will gain over the course of the novel in order to fully understand their thoughts. Paradoxically, you need to have read *Ulysses* in order to read *Ulysses*. That is, unless you have *The Guide to James Joyce's "Ulysses."* I'll tell you what a first-time reader needs to know so that you can approach the novel with confidence.

Another element of Joyce's style that brings us closer to the characters involves the narrator adopting the sort of language most natural to the individual protagonist in focus. Since Stephen Dedalus is erudite, lyrical, and paranoid, the narrator assumes those qualities in episodes where Stephen is the central character. Then, when the plot shifts focus to Mr. Bloom, the narrator reflects Mr. Bloom's more quirky, bodily, and curious characteristics by attending to sensory details and adopting a more humored attitude. We call this narrative technique of borrowing a character's idiom "the Uncle Charles Principle." This term was coined by a prominent Joycean named Hugh Kenner in ironic reference to a misfired critique of Joyce's writing style: in Joyce's first novel, *A Portrait of the Artist as a Young Man*, a line reads "Uncle Charles repaired to his outhouse" (*P* 53), stilted phrasing that prompted a critic to scoff that "people repair to places in works of fiction of the humblest order."[1] But this critic had failed to grasp that the verb "repair" (meaning "to go to a place") is a stuffy sort of word used by people like Uncle Charles, not James Joyce. In this way, the Uncle Charles Principle allows for even standard narration to assume the flavor of a character.

This combination of techniques, which Joyce called "the initial style" (*Letters* 129) of *Ulysses*, ensures that the reader experiences the plot in the characters' own language, contributing to a sense of immediacy that subtly binds us to the protagonists, Stephen and Mr. Bloom. This initial style dominates the novel's first six episodes, but our proximity to the two protagonists' minds gradually tightens and then loosens in an inverted ABC-CBA sequence.[2] As the first triad introduces Stephen, the "Telemachus" episode (A) uses inner monologue sparingly, instead foregrounding narration in order to represent the drama unfolding between Stephen and his roommates. Our access to Stephen's thoughts gains prominence in "Nestor" (B) as he teaches his class and meets with the headmaster, and it reaches a pinnacle in the largely uninterrupted inner monologue of Stephen walking alone along the beach in the "Proteus" episode (C). In reciprocal echo of these opening episodes, we first meet Mr. Bloom as he goes through his morning routine (largely left to his own thoughts) in "Calypso" (C), but our access to his inner monologue recedes somewhat as he runs errands in "Lotus-Eaters" (B) and even more so in the sixth episode, "Hades" (A), as the narrator reasserts himself to depict the social dynamics of Mr. Bloom attending a funeral with other Dubliners who treat him with various degrees of disregard. By the end of these two introductory triads, we have become intimately familiar with Stephen, Mr. Bloom, and their respective Dublin communities.

Just as we are getting comfortable with the novel's initial style, Joyce starts to mess with us. In the seventh episode, "Aeolus," a series of newspaper headlines interrupt the prose on the page. This oddity announces the emergence of "the arranger," a personality in the novel distinct from the narrator who finds immense pleasure in disrupting and embellishing the text.[3] If Mr. Bloom is the Father and Stephen is the Son, then the arranger is the Holy Ghost completing the Trinity of *Ulysses*. The term "arranger" originates from the phrase "retrospective arrangement," which appears seven times over the course of *Ulysses* and provides a clue to one of the novel's underlying methods. Only by retrospectively looking back and rereading *Ulysses* can we fully appreciate the progression of its style and the interconnected arrangement of its details. As the initial style withdraws, the arranger wields increasing control over the second half of *Ulysses*, playfully manipulating and contributing to the text. We can find the arranger's mischievous genius in the novel's most innovative features—from the panoramic effect of the "Wandering Rocks" episode to the musical prose of "Sirens," from the parodies of "Oxen of the Sun" to the catechism of "Ithaca." Nearly one-fifth of the novel is written as the script of a surreal play! All of the arranger's challenges to novelistic conventions embody literary modernism's break from tradition and spirited imperative to "make it new." While not all scholars agree on the notion of the arranger, I find it to be a useful concept for explaining the audacious stylistic flourishes that coalesce to distinguish the novel. In the Episode Guides ahead, I will point out and explain the arranger's handiwork, helping you make meaning of the novel's inventive new styles. But Joyce helps us, too: each new style builds on techniques introduced earlier in the novel. *Ulysses* therefore relies on our innate human ability to exercise memory and adapt to change.

## James Joyce's Biography and Early Works

Joyce came by his artistic impulse toward change quite naturally; indeed, an unsettled life was perhaps the most consistent element of his biography. In 1888, at the tender age of six, Joyce was uprooted from the comforts of his family home in Dublin to begin his schooling at Clongowes Wood College, a prestigious Jesuit boarding school in County Kildare. Even as the youngest student in the school, he earned renown for his academic achievement and settled into friendships with other boys. Within three years, though, Joyce was withdrawn from Clongowes after his father lost his job and could no longer pay the tuition. Over the next eleven years, constant instability influenced Joyce's formative years as his family relocated nine times, often because of eviction or to elude creditors.[4] In the midst of this domestic turmoil, adolescent Joyce began writing brief sketches he called "Epiphanies," which shaped mundane moments into literature, similar to the idea behind the "found object" sculpture of modernists such as Marcel Duchamp. Sensing significance in everyday incidents, Joyce "believed that it was for the man of letters to record these epiphanies with extreme care, seeing that they themselves are the most delicate and evanescent of moments" (*SH* 211). This interest in writing about common people and unremarkable events would define Joyce's career.

After a brief spell in Paris, Joyce returned to Dublin to be present at the death of his mother. He then spent a year drifting between studying medicine, law, and literature; he dabbled in teaching, lived sometimes at home and for other periods with friends, eventually bunking up with Oliver St. John Gogarty in the Martello tower in Sandycove. After a falling out with Gogarty in September of 1904, Joyce left the tower in the middle of the night and departed Dublin for the Continent soon thereafter. This time, his exile from Ireland would be final, and he was accompanied by Nora Barnacle, the woman with whom he would spend the rest of his life. The couple had two children as they hopped around Europe, moving from Pula to Trieste to Rome, back to Trieste, to Zurich, and eventually back to Paris.

During the first few years Joyce spent away from Dublin, he wrote the *Dubliners* short stories, which developed his interest in representing everyday sorts of people and their problems. As in the "Epiphanies," Joyce's stories sought to depict reality—even its unpleasant aspects—as accurately as possible. His uncompromising commitment to realism would present obstacles to the publication of his works in an era of lingering Victorianism and harsh censorship laws. In one clash over *Dubliners*, a publisher objected to Joyce's use of the word "bloody" (among other perceived indecencies), but Joyce held firm that he "absolutely could not alter" his word choice (*SL* 85); the character Jack Mooney must use the word "bloody" because, well, that's the kind of language guys like Jack Mooney use. Joyce conceived of his literature as a "nicely polished looking-glass" (*Letters* 64) reflecting the real world back on itself. If what the mirror shows is disgusting, don't blame the mirror.

Joyce's next major work was *A Portrait of the Artist as a Young Man*, his 1916 quasi-autobiographical novel that narrates the life of Stephen Dedalus from infancy to young adulthood. In this novel, Joyce charts the development of Stephen's consciousness from the rudimentary thoughts of a toddler to the widely read, soaring intellect that we will encounter from the beginning of *Ulysses*. To present the progression of Stephen's mind, Joyce relied on a narrative technique called free indirect discourse, which allows the narrator to present a character's thoughts and feelings while maintaining standard third-person past tense (whereas inner monologue uses first-person present tense). Joyce will continue to use this technique in *Ulysses*. By the end of *A Portrait*, Stephen's Luciferian rejection of religion, nation, and family leads him to pursue a life of freedom, artistic creation, and self-imposed exile. The sensibilities and innovations of *A Portrait* made Joyce a principal figure of the modernist literary movement by 1920, when he settled in Paris and joined a community of writers including Ernest Hemingway, Valery Larboud, Ezra Pound, Robert McAlmon, and F. Scott Fitzgerald.

In Paris, Joyce formed a particularly close friendship with Sylvia Beach, the American owner of Shakespeare and Company Bookstore on the Left Bank. When nobody in the English-speaking world would publish *Ulysses* owing to strict censorship laws, Sylvia Beach rescued the novel. What's more, she afforded Joyce unfettered freedom to revise, allowing him to compose upward of a third of *Ulysses* at the proof stage of the publication process.[5] As he added and arranged codependent details all over the novel, he displaced paragraphs and full pages of text on the printing plates. Despite the extraordinary expense Sylvia incurred by allowing these revisions, she remained steadfast in her commitment to allowing Joyce to shape *Ulysses* as he envisioned it. Now that *Ulysses* has celebrated the centenary of its 1922 first edition publication and entered its second century as a literary monument, we should honor Sylvia Beach alongside James Joyce for giving humanity the gift of this novel.

In reading *Ulysses*, you are sharing in that gift, providing yourself with an experience of human expression and self-exploration unlike any other. Let's enjoy it together.

# EPISODE GUIDES

# Chapter 1

# "TELEMACHUS" GUIDE

*U*lysses begins on the rooftop of the Martello tower in Sandycove at 8:00 a.m. on June 16, 1904. Buck Mulligan, a medical student in his twenties, looks out over this bayside suburb just south of Dublin and begins to parody the Catholic mass as he prepares to shave his face. He calls back down "the dark winding stairs" (1.6) for Stephen Dedalus to join him in the mild morning air.

Some readers might mistake Buck Mulligan for the protagonist of *Ulysses*; his wit and charisma dominate the book's first few pages. Those who have read Joyce's first novel, *A Portrait of the Artist as a Young Man*, however, have followed Stephen Dedalus from infancy through school to his young adulthood's grand aspiration to "forge in the smithy of [his] soul the uncreated conscience of [his] race" (*P* 235). Called to a life of artistic freedom beyond the encumbering "nets" of his family, his religion, and his nation, Stephen had left Dublin in April 1902 and moved to Paris. His self-imposed exile was cut short about a year later when he was called home to say goodbye to his dying mother before her passing on June 26, 1903. Nearly a year after her death, Stephen remains in Dublin, paralyzed by guilt, poverty, and frustration over his failure to realize his lofty ambitions. At this point, Stephen is more Icarus than Daedalus. Plus, his living situation is less than ideal: his roommates are Buck Mulligan, a frenemy who mercilessly needles him, and Haines, a well-meaning but naive Oxford-educated Englishman who regards Stephen as a curiosity.

The Sandycove Martello tower in relation to Dublin

Before we get into the events of the episode, we should situate "Telemachus" in the context of its two principal correspondences, Homer's epic poem *The Odyssey* and Shakespeare's *Hamlet*. *The Odyssey* begins with Telemachus, Odysseus's adolescent son, depressed and surrounded by suitors vying to marry his mother and aiming to usurp his rightful kingdom on the Greek island of Ithaca. Telemachus has grown up without a father's guidance because Odysseus/Ulysses has been away for roughly seventeen years, first fighting the Trojan War (as depicted in *The Iliad*) and then wandering around the Mediterranean on a troubled journey home (as depicted in *The Odyssey*). Shakespeare's *Hamlet* begins with Prince Hamlet mourning the death of his father and seething over his mother's hasty remarriage to his uncle, Claudius, who has usurped the prince's rightful throne. Both Hamlet and Telemachus begin their respective stories in a state of angst and dispossession, and both are sons without fathers. In these and other

ways, Stephen Dedalus fits into their lineage. They are his literary an-
cestors.

It is Buck Mulligan, however—whose character corresponds to the
usurpers Claudius in *Hamlet* and Antinous in *The Odyssey*—who oc-
cupies the spotlight at the outset of *Ulysses*. As Buck blasphemously
mocks the liturgy, Stephen emerges onto the rooftop; Buck "ben[ds]
toward him and ma[kes] rapid crosses in the air, gurgling in his throat
and shaking his head" (1.12–13), playing as if Stephen is possessed by a
demon. At this gesture specifically and at his situation generally, Stephen is "displeased and sleepy" (1.13). Buck's continued parody uses
scientific terminology to describe the miracle of transubstantiation;
he is a blasphemous atheist, a strict materialist.

You may notice that the novel's opening scene depicts a fairly unremarkable event (an obnoxious young man shaves his face while an-
tagonizing his dour roommate), but the epic setting of the tower and
Joyce's careful prose instill a sense that each detail is laden with meaning and significance. Perhaps Buck's "equine" face and "oak"-hued hair
signal that he is a Trojan horse (1.15–16), but those details also simply
describe the appearance of his head. This tension between realism and
metaphor is central to Joyce's writing; he intended to use his art to
imbue mundane events with spiritual meaning, to "convert the bread
of everyday life into something that has a permanent artistic life of its
own."[1] Through *Ulysses*'s layered correspondences, Joyce elevates ordinary people and situations into the realm of myth, and the genius
of the text allows for multiple levels of interrogation. Rest assured,
though, that you don't have to consider the figurative significance of
each detail in order to understand or even enjoy this novel—certainly
not on a first reading.

That said, we should pause a moment to consider the word
"Chrysostomos" (1.26). This one-word sentence, an interruption in
the narration, provides our first access to Stephen's inner monologue.
He notices Buck's "white teeth glistening here and there with gold
points" (1.25–26) and thinks of St. John Chrysostomos, "the Church
father famed for his rhetorical skill."[2] In Greek, "Chrysostomos" means
"golden mouthed," and Stephen here refers simultaneously to Buck's
gift of gab as well as the gold fillings in his mouth.[3] This label, the first
of two Stephen will mentally apply to Buck in "Telemachus," reveals

Stephen's incisive intelligence and erudition. His inner monologue constantly makes references that will require most readers to open Don Gifford's *"Ulysses" Annotated* for clarification. My general advice: seek explanations for the allusions that genuinely pique your curiosity, but please don't feel compelled to look up everything that you don't know. Lots of stuff is going to fly over your head. Let it.

"In friendly jest" (1.35), Buck Mulligan starts teasing Stephen over his name: Stephen (a martyr) Dedalus (a cunning inventor). Note Buck's repeated attempts to apply names and labels to Stephen in these opening pages: "Kinch" (1.8), "fearful jesuit" (1.8), "absurd" (1.34), "jejune jesuit" (1.45), "the bard" (1.73), "poor dogsbody" (1.112), "Oxford manner[ed]" (1.54), "sinister" (1.94), "hyperborean" (1.92), "lovely mummer" (1.97), "impossible person" (1.222), and "insane" (1.129). Mulligan claims that "kinch" is the best of these labels, identifying it with "the knife blade" (1.55), but he's being coy; the term also refers to an errand boy for the prostitutes in a brothel—a much more sharply barbed nickname than Buck is willing to admit.[4] Indeed, most of these labels are insults, yet their quantity demonstrates the difficulty of pinning down Stephen's protean character. The man is too complex for easy definition. Plus, these repeated efforts to name Stephen contrast with Stephen's precision in labeling Buck. Mulligan draws attention to his own "absurd" dactylic name, Malachi Mulligan, described as "tripping and sunny" with a "Hellenic ring" (1.41–42). The name "Malachi" references three individuals: a Hebrew prophet, an Irish king, and an Irish archbishop; therefore, Buck's given name primes him to lead a new spiritual movement.[5]

Finally breaking his silence, Stephen asks, "How long is Haines going to stay in this tower?" (1.49). Haines, a visiting Oxford student interested in Irish culture, woke Stephen up in the night, yelling through a nightmare about shooting a black panther. Concerned that another nightmare might prompt Haines to fire a shot, Stephen asks where Haines keeps his gun case. In fact, James Joyce (the source for Stephen) lived in the Sandycove Martello tower for part of 1904 with two other young men, Oliver St. John Gogarty (the source for Buck Mulligan) and Samuel Trench (the source for Haines). One night, Trench had a nightmare and actually shot his revolver at the fireplace beside Joyce's bed. Later that night, when Trench woke up a second time yelling about a panther, Oliver St. John Gogarty grabbed the gun from Trench, saying "Leave him to me!" and fired at the pans hanging on the wall above Joyce's head. The pans came clattering down on top of Joyce, who got up and left the tower in the middle of the night, never to return (*JJ* 175).[6] In *Ulysses*, Stephen threatens to leave the tower if Haines stays. In this way, Stephen brandishes "exile," one of the three weapons with which he armed himself back in *A Portrait* (along with "silence" and "cunning" [*P* 229]).

Buck agrees that Haines is "dreadful" (1.51), but his antagonism remains trained on Stephen. He intrusively "thrust[s] a hand into Stephen's upper pocket" (1.67–68) to borrow a "dirty crumpled handkerchief" (1.71), which he derides as "the bard's noserag! A new colour for our Irish poets: snotgreen" (1.73). Stephen remains silent, presumably unamused, as Buck elaborates on "the snotgreen sea" as "our great sweet mother" (1.78, 80). The notion of the sea-mother shifts Buck's attention to Stephen's late mother and the events surrounding her death. Buck says, "The aunt thinks you killed your mother" (1.88), referring to Stephen's unwillingness to kneel down and pray for his mother on her deathbed—a refusal of her dying wish. Buck finds "something sinister" (1.94) in Stephen and considers him overly hyperborean, a term Nietzsche uses to describe an elite intellectual class aloof from the common masses and independent of Christian morality. While we may be inclined to agree with Buck's condemnation of Stephen's cruel denial of his mother's final request, we might also find reasons to respect Stephen's integrity. In *A Portrait*, Stephen assumes a Luciferian posture in stating that he "will not serve that in which I no longer believe whether it call itself my home, my fatherland, or my church" (*P* 229); because Stephen no longer believes, praying at his mother's bedside would have been an insincere sacrilege. Paradoxically, his refusal to pray is respectful of God. For this decision, he feels immense guilt but not regret.

The paragraph beginning at line 100 conveys this guilt while initiating the reader into the novel's revolutionary technique of quickly shifting between narrative modes. This paragraph begins with a description in highly detailed realism ("the fraying edge of his shiny black coatsleeve") to lyrical free indirect discourse[7] ("pain, that was not yet the pain of love, fretted his heart") to the narration of Stephen's nightmare of his mother ("silently, in a dream, she had come to him after her death") back to description and imagery ("across the threadbare cuffedge he saw the sea . . . a dull green mass of liquid"), which Stephen then associates with the memory of his mother's death-bed ("the green sluggish bile which she had torn up from her rotting liver by fits of loud groaning vomiting"). Joyce doesn't provide much if any guidance through these shifts, but he is subtly training us in how to read this novel.

While we're on the topic of Joyce's writing style: if you are approaching *Ulysses* expecting to experience a paragon of English prose, you might be surprised by the preponderance of adverbs in the first episode. On the novel's opening page alone, we find characters doing things "gently," "coarsely," "solemnly," "gravely," "coldly," "smartly," "sternly," "briskly," "gravely" (again), "quietly," and "gaily."[8] This over-reliance on adverbs, a quirk typical of immature writers, represents our first indication that the various styles Joyce uses in *Ulysses* reflect and comment on the novel's characters and content; the angsty tension between Buck and Stephen is a product of their immaturity, so the narration adopts a characteristic of adolescent writing to suggest that these young men need to grow up.

Buck asks about the pants he handed down to Stephen, drawing attention to Stephen's embarrassing poverty and significant indebtedness (we learn in the next episode that he owes Buck £9, roughly equivalent to US$2,700 in 2020 money). Masking his antagonism as generosity, Buck offers to give him another pair of pants, but Stephen "can't wear them if they are grey" (1.120) because he is still wearing black in bereavement. Again, you might be tempted to agree with Buck over Stephen's absurd contradictions: "He kills his mother but he can't wear grey trousers" (1.122). But that's an oversimplification of the nuances of Stephen's situation: his sincere grief over the death of his mother is made all the more painful by his guilt.[9]

Buck continues to alternate between aggressive thrusts and testing embraces. He casually tells Stephen that there's gossip around town that Stephen has "g.p.i." (1.128), a euphemism for syphilis.[10] Not a rumor you want out there. Buck then shoves a mirror in Stephen's face and demands he look at himself. We get our first sustained access to Stephen's inner monologue: "Hair on end. As he and others see me. Who chose this face for me? This dogsbody to rid of vermin. It asks me too" (1.136–37). Stephen eventually offers a witticism, identifying the broken mirror as "a symbol for Irish art. The cracked lookingglass of a servant" (1.146). This symbolism conveys Joyce's own rejection of the early twentieth-century Irish literary movement as introspective, warped, self-pitying, and submissive. This pithy expression reminds Buck of Stephen's cleverness, and he seeks to ingratiate himself out of fear that Stephen might disparage him through an unflattering depiction in a future work of literature. Sorry, Mulligan/Gogarty. Too little, too late.

Hoping to ease the tension of their intellectual dueling and mutual distrust, Buck entices Stephen to join his materialist movement and Hellenize Ireland. He links his arm with Stephen's (as Cranly did toward the end of *A Portrait*) and attempts to shift Stephen's attention toward a common enemy, the Englishman Haines, suggesting they "give [Haines] a ragging" (1.163), launching Stephen's mind to imagine the scene of Clive Kempthorpe's hazing at Oxford. Stephen, a pacifist, would prefer to "let [Haines] stay" (1.177) rather than to instigate this sort of violence. He also seems to associate this sort of chauvinism with the phrases "to ourselves" (the Sinn Fein Irish independence movement), "new paganism" (a Romantic Celtic revival), and "*omphalos*" (an esoteric Greek word explained by Stuart Gilbert to mean the Delphic navel of the Earth), a "seat of prophetic power."[11] In this context, Buck seems to have conceived of the Martello tower as a new Delphi (and, to be fair, it does resemble a huge belly button). Stephen "free[s] his arm quietly" (1.182) from Buck's embrace in silent rejection of these appeals. When forced to choose between union and independence, Stephen will almost always choose the creative freedom afforded by independence.

Faced with this rejection, Buck asks, "What have you against me now?" (1.180). Stephen explains that he was offended when Buck once referred to him as "only Dedalus whose mother is beastly dead" (1.198–99). Buck explains that he "didn't mean to offend the memory of [Stephen's] mother" (1.214–15)—as a medical professional, he is desensitized to death. But Buck has misunderstood Stephen, who is "not thinking of the offence to [his] mother" but rather "of the offence to [himself]" (1.218, 220). Here, Stephen might mean that he was offended by Buck's callous and harsh language, but we might also take him to mean he was offended by Buck saying, "It's *only* Dedalus" (emphasis mine), thus minimizing Stephen's importance. "Impossible person" (1.222) indeed. Buck accuses Stephen of having "the cursed jesuit strain in [him], only it's injected the wrong way" (1.209), meaning that Stephen is zealously devout in his disbelief. As the scholar Sam Slote puts it, Stephen "has one more net to fly by, the net of his own pretentious egoistic self-determination."[12]

Haines calls to Mulligan from within the tower, and Buck heads down to make breakfast. As he descends the stairs, he pauses to implore Stephen to "give up the moody brooding" (1.235–36), echoing Claudius in *Hamlet* and Antinous in *The Odyssey*. Stephen hears Buck singing Yeats's "Who Goes with Fergus?" in the stairwell. Coincidentally, Stephen sang exactly this song at the request of his crying mother on her deathbed, so Buck's unfortunate song choice prompts Stephen to remember his mother's life and death even more poignantly. Take note here that "a cloud began to cover the sun" (1.248) at around 8:15 a.m.; we will see this same cloud in the "Calypso" episode, which also begins at 8:00 a.m. but across town in the home of Mr. Leopold Bloom. After thinking of *Turko the Terrible*, a popular pantomime about a magical kingdom, Stephen broods on memories of his mother and recalls again her reproachful appearance to him in a dream. He mentally recites a Latin prayer for the dying (*"Liliata rutilantium . . ."* [1.276–77]). Horrified by these haunting images, he exclaims within his inner monologue, "No, mother! Let me be and let me live" (1.279). This assertive statement echoes Telemachus standing up to his mother, Penelope, in the first book of *The Odyssey*.

From within the tower, Buck calls up to Stephen that "breakfast is ready" (1.284). Stephen is so traumatized by his dark thoughts regarding his mother that he will gladly escape them by going into the tower; he even hears Buck's voice as "friendly" (1.283). Buck's head pops out of the staircase to tell Stephen that Haines is charmed by his witticism about the cracked mirror and encourages Stephen to get money from the Englishman. Stephen announces that he will receive his monthly salary from his job as a schoolteacher this morning, and Buck's spirits lift as he foresees getting "glorious drunk" (1.297) on Stephen's tab later in the day. Mulligan descends the stairs again, and Stephen notices that Buck left his shaving bowl on the parapet. He contemplates whether to "bring it down? Or leave it there all day" as an emblem of their "for-gotten friendship" (1.307–08). He decides to do Buck this favor, and carrying the bowl reminds him that he also "carried the boat of incense then at Clongowes" (1.311) as a schoolboy. He contemplates his physi-cal and spiritual development since those days, thinking "I am another now and yet the same" (1.311–12). Questions over the continuity of identity will arise in characters' minds repeatedly over the course of the novel. Regardless of whether Stephen is the same as he was as a child, he remains "a server of a servant" (1.312); he serves Buck, a servant of Ireland, in turn a servant of England, just as he served the Clongowes priests, servants to Rome. Presented with these heavy, systemic layers of subservience, perhaps we now begin to appreciate the strength of spirit and unwavering commitment required of Stephen to free himself.

The setting shifts to "the gloomy domed livingroom of the tower" (1.313), where Buck prepares a pan-fried breakfast for the three young men. Smoke from the stove begins to fill the room, and Buck asks Haines, the shadowy "tall figure" (1.319) sitting on the hammock, to open the door. Haines asks the whereabouts of the key to the tower, and Buck responds that "Dedalus has it" (1.323) because he pays the rent. In fact, the key is already in the lock, and Haines turns it to open the door to the morning's "light and bright air" (1.328). Buck finishes cooking, again parodies religious language in his mock blessing, and then curses when he realizes that "there's no milk" (1.336) for his tea because the milkwoman is late in her delivery to the tower. Contrast-ing with Stephen's more cosmopolitan suggestion that they use lemon to flavor their tea, Buck "wants Sandycove milk" (1.342–43).

English Haines announces the milkwoman's approach and com-ments on the strength of Buck's tea, prompting Mulligan to quote from a crude Irish folk song: "when I makes tea I makes tea, as old mother Grogan said. And when I makes water I makes water" (1.357–58). Making water means urinating, so "don't make them in the one pot" (1.362). Tongue in cheek, Buck then presents this lyric as an item for inclusion in the book Haines plans to write about Irish culture. Haines's interest in the Irish is condescending but not malicious. Buck tries to involve Stephen in the joke of elevating Mother Grogan's scat-ological humor to the lofty heights of the Hindu sacred text of the Upanishads or the Welsh *Mabinogion*'s tales; Stephen "gravely" (1.372) declines to play along. Rather, he suggests that Mother Grogan more likely shares kinship with Mary Ann, a bawdy character from Irish folk songs. Buck slices bread and sings a song featuring Mary Ann.

With imagery that alludes to Athena's entrance in book 1 of *The Odyssey*, the milkwoman enters the tower. Stephen's inner monologue vividly imagines this old woman milking the cows this morning and identifies her as the archetypal Old Mother Ireland, worn haggard from centuries of oppression. In "scornful silence" (1.418), Stephen's thoughts reveal his resentment toward the Irish Mother's preference of Dr. Buck over him. Haines speaks Irish to her, which she mistakes for French, evidencing the shortcomings of an Irish Mother who does not recognize her own language. Certainly, there's a touch of irony in Haines speaking Irish, and the Englishman suggests that they "ought to speak Irish in Ireland" (1.431–32)—a rather patronizing opinion, especially given that the English outlawed the language. Buck pays most of the bill while munching on the bread he gluttonously "buttered on both sides" (1.447). The milkwoman leaves.

The men then review the day's agenda: Stephen will go teach (and receive his monthly salary) this morning, Buck is eager to drink on Stephen's tab, and Haines needs to visit the National Library, but first they must wash themselves with a swim in the bay. Stephen is teased for rarely bathing; we learn in the "Ithaca" episode that his last bath occurred eight months ago. His hydrophobia may be rooted in a rejection of his baptism, or perhaps he avoids water owing to the trauma of being shouldered into pond scum as a kid back at Clongowes. To justify not bathing, Stephen suggests that "all Ireland is washed by the gulfstream" (1.476). As they prepare to leave the tower, Haines says to Stephen, "I intend to make a collection of your sayings if you will let me" (1.480). Stephen attributes Haines's interest in Irish culture to an effort to "wash and tub and scrub" (1.481) away his English guilt. Stephen's inner monologue notes Haines's "Agenbite of inwit" (1.481), which means "remorse of conscience" in Middle English. He associates Haines's Hibernophilia with Lady Macbeth's sleep-washing of her bloody hands ("yet here's a spot" [1.482]).[13] So, Stephen recalls centuries-old expressions of guilt in his oppressor's language to imply the longevity of English subjugation of the Irish. He's off-the-charts smart.

With a covert kick under the table, Buck begins to hype Stephen's theory about Hamlet, hoping that Stephen will play along. Rather rudely, Stephen asks if he would profit financially from contributing his witticisms to Haines's project. Haines ducks the awkwardness of Stephen's blunt solicitation and walks away, and Buck then rebukes Stephen's tactlessness. Remember, though, that Stephen is poor. His family is destitute. At the forefront of his mind, "the problem is to get money. From whom? From the milkwoman or from him. It's a toss up, I think" (1.497–98). Regardless of whether he seeks income from poor Old Ireland or wealthy England, he "see[s] little hope" (1.501) from either. Buck offers himself as a potential source of support.

In anticipation of a swim in Forty Foot bathing area, "Mulligan is stripped of his garments" (1.510) (an allusion to the Stations of the Cross), and Stephen prepares to walk to his teaching job in Dalkey by putting on his wide-brimmed "Latin quarter hat," "taking his ash-plant" walking cane, and dropping "the huge key in his inner pocket" (1.530). They descend the ladder to the ground, and, walking to the water, Haines inquires about the tower. Buck explains that they were built by the English to defend the coast against an anticipated Napoleonic invasion; he also claims that their tower is "the *omphalos*" (1.544), meaning both the architectural source for the other towers and the center of his secular Irish literary movement.

Haines comments that the tower and the rocky coast of Sandycove remind him of Elsinore (the setting for much of Shakespeare's *Hamlet*) and presses Stephen on his Hamlet theory, but Buck claims to need "a few pints" (1.548) before he can listen to the absurd complexity of Stephen's argument: "He proves by algebra that Hamlet's grandson is Shakespeare's grandfather and that he himself is the ghost of his own father" (1.555–56). Baffled, Haines offers halting comments on *Hamlet*, receiving no reply from Stephen. Haines tosses out "a theological interpretation" of the play, "the Father and Son idea. The Son striving to be atoned with the Father" (1.577–78). These ideas pertaining to father-son consubstantiality seem inadequately developed here, but they will be expounded upon in the "Scylla and Charybdis" episode when Stephen finally delivers his much anticipated *Hamlet* lecture in the National Library.[14]

Buck recites his "Ballad of Joking Jesus" as he "caper[s]" (1.600) down to the water. More blasphemy. More pee jokes. We might begin to see Buck as something of a one-trick pony. But he is funny enough, as Haines laughs at Buck's clowning before checking himself now that he's walking alone with Stephen. Haines attempts to engage Stephen on questions of religious faith and a "personal God" (1.613), but Stephen's treatment of Haines echoes Hamlet's toying with Polonius. Haines removes from his pocket "a smooth silver case in which twinkled a green stone" (1.615–16), which may symbolize emerald Ireland as a charming trinket in England's possession. Still, Stephen accepts the cigarette Haines has offered. Stephen's silent monologue imagines Buck and Haines returning to the tower in the dark this night and presciently foresees Buck asking for the key. Stephen claims legitimate possession because he paid the rent; in the schema, Joyce listed "the dispossessed son in struggle" as the meaning for the "Telemachus" episode (see appendix D). As the scholar Stanley Sultan explains in his book *The Argument of "Ulysses,"* "the struggle is for rule of the Martello tower, the common home of the poet and the scientist, [and] the symbol of control is, quite properly, the key. Ancient tradition held that the poet rules Ireland, that he sits on the right hand of the king in council, and that his wisdom prevails. Correspondingly, Stephen possesses the key. But today it changes hands."[15] As we shall soon see.

You have to admire Haines's persistence in trying to engage Stephen, who is more or less ignoring the Englishman. Stephen realizes, however, that his antipathy toward Haines might be unfair; the Englishman may be a dolt, but he is "not all unkind" (1.635). As a result, Stephen relaxes his posture and explains that he serves "two masters, . . . an English and an Italian"—the British Empire and the Roman Catholic Church—"and a third [Ireland] . . . who wants [him] for odd jobs" (1.638, 641). Haines, expressing his English guilt while avoiding personal responsibility, says that "we feel in England that we have treated you rather unfairly. It seems history is to blame" (1.648–49). In today's parlance, Haines is struggling to unpack his privilege.

The reference to "history" sends Stephen's mind, which is already spinning with Christian theology, into thoughts of church history, particularly its engagement of the controversy and various heresies surrounding the Trinity and consubstantiality of the Father and the Son. Stephen notes the connection between these tidbits of Christian theological debate and the "words Mulligan had spoken a moment since"

(1.660–61) when he mocked Stephen's *Hamlet* theory. The heavy father-son motif here at the outset of the novel points to Stephen's own father, Simon Dedalus, a man woefully inadequate to meeting his son's needs. We'll spend some time with Simon in the episodes ahead.

Haines's anti-Semitism brings Stephen crashing back to Earth from his inner monologue's elevated plane. Fear of the influence of "German jews" (1.667) hints at the hostile environment endured by the novel's second protagonist, Mr. Leopold Bloom, a Jewish man whom we will meet in the novel's fourth episode. Stephen passes by a businessman and a boatman, overhearing their discussion of the drowned corpse expected to be swept in with the afternoon tide, and he imagines the "swollen bundle" (1.676) appearing on shore. They make it to the bathing area, where a young man carefully navigates the rocks "frogwise" (1.680) and an old priest pops out of the water. Mulligan mockingly crosses himself as the priest scuttles past. Mulligan knows the unnamed young man, and they share the latest news from Bannon, a mutual friend, who has a new romantic interest, a "sweet young thing…photo girl" (1.685)—we will soon learn the identity of this young woman. They also discuss Seymour, another friend, who has changed his career from medicine to the military and is apparently involved with a rich redheaded girl. The stereotype that "redheaded women buck like goats" (1.706) establishes the misogyny present in this society.

Buck again references Nietzsche and strips down. The young man in the water does the backstroke. Haines smokes. Stephen begins to leave (he does not bathe), but Buck calls him back, issuing a command: "Give us that key, Kinch." He veils his aggression by supplying a practical purpose for this demand: "to keep my chemise flat" (1.721). Stephen, despite his earlier assertion that "it is mine. I paid the rent" (1.631), relinquishes his ownership of the tower by laying the key across Buck's shirt. Perhaps emboldened, Buck also demands money "for a pint" (1.724), and Stephen again obliges. Haines bids Stephen farewell, and Buck and Stephen agree to meet at The Ship, a pub in town, at 12:30 p.m.

As Stephen begins his walk to the school in Dalkey, he hears the bell in a nearby tower chime three times, signifying that the time is now 8:45 a.m. (three chimes for each quarter past the hour). Stephen hears these chimes as three lines of Latin from the Catholic deathbed prayer recalled earlier in the episode; the Latin translates to "May the glittering throng of confessors, bright as lilies, gather about you. May the glorious choir of virgins receive you."[16] Stephen remains utterly haunted by the memory of his mother's death.

Downcast and dispossessed, Stephen inclines himself to self-imposed exile, realizing that he "will not sleep here tonight. Home also [he] cannot go" (1.740). Buck calls to him from the water, and Stephen waves in reply before silently sniping Buck with a final label: "Usurper" (1.743).

## Further Reading

Knuth, Leo. "How Stately Was Plump Buck Mulligan?" *James Joyce Quarterly* 7, no. 3 (Spring 1970): 204–09.

In case you weren't convinced of the depth of scholarship that exists on *Ulysses*, this article is entirely devoted to the novel's first word: "Stately."

Lawrence, Karen. "The Narrative Norm." Chap. 2 in *The Odyssey of Style in "Ulysses."* Princeton, NJ: Princeton University Press, 1981.

This chapter introduces the principal stylistic techniques employed in the opening episodes of *Ulysses*, including free indirect discourse, stream-of-consciousness, and the "linguistic sympathy" between the characters and the narrative voice. Lawrence interprets the narrator's overreliance on adverbs in "Telemachus" as characterizing the immaturity of Stephen and Buck, our first hint that the many styles of the novel inform our understanding of its content.

Steinberg, Erwin R. "Introducing the Stream-of-Consciousness Technique in *Ulysses.*" *Style* 2, no. 1 (1968): 49–58.

This essay notes the sparing use of Stephen's stream-of-consciousness in "Telemachus" and explains how Joyce effectively prepares the reader for the prominence of this technique later in the novel.

Tanyol, Denise. "Mummery, Murmuring Memory, Mum: Buck Mulligan as Resurrector in *Ulysses.*" *James Joyce Quarterly* 41, no. 1/2 (Fall 2003–Winter 2004): 111–26.

After surveying various critical opinions on the character of Buck Mulligan, this essay focuses on the word "mummer" to suggest an association with mumming plays. These plays traditionally include a death and resurrection, which Tanyol connects to Buck's instigation of the resurrection of Mrs. Dedalus in Stephen's thoughts.

# Chapter 2

# "NESTOR" GUIDE

The "Nestor" episode depicts Stephen at work as a teacher in a private boys' school in Dalkey, which is about a twenty-minute walk south from the Martello tower. We know Stephen departed the tower no sooner than 8:45 a.m. (the bells chimed three quarters past the hour at the end of "Telemachus"), so he presumably arrives a few minutes past 9:00 a.m. We can assume that he is late to work.

The narrative joins Stephen around 9:40 a.m., in the midst of his lesson. His teaching is uninspired. He quizzes the boys on memorized historical facts related to the costly victory won by the Greek King Pyrrhus over the Romans at Asculum. From this battle, we get the term "pyrrhic victory," like winning a soccer match but losing three starters to season-ending injuries in the process; in short, "another victory like that and we're done for" (2.14). By Stephen's need to "glance at the name and date in the gorescarred book" (2.12–13), we gather that he is unprepared for class. We've all been there.

As Stephen teaches, his inner monologue reveals the background activity of his remarkable mind: he thinks of William Blake's characterization of history as romanticized and "memory fabled" (2.8), he wrestles with Aristotle's ideas regarding history and events as the only possible outcomes ("was that only possible which came to pass?" [2.52]), and he vividly imagines General Pyrrhus leaning on a spear and speaking to his officers on "a hill above a corpsestrewn plain" (2.16). We will spend more time with Stephen's layered and erudite thoughts

25

Mr. Deasy's school in relation to the Sandycove Martello tower.
*Photo of Mr. Deasy's school / Summerfield House courtesy of Marc Conner.*

during these next two episodes, so you might want to keep your copy of Gifford's book of annotations handy if you want explanation for each of his allusions. Here, I'm more interested in helping you build momentum and confidence as we continue to gain a foothold in this beautiful beast of a novel.

The students laugh at Armstrong, a boy who seems more interested in sneaking bites of his figrolls than learning his history, and Stephen silently acknowledges his own "lack of rule" (2.29) in the classroom. Perhaps he isn't delivering an educational experience worthy of the tuition "fees their papas pay" (2.29). Stephen's cleverness in defining a pier as a "disappointed bridge" (2.39) goes right over his students' heads, but he intends to remember this witticism "for Haines's chapbook" (2.42). At this thought, he registers some self-loathing for his willingness to play the role of "a[n Irish] jester at the court of his [English] master," merely an intellectual entertainer seeking his "master's praise" (2.45–46).

Stephen abandons the history lesson in favor of poetry. A boy recites a section of Milton's "Lycidas," which reinforces the drowning motif established in "Telemachus." Stephen remembers the year he spent in Paris reading Aristotle in French: "the studious silence of the library of St. Genevieve where he had read, sheltered from the sins of Paris, night by night" (2.69–70). This image of Stephen contentedly surrounded by other "fed and feeding brains" (2.71) contrasts with the suffocating atmosphere of the tower (and perhaps Dublin in general) that stifles him here. Prior to dismissing the boys to get ready for field hockey, Stephen concludes his lesson with a nonsensical riddle, the answer to which is "the fox burying his grandmother under a hollybush" (2.115), suggesting Stephen's feelings of culpability for his own mother's death. Stephen then gives extra math tutoring to a struggling student named Cyril Sargent. Looking at the "lean neck" and "tangled hair" of the "ugly" boy (2.139), he muses on the love and protection young Sargent has received from his mother. Echoing Cranly from *A Portrait*,[1] Stephen reflects that a mother's love may be "the only true thing in life" (2.143). He thinks of the Irish Saint Columbanus's mother, over whose "prostrate body" (2.144) the priest had to step as he departed for his missionary work "grievously against her will."[2] His mind returns to his own mother and her haunting appearance to him in a dream with "an odour of rosewood and wetted ashes" (2.145–46). Stephen then imagines the fox from his riddle: "with merciless bright eyes [he] scraped in the earth, listened, scraped up the earth, listened, scraped and scraped" (2.149–50). The repeated scraping and listening might signify that the fox, after "burying his grandmother," is now trying to exhume her, listening for signs of life. Likewise, Stephen, after "merciless[ly]" refusing his mother's dying wish, obsessively brings her back to life in his tortured thoughts.

As Stephen works the math problem for Sargent, he recalls Mulligan's taunt that "he proves by algebra that Shakespeare's ghost is Hamlet's grandfather" (2.151–52). Stephen also sees a bit of his younger self in Cyril's "sloping shoulders" and "gracelessness" (2.168). They wrap up the extra help session, and Stephen dismisses Cyril to join his classmates at field hockey (an English sport, forecasting Headmaster Deasy's politics).

We meet Mr. Deasy, the correspondent to King Nestor, with his "angry white mustache" (2.188) and "illdyed head" (2.197–98). Deasy sorts the boys into teams and gets the game under way. He tells Stephen to wait for him in his study for their "little financial settlement" (2.207). Deasy enters and pays Stephen his monthly salary of £3 12s. in two £1 notes, a sovereign coin (also worth £1), two crown coins (worth 5 shillings each), plus two shilling coins. This wage is roughly equivalent to US$1,000 in today's spending power (for more information on money in *Ulysses*, see appendix C). Stephen collects his payment with "shy haste" (2.223–24), and Deasy advises him to organize and save his money in a "little savingsbox" (2.218) machine like his. After prodding himself to "answer something" (2.231) to Deasy's unsolicited advice, Stephen replies that his savingsbox "would be often empty" (2.232). Deasy continues to lecture him on fiscal prudence, citing Shakespeare: "put but money in thy purse" (2.239). Of course, Stephen recognizes that Deasy has taken this line completely out of context; in *Othello*, the treacherous Iago says this phrase repeatedly as he manipulates Rodrigo. Deasy's knowledge of Shakespeare (and most other things) is superficial. Deasy also demonstrates that he is a West Briton, an Irish supporter of England, as he continues to espouse the English virtue of financial discipline, claiming that "I paid my way" (2.251) is the "proudest word you will ever hear from an Englishman's mouth" (2.244–45). Stephen's inner monologue silently mocks Deasy ("Good man, good man" [2.252]) before cataloguing his own debts owed to at least ten people around town, totaling more than £25—roughly US$7,500 today.[3] In the face of this mountain of debt and out of youthful irresponsibility, Stephen thinks that "the lump" of money he just crammed into his pocket is "useless" (2.259) to even begin paying off what he owes . . . plus, we know that he plans to go drinking this afternoon.

Deasy then shifts focus to the history of the Irish independence movement, making assumptions about Stephen's politics and generally striking the wrong chords. You might take a look at these pages and note how little Stephen says in this conversation. In *The Odyssey*, Telemachus leaves Ithaca in search for news of his long-lost father, first visiting King Nestor, a wise old man and former comrade of Odysseus's. Deasy's correspondence to Nestor is ironic; his failure as a suitable mentor to Stephen is emphasized by the erroneous historical information he spouts throughout the conversation; even Deasy's account of his own Blackwood family history is riddled with inaccuracies, as Robert Martin Adams thoroughly documents in his book *Surface and Symbol*.[4]

Deasy asks a favor of Stephen: he has written a letter on the topic of foot-and-mouth disease, a viral contagion that can decimate entire populations of cattle, and he'd like for Stephen to arrange for its publication in a Dublin newspaper. As Deasy finishes copying the letter on his typewriter, Stephen looks around at the pictures of famous horses adorning Deasy's walls and recalls a day of horse-race gambling with Cranly. He hears shouts and a whistle from the field hockey game outside, leading his mind to conflate the "battling bodies" (2.314) of the boys playing sports with the "slush and uproar of battles, the frozen deathspew of the slain, a shout of spearspikes baited with men's bloodied guts" (2.317–18). In this passage, we may find "barely disguised World War I imagery—bayonets, grenade blasts, mud, trench warfare."[5] When combined with the earlier image of Pyrrhus surveying "a corpsestrewn plain" (2.16), we might be reminded that the Great War was raging around Joyce as he composed "Nestor" in 1917 while living in neutral Switzerland.[6]

Deasy finishes copying the letter and hands both copies to Stephen, who skims it to get the gist that foot-and-mouth disease threatens the export of Irish cattle and that Deasy's cousin in Austria claims that veterinarians there have developed a cure. Deasy tells Stephen that he has encountered difficulties in getting the government's attention on this issue, blaming conspiratorial intrigues and the covert influence of the Jews. Deasy's anti-Semitism, similar to Haines's in the previous episode, imagines Jews operating in the shadows and signaling "a nation's decay" (2.348): "As sure as we are standing here the jew merchants are already at their work of destruction" (2.349–50). These statements reinforce the hostile social context into which Joyce will place Mr. Bloom. Stephen silently recalls a memory of Jewish businessmen in Paris. While this passage includes derogatory stereotypes, it seems that Stephen expresses an overall attitude of sympathy, especially since he immediately speaks up to defend Jewish merchants as being no different from their gentile counterparts. Deasy retorts that "they sinned against the light" (2.361), alluding to the Christian belief that the Jewish people are guilty of deicide, the murder of Jesus/God. The idea of the mythological Wandering Jew makes its first appearance in the novel, foreshadowing Mr. Bloom's eighteen hours of wandering around Dublin. You can be sure that Joyce will put his own spin on this old trope.

In response to Deasy's assertion that the Jews "sinned against the light," Stephen asks "Who has not?" (2.373), literally dropping Deasy's jaw. Stephen's inner monologue wonders, "Is this old wisdom?" (2.376), indicating the failure of Deasy/Nestor to serve as the father figure Stephen/Telemachus seeks. Explaining Deasy's shortcomings, Richard Ellmann explains in his book *"Ulysses" on the Liffey* that "what he offers to Stephen, as worldly wisdom, is archaic conservatism in politics, and conserved wealth in finance—kingdoms of the past and of the future. Stephen seeks a different kingdom, that of the 'now, the here.'"[7] As such, Stephen offers his rebuke of history, saying that "history is a nightmare from which I am trying to awake" (2.377). He means both the nightmare of Ireland's history of subjugation and his personal inability to escape the haunting history of his mother's death. Deasy proposes a Victorian platitude that "history moves toward one great goal, the manifestation of God" (2.381). But "God to Stephen is not the final term in a process . . . but rather a 'shout in the street,' some totally unexpected and unforeseeable manifestation."[8] Stephen, "shrugging his shoulders" (2.386), accepts his incompatibility with Deasy. Deasy spews a misogynistic diatribe, scapegoating female figures from the Bible (Eve), Homer (Helen), early Irish legend (twelfth-century King Dermot MacMurrough's wife), and contemporary Irish politics (Kitty O'Shea). Stephen is done here. He makes ready to leave.

Deasy is wrong on many things, but he is correct about Stephen's unhappiness and in predicting that Stephen "will not remain here very long at this work" (2.401–02). Stephen doesn't argue, claiming that he's "a learner rather" than a teacher (2.403). He silently questions what more he will learn here—with Deasy specifically and in Dublin generally. Deasy offers another pearl of trite wisdom: "To learn one must be humble. But life is the great teacher" (2.406–07). Proud, insecure young Stephen could stand to learn about humility, but we can't blame him for dismissing Deasy in the context of his intellectual vapidity, anti-Semitism, and misogyny. Yet, "still [Stephen] will help him" (2.430) with the publication of his letter, imagining that Buck will have a new mocking label for him: "the bullockbefriending bard" (2.431).

As Stephen walks away from the school, Deasy calls and hustles after him to jab a final anti-Semitic barb: "Ireland, they say, has the honour of being the only country which never persecuted the jews . . . because she never let them in" (2.437–38, 442). The revolting description of Deasy's "coughball of laughter leap[ing] from his throat dragging after it a rattling chain of phlegm" (2.443–44) emphasizes the novel's rejection of prejudice.

Stephen leaves the school to catch a northbound train from the Dalkey station. We will next see him walking along Sandymount Strand, enjoying some time alone with his own thoughts.

## Further Reading

Adams, Robert Martin. "Deasy." In *Surface and Symbol: The Consistency of James Joyce's "Ulysses."* New York: Oxford University Press, 1967.

In this section of *Surface and Symbol*, Adams identifies Mr. Deasy's many factual errors in his conversation with Stephen.

Feinstein, Amy. "Usurers and Usurpers: Race, Nation, and the Performance of Jewish Mercantilism in *Ulysses*." *James Joyce Quarterly* 44, no. 1 (2006): 39–58.

After establishing the prominence of racial nationalism around the turn of the century, Feinstein explains Joyce's satire of the trope of the usurious Jewish moneylender as a means of criticizing the immorality and greed of British imperialism. Mr. Deasy in "Nestor" voices the scapegoating of Jews for the ills of free-market capitalism.

Spoo, Robert. "Jules Laforgue and the Nightmare of Stephen Dedalus." *James Joyce Quarterly* 26, no. 3 (Spring 1989): 445–49.

This essay evaluates two potential sources for Stephen's famous statement that "history is a nightmare from which I am trying to awake." Based on wider similarities between Laforgue and Stephen Dedalus, Spoo argues that the French poet is the most likely influence in Stephen's mind.

# Chapter 3

# "PROTEUS" GUIDE

The "Proteus" episode presents the erudite musings of Stephen Dedalus as he walks along Sandymount Strand just before 11:00 a.m. Dense and difficult to follow, "Proteus" is where most first-time readers of *Ulysses* throw in the towel. Don't. Despite the fact that even the most serious Joycean could spend an entire career reading deeply in this episode, you needn't get bogged down if you don't want to. In this guide, I'll give you what you need to continue your momentum toward meeting Mr. Bloom in the next episode. Of course, if you like Aristotelian philosophy and enjoy following the ricochets of Stephen's mind, pull out the Gifford and have at it! Otherwise, I'll aspire to concision in presenting the episode's main ideas and highlights.

After leaving Mr. Deasy's school, Stephen takes the train north from Dalkey and makes his way to the shore of Dublin Bay, needing some quiet time after a relatively tense morning.[1] As Stephen contemplates the "ineluctable modality of the visible" (3.1), it is worth noting that his eyesight is severely impaired, limiting what he can literally see. Stephen is also unable to see his future—both in the near-term (where will he sleep tonight having left the tower? Will he continue to work for Mr. Deasy?) and in the long-term (how long can he remain isolated and disesteemed in Dublin?). Stephen's walk in "Proteus" is an inverted echo of his euphoric walk on the strand in *A Portrait*, when he "burned to set out for the ends of the earth" and proclaimed that

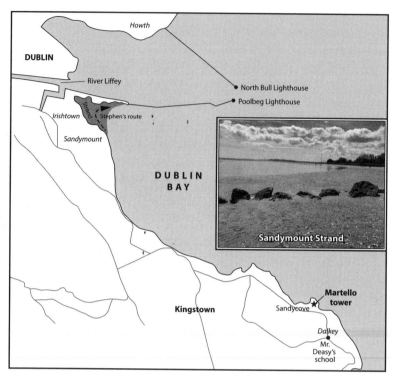

Stephen's walk along Sandymount Strand in relation to Dublin,
Mr. Deasy's school, and the Sandycove Martello tower

he "would create proudly out of the freedom and power of his soul"
(*P* 157). That adventure seems to have ended in a blind alley.

In *The Odyssey*, Menelaus describes to Telemachus his ambush of
the shape-shifting sea god Proteus. Difficult to pin down, Proteus
changes into a lion, a snake, a leopard, a boar, water, and a tree. Menelaus holds on, and the elusive old god finally returns to his normal
form and tells truths about the journey home from Troy. From Proteus
(via Menelaus), Telemachus learns that his father is alive but trapped
on Calypso's island. Just as Proteus repeatedly shifts his shape, this
episode's immersion in Stephen's inner monologue demonstrates the
changeability of the human mind. In "Proteus," Stephen constantly
changes his focus and his attitude, shifting between intellectual playfulness and bitter despair, modulating between contemplation, imagination, and memory. As he varies his mentality, his inner monologue

adopts different styles, syntactical rhythms, and prosody. As J. Mitch-ell Morse explains, this episode depicts how "the metamorphosis of lit-erary styles . . . both reflects and produces the endless metamorphosis of our ways of thinking."[2]

Stephen opens his monologue with philosophical musings on Aris-totle's notion that ideas originate from sensory experience of the exter-nal world, deriving "thought through [his] eyes" (3.1–2). He examines the relationship of sight, object, and color, then closes his eyes to walk blindly as he ponders sound, time, and space. On the opening page alone, Stephen's mind adopts the shape of "Aristotle, Boehme, Ham-let, Blake, perhaps Lessing, perhaps Gutzkow, and an upside-down Berkeley."[3] When he reopens his eyes, he confirms that the world was "there all the time without" him (3.27), betraying a shade of solipsism. He observes midwives coming down the stairs from Leahy's terrace to the strand. Stephen contemplates his own birth and imagines that one of the women has in her bag a dead fetus with its umbilical cord, prompting him to reconsider the omphalos idea from "Telemachus." He whimsically imagines the cords linking everyone back to Adam and Eve, as if to a telephone operator. Stephen then contemplates his own parentage and creation, leading him to consider again the Chris-tian theological notion of father-son consubstantiality as well as the heretic Arius, previously linked in his thoughts with Buck Mulligan.

The style of the episode favors Stephen's interior monologue by a ratio of nearly eight to one, but moments of third-person narration in-terrupt his thoughts and ground Stephen in the setting on the strand.[4] For example, the narrative description that "airs romped round him, nipping and eager airs" (3.55) briefly removes the focus from Stephen's thoughts and places it on the external world even as the narrator, by the Uncle Charles Principle, borrows Stephen's idiom in quoting *Hamlet*. Stephen reminds himself to deliver Mr. Deasy's foot-and-mouth disease "letter for the press" (3.58) and to meet Buck at The Ship at 12:30. With biting self-deprecation, he advises himself not to drink away his "money like a good young imbecile" (3.59). Stephen then slows his walk to consider whether he might visit his Aunt Sara and Uncle Richie Goulding at their nearby home (and perhaps to ask if he can sleep there tonight). Stephen imagines his father Simon's mockery of Uncle Richie's stammer: "And and and tell us Stephen, how is Uncle Si?" (3.64–65). Yes, this is Stephen's parody of Simon parodying Richie Goulding. We remain in Stephen's imagination as he mentally sees himself arriving at the Goulding home (some first-time readers might mistake this vignette for something that actually happens; it doesn't. Stephen physically remains on the strand for the entirety of this episode). The imagined visit with his relatives begins with their delay in opening the door (for fear that he is a bill collector). Uncle Richie offers Stephen a whiskey and insists that he sit down (despite the absence of an extra chair) and have a meal (despite the absence of any food in the house). Stephen then imagines his uncle whistling a tune from an opera about a fallen family. Apropos.

The reverie ends, and Stephen's attention returns to the present, which he prefers to the imagined future, thinking "this air is sweeter" (3.104). He laments the many "houses of decay" (3.105) in his life and chastises himself for the aggrandizing lies he told his Clongowes schoolmates about his family, thinking, "Come out of them, Stephen. Beauty is not there" (3.106–07). We are left to discern whether by "them" he means the lies, his family, or the Clongowes elite. He also finds no beauty in the Dublin library, where he read the prophetic writings of Joachim Abbas. The word "rabble" in this dense paragraph recalls Joyce's 1901 essay "The Day of the Rabblement," wherein he rails against the Irish Literary Theatre for its parochialism; the essay opens with the notion that "the artist, though he may employ the crowd, is very careful to isolate himself."[5] After thinking of Jonathan Swift's misanthropic madness, Stephen rejects his own crowd of intellectual sparring partners, "Temple, Buck Mulligan, Foxy Campbell" (3.112). He blasphemes and thinks about Occam and the Eucharist. Stephen then trains this bitterness on himself as he mocks his season of piety, his sins of simony, his misogyny, his youthful literary pretentions, and his delusions of grandeur. While he may be feeling the sting of his failure to achieve his lofty goals, we have to feel that Stephen is relentlessly hard on himself in this passage of thought. He is lost and in despair.

Stephen's attention returns to his present experience as he walks from the sand to the tideline's "crackling mast, razorshells" (3.147–48), navigating between "a pocket of seaweed" (3.151) and a beer bottle half-buried in the sand. Stephen then stops, realizing he has, in his state of thoughtful distraction, already "passed the way to aunt Sara's" (3.158).

He shifts his focus to memories of Paris, where he met two Irish expatriates, Patrice and Kevin Egan. Stephen mocks his failed medical studies and his current projection of cosmopolitanism by wearing a Latin Quarter hat around Dublin and casually name-dropping Left Bank street names. He reveals a measure of paranoia in carrying a punched ticket as an alibi if he were to be arrested on suspicion of murder. Stephen recalls a scene from his time in Paris indicative of the depths of poverty and hunger he suffered there: at the door of a closed post office, he pleaded with an officer to reopen and cash a money order his mother had sent him so that he could buy a meal. When the officer refuses, Stephen imagines "shoot[ing] him to bloody bits with a bang shotgun" (3.187–88) and then apologizing and helping put the officer back together. He again castigates himself for his failure to achieve his goals and shamefully remembers pretending not to speak English in order to avoid tipping the porter upon his arrival back in Dublin. Stephen then mentally paints a morning scene of "Paris rawly waking, crude sunlight on her lemon streets" (3.209). If you've experienced one of those bright Paris mornings, you know that his description nails it.

Stephen thinks again of the Egans, Irish revolutionaries in exile, and recalls snippets of his conversations with them. Prompted by the thought of exile, he turns to face south, where the tower stands across the bay. He imagines the interior scene of the tower and that Haines (the "panthersahib" gentleman) and Buck (his "pointer" dog) would not answer Stephen's call from outside of the tower (3.277–78). Knowing that Buck now "has the key," Stephen confirms that he "will not sleep there when this night comes" (3.276). They can "take all, keep all"; Stephen claims to be undaunted by loneliness and isolation so long as his "soul walks with [him]" (3.279). He climbs and sits on a rock and notices a dog carcass nearby. Then, a live dog named Tatters runs along the strand, spurring a moment of cynophobic panic. Stephen decides to sit still and respect the dog's right to liberty. He thinks of Viking invaders on these shores, then compares Buck Mulligan's courage to his own cowardice, thinking, "He saved men from drowning and you shake at a cur's yelping" (3.317–18). He probes himself as to whether he would "do what he did" (3.320), and the best he can muster is "I would want to. I would try" (3.323). Despite this unfavorable comparison, Stephen affirms that "I want his life to be his, mine to be mine" (3.327–28). But then he is again haunted by the idea of drowning and the related memory of his mother's death. The text departs from Stephen's inner monologue as it spends a few paragraphs narrating Tatters's adventure on the beach, including encountering the dog's carcass and digging in the sand, which recalls the fox burying his grandmother in Stephen's riddle from the previous episode.

The narrative shifts back to Stephen as he suddenly remembers pieces of a shadowy dream from the previous night, and his inner monologue attempts to reassemble it: "After he woke me last night same dream or was it? Wait. Open hallway. Street of harlots. Remember. Haroun al Raschid. I am almosting it. That man led me, spoke. I was not afraid. The melon he had he held against my face. Smiled: creamfruit smell. That was the rule, said. In. Come. Red carpet spread. You will see who" (3.365–69). When Frank Budgen inquired into the appearance of "almosting" in this passage, Joyce described the word as representing the "Protean character" of the entire episode: "Everything changes, land, water, dog, time of day. Parts of speech change, too. Adverb becomes verb."[6] Beyond this anthimeria expressing the elusiveness of our subconscious experiences, the content of Stephen's dream foretells events and associations that will be revealed later in *Ulysses*. Stephen will visit a "street of harlots" in the brothel district around midnight tonight. Mr. Bloom will be briefly identified with Haroun al Raschid (see 15.4325), a wise Persian king who walked in disguise among everyday people. In the early morning hours, Mr. Bloom will lead Stephen to his home and spread out the "red carpet" of hospitality. In one reading of the passage's last sentence, the text directly addresses the reader to promise that "you will see who" is foretold in this prophetic dream as the novel unfolds. Like Proteus revealing that Telemachus's search for his father is not in vain, this dream suggests that Stephen may yet experience the grace of fatherly care.

The gypsy cocklepickers who brought Tatters to the strand are described in detail, and Stephen takes a multilayered interest in the woman. They pass him by with "a side eye at [Stephen's] Hamlet hat" (3.390). Stephen then begins to compose lines of poetry in his head and searches his pockets for some scrap paper. Realizing he has twice forgotten to take slips from the library, he tears a blank corner off of Deasy's letter on foot-and-mouth disease and begins to compose a few lines of verse (about a vampire kissing a woman? the angel of death visiting his mother? a romantic encounter? not entirely clear here). Then the text offers a rather poignant paragraph: "Touch me. Soft eyes. Soft soft soft hand. I am lonely here. O, touch me soon, now. What is that word known to all men? I am quiet here alone. Sad too. Touch, touch me" (3.434–36). This passage might be Stephen expressing his vulnerability, loneliness, and deep desire for companionship and love (the "word known to all men" as controversially specified in the "Scylla and Charybdis" episode of Hans Walter Gabler's 1984 edition of *Ulysses*),[7] or these lines may be part of the poem he is drafting. Stephen has completed his writing for the day when the narrator reports that "he lay back at full stretch over the sharp rocks, cramming the scribbled note and pencil into a pocket" (3.437–38). The text quickly returns to Stephen's self-conscious inner monologue as he thinks, "That is Kevin Egan's movement I made" (3.439) when he tilted down his hat.

The sun of the "faunal noon" (3.442–43) shines on Stephen before he recalls a snippet of "Fergus's Song" from earlier this morning and looks at his boots, Buck Mulligan's hand-me-downs (or foot-me-downs, as the case may be). In an efficient synecdoche, Stephen reflects that they once held a "foot I dislove" (3.448–49). He muses briefly on the homoeroticism of his relationships with both Mulligan and Cranly. His mind pings from *The Tempest* to Proteus to Lucifer to Ophelia before observing that he is ready for a drink. Stephen contributes his own waters to the rising tide and imagines the scene of the drowned man being pulled from the sea. He notes that next Tuesday will be the summer solstice, and he thinks of Queen Victoria in derogatory terms. He observes that his "teeth are very bad" (3.494) and momentarily considers using the salary he collected this morning toward a visit to a dentist. As he tongues his rotting teeth, we note the episode's recurrent motif of decay, including that of his family, the dog carcass, the imagined corpse of the drowned man, and his ambitions.

Needing to pick his nose, Stephen searches for his handkerchief and realizes he must have left it back at the tower. Stanley Sultan notes that "in medieval science, the nose was considered the passage to, and an expurgative of, the brain. In a sense Stephen has been 'picking at' his mind during the chapter—his nose-picking is a counterpart to his brooding meditation."[8] He leaves the booger on a rock, then has a moment of self-consciousness and peeks over his shoulder to see if anyone saw. Richard Ellmann suggests that this backward glance exposes the absurdity of Stephen's toying with subjectivism earlier in the episode and "implies that art is not self-isolation, that it depends upon recognition of other existences."[9] Nobody is behind him, anyhow, although Stephen does see a tall ship with "crosstrees" (3.504), imagery that portends crucifixion and signals Stephen's grand self-identification as a martyr for art and freedom of thought. The ship is the *Rosevean* and—like almost everything else we've encountered in *Ulysses*'s opening triad of episodes—it will appear later in the novel.

Like Stephen, this ship is due in Dublin.

## Further Reading

Livorni, Ernesto. "'Ineluctable Modality of the Visible': Diaphane in the 'Proteus' Episode." *James Joyce Quarterly* 36, no. 2 (Winter 1999): 127–69.

This essay engages the use of inner monologue in presenting Stephen's aesthetic philosophy and investigates the sources (Aristotle, Aquinas, Dante, Cavalcanti, etc.) for Stephen's thoughts on space, sight, and language.

Rimo, Patricia A. "'Proteus': From Thoughts to Things." *Studies in the Novel* 17, no. 3 (Fall 1985): 296–302.

Rimo frames Stephen's inner monologue in "Proteus" as processing the relationship between the intellect (male) and the material (female). Although Stephen seems more comfortable with the masculine world of ideas, Rimo suggests that his thoughts in this episode ultimately shift their focus toward the physical world as the text anticipates the change to the more worldly Mr. Bloom in the subsequent episode.

Steinberg, Erwin R. "The 'Proteus' Episode: Signature of Stephen Dedalus." *James Joyce Quarterly* 5, no. 3 (Spring 1968): 187–98.

This essay explicates various threads of Stephen's thoughts in "Proteus" by identifying the philosophers (Aristotle, Boehme, etc.), the authors (Blake, Shakespeare, etc.), and the memories (Kevin Egan, Clongowes, etc.) that are on his mind during his walk along the beach. Steinberg ultimately affirms the success of this episode's stream-of-consciousness by its coherence to our understanding of Stephen's character developed elsewhere in the novel.

# Chapter 4

# "CALYPSO" GUIDE

Just as book 5 of *The Odyssey* shifts focus from Telemachus to Odysseus, the "Calypso" episode restarts the story of *Ulysses* in Mr. Bloom's home (7 Eccles Street) at 8:00 a.m. on the morning of June 16, 1904.

Leaving behind Stephen's intensity and density of thought, you'll likely find Mr. Bloom's arrival on the page a relief. Joyce created each protagonist with a unique mode of thought, as reflected in the distinct styles of their inner monologues. Whereas Stephen's mind works like a magnet, drawing together everything he knows about a particular topic (and he knows a lot), Mr. Bloom's mind is stimulated by the sensory world as he hops from tangential point to point. Frank Budgen, a friend of Joyce's and an early scholar of *Ulysses*, describes their different styles of thinking: "Stephen's, hither and thither darting, swallow-like; Bloom's, nose on the ground, like a dog on the scent."[1] Given that "Proteus" and "Calypso" appear back to back, these different patterns of inner monologue are thrown into stark relief, serving to characterize and distinguish the novel's heroes. For example, whereas Stephen's musings about sight at the beginning of "Proteus" resemble an epistemological pinball machine, Mr. Bloom at the outset of "Calypso" simply uses his sense of sight to watch his cat and make mental observations about her movements and physical features. As we begin the novel's second triad of introductory episodes, the narrative voice also changes, adopting Mr. Bloom's comic sensibility and groundedness in the physical world (as prescribed by the Uncle Charles Principle explained in my introduction).

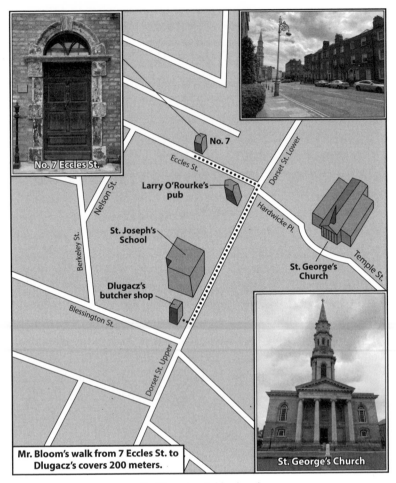

Mr. Bloom's neighborhood

Through the combination of these narrative elements, Mr. Bloom's characteristic curiosity is highlighted as he wonders about his cat's nature and view of the world. He also bends down to the cat's level and cares for her by providing milk, acts of humility and empathy that help to define Mr. Bloom as generous and kind. The "Calypso" episode also begins with recognition of Mr. Bloom's bodily appetites as he prepares breakfast for his wife in the kitchen of their north Dublin home. We find an immediate contrast to Stephen, about whose preferred foods we know nothing. As the episode's first page continues, you might notice other echoes of moments in the "Telemachus" episode, but they are all repeated with differences that signal the shift to the novel's new protagonist: the "green stones" (4.35) here in "Calypso" describe the cat's eyes rather than serving as symbols of Irish subjugation under English rule (as in the green gem on Haines's silver cigarette case); the "tower" (4.29) figures into Mr. Bloom's curiosity about his cat's perception of his relative height, not an esoteric figuration of the omphalos of an Irish intellectual movement; Mr. Bloom's milk jug is uneventfully filled by Hanlon's milkman, whereas the milkwoman in "Telemachus" represents Athena and the shortcomings of an archetypal Irish mother. While Stephen seems to exhaust all knowledge in his allusion-laden inner monologue, Bloom conveys inexhaustible wonder. His mind has a lighter air than Stephen's, yet it is no less active.

Whereas Buck blasphemes and teases as he prepares breakfast in the tower, Mr. Bloom carefully arranges the plate for his wife's breakfast in bed. As we learn more about the status of the Blooms' marriage, some readers will find Mr. Bloom's subservience to Molly odd—perhaps even degrading—but he conveys no resentment over what seems to be a routine conjugal favor. He hungrily but thoughtfully weighs his own breakfast options and decides on a pork kidney from Dlugacz's butcher shop around the corner from his home.[2] He goes up the staircase from the kitchen (located in the basement level of the house) and "softly" (4.52) tells Molly (still in bed) that he's going out and asks if she wants something beyond buttered bread for her breakfast. She grunts her first word of the novel, "Mn" (4.57), a muffled "no." As she turns over in bed, Bloom hears the jingle (4.59) of the bed's loose brass rings. Mr. Bloom recalls that Molly's father, Brian Tweedy, purchased the bed at an auction in Gibraltar, where he was stationed as an officer of the British army during Molly's childhood. He parodies the soldier's bravado but ultimately finds the good in his father-in-law.

Preparing to leave the house and still thinking about old Tweedy's lucrative stamp collecting, Mr. Bloom takes his Plasto's high grade ha[t] (the "t" has worn off) from the peg and checks inside the headband to make sure that the "white slip of paper" (4.70) remains hidden there. We will learn in the next episode that this card allows Bloom to access a secret post office box—Mr. Bloom is not as simple as he initially seems. As he steps out the front door, he searches his pockets for the key. He feels in his pocket his talismanic shrunken potato, but he realizes the housekey is in his other pants (he is wearing his black suit for the funeral of his friend Paddy Dignam that he will attend later this morning). Deciding that there's "no use disturbing" Molly by going back in to retrieve the key, he leaves the door ever so slightly ajar that it "looked shut" (4.73–76). Like Stephen, he is entering the day without a key to his home. But these sorts of similarities highlight their differences: Mr. Bloom's keylessness results from an act of generosity, whereas Stephen's keylessness is rooted in defiant self-imposed exile.

Mr. Bloom enters the streets of Dublin this sunny Thursday morning, and we begin to see the city through his keenly observant eyes. Most people fail to look closely at the things routinely seen, but Mr. Bloom notes many details as he walks through his own neighborhood, including a neighbor's "loose cellarflap" (4.77), the sun's orientation to the steeple of St. George's Church, and a bread van making deliveries. Interspersed in these observations, his mind wonders about why one feels hotter in a black suit; he is incorrect in guessing "conducts, reflects," and "refracts" (4.79–80); rather, black absorbs heat. Richard Ellmann terms these sorts of mental errors "bloomisms."[3] His later inclusion of Edom alongside Sodom and Gomorrah (see 4.222) is another such "bloomism." Continuing on, Mr. Bloom notes his wife's preference for day-old loafs and imagines walking through a Middle Eastern market. He quickly dismisses his reverie as overly romanticized and recognizes its origins in the illustrated title page of a travel book he owns. He then thinks about sun imagery in Irish nationalist newspapers. Get accustomed to these mental jumps; we will spend the better part of the day with access to Mr. Bloom's inner monologue.

As he turns the corner from Eccles Street to Dorset Street, he passes Larry O'Rourke's pub and smells "whiffs of ginger, teadust, biscuit-mush" (4.107). He muses on Mr. O'Rourke, decides not to solicit him for an ad (Bloom works as an advertising agent), and recalls Simon Dedalus's imitation of him (Mr. Bloom knows Stephen's father). Bloom greets Mr. O'Rourke and contemplates the economics of pubs. He passes Saint Joseph's National school and is distracted from his mental math by hearing the ABCs ("ahbeesee . . .") (4.137) recited through a classroom's open windows. Although he is "displeased" that his pub mathematics are left "unsolved," he has the maturity to "let them fade" (4.142). He finds sensory solace in arriving at the butcher where he "breathed in tranquilly the lukewarm breath of cooked spicy pigs' blood" (4.143–44). Of course, it is worth noting that Mr. Bloom is Jewish, and he is about to buy pork from a Jewish butcher—not kosher. In Dlugacz's, Bloom is pleased to wait behind a young woman as she places an order for sausages—she works as a housekeeper next door to him. He admires "her vigorous hips" (4.148) and hopes to hurry with his own order so that he can walk behind and ogle her "moving hams" (4.172). Also not kosher.

He notes the Jewish newspaper sheets Dlugacz uses to wrap up the woman's sausages and recalls his previous employment working as a cattle trader. He places his order and silently encourages the butcher to "make hay while the sun shines" (4.174) so he can catch up to the woman, whom he recalls seeing "cuddling" (4.178) with a burly policeman. He pays threepence for his kidney—one of the "inner organs of beasts and fowls" (4.1–2) Mr. Bloom most enjoys—and leaves the shop. He is too late to walk behind the woman.

As he heads home, he reads on the butcher paper a prospectus for Agendath Netaim, a Zionist investment opportunity that touts the land's fertility. He wonders about Jewish friends of his, Citron and Mastiansky, with whom he has lost touch. He thinks about produce. Then, "a cloud began to cover the sun slowly, wholly" (4.218); this is the same cloud that covered the sun in the "Telemachus" episode (see 1.248), representing the novel's first direct incident of parallax, the phenomenon of the same object being observed from different viewpoints. The cloud casts a shadow on Bloom's mind (just as it does on Stephen's), and he thinks of Israel as "a dead land, grey and old" (4.223), starkly contrasting with the idyllic portrayal of Palestine in the Agendath Netaim ad as a land teeming with life. This dramatic swing of thought exemplifies Bloom's cyclical mind. In both his mental processes and his character, Mr. Bloom embodies contradictions: he is ordinary and extraordinary, an amateur scientist with "a touch of the artist" (10.582), an Everyman and a good man, which not every man is. He is admirable but deeply flawed. In short, he is human.

Horrified by his mind's image of Palestine, Bloom hurries home, thinking, "Well, I am here now. Yes, I am here now" (4.232–33), re-affirming that he considers Ireland to be his home despite his Jewish ethnicity. He is also drawn home by Molly, his Penelope, wanting to "be near her ample bedwarmed flesh" (4.238–39). His equilibrium is restored by these thoughts of home. The text then personifies the morning sunlight as running "swiftly, in slim sandals," which suggests Hermes (who, in *The Odyssey*, tells Calypso she must release Odysseus), and "a girl with gold hair on the wind," which suggests Bloom's daughter, Milly (4.240–42). Erwin Steinberg suggests that this passage, which doesn't quite fit the prevailing style of the episode, reveals "a narrator who has not yet settled into Bloom's idiom, who uses his own style, or, perhaps, a style more appropriate to a happy Stephen than to Bloom."[4]

Arriving back home, Mr. Bloom collects the morning mail: a card from Milly to Molly, a letter from Milly to Bloom, and a letter addressed to "Mrs Marion Bloom" in a "bold hand" (4.244). Bloom recognizes "at once" (4.244) that this letter is from Blazes Boylan, the man set to manage Molly's upcoming concert tour (she is a prominent soprano in the Dublin music scene). Molly's name on the envelope should by proper etiquette appear as Mrs. Leopold Bloom; Boylan has effectively removed Leopold from the marriage. Indeed, Blazes Boylan will make good on that envelope's clerical promise by cuckolding Mr. Bloom this very afternoon. Molly's correspondence to loyal Penelope is ironic.

Bloom enters the bedroom and gives Molly her mail. While he is at the window "letting the blind up," he watches Molly in the reflection of the window as she "tuck[s Boylan's letter] under her pillow" (4.257) to read in private once Bloom has left the room. He clears an armful of Molly's dirty laundry onto the bed. As Bloom makes his way back downstairs to finish preparing breakfast, Molly tells (commands?) him to "scald the teapot" (4.270). Molly calls him Poldy, short for Leopold, though perhaps de-lionizing by removing the Leo from his name. Back in the kitchen, Bloom makes the tea as instructed, puts the kidney in the pan on the coals, lets the cat lick the butcher paper, and then opens and skims Milly's letter. He takes the full breakfast tray up to Molly in bed. There, he notices Molly's ample figure and "a strip of torn envelope peep[ing] from under the dimpled pillow" (4.308), evidence that she has read Boylan's letter while he was downstairs. Knowing full well who it was from, he asks anyway, and Molly confirms that Boylan is going to visit the house that afternoon to review the tour program. We also learn that Mr. Bloom will attend Paddy Dignam's funeral at eleven this morning.

Molly then asks Bloom to explain a word she read in a book. The word is "metempsychosis," and Bloom initially explains that it is Greek, meaning "the transmigration of souls" (4.342), but Molly dismisses this pedantic definition, saying "O, rocks!... Tell us in plain words" (4.343). Bloom goes on to explain reincarnation in simpler terms. He also offers to swap out Molly's book, *Ruby: The Pride of the Ring* (a cheap romance novel about a circus), for a more smutty read. Bloom admires the picture framed over their bed, *The Bath of the Nymph*, and correlates the nymph in the painting with Molly, thinking "not unlike her with her hair down: slimmer" (4.371). Beyond the similarities between the nymph and Molly, both women correspond to Calypso, the nymph in *The Odyssey* who holds Odysseus captive. Bloom/Odysseus is perhaps imprisoned (by psychological forces yet to be revealed) in a state of deference to Molly: bringing her breakfast in bed, running errands for her, following her commands, and resigning himself to her impending adultery. Questions around the causes, consequences, and sustainability of this dynamic within the Blooms' marriage are central to *Ulysses*.

Molly smells something burning, and Bloom, having forgotten about his kidney on the stove, hurries back downstairs. He salvages his breakfast and sits down to eat with a cup of tea. He reads his daughter's letter to him in full: Milly thanks him for her birthday presents (she turned fifteen yesterday, June 15) and provides a brief update on her social life down in Mullingar, County Westmeath, where she is working in a photography shop. One detail stands out to Mr. Bloom: "there is a young student comes here some evenings named Bannon" (4.406–07). You may remember Buck Mulligan's conversation with the guy at Forty Foot bathing area who reports that their mutual friend Bannon "found a sweet young thing down [in Westmeath]. Photo girl he calls her" (1.684–85). Photo girl is Milly Bloom. So, in another instance of parallax, Bloom's daughter is involved with a young man in Buck Mulligan's circle of friends. Even without knowing anything about Bannon, Bloom responds paternally to this news "with troubled affection" (4.432). Milly's letter also references a popular song, "Seaside Girls," that will return to Bloom's mind over the course of the day. In setting Mr. Bloom beside Stephen, the text presents a protopostmodern leveling of culture whereby we might find as much meaning in snatches of pop songs as in lines of Aquinas.

Singing a few lines of the song to himself, Bloom recalls the "torn envelope" (4.439) of Boylan's letter, as well as its addressing of "Mrs Marion" (4.444); in this way, he conflates Milly's blossoming sexuality with Molly's impending sexual encounter with Boylan. His body responds to these developments as "a soft qualm, regret, flowed down his backbone, increasing. Will happen, yes. Prevent. Useless: can't move" (4.447–48). We might admire his wisdom in passivity here: if Molly wants to have an affair, Bloom is ultimately powerless to stop her. He could intervene this afternoon, sure, but she would find a way around him tomorrow or the day after. Same thing with Milly's involvement with the Bannon boy. Bloom will later think, "Woman. As easy stop the sea" (11.641). Molly will later think, "I knew I could always get round him" (18.1579–80). Both are right.

Reflecting on Milly's birthday, he "remember[s] the summer morning she was born, running to knock up [the midwife] Mrs Thornton" (4.416–17). This same midwife delivered the Blooms' second child but "knew from the first poor little Rudy wouldn't live. . . . He would be eleven now if he had lived" (4.418–20). The Blooms' infant son was born on "29 December 1893" (17.2280–81) and died in infancy at only eleven days old (so, Rudy would actually be ten and half years old, not eleven). Pangs related to Rudy will arise throughout the day in the thoughts of Mr. Bloom. The loss of this child has profoundly impacted their marriage for a decade, and we will later see evidence of Mr. Bloom's feelings of responsibility for Rudy's death (see 6.329). So, we might reconsider the parallel to *The Odyssey*, how Calypso craves Odysseus for a husband. Perhaps Bloom's guilt over the loss of Rudy manifests itself in his apologetic subservience to Molly, and Molly/Calypso desires for Bloom/Odysseus to reassert himself as the husband she married. Perhaps the correspondence for Calypso in *Ulysses* is neither Molly nor the nymph picture but rather the disconnect within the marriage. This underlying dysfunction between Leopold and Molly Bloom imprisons each in isolation from the other. In *The Odyssey*, the gods determine that Odysseus deserves to be released from his imprisonment so that he may continue his journey home to Ithaca and his wife, Penelope. The journey of *Ulysses* culminates in Mr. Bloom's return home in the "Ithaca" episode, and the novel concludes with Molly's monologue in "Penelope"—the title of the novel's final episode suggests that enough will have changed over the course of the day that the marriage has been freed from its years of captivity. Maybe. Joyce's penchant for irony prevents any such reading as certain, and your own experience of this novel will yield its own opinions and reactions.

Mr. Bloom feels "a gentle loosening of his bowels" (4.460) and grabs some reading material for a trip to the outhouse. In stark contrast to the way the text obscures Stephen's urination at the end of "Proteus," the narrator in "Calypso" offers excessive details regarding Mr. Bloom's bowel movement. In his backyard, Bloom considers improvements to his garden but, in another example of his cyclical thinking patterns, cites his recent bee sting to suggest that "gardens have their drawbacks" (4.483). Then Bloom asks himself, "Where is my hat, by the way?" (4.485), which will send a hyperdiligent reader back a few pages to examine Bloom's return home in lines 243–47. For all of the narrator's attention to Bloom's exit (ha[t], potato, key, leaving the door slightly ajar, etc.), the text offers no description of his entrance from the time he collects the mail until he enters the bedroom. These sorts of "narrative skips," as Hugh Kenner calls them,[5] compel the reader to consider what is missing and why. In this instance, we can assume that Bloom is sufficiently distracted by the appearance of Boylan's letter—"his quickened heart slowed at once" (4.244)—that he takes no note of where he put his hat.

Seated in the outhouse, Mr. Bloom reads a short story titled "Matcham's Masterstroke" by Mr. Philip Beaufoy and considers his own literary prospects. Obviously humored and intrigued by his wife, Bloom "used to try jotting down" (4.519) snippets of Molly's dialogue out of context, similar to the idea of Joyce's own "Epiphanies." Bloom remembers the night of the bazaar dance a few weeks ago when Molly first met Boylan. He also remembers her questions about Boylan's financial standing the following morning. He considers the changes that occur with the time of day. Then, echoing the end of "Telemachus," we again hear three chimes signaling that the time is 8:45. Whereas Stephen's mind translated the chimes into three lines of a Catholic prayer for the dying, recalling his mother's deathbed, Bloom hears them as straightforward onomatopoeia:

*Heigho! Heigho!*
*Heigho! Heigho!*
*Heigho! Heigho!* (4.546–48)

This instance of parallax (the two men responding differently to the same hour's bell chimes) demonstrates that, again, Bloom and Stephen's distinctions will be highlighted by the manner in which they perceive similar events, objects, and ideas. The contrast between the two protagonists is further emphasized in their respective last words of the opening episodes: Stephen's last word in "Telemachus," "Usurper" (1.743), reveals his paranoia and self-absorption, whereas Mr. Bloom's last words, "Poor Dignam!" (4.551), convey a spirit of compassion. This impulse toward empathy represents an important touchstone as Joyce begins to redefine the epic hero in the character of Mr. Bloom.

## Further Reading

Brevda, William. "The Ha in Hat: Joyce's *Ulysses*." *Joyce Studies Annual* (2019): 3–32.
  This essay examines the layered social and symbolic meanings of the many hats worn by characters in *Ulysses*, including a thorough examination of Mr. Bloom's bowler hat.

Mook, Lorne. "Distance from Etiological Sites in the 'Calypso' Episode of *Ulysses*." *James Joyce Quarterly* 39, no. 4 (Summer 2002): 775–85.
  This essay notes the various ways that the style of narrative mediation in "Calypso" creates distance despite the relative clarity of this episode in comparison to the more difficult chapters of the novel.

Rando, David. "The Cat's Meow: *Ulysses*, Animals, and the Veterinary Gaze." *James Joyce Quarterly* 46, no. 3/4 (Spring-Summer 2009): 529–43.
  From Mr. Bloom's first interaction with his cat, he exhibits care and concern for animals; Rando's essay traces this aspect of his character and examines the discourse of and about animals in *Ulysses*.

Wellington, Fredrick V. "A Missing Conversation in *Ulysses*." *James Joyce Quarterly* 14, no. 4 (1977): 476–79.
  Using Hugh Kenner's method of deducing through close reading what Joyce has left out of the text, this short essay recreates the details of the conversation that must have occurred between Mr. Bloom and Molly after his visit to the outhouse and before he left home for the day.

## Chapter 5

# "LOTUS-EATERS" GUIDE

The "Lotus-Eaters" episode depicts Mr. Bloom's morning errands in the streets of Dublin between approximately 9:30 and 10:25.[1] Mr. Bloom has walked roughly one and a quarter miles south from his home, paralleling Stephen's concurrent commute from the tower to Mr. Deasy's school. Beyond the similarity of these off-page walks, "Lotus-Eaters" and "Nestor" share other qualities: both episodes begin *in medias res* and depict the protagonist's inner monologue during interactions with other people and a wider world. Just as we saw Stephen's interior monologue while teaching his students and meeting with Mr. Deasy, we now access Bloom's thoughts as he visits the post office and distractedly engages with M'Coy, Sweny, and Bantam Lyons. As Joyce continues to train us in how to read this novel, we now must discern dialogue, inner monologue, and third-person narration without much explicit delineation therebetween.

In *The Odyssey*, Odysseus sends members of his crew to scout an island. They discover the Lotus-Eaters, peaceful people who spend their days munching on lotus flowers. After partaking of the heady fruit, the scouts forget their mission and lose all desire to return home. Odysseus goes inland to find his men; when they refuse to leave, he drags them back to the ship, ties them below deck, and orders the rest of his crew to shove off. You may notice in the opening paragraph of the "Lotus-Eaters" episode that Bloom/Odysseus "walked soberly" past a boy smoking, "lolled" (5.5) by the nicotine, and a poor young girl

51

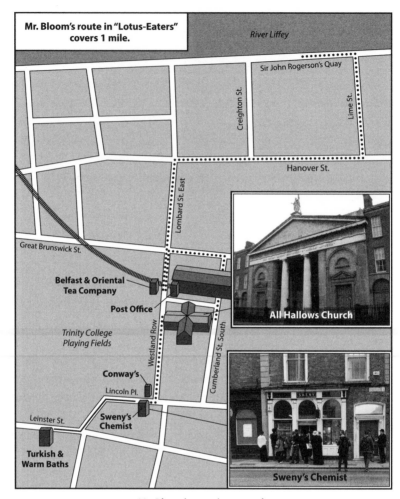

**Mr. Bloom's route in "Lotus-Eaters" covers 1 mile.**

River Liffey

Sir John Rogerson's Quay

Creighton St.

Lime St.

Hanover St.

Lombard St. East

Great Brunswick St.

Belfast & Oriental Tea Company

Post Office

Trinity College Playing Fields

Westland Row

Cumberland St. South

Conway's

Lincoln Pl.

Leinster St.

Sweny's Chemist

Turkish & Warm Baths

All Hallows Church

Sweny's Chemist

Mr. Bloom's morning errands

sitting "listlessly" (5.7). He considers telling the boy that "if he smokes he won't grow" (5.7–8), but these children are not his crew to rescue; rather, Bloom empathizes with what he supposes to be the boy's tough life. He imagines a scene of the boy pleading with his father "outside pubs to . . . come home to ma, da" (5.9), identifying alcohol as one distraction from the pains of reality. The "Lotus-Eaters" episode is full of many such intoxicating distractions—from gambling to religion, from teas to titillation—which reflect Mr. Bloom's own desire for distraction from his wife's impending adultery. Along these lines, the episode is steeped in opiated diction, such as "lazy" (5.30), "idleness" (5.34), "hypnotised" (5.73), "narcotic" (5.272), "opium" (5.327), "stupefies" (5.350), "lulls" (5.367), "placid" (5.410), "lethargy" (5.474), and "pleasure" (5.505), all of which contribute to the rhetorical effect of numbing the pain of Bloom's reality.

The opening of "Lotus-Eaters" joins Mr. Bloom as he walks "along sir John Rogerson's quay" (5.1) on the south bank of the Liffey; he will cover about a mile over the course of this episode. Bloom's first order of business on this warm morning, as hinted at in the "Calypso" episode, is to visit the post office to see if his secret pen pal has responded to his latest letter. Looking through the window of the Belfast and Oriental Tea Company, Bloom removes his hat under the auspices of running his "hand with slow grace over his brow and hair" (5.22) but sneakily, "quickly" (5.25) removes from his hatband the hidden name-card bearing his pseudonym, Mr. Henry Flower. He returns his attention to the tea shop and entertains an imagined scene of the "lethargy" (5.34) of the Far East that echoes his similarly exoticized reverie in "Calypso." He remembers seeing a photo of a man floating in the Dead Sea, unable to sink because of the water's high salinity, and he half-recalls a high school physics lesson on Archimedes' Principle (a solid body immersed in a liquid undergoes an apparent loss of weight equal to the weight of the liquid displaced), which he then conflates with the Law of Acceleration and Newtonian ideas on gravity. This bloom-ism exemplifies both his curious mind and almost-knowledge. He gets things wrong, sure, but we can appreciate his unique activity of mind in considering physics concepts as he goes about his day. Mentally lively but often mistaken, he is an amalgamation of quirks and idiosyncrasies. But aren't we all?

Crossing the road to the Westland Row Post Office, Bloom wonders about the woman he waited behind at Dlugacz's and lightly taps his leg with the newspaper he has rolled into a baton. He puts on a careless air to disguise his anxiety as he takes a furtive glance into the post office and is glad to find it empty. Why all the secrecy? Three episodes hence, we will learn that Mr. Bloom placed a want ad in the newspaper under the name Mr. Henry Flower for a "smart lady typist to aid gentleman in literary work" (8.326–27). He printed the Henry Flower card to prevent him from having to say his fake name aloud in the post office, where an acquaintance might overhear. This sort of delayed clarification exemplifies how you need to have already read *Ulysses* in order to read *Ulysses*. Anyhow, Bloom gives this card to the postmistress and is somewhat surprised when she hands him a letter from Martha Clifford, the fourth such correspondence he has received from his illicit pen pal. Bloom puts the letter in his pocket, looks at a British army recruiting poster, and leaves the post office. This passage of Bloom's inner monologue also includes the first hint that he is a "mason" (5.75), a member of the secret society of Freemasonry.

Take a moment to appreciate the vivid clarity of the third-person narration as Bloom's "hand went into his pocket and a forefinger felt its way under the flap of the envelope, ripping it open in jerks" (5.77–78). Just as he is removing Martha's letter, a man named M'Coy stops him. Bloom is irked at being delayed in reading the letter but behaves pleasantly enough. They exchange comments on Paddy Dignam's unexpected death, but Bloom is distracted by an attractive, high-class woman climbing into a carriage across the street. As we saw in the butcher's shop earlier in the morning, Bloom has a bit of a lecherous streak in him. Here, he is hoping to catch a glimpse of the woman's "silk flash rich stockings white" (5.130), but a passing tram comically thwarts his view at "the very moment" (5.133) he might have indulged this particular fetish. Readers of Joyce's *Dubliners* stories will recognize many names in Bloom's conversation with M'Coy, including Bob Doran ("The Boarding House"), Hoppy Holohan ("A Mother"), and Bantam Lyons ("Ivy Day in the Committee Room"), as well as M'Coy himself ("Grace"). There is continuity in Joyce's Dublin, and his characters' lives have followed natural trajectories. For example, in "The Boarding House," poor Bob Doran was trapped into marrying Polly Mooney, and the result is an unhappy homelife from which he distracts himself by going on periodical drinking benders. This sort of intertextual connectivity within Joyce's works contributes to the unprecedented verisimilitude of the fictional Dublin depicted in *Ulysses*.

Looming in the background of Bloom's conversation with M'Coy is the fact that their respective wives are rival soprano prima donnas competing for music hall gigs. In this context, Bloom is pleased to tell M'Coy the news of Molly's planned concert tour, but doing so reminds him of this afternoon's meeting between his wife and Blazes

Boylan, especially when M'Coy asks Bloom, "Who's getting it up?" (5.153). Possibly a double entendre, this exact question will be asked of Bloom again later in the day, raising the prospect that other Dubliners are aware of Boylan and Molly's affair, making Bloom the butt of a joke going around town. Even the newspaper ad for Plumtree's Potted Meat seems to be teasing Bloom: potted meat, a food product, also carries sexual innuendo. We will later learn that Molly and Boylan enjoy some potted meat together in bed this afternoon. Literally. And figuratively.

M'Coy asks Bloom the favor of putting his name down at Dignam's funeral, and the two men part ways. Alone again, Bloom congratulates himself on ducking M'Coy's trick of borrowing luggage from people and then pawning it off. He then thinks about seeing a performance of the play *Leah* tonight. This play invokes themes of anti-Semitism and suicide, which brings Bloom's mind to his Jewish father, who enjoyed this play and who took his own life by poison (more on this topic to come in the next episode, "Hades"). Bloom also offers his own *Hamlet* theory: "Perhaps [Hamlet] was a woman. Why Ophelia committed suicide" (5.196–97). He reveals that he was born in 1866, making him thirty-eight years old. He walks by some cab horses contentedly munching oats "with their long noses stuck in nosebags" (5.216) and notes the animals' temporary escape from an otherwise unpleasant existence. He passes a cabman's shelter and draws a comparison between the monotonous lives of these horses and the cabbies who drive them. He also recalls for the second time (see 4.327) a line from the opera *Don Giovanni*: "*voglio e non*" *vorrei* (5.224), which translates as "I want to and I wouldn't like to," reflecting Bloom's paralysis in the face of Molly's affair. He gets tripped up by this phrase throughout the day.

Bloom turns down a side street and finally reads Martha's letter to Henry Flower. If Bloom was worried that he "went too far" (5.59) in his last letter, it seems Martha is rising to meet the edgier tone of their flirtation. The letter contains a slew of typographical and grammatical errors; ironically, Martha falls far short of the "smart lady typist" sought in the initial want ad. While titillated by the letter, Bloom foresees the arc of this relationship: Martha will pursue this tryst while trying to maintain the appearance of the scrupulous Catholic woman, which Bloom describes as the back-and-forth of a "usual love scrimmage" (5.271). Bloom therefore resolves not to meet Martha in person, but he will continue to indulge the excitement of the written correspondence, especially now that Martha has dabbled in suggestions of masochism, which strikes Bloom's fancy (as we will see in the "Circe" episode). We might also weigh Bloom's epistolary infidelity against Molly's affair on a moral scale.

Removing the pin from the flower Martha included in her letter, Bloom thinks about pins and women while attempting to discern the meaning of various phrases from the letter. He then tears into bits the envelope bearing Henry Flower's name and ponders the similar ease with which someone could tear up a check. He remembers a massive check cashed by a member of the Guinness family, prompting a resumption of his mental math pertaining to Dublin's pub economy from earlier in the morning. Again, he gets it almost right. Since Mr. Bloom took a detour down a side street to read Martha's letter in private, he cuts through a path alongside All Hallows Church and decides to go into the sanctuary for a moment of quiet reflection. He sees a poster for a sermon on missionary work abroad to be delivered by Father Conmee (the former rector of Clongowes Wood College from whom young Stephen Dedalus sought help in *A Portrait*). Typical of Bloom, he notes the sensory experiences of the church, such as "the cold smell of sacred stone" (5.338), the mystical effect of hearing the Latin, the eating of the host, and the appeal of drinking wine—more "aristocratic" than the Guinness that the congregants "are used to" (5.386–87). Also typical of Bloom, he has a relatively harmless but still unsavory thought that a church is a "nice discreet place to be next some girl" (5.340–41). Bloom thinks about miracles and the practical effects of going to mass. He offers bloomisms in his erroneous explanation of church iconography: INRI is "Jesus of Nazareth, King of the Jews" rather than "iron nails ran in" (5.374), and IHS are the first three letters of the name "Jesus" in Greek, not "I have suffered" (5.373).[2] Bloom has humorously pragmatic thoughts on the church as he deconstructs the pageantry of the mass and generally considers religion to be the opium of the people. We saw in "Calypso" that Bloom is not a practicing Jew, and we now see that he is far from an observant Catholic. As Robert Martin Adams points out, by creating Mr. Bloom as someone "outside the traditions of all faiths, just as naive about Haggadah as about the ceremonies in All Hallows, Joyce gains [an] ironic perspective on the various religious formulas."[3] Bloom reduces the church to a "wonderful organization" (5.424) that "rake[s] in the money" (5.435) by giving people the punishment and forgiveness they crave for their misdeeds. You might contrast Bloom's irreverent though whimsical thoughts on religion with Stephen's solemn rejection of faith.

Before they pass around the collection plate, Bloom stands up to leave and notices that two buttons on his waistcoat have been open all morning. He generalizes that women enjoy the unexpected exposure of a man's skin. Leaving the church, he checks the time: "quarter past" (5.462) = 10:15. He decides he has "time enough" (5.462) to get Molly's lotion made at Sweny's Chemist down the street; however, he realizes to his frustration that the recipe for the lotion is in his other trousers, as is the key to his home (which he had reminded himself to get earlier in the morning). In another example of his circular thinking, he begins to curse the funeral (the reason he is wearing his black suit rather than his normal pants) but checks himself by remembering poor Dignam: "it's not his fault" (5.469). Mr. Bloom finds balance by oscillating between extremes and returning to the type of centered thinking that characterizes a more mature, open-hearted person.

In a wonderful bit of problem solving, Bloom realizes that the chemist can look up the recipe for Molly's lotion in his prescription book based on the date he last had it made. He recalls paying with a sovereign (a £1 coin), which would be memorable for a middle-class guy like Bloom—similar to using a $100 bill in American currency (although a sovereign actually would have been closer in value to $300). So, Bloom deduces that he must have last bought Molly's lotion on the first or second of the month, right after his bimonthly pay "about a fortnight ago" (5.485). He muses on the miraculous paradox of nature providing cures in poisons as he enters Sweny's and does his best to remember the ingredients to the lotion. His mind pops from memories of Molly from this morning to Martha's letter, leading to the idea of taking a bath prior to the funeral and, ahem, "combining business with pleasure" (5.504–05). He adds a bar of lemon soap to his purchase from Sweny's and arranges to pay when he returns later in the day to collect Molly's lotion. He exits the shop with the rolled newspaper under his arm.

On the street, an unhygienic man named Bantam Lyons, who M'Coy mentioned was in the pub across the street, appears at Mr. Bloom's armpit (Mr. Bloom is 5 feet, 9½ inches tall [see 17.86–87], well above average height for his era).[4] Lyons pokes Bloom in greeting and asks to borrow his newspaper so that he can check on the horses racing in this afternoon's Ascot Gold Cup, a major English flat racing event. Bloom, facing a tight timeline if he wants to bathe and make it to the Dignams' house by 11:00, hopes to "get shut of [Bantam Lyons]" (5.530) quickly and offers the paper to him, saying, "I was just going to throw it away" (5.534). Bantam Lyons eyes Bloom questioningly, then says "I'll risk it" (5.541) and speeds off. This exchange is inscrutable both to Bloom and to the first-time reader. We will later learn that a horse named Throwaway is running in the Gold Cup at twenty-to-one odds, and Bloom, saying that he was going to throw away his newspaper, has just unwittingly given Bantam Lyons a tip on this longshot. This misunderstanding will reverberate later in Bloom's day.

On his way to the bathhouse, Bloom the ad man critiques the design of an advertisement poster for college sports. He celebrates the pleasant weather of this morning, which he thinks would be perfect for playing the English game cricket. The episode closes with a paragraph of free indirect discourse as Mr. Bloom imagines himself naked in the bathtub. He sees his genitals as a "languid floating flower" (5.571–72), recalling both his *nom de plume* and the lotus so subtly influential throughout the episode. Of course, there's also heavy irony in Mr. Bloom, a father of one child, viewing his penis as the "limp father of thousands" (5.570).

### Further Reading

Benstock, Shari. "The Printed Letters in *Ulysses*." *James Joyce Quarterly* 50, no. 1/2 (Fall-Winter 2013): 167–79.

By the end of "Lotus-Eaters," the reader has encountered Mr. Deasy's letter to the press, Milly's correspondence to her parents, Boylan's letter to Molly, and Martha's letter to Henry Flower; other letters are forthcoming in the episodes ahead. This essay examines the distinct voices of these letters and their varying ways of relating to the larger text.

Christensen, Andrew G. "*Ulysses*'s Martha Clifford: The Foreigner Hypothesis." *James Joyce Quarterly* 54, no. 3/4 (Spring-Summer 2017): 335–52.

After surveying various theories pertaining to the identity of Martha
Clifford, this essay focuses on the errors in Martha's letter, proposing that
Mr. Bloom's pen pal is an immigrant to Ireland.

Finn, Anna M. "A Bloom without a Flower, or How to Read 'Lotus Eaters.'"
*James Joyce Quarterly* 52, no. 3/4 (Spring-Summer 2015): 623–35.

Finn presents the floral motif of this episode in terms of its Homeric correspondences, its nod to Victorian flower dictionaries, and its metaphori-
cal meanings in Bloom's thinking at this hour.

# Chapter 6

# "HADES" GUIDE

The "Hades" episode depicts Mr. Bloom's attendance of Paddy Dignam's funeral during the eleven o'clock hour of June 16, 1904. Along with Martin Cunningham, Jack Power, and Simon Dedalus (Stephen's father), Mr. Bloom departs from the Dignams' home in a procession of horse-drawn carriages that will traverse the city of Dublin to Prospect Cemetery in Glasnevin. "Hades" is the final episode in the novel's pair of opening triads in their reciprocal ABC-CBA structure, mirroring "Telemachus" in its presentation of the protagonist within a dramatic group. Bloom's social isolation from the other funeral-goers recalls Stephen's sense of exile from those with whom he interacts at the tower.[1] Indeed, Robert Martin Adams's description of Bloom in "Hades"—"less alone physically, more alone spiritually"[2]—could just as easily apply to Stephen's situation in the company of Buck and Haines. Similar also to "Telemachus," the third-person narrator asserts greater control in navigating the social drama of "Hades," even going so far as to detach from Bloom's perspective twice in order to narrate conversations occurring outside his hearing. In this way, "Hades" concludes the introductory triads in the initial style while briefly hinting toward the stylistic shifts and narrative disruptions ahead.

In Homer's *Odyssey*, Odysseus visits the land of the dead to learn from the prophet Tiresias how he might return to his home in Ithaca. In Hades, Odysseus encounters many deceased comrades and loved ones, and he learns from Tiresias that he will find suitors courting his

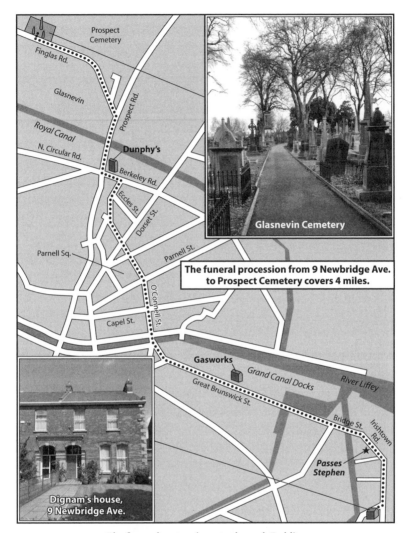

The funeral cortege's route through Dublin.
*Photo of Glasnevin Cemetery courtesy of Anne Stuzin.*

wife when he returns home to Ithaca. Likewise, Mr. Bloom in this episode confronts the memories of departed loved ones and wrestles with thoughts of his own troubled homelife. The first spirit to appear to Odysseus in Hades is Elpenor, a member of his crew who recently died in a drunken accident; Elpenor corresponds to Paddy Dignam, who died of heart complications related to alcoholism. Just as Odysseus goes out of his way to give Elpenor a proper funeral, Mr. Bloom here makes the effort to attend the funeral of a man with whom he seems to share only a thin acquaintance.

Between the end of "Lotus-Eaters" and the beginning of "Hades," Mr. Bloom bathed and then took a tram toward the Dignams' home at 9 Newbridge Avenue in Sandymount. The episode begins *in medias res* as Martin Cunningham, Jack Power, and Simon Dedalus enter the carriage; when Bloom takes the fourth and final seat, you may sense that the other men are not excited to have him join their group. Bloom observes that he's sitting uncomfortably on his bar of lemon soap and intends to "shift it out of" his hip pocket when presented with "an opportunity" to do so discreetly (6.22–23). As the carriages set forth, the men discuss the route the driver will take through town, and Mr. Dedalus notes with appreciation the continued observance of "a fine old custom" (6.36) of Dublin citizens lifting their hats out of respect for the deceased as the hearse passes by.

Mr. Bloom spots Stephen Dedalus as the carriage passes by "a lithe young man, clad in mourning, a wide hat" (6.39–40); Stephen is heading into town after his walk on the strand in "Proteus." Bloom points him out to Simon, who launches into a rant about his in-laws and Buck Mulligan, a "contaminated bloody doubledyed ruffian" (6.64) corrupting his son. Bloom silently absorbs Simon's "angry" (7.72) outburst, accepting that a father has the right to be "full of his son" (6.74). For the second time today, Bloom poignantly imagines "if little Rudy had lived" (6.75) that he'd be eleven years old now, dressed in an Eton suit, and sounding his voice in their home. Bloom thinks of his own thwarted paternal impulse to have "something to hand on" (6.74–75) to future generations, echoing Stephen's contemplation of paternity and his own future in "Proteus." He recalls the morning of Rudy's conception and Molly's consequent pregnancy; he silently mourns the loss of Rudy but finds some solace in thinking of his daughter Milly, even if that comfort is twinged with reminders of her emerging womanhood.

As the carriage rocks, the men object to the rickety ride supplied by Corny Kelleher, an acquaintance who works for the funeral home. As their inspection of the carriage continues, the men notice "crumbs" (6.97), as well as, perhaps, unspecified evidence of a sexual event. They note the other attendees of Dignam's funeral before stopping at "the grand canal" (6.120), the first correspondence to the rivers surrounding Hades in Greek mythology. Looking at the gasworks facility, Mr. Bloom notes that its gases purportedly cure whooping cough and expresses silent gratitude that Milly had a relatively healthy childhood. Seeing a dog shelter in the distance triggers the memory of his late father's suicide letter, imploring Leopold to "be good to Athos" (6.125), his dog. It begins to rain but only briefly.

The men begin to mock the pontification of Tom Kernan, who, like Martin Cunningham and Jack Power, first appeared in the *Dubliners* story "Grace." In their parody of Kernan's speech, we see for the first time the phrase "retrospective arrangement" (6.150), a term that appears seven times in the novel and may signal Joyce's hint of how *Ulysses* works. David Hayman suggests that the "arranger" of this "retrospective arrangement" knows everything in the novel and systematically organizes the details, references, thematic echoes, and revelations in a manner that builds coherence and amplifies meaning. As a reader gains knowledge of the text, *Ulysses* makes more sense; in this way, the technique of "retrospective arrangement" offers rich rewards to the repeat-reader of the novel.

Martin Cunningham raises the topic of the speech delivered by Dan Dawson, the owner/baker of the Dublin Bread Company and a merchant-politician.[3] Bloom feels in his coat pocket the book he plans to swap for Molly; he will exchange this book in the "Wandering Rocks" episode. Simon Dedalus asks where Dan Dawson's speech was printed, so Bloom pulls out his newspaper to share with him. Mr. Dedalus brusquely declines to look at it, keeping Bloom on the outside of the conversation. Mr. Bloom silently considers the obituaries "down the edge of the paper" (6.157). Just as diction related to narcotics suffused the "Lotus-Eaters" episode, the stench of death wafts through "Hades," from whiffs as pungent as when Bloom thinks of his dead son to those as mild as his consideration of cheese being the "corpse of milk" (6.982).

For the second time (see 5.385), Mr. Bloom expresses some paranoia about whether he "tore up the envelope" (6.168) of Martha Clifford's letter (we know he did; see 5.300) and checks for the letter itself in his pocket. The carriage passes locations Bloom walked by about "an hour ago" (6.173) in the "Lotus-Eaters" episode. He imagines a device that could automatically switch the tram track, but he displays his characteristic compassion by worrying that the invention would result in the elimination of the pointsman's job. He sees billboards for local performances and again considers seeing *Leah* tonight; he thinks, "I said I" (6.185), abbreviating that he told Molly that he would indeed see the play this evening, which effectively signals to her that he will not interrupt her meeting with Boylan. He remembers that Blazes Boylan "is coming in the afternoon" under the auspices of discussing "her songs" (6.190). The choppy, unfinished style of Bloom's inner monologue here reflects his avoidance of sustained thoughts related to Molly's impending infidelity. In the first of many coincidences in the novel, just at that moment the other men in the carriage see Boylan emerging from the Red Bank, a restaurant known for its seafood and, auspiciously, its oysters. Anxiously distracting himself by looking down at his nails, Bloom silently questions Boylan's appeal.

Mr. Power asks, perhaps with some malice, "How is the concert tour getting on, Bloom?" (6.212). As Bloom begins to answer, Mr. Power pointedly inquires if Bloom himself will be accompanying Molly on the tour. It seems that the budding illicit romance between Boylan and Molly has been the subject of Dublin gossip, and these fellows enjoy digging the knife into Bloom's side. In any event, Bloom will not be traveling with Molly on the tour because he is visiting Ennis in County Clare to honor the anniversary of his father's death and pay for the upkeep of the gravesite. Bloom thinks of Molly, imagining that she is now out of bed and doing her hair while their housekeeper, Mrs. Fleming, cleans the house. Bloom's inner monologue silently volleys back a bit of gossip about Mr. Power, who reportedly is having an affair with a barmaid.

The men notice Reuben J. Dodd, a Jewish moneylender, as the carriage passes him in the street. Simon Dedalus curses him, Mr. Power laughs, and Martin Cunningham suggests that "we have all been there" (6.259), meaning in debt, then looks at Bloom and corrects himself—"well, nearly all of us" (6.261). The implication is that Jewish Mr. Bloom has never owed money to a Jewish moneylender. Eager to disassociate himself from Reuben J. Dodd, Bloom begins to share a story about Dodd's son falling into the river, but he stumbles in his narration, and Martin Cunningham "rudely" (6.277) hijacks the story (Dodd rewarded the boatman who saved his son with a florin coin worth 2 shillings—a relatively small sum—roughly US$30 today). The other men make sure that Mr. Bloom is kept on the outside of the joke, and the anti-Semitism clouding the air of the carriage remains heavy.

As the procession passes Nelson's Pillar, we hear a girl selling "eight plums a penny" (6.294), which will figure into Stephen's "Parable of the Plums" at the end of the "Aeolus" episode. The men turn their attention to Paddy Dignam, celebrating his good humor in life and mourning the suddenness of his death. Dignam died of complications related to his alcoholism, which the men euphemize as a "breakdown" of the "heart" (6.305). Mr. Bloom, ever humane, finds solace in the fact that Dignam died quickly, with no suffering. The other men in the carriage, however, stare at Bloom with shocked "wideopen eyes" (6.312); for Catholics, a sudden death affords no opportunity for the sacrament of last rites and the final absolution of sins. Therefore, Paddy Dignam's sudden death means his soul was unprepared for heaven. Mr. Bloom, trying only to be sympathetic, once again finds himself silently but undoubtedly ostracized.

A hearse carrying the "tiny coffin" (6.322) of a dead child passes by their window, and Bloom's thoughts return to Rudy. His mind acknowledges the conventional belief that "if it's healthy it's from the mother. If not from the man" (6.329), revealing his sense of responsibility for Rudy's death. So, Bloom is already in a dark place when Mr. Power and Mr. Dedalus begin to rail against suicide as the "greatest disgrace to have in the family" (6.338). "Sympathetic" (6.344) Martin Cunningham, who knows of Bloom's father's suicide, attempts to temper and thwart the conversation. Mr. Bloom considers speaking up but remains silent. He silently reciprocates Cunningham's compassion by thinking of "that awful drunkard of a wife of his" (6.349–50), who pawns their furniture every Saturday. As S. L. Goldberg explains, Mr. Bloom and Martin Cunningham are subtly bound by "their common sympathy of heart, their common pain, and their common silence."[4] In silence, Mr. Bloom recalls the scene of his father's deathbed, including the "redlabelled bottle" (6.359) of aconite, the "yellow streaks on his face" (6.362–63), the coroner, the sunlight, and the suicide letter.

The cortege reaches the north side of the city, close to Bloom's neighborhood, and Mr. Bloom hears "a streetorgan" (6.372) playing "Has Anybody Here Seen Kelly?" (a rare anachronism in the novel—the song didn't appear until 1908). He thinks about the Mater Misericordiae hospital on Eccles Street, the hospice ward there, and the medical student who took care of the bee sting Bloom suffered a few weeks back. This young doctor's name is Dixon, and we will see him later at the maternity hospital in the "Oxen of the Sun" episode. The carriage stops for a herd of cattle to pass on their way to boats bound for Liverpool. Mr. Bloom knows the cattle trade from his previous employment as an actuary for Mr. Cuffe and suggests the idea of running a cattle tramline from the farmland to the boat docks, thus clearing the roads of these herds. Martin Cunningham agrees. Feeling some traction in the social group, Bloom also offers the idea of "municipal funeral trams" (6.406) to the cemetery. After some debate, the men agree with this idea, too, especially since it would eliminate unpleasant scenes of hearse carriages hitting a bump and knocking the coffin and corpse out into the road. Bloom imagines such a macabre scene, and Mr. Power points out Dunphy's pub, where funeral-goers customarily stop off for a postburial drink.

The carriage passes over the Royal Canal (another correspondence to the rivers of the underworld), where a man on a barge salutes Dignam (this bargeman will briefly reappear in "Wandering Rocks"). Bloom again considers visiting his daughter down in Mullingar "as a surprise" (6.450) but decides he shouldn't arrive unannounced for fear that he might catch her with her "pants down" (6.485). Mr. Power points out the site of the Childs murder, a famous and enthralling case that attracted the attention of seventeen-year-old James Joyce. The accused was found not guilty because the prosecution had "only circumstantial" (6.473) evidence; as Martin Cunningham says, "Better for ninetynine guilty to escape than for one innocent person to be wrongfully condemned" (6.474–75).

The funeral procession arrives at Prospect Cemetery, and the men exit the carriage. Bloom moves the lemon soap from his hip to the inner handkerchief pocket of his coat. He notices the funeral's "paltry" (6.498) attendance and walks behind the other men toward the mortuary chapel. For the first time, the narrative perspective shifts from Bloom to the other men as Cunningham informs Mr. Power of Mr. Bloom's father's suicide. This is the "first [Power] heard of it"

(6.532), and he seems genuinely sorry, even if he doesn't feel moved to apologize. He looks back to see the "dark thinking eyes" (6.533) of Mr. Bloom, who is walking and speaking with Tom Kernan, a Protestant whose pretentions were the subject of the other men's ridicule earlier during the carriage ride. Mr. Bloom inquires into the state of Paddy Dignam's finances. Tom Kernan explains that Dignam's life insurance policy had been heavily borrowed against and that Cunningham and Ned Lambert are working to arrange things for the Dignam children. Bloom is concerned for the widow and her five children and contemplates the loss of a spouse. He assumes that Molly would remarry if he died—probably not to "him," meaning Boylan, "yet who knows" (6.548–49). Mr. Dedalus greets Ned Lambert, who informs Simon that they are "whip[ping]" (6.564) up a collection to support the Dignam family until the insurance begins to pay out. Broke, Simon Dedalus dodges the appeal; after all, he has his own destitute family to worry not enough about. The funeral moves into the mortuary chapel. Bloom thinks about Dignam's last moments. We might notice that Bloom seems not to know Dignam very intimately; his inner monologue offers little insight into the nature of their acquaintance and no details of their friendship. Attending the funeral of a fellow he only slightly knew emphasizes his generous and empathetic character. Also characteristic of Bloom, the pragmatism of his inner monologue considers various aspects of the religious ceremony (the Latin, the holy water, the altar boys, the liturgy, etc.).

In an interesting passage in terms of style, the third-person narrator's language is conflated with Mr. Bloom's inner monologue: the narrator describes the priest reading the prayers "with a fluent croak" (6.594) and as having a "toad's belly" (6.591), while Bloom notes that the priest has "eyes of a toad too" (6.605). While blurring the lines between subjectivity and objectivity, this narrative effect also brings us into even closer alliance with Mr. Bloom because, as S. L. Goldberg explains, "the narrative point of view has shifted entirely behind Bloom's and serves as a tacit endorsement of it."[5] The silent travails of the carriage ride have bonded us to Mr. Bloom, and the narrative style here reflects that camaraderie.

They wheel the coffin out of the chapel and toward the gravesite. Simon nods toward the burial site of his late wife, expresses his readiness to join her in death, and begins "to weep to himself quietly" (6.647). Mr. Bloom and Tom Kernan, again walking behind the others, comment briefly on the Catholic rituals in which they are unpracticed. Kernan compares the Catholic liturgy unfavorably to the Protestant service, and Bloom thinks about death in its most practical terms: the heart is a pump, and "once you are dead you are dead" (6.677). Bloom's disbelief in God and an afterlife is notably matter-of-fact compared to Stephen's Luciferian revolt and heroic martyrdom. As the caretaker's assistant, Corny Kelleher, joins Bloom and Kernan, the narrative perspective again drifts briefly away from Bloom, this time to John Henry Menton, a lawyer and former employer of Paddy Dignam, who recognizes Bloom's face and asks Ned Lambert who he is. Ned identifies Bloom through his marriage to Molly. Menton remembers Molly as a "finelooking woman" (6.696) and fondly recalls dancing with her years ago. Menton inquires further, remembering that Bloom used to work for Wisdom Hely's stationer and recalling also that he once quarreled with Bloom over a game of lawn bowling years ago. Lambert tells him that Bloom now works in advertising, and Menton questions why Molly, with all her talent, charisma, and good looks, would have married "a coon like that" (6.704–05). Resentful of Bloom winning Molly's hand in marriage, Menton corresponds to Ajax in *The Odyssey*, who carries a grudge against Odysseus for winning Achilles's armor and therefore snubs him in Hades.

John O'Connell, the caretaker, joins the funeral and greets the men in attendance cordially, even offering a joke to lighten the mood. Bloom's mind hops around from topic to topic, including his plan to work on "Keyes's ad . . . after the funeral" (6.741–42), his surreptitious correspondence with Martha, the signs of aging, ghost stories, amorous "love among the tombstones" (6.758–59), and the creative idea of burying people upright rather than lying down in order to save space. He considers the fecundity of the soil in and near a cemetery and morbidly imagines flesh decomposing beneath the ground. We overhear O'Connell discussing business with Corny Kelleher.

Then, Mr. Bloom prompts one of the novel's great mysteries: "who is that lankylooking galoot over there in the macintosh?" (6.805). Many Joyce scholars, and Bloom himself, take an interest in the identity of the man in the brown macintosh. Because he brings the number of funeral attendees to thirteen, some think he is Jesus with the twelve apostles, while others think he is the Grim Reaper: "the chap in the macintosh is thirteen. Death's number" (6.825–26). Or perhaps he is James Joyce subtly painting himself into the composition like Jan van Eyck or Diego Velázquez. Given that the man in the brown macintosh has seven subsequent appearances in the remaining episodes of the novel, perhaps he is simply a fixture of the modern urban experience, the person who randomly pops up in places but whom nobody seems to know, as Stuart Gilbert posits: "he is the hunchback one never fails to see in the left-hand corner seat of the front row of the gallery on every first night, the bearded Russian priest who never misses an international football match, that old woman in a moleskin coat with a packet of peppermint lozenges."[6] You can have fun investigating this mystery or elect to set it aside at your pleasure. While perhaps an enticing thread to follow, it seems to me a puzzle intentionally lacking the pieces required for a solution. Robert Martin Adams suggests, "It doesn't seem in the least uncomfortable to accept the notion that he is an enigma without an answer."[7] Even so, be on the lookout for his reappearances in future episodes.

Bloom admires the "nice soft tweed" (6.828) of Ned Lambert's suit before Dignam's coffin is lowered into the earth. He thinks about the moment of death and the inevitability of being forgotten as acquaintances eventually "follow" (6.855) the deceased into the grave. Thinking of his own death for a moment, he glances toward the plot on the cemetery grounds he has purchased for his family, where his "poor mamma, and little Rudy" (6.863) are buried but not his father; suicides are "refuse[d] christian burial" (6.346). As the gravediggers begin shoveling dirt onto Dignam's coffin, Bloom thinks with panic that perhaps he isn't actually dead. Maybe they should put a "telephone in the coffin" or a "flag of distress" (6.868–69) just in case. As the earth fills Dignam's grave, the funeral-goers put on their hats and prepare to go about their lives: "out of sight, out of mind" (6.872). Joe Hynes, a newspaperman, asks Mr. Bloom's "christian name" (6.881) for the funeral notice—folks seem to know him only by his last name. Bloom asks Hynes to "put down M'Coy's name too" (6.882). Promise kept. He imagines M'Coy thanking him for this favor and thinks, "Leave him under an obligation: costs nothing" (6.890), which Marilyn French cites as an example of Bloom's "distasteful habit of rationalizing the impulse behind his kind acts by imagining that he will derive some practical advantage from them."[8] Fair enough.

A bit of confusion arises as Hynes asks the name of the man "over there in the . . . Macintosh" (6.891–92, 894), Bloom finishes. Hynes jots down "M'Intosh" (6.895), mistaking it for the mystery man's name. The gravediggers finish their work, and Hynes and Power head over to pay respects at Parnell's grave. Bloom walks off by himself, thinking about visiting his father's grave at the end of the month and his obligation to pay the gardener who tends the plot. Bloom considers more interesting information to engrave on tombstones, such as the profession or particular talents of the deceased. Looking out on the innumerable tombstones in the huge cemetery, he has the sublime thought that "all these here once walked round Dublin" (6.960). He imagines playing voice recordings of the deceased to keep them in memory. Bloom is halted by a fat, old gray rat toddling by a crypt and thinks again about decay and what happens to a corpse after death "no matter who it was" (6.981). Bloom's thought that "drowning they say is the pleasantest" (6.988) death echoes Stephen's thought that "seadeath mildest of all deaths" (3.482), suggesting further similarities between the two men despite their obvious differences and contributing to our growing eagerness to see them meet.

Approaching the gates of the cemetery, Bloom's mood lifts as he turns "back to the world again" (6.995). In stark contrast to Mr. Dedalus's fatalism earlier in the episode, Bloom has "plenty to see and hear and feel yet" (6.1003). He notices John Henry Menton, who had earlier noticed him, and likewise recalls their dispute during the game of lawn bowling. Here, a pun on "the bias" refers to both the curved shot of a weighted bowl as well as to Menton's anti-Semitic "hate at first sight" (6.1012) of Bloom. Menton's embarrassed anger over losing the game was apparently compounded by "Molly and Floey Dillon linked under the lilactree, laughing" (6.1013) as they watched. Bloom notices that Menton's hat has a dent in its side and politely points it out to him. Menton stares at Bloom blankly before Martin Cunningham breaks the tension. Menton reluctantly says, "Thank you" (6.1026), and Bloom falls back, dejectedly "chapfallen" (6.1027) by Menton's rudeness. Bloom concludes the episode with silent slights against Menton, calling him in his inner monologue "sappyhead" and "oyster eyes" (6.1031) and sarcastically noting "how grand" Menton was in deigning to say "thank you" (6.1033). He takes the high road, imagining that he will "get the pull over him" (6.1032) in the long run; indeed, with Molly as his wife, he already has.

## Further Reading

Abbott, H. Porter. "The Importance of Martin Cunningham." *James Joyce Quarterly* 5, no. 1 (1967): 47–52.

    While harsh on Martin Cunningham's pomposity and assertiveness, this essay also highlights the character's ability to affect change and his capacity for empathy. Abbott explains Cunningham as one of the novel's more fully formed minor characters and a tile in the mosaic of Joyce's portrait of humanity.

Duffy, Enda. "Setting: Dublin 1904/1922." In *The Cambridge Companion to "Ulysses,"* edited by Sean Latham, 81–94. New York: Cambridge University Press, 2014.

    Most of the characters in *Ulysses* come from the Catholic middle class that was just emerging in Dublin at the beginning of the twentieth century, and this essay offers helpful context for understanding the precarious status of this socioeconomic group. Duffy also provides historical context for the Irish nationalist movements that are evident in the novel.

Rowan, Jonathan Bricke. "Who Is M'Intosh?" *James Joyce Quarterly* 51, no. 4 (2014): 631–40.

    Rather than searching for a person, Rowan argues that M'Intosh is emblematic of the incertitude that *Ulysses* presents as a central aspect of the human experience.

Somer, John. "The Self-Reflexive Arranger in the Initial Style of Joyce's *Ulysses*." *James Joyce Quarterly* 31, no. 2 (Winter 1994): 65–79.

    After establishing explanations and opinions of other scholars on the arranger as a presence in the text, Somer focuses on distinguishing between the functions of the narrator and the arranger and the way that *Ulysses*'s self-referentiality complicates its realism. Somer demonstrates the more subtle influence of the arranger within the novel's first six episodes.

# Chapter 7

# "AEOLUS" GUIDE

The "Aeolus" episode, with its inclusion of newspaper headlines, represents the first of many chapters in which Joyce pushes the boundaries of the novel as a genre of literature. How is the experience of reading fiction altered by the introduction of another form's conventions? Is a novel still a novel if one-fifth of it is presented as a dramatic script? What if it also contains a catechism? Joyce's contemporary T. S. Eliot addresses these questions in his essay "*Ulysses*, Order, and Myth": "If [*Ulysses*] is not a novel, that is simply because the novel is a form which will no longer serve."[1] Eliot understood that Joyce was creating a new sort of modernist literary art more capable of expressing "the immense panorama of futility and anarchy which is contemporary history."[2] In his revolutionary redefinition of the novel, Joyce saw all types of language—from Dublin slang to Deuteronomy, from advertising slogans to Virgil's *Eclogues*—as fodder for the great project of *Ulysses*. In the case of this episode's newspaper headlines (which Joyce added to the text at a late stage of the writing/revision process),[3] we immediately notice their effect of simultaneously interrupting and framing the prose and narration, signifying the text's alternately helpful and ironic relationship with the reader. Since "Aeolus" is the first episode of *Ulysses* to engage the consciousness of both Stephen and Mr. Bloom, the headlines suggest that the stories of these two men, like separate articles in a newspaper, can be brought together into a unified whole.

The newspaper office and other locations relevant to this episode

In terms of the correspondence to Homer, the episode is named for Aeolus, the keeper of the winds, who gives Odysseus a magical sack of winds; appropriately, this chapter is filled with the hot air of political speeches, frequent gusts of rhetorical devices, and the inflated discourse of newspapers and newspapermen. In the schema, Joyce identified the lungs as the organ for this episode; indeed, "Aeolus" features lots of comings and goings (inhales and exhales), and the diction is suffused with references to air and wind. In Homer's *Odyssey*, Odysseus and his crew have nearly returned home; they can even see men tending fires on the shores of Ithaca. Relieved, and exhausted from sailing for two weeks straight, Odysseus takes a nap. While he's sleeping, Odysseus's men assume with jealousy that Aeolus's sack contains treasure; after griping about unfair distribution of wealth, they open the sack, letting loose the winds and blowing the ship all the way back to Aeolus's island. In correspondence to this frustrating moment in *The Odyssey*, the "Aeolus" episode includes a few near-misses as Bloom attempts to do his job as an advertising agent and has a fleeting encounter with Stephen outside of the newspaper offices.

In the preceding "Hades" episode, the narration briefly detached from Mr. Bloom to depict conversations outside his earshot; here, the narrator at the beginning of "Aeolus" presents a wider panoramic perspective in describing various scenes occurring in Dublin independent of Mr. Bloom and in highly stylized prose. By depicting activity at the terminus of the city's tramlines, outside the general post office, and on the docks, the text displays an interest in exploring the city without Stephen or Bloom, an interest in Dublin and Dubliners that the novel will fully indulge in the "Wandering Rocks" episode ahead. This bird's-eye narrative perspective in these opening paragraphs, combined with the headlines' metatextuality, signal the emergence of "the arranger," a mischievous creator, distinct from the narrator, who will increasingly manipulate the text.

By noon, the funeral-goers have returned from Glasnevin Cemetery (likely by way of Dunphy's pub) to the center of Dublin, where Mr. Bloom immediately gets to work on placing an advertisement for House of Keyes tea shop in the *Evening Telegraph* newspaper. Bloom's job involves brokering the sale of advertising space in newspapers by first pitching the idea for the advertisement to the business owner, then negotiating with the officers of the newspaper for the price and length of time that the advertisement will run. Bloom's sort of newspaper advertisements were a relatively recent innovation,[4] first appearing in the 1880s when an increasingly literate populace began widely reading cheap daily newspapers.[5] The advertising industry "becomes an indispensable aid to modern trade precisely at the time of *Ulysses*," the literary sociologist Franco Moretti explains, "because of the definitive crisis of the automatic balance between supply and demand."[6] William T. Stead, a prominent journalist, wrote a book in 1899 titled *The Art of Advertising: Its Theory and Practice Fully Described*, offering a glimpse into both the economic importance of the nascent advertising industry and the aura of suspicion surrounding the advertising agent in Bloom's era. Indeed, the defensive tone of Stead's book implies that at the turn of the century, Great Britain was a hostile environment for pioneering ad men such as Mr. Bloom:

> The Advertising Agent is eminently a modern institution. He is the product of a democratic age. He has sprung into existence almost in the lifetime of a single generation. . . . The Advertising Agent is the nerve-centre of modern industry. . . . The advertiser is often a modern Ishmaelite, every man's hand is against him. The Advertising Agent must devise methods by which he can overcome this feeling of repulsion.[7]

Stead uses the Semitic allusion to the "Ishmaelite" to explain that the advertising canvasser was viewed as an outsider, an object of "repulsion" and mistrust. Stead's description of the adman in this era provides further context for the isolation Mr. Bloom experiences in Dublin and helps explain the exclusion he experiences in the newspaper offices.

At the beginning of "Aeolus," Bloom meets first with Red Murray, who cuts out a previous ad the paper ran for Keyes. Murray, who has no authority in the matter, suggests that Bloom can offer Keyes "a par" (7.34), meaning a paragraph of free advertisement posing as a news story. Murray then points out the "stately figure" (7.42) of Mr. Brayden, a respected barrister and an editor of the *Freeman's Journal*. Bloom silently thinks of a song from the opera *Martha*; he will hear this same song performed by Simon Dedalus in the Ormond Hotel bar a few hours later in the "Sirens" episode. Mr. Bloom takes the Keyes ad clipping to the foreman, Nannetti. In addition to working for the newspaper, Nannetti is a city councilor tipped by Bloom to become Dublin's "lord mayor" (7.106); Nannetti will indeed become mayor in 1906. In Nannetti's office, Bloom finds Hynes submitting his report on Dignam's funeral. Hynes owes Bloom 3 shillings, so Bloom gives a subtle hint that he can "draw the cashier" (7.113) before he goes to lunch; maybe Hynes would like to "catch him" (7.116), receive his pay, and then repay the "three bob [Bloom] lent him" (7.119) three weeks ago. Hynes either doesn't get the hint, or he's aloof to his debt.

Mr. Bloom tactfully explains to Nannetti his idea for the ad's design—"two crossed keys here. A circle. Then here the name. Alexander Keyes, tea, wine, and spirit merchant" (7.142–43). This imagery suggests the House of Keys parliament on the Isle of Man, representing a form of home rule and independence from Britain.[8] Thus, Mr. Bloom's idea for the ad makes a covert political statement. Mr. Bloom is aware that a Kilkenny newspaper ran a similar ad design, and he will seek a copy at the National Library. Nannetti likes the idea and agrees to run the ad if Keyes renews his lease on the print-space for three months. So, Mr. Bloom has the terms of a deal to broker.

Bloom's mind returns to the encounter with Menton at the end of the "Hades" episode, and he thinks he should have said, after Menton popped out the dent in the hat, something like "looks as good as new now" (7.173). So very human of Bloom to replay and revise a moment of social tension from earlier in the day. Amid the din of the printing press, Mr. Bloom hears the "sllt" (7.174) of the machine and thinks "everything speaks in its own way" (7.177). Bloom also lingers to marvel at the speed of the typesetter laying out the letters backward. The text in the novel reads "mangiD kcirtaP" (7.206) in imitation of the way the type would be laid, but, of course, the letters themselves would also be backward (e.g., "b" would look like "d"). For all of its clever inventiveness, this little moment demonstrates the text's limitations in representing exactly what Joyce is trying to do. Without question, *Ulysses* pushes the boundaries of what literature can represent to a reader.

Keyes's teahouse is in Ballsbridge, a southeastern suburb of Dublin, and Bloom smartly decides he "better phone him up first" so he doesn't "tram it out all the way and then catch him out" (7.218–19) of the shop. He heads downstairs to the office where the telephone is located and moves the lemon soap from his breast coat pocket back "into the hip pocket of his trousers" (7.228–29). The smell of the soap reminds him of Martha Clifford's question about what perfume his wife wears, which prompts him to consider popping home to see Molly before her meeting with Boylan, but he decides against it.

Bloom enters the office of the *Evening Telegraph* to find Simon Dedalus, Myles Crawford, Ned Lambert, and a man called "professor MacHugh" laughing at the terribly inflated language of Dan Dawson's speech given the previous day, which was published in the paper that morning and which the men in the carriage had discussed on the way to Dignam's funeral. J. J. O'Molloy, a "mighthavebeen" lawyer with a "gambling" problem (7.303), enters the office and is greeted warmly by the other men. Note that Bloom received no such greeting. Simon Dedalus exclaims, "Shite and onions!" (7.329) over Dawson's speech and claims he "must get a drink after that" (7.351–52), prompting an excursion with Ned Lambert to The Oval pub just down the street. Myles Crawford and professor MacHugh (who is scholarly but not actually a professor) remain behind, and Bloom asks to use the phone. A man named Lenehan (seen in the *Dubliners* story "Two Gallants") enters, offering Sceptre as his pick to win the Gold Cup (7.389).

We overhear Bloom's side of the phone call and learn that Mr. Keyes has stepped out of his shop to visit Dillon's "auction rooms" (7.412), which happens to be just around the corner from the newspaper offices. Bloom, in a rush to "catch him" (7.413) in town and therefore save himself the trip to Ballsbridge, pops out of the office and collides with Lenehan, who makes a bit of a scene, "rubbing his knee" (7.421). Bloom tells Crawford that he's "running round to Bachelor's walk . . . about this ad of Keyes's" (7.430–31), subtly hinting that he'll need Crawford's final approval for this ad (so please don't leave before he returns). Crawford, like Aeolus, sends Bloom off: "Begone! he said. The world is before you" (7.435). Mr. Bloom hurries out, followed by "capering newsboys in Mr. Bloom's wake . . . mocking" (7.444) his walk behind him. Mr. Bloom's gait has elsewhere been compared to "a flurried stork's legs" (4.384), and here he is described as having "flat spaugs" (7.448)—big, clunky feet—even as Lenehan caricatures Bloom as moving in the style of a "mazurka" (7.450)—a lively, sweeping Polish folk dance. By this point in the novel, you have probably begun to form an image of what Mr. Bloom looks like, and here you can try to imagine his distinctive manner of walking.

Crawford suggests they all go to meet Simon and Ned at The Oval, and professor MacHugh begins a meditation on empire. By analogy, the Irish are to Britain what the Greeks were to Rome: a colonized people with a richer culture than their conqueror. Later, MacHugh's delivery of Taylor's speech will compare the Irish subjugation under the English to the Egyptian oppression of the Jews. Lenehan demands silence (and does not receive it) for his new riddle: "What opera resembles a railwayline?" (7.512); the answer is *The Rose of Castile*.

Stephen Dedalus enters the office to deliver Mr. Deasy's letter on foot-and-mouth disease. With Stephen's arrival, we now have access to his inner monologue for the first time since we left him at the end of "Proteus," and the reading gets more difficult as a result. Remember that Stephen tore off a bit of Deasy's letter to compose a few lines of poetry on the rocks of Sandymount Strand—Mr. Crawford notices the tear, and Stephen mentally recites the quatrain he wrote:

> On swift sail flaming
> From storm and south
> He comes, pale vampire,
> Mouth to my mouth. (7.522–25)

Stephen, "blushing" (7.530), is embarrassed to serve as courier for Garrett Deasy, but he has fulfilled his promise. We might here perceive a similarity to Bloom inserting M'Coy's name into the list of funeral attendees in the "Hades" episode; both Stephen and Bloom honor trivial though somewhat unpleasant commitments.

The men in the office discuss Deasy and his wife, who is evidently a difficult woman and from whom Mr. Deasy is now separated; this information provides context for Deasy's misogyny in the "Nestor" episode. The men wistfully discuss Irish history, we see a few other inner echoes from Stephen's morning, and Lenehan again presses his riddle. There's a celebration of all the diverse talent present in the room (which is slightly absurd, because J. J. O'Molloy is a failing lawyer, professor MacHugh is not actually a professor, Stephen is to this point an unsuccessful poet, and Lenehan is, well, yappy). The professor lists Bloom as a representative of "the gentle art of advertising" (7.608), and Burke suggests Molly's talent for singing, which draws a "loud cough" (7.611) from Lenehan, who we might assume appreciates Molly principally for her other "talents" (7.605).

Crawford implores Stephen to write for the newspaper, saying, "You can do it. I see it in your face" (7.617), which recalls Stephen's memory of Father Dolan saying he could "see it in your face" when falsely accusing Stephen of being a "lazy idle little schemer" (7.618) in *A Portrait* (see *P* 43). Crawford presses Stephen to write something "with a bite in it. Put us all into it, damn its soul" (7.621). Given that all of the men in this episode are thinly veiled depictions of real Dubliners, it feels like *Ulysses* is a resounding answer to Crawford's call. Crawford cites a piece about the Phoenix Park murders written by Ignatius Gallaher (from the *Dubliners* story "A Little Cloud") as an exemplar of journalistic excellence because of its use of code to elude British censors, but Crawford's explanation is riddled with errors. As Robert Martin Adams explains, "the editor has all of the actors in the drama mixed up (as well as the dates), and even when he accidentally gets a name straight—'Tim Kelly,' for example—immediately corrects himself into an error—'or Kavanagh I mean.' His geography is also oddly oriented."[9] So, like Mr. Deasy a few hours earlier, Mr. Crawford's inadequacies as Stephen's potential mentor are reinforced by his factual inaccuracies.

The phone in the office rings: Mr. Bloom is calling from Dillon's, where he is trying to close the deal with Keyes. When MacHugh tells Crawford that Bloom is on the phone, the editor rudely says, "Tell him to go to hell" (7.672) and continues speaking to Stephen. Stephen, for his part, is distracted from Crawford's exposition by his own mental editing of the poem he started that morning; he is not interested in the world of journalism. J. J. O'Molloy and Crawford debate the contributions to the Irish cause of various men of law and letters. The discussion turns to the rhetorical skill of the lawyer Seymour Bushe in the Childs murder case. The topic of fratricide prompts Stephen's mind to wander to *Hamlet*: King Hamlet was asleep when Claudius poisoned him, yet he knows who did it: "how did he find that out?" (7.751). Good question. Then, in a brief stylistic interruption, the text parodies Dickensian prose: "I have often thought since on looking back over that strange time that it was that small act, trivial in itself, that striking of that match, that determined the whole aftercourse of both our lives" (7.763–65). This stylistic parody predicts the arranger's subversive influence on the second half of the novel, where the initial style recedes and pastiche emerges as the new normal of Joyce's style in *Ulysses*.

J. J. O'Molloy tells Stephen that he is being discussed by elders of the Dublin intelligentsia, including Professor Magennis and A. E., and asks Stephen's opinion of the theosophical crowd. Young and insecure as ever, Stephen desperately wants to know "what did he say about me?" (7.789–90) but refrains from asking. MacHugh raises a new topic: a speech he heard by John F. Taylor about the revival of the Irish language, which he lauds as one of the best displays of oratory he has ever heard. From memory, he goes on to recite the speech, which compared the Irish (who adopted the language of their English oppressors) to the Jews (who maintained their own language and culture in the face of Egyptian pressure). Stephen, remembering in his inner monologue that "I have money" (7.884) on this payday, offers to stand a round of drinks. The other men respond with enthusiasm. Remember that Stephen was supposed to stand rounds for Mulligan at The Ship at 12:30. That is not going to happen. Stephen sent a telegram to Mulligan at the pub to renege on their appointment. Lenehan suggests they go to "Mooney's" (7.892), a pub just down the street (and, incidentally, only a few doors down from The Ship). Crawford agrees to publish Deasy's letter about "foot and mouth" (7.902).

As the group leaves the offices, Stephen begins to tell a story about "two Dublin vestals, . . . elderly and pious" (7.923). As suggested by Stephen's inner monologue thinking, "Dubliners" (7.922), this story, which Stephen calls "*A Pisgah Sight of Palestine* or *the Parable of the Plums*" (7.1057–58), seems like the first draft of a *Dubliners* short story in its depiction of an anticlimactic slice of everyday life. By calling it a parable, Stephen implies that, despite the story's ambiguous ending and obscure meaning, moral lessons might be available to a reader willing to apply careful interpretive thought.[10] Much the same could be said of *Ulysses* itself: part of the novel's genius lies in its endless promise for those who reread and reconsider its wisdom. Anyhow, the men seem more bemused than impressed as they listen to Stephen's story about the old women climbing the steep stairs to the top of Nelson's Pillar and "spitting the plumstones slowly out between the railings" (7.1026–27).

As the men enter the street on their way to the pub, they encounter a "breathless" (7.963) Mr. Bloom. Because Crawford refused Bloom's phone call, Bloom had to run from Dillon's in hopes of catching Crawford and finalizing the deal. Keyes has counteroffered a two-month renewal (Nannetti had asked for three), as well as a request for a par, and Bloom wants to know whether the paper will accept this deal. Crawford tells Bloom to tell Keyes "he can kiss my arse" (7.981). Bloom, recognizing that the group is "off for a drink" (7.983), prudently realizes that he is unlikely to get his way by standing between Crawford and a pint. He offers to design the ad on spec. Crawford improves on his earlier reply: Keyes can kiss his royal Irish arse. During this exchange, Bloom's inner monologue focuses on Stephen; he wonders "is that young Dedalus the moving spirit" (7.984–85) of the daydrinking and notes his good but sandy boots. His curiosity and concern for this "careless chap" (7.987) predict the action of the novel's later episodes.

As the men continue their walk down the street, Crawford rebuffs J. J. O'Molloy's plea for help paying a gambling debt, and Stephen resumes his story. As he finishes, he gives "a sudden loud young laugh as a close" (7.1028), betraying his awkward insecurity. The men seem more interested in Stephen's promise of drinks than in his story. Still, the professor sees in Stephen a new Antisthenes; MacHugh is more right than he knows, as we might also wonder whether Stephen is "bitterer against others or against himself" (7.1046–47).

## Further Reading

Benstock, Shari, and Bernard Benstock. "Narrative Sources and the Problem of *Ulysses*." *Journal of Narrative Technique* 12, no. 1 (1982): 24–35.

The Benstocks engage the change in narrative voice that emerges in "Aeolus" and the various scholarly approaches to these innovations.

Lawrence, Karen. "'Aeolus': Interruption and Inventory." *James Joyce Quarterly* 17, no. 4 (Summer 1980): 389–405.

This essay interprets the metatextuality of the headlines and the emphasis on rhetoric in this episode, drawing attention to the self-questioning effect that these disruptions have on the initial style.

Mikics, David. "History and the Rhetoric of the Artist in 'Aeolus.'" *James Joyce Quarterly* 27, no. 3 (Spring 1990): 533–58.

This essay argues that Bloom's mix of political idealism and pragmatism cut through the inflated rhetoric of this episode. These elements foreshadow the influence of Bloom on Stephen later in the novel in softening his rigid resistance to politics and history.

Smith, Eric D. "How a Great Daily Organ Is Turned Out: 'Aeolus,' *Techne*, and the Recording of *Ulysses*." *James Joyce Quarterly* 41, no. 3 (2004): 455–68.

This essay engages the attitude of *Ulysses* toward modern technology. The "Aeolus" episode, with its machinery, telephone calls, and newspaper headlines, most directly comments on the relationship between the technological and the natural. This essay also notes that Joyce chose a passage from "Aeolus" for his only recorded reading of *Ulysses*.

## Chapter 8

# "LESTRYGONIANS" GUIDE

With Stephen heading off at the end of "Aeolus" for a few pints, Mr. Bloom is once again the sole focalized character in the "Lestrygonians" episode. With a two-to-one ratio of inner monologue to narration, "Lestrygonians" represents the episode with the most prevalent access to Bloom's interiority,[1] leading some scholars, such as Erwin Steinberg and James Maddox, to consider this episode to be Bloom's "Proteus."[2] The sense of intimacy with Bloom is enhanced by a retreat from the stylistic innovations of "Aeolus" and a comforting return to the now-familiar initial style. We experience in this episode the essential Mr. Bloom: he exhibits behaviors, considers concepts, and recalls memories that we can now appreciate as central to his character. We join him around 1:00 p.m. as he moves south on O'Connell Street from the newspaper office toward the River Liffey. Given that it is lunchtime and Mr. Bloom is hungry, the "Lestrygonians" episode is peppered with references to food, similar to how "Aeolus" is suffused with references to wind. The schema lists "peristaltic prose" as the technique of this episode, referring to the way intestinal muscles alternately contract and relax as they push food along in digestion; "Lestrygonians" mimics peristalsis as Bloom moves in starts and stops through the belly of downtown Dublin.

From the outset of the episode, food is on Bloom's mind as he passes Graham Lemon's candy shop. He accepts a flyer from a young

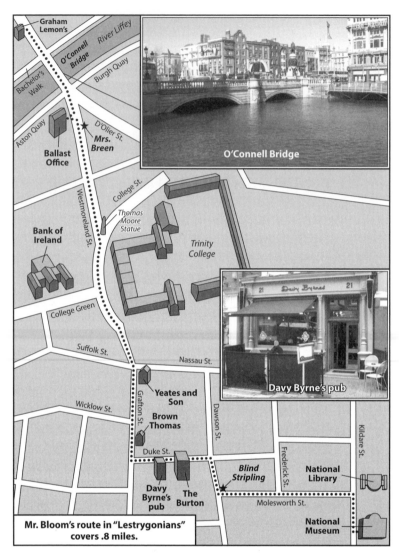

Mr. Bloom's walk to lunch

YMCA evangelical and initially mistakes the "Bloo" of "Blood of the lamb" (8.9) for his own name, "Bloo[m]." He skims the rest of the flyer's contents: "Are you saved? . . . Elijah is coming" (8.10–13). He dismisses this sort of proselytizing advertisement as a for-profit "paying game" (8.17). As he approaches the River Liffey, he glances down Bachelor's Walk to his right to see Dilly Dedalus, Stephen's little sister, "still outside Dillon's auctionrooms" (8.28) waiting on her father. She appears "underfed" and her "dress is in flitters" (8.41). Bloom presumes that she is selling off furniture and reflects on the collapse of the Dedalus household since the passing of Stephen's mother. He notes the folly of large Catholic families with too many mouths to feed, although these criticisms may expose his defensiveness over having just one surviving child.

Crossing O'Connell Bridge, Bloom observes a barge carrying Guinness stout for export to England and notes that "sea air sours it" (8.45–46), which might explain why Guinness famously tastes better in Ireland. He considers with disgust the occurrence of rats falling into the vats of beer where they "drink till they puke" (8.49). He exclaims, "Imagine drinking that!" (8.47–49) but reasonably reconciles himself to the bliss of ignorance: "Well, of course, if we knew all the things" (8.50). He watches hungry gulls flapping in hope of food and tosses into the river the crumpled up "Elijah is coming" flyer (we will see this paper vessel later as it voyages down the Liffey). He contemplates prosody and quotes a passage from *Hamlet* that has coincidental relevance to Stephen's Shakespeare theory to be unspooled in the subsequent "Scylla and Charybdis" episode. Charitable, Mr. Bloom stops to buy two Banbury cakes to toss into the water for the gulls.

Resuming his walk across the bridge, he sees an ad for Kino's trousers affixed onto a rowboat anchored in the river. He admires the cleverness of the ad's visibility and thinks of other smart ads he's seen. In a moment of panic, he wonders whether Boylan has an STD but decides "no, no. I don't believe it" (8.106); he encourages himself to "think no more about that" (8.108). Anxious over the approach of the 4:00 meeting between Boylan and Molly, he notes that the current time is after 1:00 p.m. because the "timeball on the ballastoffice is down. Dunsink time" (8.109)—more on this ahead. As the clock ticks toward his cuckolding, Bloom thinks of this morning's conversation with Molly about metempsychosis and her "O rocks!" (8.112) rejection of pretentious vocabulary. Bloom then argues with himself over whether or not Molly is "witty" (8.116).

Mr. Bloom sees men walking toward him wearing sandwich boards and tall hats bearing the letters H-E-L-Y-S, for Wisdom Hely's stationery shop (where Bloom previously worked)[3] and criticizes the ineffectiveness of this kind of ad. He wonders if the H-E-L-Y-S men work for "Boyl: no, M'Glade" (8.130); here, we subtly learn that Blazes Boylan runs an advertising firm, and we notice that Bloom avoids even thinking Boylan's name in full. In most cases, Bloom will refer to Boylan by pronouns, such as in the "if he" (8.102) passage on the previous page. Bloom thinks of advertising ideas he suggested to Mr. Hely during his employment there, including "a transparent showcart with two smart girls sitting inside writing letters" (8.131–32) that would "catch the eye at once" (8.134). His inner monologue recalls moments from his professional and personal history, leading him to muse that he was "happier then" (8.170). His phrase "stream of life" (8.176) suggests the fluid relationship between present experience and memories of the past.

Mr. Bloom struggles to recall the name of a "priestylooking chap . . . Pen something" (8.176–78) — more on this ahead, as well. He remembers Molly's relationships with Bartell d'Arcy and Professor Goodwin, men involved in the Dublin music scene, both of whom will appear in the list of Molly's suitors presented in the "Ithaca" episode. His absorption in memories of Molly is interrupted when Bloom bumps into his ex-girlfriend, Mrs. Breen, formerly Josie Powell. They ask about one another's families, and Bloom's inner monologue reveals his smooth conversational skills and strategies; he generally seems more comfortable and confident socializing with women than with men. Mrs. Breen shares with Mr. Bloom the trouble she's having with her slightly unhinged husband, who last night woke up from a nightmare saying, "The ace of spades was walking up the stairs" (8.253). Mr. Breen is currently meeting with John Henry Menton to research the applicability of libel laws to a postcard he received this morning that reads "U. p: up" (8.258). Although the meaning of this card is unclear, Mr. Breen has clearly taken offense; Richard Ellmann suggests that the card "implies that in erection he emits urine rather than sperm."[4]

Bloom shifts the topic of conversation to their mutual friend Mina Purefoy (after mixing up her name with Philip Beaufoy, the author of the story he read in the outhouse this morning). Mrs. Purefoy is "three days bad" (8.282) in the throes of a difficult childbirth at the Holles Street Maternity Hospital (Mr. Bloom will visit the hospital around 10:00 p.m. tonight to check on Mrs. Purefoy's condition). A Dublin eccentric named Cashel Boyle O'Connor Fitzmaurice Tisdall Farrell passes by Bloom and Mrs. Breen, wearing a too tight hat; carrying a coat, a stick, and an umbrella; and walking outside the lampposts. Mrs. Breen then spots her husband and takes off after him. Resuming his walk southward, Bloom muses that "Alf Bergan or Richie Goulding" (8.320) might be responsible for the U. p: up postcard. He passes by the offices of the *Irish Times* and considers dropping in to collect any new responses to Henry Flower's want ad for a "smart lady typist to aid gentleman in literary work" (8.326–27). He recalls a few phrases from Martha Clifford's letter, as well as the response he received from Lizzie Twigg—more on her to come.

He thinks about newspapers, hunting, and fancy women, such as the one he ogled this morning climbing into the car and Mrs. Miriam Dandrade, who once sold him "old wraps and black underclothes" (8.350) when he and Molly ran a business selling secondhand clothes and theatrical costumes. He stops to consider his dining options, notes that he needs "to look up that ad in the national library" (8.370), and therefore opts to eat at the Burton because it is on the way. He moves along, remembering that he forgot to "tap Tom Kernan" (8.372) for a deal on some tea. Notice Joyce's "peristaltic" technique in the stop-and-start quality of Bloom's physical and mental passage through this episode.

Bloom thinks again of Mina Purefoy and her "Methodist husband" (8.358), laments the awful pain of childbirth, and proposes a social savings plan whereby the state would give everyone £5 at birth to grow at interest over the lifespan to a "tidy sum" (8.386). As we will later see in greater detail, Bloom leans toward socialism. He thinks of pregnancy, the relief of delivery, and their midwife, Mrs. Thornton. As he passes the Irish House of Parliament, he sees a flock of pigeons and imagines them plotting out "who will we do it on?" (8.402), like an aerial bombing formation fixing its target. He recalls climbing trees with childhood friends, then sees a line of policemen marching back into the street after their lunch. He continues through the heart of Dublin, crossing "under Tommy Moore's roguish finger" (8.414), a prominent feature on the statue of this Irish poet, singer/songwriter, and entertainer. He thinks about Irish nationalist efforts and regrets getting "swept along with those medicals" (8.428), although he is glad to have met Dixon "who dressed that sting for me" (8.430); Bloom has recalled this bee sting twice already (in "Calypso" and "Hades"), and he will see Dixon during Bloom's visit to the Holles Street Maternity Hospital in the "Oxen of the Sun" episode. As he passes by Trinity College's "surly front" (8.476), Bloom enters a rather gloomy mental space, reflecting on the monotony of life and the endless cycle of births and deaths: "cityful passing away, other cityful coming" (8.485). He reaches the nihilistic thought that "no-one is anything" (8.493), but he has enough maturity to moderate these swings and sufficient self-awareness to acknowledge that his mood is influenced by this being "the very worst hour of day" (8.494).

He thinks of John Howard Parnell, brother to the late politician Charles Stewart Parnell, and then, coincidentally, sees him right there on the street. Bloom imagines that Parnell is on his way to "drop into the D. B. C. probably for his coffee, play chess there" (8.510), which is exactly what we will see him doing in the "Wandering Rocks" episode. Then, the poet A. E. and his literary associate Lizzie Twigg ride past Bloom on bicycles, and we catch a snippet of their conversation—"of the twoheaded octopus ..." (8.520)—as they cycle by him. Mr. Bloom, having thought about these individuals a few minutes earlier, is astounded by this second coincidence. Bloom supposes they are discussing "something occult" (8.530) and muses about the taste and fashion of aesthetes.

Bloom stops at Yeates and Son opticians and weighs whether to "get those old glasses of mine set right" (8.554) or to take a "chance on a pair in the railway lost property office" (8.556). You may recall that Mr. Bloom also has a "lost property office secondhand waterproof" (4.67) coat at home; apparently, Mr. Bloom shops in the lost-and-found. He squints as he tries to see a distant clock, then "held out his right hand at arm's length" for the optical trick whereby "his little finger blotted out the sun's disk" (8.564–66). As he resumes his walk, he thinks, "Now that I come to think of it that ball falls at Greenwich time" (8.571), realizing his earlier mistake in thinking that the time-ball at the Ballast Office is on Dunsink time (see 8.109). His thoughts about parallax draw an unintentional but appropriate connection: Hugh Kenner in his book *"Ulysses"* points out that "Greenwich Time and Dunsink Time differ by twenty-five minutes because astronomers in those two places observe the sun from stations separated by 6¼° of longitude; this is, precisely and technically, parallax."[5]

Molly's impending affair with Boylan returns to the forefront of Bloom's thoughts as he remembers an evening two weeks ago when he, Molly, and Boylan walked together after a performance. As Molly hummed "The Young May Moon," Boylan and Molly made clear their reciprocal interest in each other, and Bloom noticed: "He other side of her. Elbow, arm. He. Glowworm's la-amp is gleaming, love. Touch. Fingers. Asking. Answer. Yes" (8.589–91). Tortured, Bloom attempts to shake the memory of their flirty exchange of hand squeezes, thinking, "Stop. Stop. If it was it was" (8.592). He then spies Bob Doran bobbing drunkenly through the street and "sloping into the Empire" (8.599), a pub, to continue his bender. After hearkening back to theatrical performances a decade ago, Mr. Bloom returns to his thought that he was "happier then" (8.608) in the era prior to the loss of Rudy. He thinks, "Could never like it again after Rudy" (8.610), hinting toward the fact that the Bloom marriage has experienced "a period of 10 years, 5 months and 18 days during which carnal intercourse had been incomplete" (17.2282–83). Clearly, Rudy's death left a deep wound and profoundly impacted Bloom's relationship with Molly. Knowing that the Blooms have shared a largely sexless marriage since Rudy's death provides important context for the conditions leading to the affair with Boylan; perhaps Bloom's recognition of his inability to fulfill his husbandly duties compels him to accept that Molly would naturally seek satisfaction elsewhere. Reaching Grafton Street, he window-shops outside Brown Thomas, a posh fabric store, and considers getting Molly a pincushion for her birthday (September 8), still "nearly three months off" (8.629). Even in the midst of this hour's gloominess over what will occur later in the afternoon, Mr. Bloom thinks of Molly with care.

You might notice the poetry of the passage "Perfume of embraces all him assailed. With hungered flesh obscurely, he mutely craved to adore" (8.638–39). In these sorts of highly stylized bits of narration (Joyce told Frank Budgen that he spent a full day working on these two sentences),[6] the idiom is distinct from both Bloom's inner monologue and the standard third-person narrator who has grounded the text in objectivity to this point. Some scholars refer to this new voice as the "second narrator," and Wayne Booth calls him an "implied author," but I follow David Hayman and Hugh Kenner in attributing these poetic narrative flourishes to the novel's arranger. When Joyce explained these two sentences to Budgen, he noted "how many different ways they might be *arranged*" (my emphasis).[7] While the author is the one ultimately doing the arranging, the notion of *Ulysses* having an arranger seems useful and efficient in explaining the stylistic innovations and intratextual puzzles that increasingly influence the text. This example and other such moments of stylized narration here in "Lestrygonians" predict this poetic technique's predominance in the "Sirens" episode ahead. As we have seen throughout the first half of the novel, Joyce briefly introduces new tricks prior to making those innovations the main attraction in subsequent episodes. He nudges the reader along, training us in how to read *Ulysses* as we go.

Mr. Bloom turns onto Duke Street and pops into the Burton restaurant, where he witnesses barbarous table manners from the lunchtime crowd eating there. These men correspond to the cannibalistic Lestrygonians in *The Odyssey*, who capture some of Odysseus's men, tear them "limb from limb" (8.684), and scarf them down. Mr. Bloom, polite even in his disgust, "raised two fingers doubtfully to his lips. His eyes said: —Not here. Don't see him" (8.694–95). Mr. Bloom is deftly acting as if he's searching the restaurant for someone he's supposed to meet, and he uses not seeing that imaginary person as a polite excuse to leave. He opts instead to "get a light snack in Davy Byrne's" (8.697) down the street. On his way, he thinks of vegetarianism.

Once inside Davy Byrne's "moral pub" (8.732), Mr. Bloom is greeted by Nosey Flynn, a mouthy fellow perched in a corner of the pub. Mr. Bloom orders a glass of burgundy and a gorgonzola cheese sandwich. Seeming to know the gossip about Boylan and Molly, Nosey Flynn asks about Molly's upcoming performances and twists the Blazes Boylan knife into Bloom, asking, "Who's getting it up?" (8.773)—the same double entendre used by M'Coy earlier (see 5.153). Bloom avoids answering the question directly, and he is made uncomfortable by hearing Blazes Boylan's name just as "a warm shock of air heat of mustard hanched on Mr. Bloom's heart" (8.789). Mr. Bloom, counting down the hours until Molly's meeting with Boylan at 4:00, checks the clock: "two. Not yet" (8.791). Bloom needs a drink: "Wine. He smellsipped the cordial juice and, bidding his throat strongly to speed it, set his wineglass delicately down" (8.794–96). Nosey Flynn scratches his crotch and praises Blazes Boylan as "a hairy chap" (8.807–08). They discuss the Gold Cup horse race to be run today, and Bloom considers telling Nosey Flynn about Lenehan's pick but decides against it. Mr. Bloom, not a gambler, doesn't want to encourage another person's bad habit. He watches Nosey Flynn's runny nose with its "dewdrop coming down" (8.845). Mr. Bloom focuses on his wine and sandwich and plans to go home around six o'clock, by which time he expects Molly will be done with Boylan: "Six. Time will be gone then. She" (8.853). Bloom distracts himself from this thought by wondering how humans discovered that some foods are safe, such as oysters, which look "like a clot of phlegm" (8.864), whereas others, such as certain berries, are poisonous. He imagines himself as a waiter in a fancy restaurant.

Two flies stuck together on the window buzz as they copulate, which prompts Mr. Bloom to remember in detail his intimate picnic date with Molly on Howth Head, a hilly peninsula overlooking Dublin Bay from north of the city. In "Penelope," Molly will remember this same scene but will be clear that Poldy proposed there. This memory leads Bloom to think "Me. And me now" (8.917), comparing his happiness on that passionate afternoon with his despondency today in the face of imminent cuckolding. The "and" between Bloom's former "me" and his "me now" resolves his questioning of identity earlier in the episode, when he asked, "Or was that I? Or am I now I?" (8.608). Here, the "and" implies that the answer to both questions is yes. Bloom's act of memory—recalling the experience of his previous self—provides continuity between his past "and" his present despite change and the passage of time. In the next episode, Stephen will offer similar thoughts regarding the role of memory in linking our experiences into a coherent identity: "I . . . am I by memory" (9.208).

Bloom's attention shifts to the beautiful curve of the oak of the bar, then to the curves on the statues of the "shapely goddesses" (8.920) in the National Museum. He wonders about the anatomical realism of those statues and resolves to covertly examine their private parts when visiting the museum later today. Then, "a quiet message from his bladder" (8.933) sends Mr. Bloom to the restroom, but the narrative perspective remains behind to overhear the other men's gossip about Bloom. Davy Byrne inquires into Bloom's profession, and Nosey Flynn explains that "he does canvassing for the *Freeman*" (8.940–41). Flynn alludes to Molly's "well nourished" large breasts as "plovers on toast" (8.952). He goes on to claim that Mr. Bloom is a Freemason, a member of the secretive "ancient free and accepted order" (8.962), and that they "give him a leg up" (8.963) by supplementing his income beyond what he makes in advertising. After the text represents Davy Byrne's yawn as "Iiiiiichaaaaaaach!" (8.970), the two men praise Mr. Bloom for his moderation and kindness and then cast anti-Semitic aspersions on his rumored aversion to signing a contract.

Paddy Leonard, Tom Rochford, and Bantam Lyons enter Davy Byrne's pub. Paddy Leonard offers to stand a round and is flabbergasted that both men pass up a drink: Rochford asks for "a glass of fresh water" (8.1003) to aid his indigestion, and Bantam Lyons orders a ginger ale, a temperance beverage. These men, plus Nosey Flynn, discuss their wagers on this afternoon's Gold Cup, and Bantam Lyons claims to have a hot tip on the race. You'll remember that Lyons stopped Mr. Bloom for a look at his newspaper at the end of the "Lotus-Eaters" episode; in that exchange, he misinterpreted Bloom's "I was just going to throw it away" (5.534) as a tip on the horse Throwaway, and here, as Bloom leaves the pub, Lyons tells the other men that "that's the man now that gave it to me" (8.1023). Paddy Leonard is incredulous.

The narrative perspective shifts back to Mr. Bloom as he returns to the streets of Dublin and makes his way toward the library to procure the art for the Keyes ad from the back issues of the *Kilkenny People*. His mood has improved after drinking the glass of burgundy, and he does a bit of mental accounting to tally up his anticipated income, which totals £5 6s. or "five guineas about" (8.1058–59) — roughly US $1,600 in today's money. Mr. Bloom decides he's in good enough financial shape to consider buying Molly a new "silk petticoat" (8.1061) to match her new garters. The thought of Molly's undergarments prompts his mind to turn again to Boylan's visit "Today. Today. Not think" (8.1063). He distracts himself from those unpleasant thoughts by considering organizing his own concert tour with Molly, taking her to "tour the south" (8.1064), as well as the beach towns of England.

He passes another sweetshop and a bookstore before coming to an intersection where "a blind stripling stood tapping the curbstone with his slender cane" (8.1075). Mr. Bloom kindly helps the young blind man cross the street, bookending the episode with acts of charity (remember his feeding of the gulls at the beginning). As they cross the street together, Bloom tries to set the man at ease with "a common remark" (8.1093) and silently wonders how a blind person experiences the world—do different colors have different feels? He experiments on himself, feeling his own dark hair and light skin, and then wonders "what dreams would [the blind] have, not seeing" (8.1144–45). In an exquisite example of the novel's mimesis, Bloom finally remembers the "Pen something" (8.178) name that eluded him earlier: "Penrose! That was that chap's name" (8.1114). Mr. Bloom plans to respond to Martha Clifford's letter and considers cosmic justice and reincarnation. He calls Reuben J. Dodd a "dirty jew" (8.1159) and notes that the Mirus bazaar will occur today, involving a viceregal cavalcade (which we will see in the "Wandering Rocks" episode) and a fireworks display (which we will see in the "Nausicaa" episode).

In *The Odyssey*, Odysseus narrowly escapes certain doom at the hands of the barbaric Lestrygonians, and Mr. Bloom has his own brush with disaster here at the end of the episode. As he approaches the library, Mr. Bloom glimpses a "straw hat in sunlight. Tan shoes. Turnedup trousers. It is. It is" (8.1168) . . . Blazes Boylan. Bloom's choppy thoughts and the "flutter of his breath" (8.1176) convey his panic as he moves with "long windy steps" (8.1173) toward the museum, where he can examine the goddess statues as previously planned. To avoid eye contact with Boylan, Mr. Bloom feigns fixation on the architecture of the museum, then searches his pockets for the lemon soap. The jumpy style reinforces Bloom's anxiety with sentences that flit between third-person narration and Bloom's inner monologue, such as "his hand looking for the where did I put found in his hip pocket soap" (8.1191).[8] Mercifully, he reaches the gate of the museum, "safe" (8.1193) from what we can only assume would have been an excruciating encounter with the man who will spend the late afternoon having sex with his wife.

## Further Reading

Gunn, Daniel P. "Beware of Imitations: Advertisement as Reflexive Commentary in *Ulysses*." *Twentieth Century Literature* 42, no. 4 (Winter 1996): 481–93.

After surveying various critical approaches to the appearance of advertisements in *Ulysses*, Gunn argues that their inclusion represents a form of self-referential, embedded commentary on the novel itself. The advertisements are consistent with the overall interest in the transformation of language, symbolism, and the blending of high and low culture.

Wicke, Jennifer. "Modernity Must Advertise: Aura, Desire, and Decolonization in Joyce." *James Joyce Quarterly* 50, no. 1/2 (Fall-Winter 2013): 203–21.

Wicke presents the interdependent relationship between modernism and mass culture, explaining Joyce's success in mediating between high art and pop culture. The ability of *Ulysses* to blend and level these different modes serves to confound hierarchy in a manner that prompts and predicts decolonization.

Yared, Aida. "Eating and Digesting 'Lestrygonians': A Physiological Model of Reading." *James Joyce Quarterly* 46, no. 3/4 (Spring-Summer 2009): 469–79.

This essay examines stylistic effects and analyzes specific details in explaining how the "Lestrygonians" episode represents a digestive tract. Mr. Bloom's movements and thoughts are identified as occurring within the stages of digestion.

# Chapter 9

# "SCYLLA AND CHARYBDIS" GUIDE

The "Scylla and Charybdis" episode of *Ulysses* takes place in the National Library, where Stephen Dedalus delivers his much-anticipated (though sparsely attended) lecture on Shakespeare and *Hamlet*. Excepting the second half of "Aeolus," the novel has large-ly been focalized in Bloom's mind since the end of "Proteus," so this episode's return to Stephen's thoughts, with their characteristic intel-lectual density, social paranoia, and discursive loftiness, can be some-what jarring, perhaps even off-putting. Some readers may be tempted to quit. Don't!

As with "Proteus," my goal is to get you through this episode and on to the rest of the book; indeed, a comprehensive guide to this episode would necessitate literally thousands of explanations and revelations; just about every line contains a Shakespearean allusion (not to men-tion heavy doses of Aristotle, Aquinas, Dante, Wilde, Brandes, et al.). As a frame of reference, "Scylla and Charybdis" requires sixty-six pages of annotations in the Gifford versus the thirty-two pages that gloss "Lestrygonians," an episode of nearly equal length. So, this episode is twice as dense as the rest of *Ulysses*, which is saying something. Any devotee of Shakespeare should use the Gifford to appreciate and enjoy Joyce's mastery of (over?) the Bard. Given that "Scylla and Charybdis" is the final chapter of the first half of the book and a dividing line in

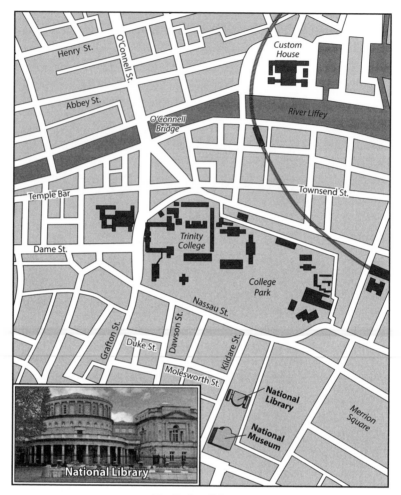

The National Library

terms of style, this Episode Guide is primarily interested in helping the first-time reader successfully make the turn to the novel's back nine.

In *The Odyssey*, Odysseus passes through a treacherous, narrow strait: on one side is Scylla, a murderous, multiheaded monster on the jagged rocks; on the other side is Charybdis, a giant sea beast that creates a whirlpool to capture its prey. Likewise, Stephen's lecture navigates between various pairs of powerful forces: the ideas of Aristotle and Plato, the impulses of youth and maturity, the relationship between the artist and his/her art, and the disciplines of dogmatic scholasticism and spiritual mysticism. In addition to *The Odyssey*, Shakespeare's *Hamlet* emerges as a prominent correspondence in this episode. For much of Shakespeare's play, Prince Hamlet wrestles with how to proceed in avenging the murder of his father by his uncle, Claudius, who has usurped the prince's rightful throne. Hamlet probes and dodges, invents and confronts. Likewise, Stephen suffers slights, carefully weaves his theory on Shakespeare, and is uncertain of his path forward. As Hugh Kenner explains, Stephen "is aware that he is Hamlet, but his awareness is put to the wrong uses. It provides him with no insight. It merely feeds his morbidity. It is a role in which he is imprisoned."[1]

In terms of style, the episode represents a nexus between the initial style and the more innovative episodes to come. Through the Uncle Charles Principle, the narrative voice assumes qualities that we have come to associate with Stephen, such as lyricism and caginess. Marilyn French explains that Stephen, keenly aware that he is delivering a performance here in the library, becomes the episode's "author and stage director" in addition to being a character in the drama.[2] Consequently, his inner monologue addresses himself in the second person with cues and director's notes, such as "Local color. Work in all you know" (9.158) and "I think you're getting on very nicely. Just mix up a mixture of the theolologicophilolological" (9.760–61). The style of "Scylla and Charybdis" also indulges further in the sort of wordplay we identified and attributed to the arranger in "Lestrygonians." We see an example of the arranger's work in the episode's first few lines: first, he borrows diction from *Twelfth Night* in describing Lyster's dance-like gait as "a step a sinkapace" (9.5–6) and "corantoed" (9.12); then, the arranger riffs on the narrator's reporting of "said he, creaking to go" (9.9), as well as Lyster's dialogue of "true in the larger analysis" (9.11), to recombine these elements into the tightly arranged phrase "twicreakingly analysis he corantoed off" (9.12).[3] These sorts of inter- and intratextual flourishes suffuse the episode.

After spending about an hour drinking with the newspapermen in Mooney's pub, Stephen has arrived at the National Library sometime before 2:00 p.m. and is speaking in the librarian's office with members of Dublin's literary elite, including Lyster ("the quaker librarian" [9.1]), John Eglinton (a critic and essayist), and, in the shadows of the office, George Russell (the poet and theosophist also known as A. E.). Mr. Best (another librarian) will soon join them, and Buck Mulligan will also eventually enter the conversation (his late arrival and interruption is retribution for Stephen skipping their planned rendezvous at The Ship). From the beginning, Eglinton treats Stephen "with elder's gall" (9.18–19) as he bitterly teases Stephen over his idea of rewriting *Paradise Lost* as *The Sorrows of Satan*. Eglinton appeals to George Russell, "the face bearded amid darkgreener shadow" (9.30), to join in his mockery of Stephen's delusions of grandeur, but Russell remains silent. Stephen directs himself to "smile Cranly's smile" (9.21) in the face of Eglinton's antagonism, hoping to channel some of his old friend's unbothered charm. In "Proteus," we saw Stephen mock himself for his own "follies" (9.35), so he resolves to "persist" (9.42) in unspooling his *Hamlet* theory despite Eglinton's hostility.

It's worth considering that Joyce likewise persists with his own bold aspirations to literary glory. When Eglinton claims that "our young Irish bards . . . have yet to create a figure which the world will set beside Saxon Shakespeare's Hamlet" (9.43–44), we might perceive Joyce's implied promotion of his characters Stephen Dedalus and Leopold Bloom as exactly the figures Eglinton here calls for. Later in the episode, it is suggested that the Irish "national epic has yet to be written" (9.309), and it now seems clear that *Ulysses* has filled that void. Joyce was not bashful about the work of genius he had created in *Ulysses*, and he was quite confident of the place his novel would occupy in the pantheon of literature. In this episode (and, later, in "Oxen of the Sun"), Joyce is staking his claim to a seat beside Shakespeare and Homer.

In the librarian's office, Stephen enters the philosophical fray in defense of Aristotle. Excited by the intellectual dueling, he directs himself to "unsheathe your dagger definitions" (9.84) and speaks "with tingling energy" (9.147). We learn that Haines already visited the library but left to purchase a book of Irish poetry. The conversation narrows its focus to *Hamlet*, and Stephen poses the central question his lecture will answer: "Who is King Hamlet?" (9.151). Essentially, Stephen's theory is biographical in nature: rather than playing the part of Prince Hamlet as is generally supposed, Shakespeare is King Hamlet, husband to an unfaithful wife (Anne Hathaway/Gertrude) and cuckolded by his own villainous brother (Richard Shakespeare/Claudius).

William Shakespeare/King Hamlet speaks directly to his son, Hamnet Shakespeare/Prince Hamlet. Furthermore, Shakespeare's own father, John Shakespeare, has died just prior to the composition of *Hamlet*, so "being no more a son, [Shakespeare] was and felt himself the father of all his race, the father of his own grandfather, the father of his unborn grandson" (9.867–69). This passage serves to explain (more or less) the paradox Buck Mulligan promised back in "Telemachus": Stephen's *Hamlet* theory "proves by algebra that Hamlet's grandson is Shakespeare's grandfather and that he himself is the ghost of his own father" (1.555–57). Furthermore, Shakespeare must have felt himself "the father of all his race" given his prodigious talent for creating human life in art; indeed, "after God Shakespeare has created most" (9.1028–29). This aspect of the argument jibes with Stephen's own aesthetic theory of "the artist, like the God of the creation" (*P* 199). As Karen Lawrence explains, Stephen's theory is both biographical and autobiographical; his "elaborate reading of Shakespeare is, of course, an expression of his own feelings about paternity, betrayal, and the relationship between the artist and his work."[4]

A. E./Russell objects to Aristotelian Stephen's effort to reduce art (the ideal) to an embodiment of the artist (the real), scorning the "peeping and prying into greenroom gossip of the day, the poet's drinking, the poet's debts. We have *King Lear*: and it is immortal" (9.187–88). The thought of "the poet's debts" prompts Stephen to recall that A. E./Russell lent him a pound ("A. E. I. O. U." [9.213]) and that he "spent most of it in Georgina Johnson's bed" (9.195). He feels "agenbite of inwit" (9.196), guilt, for squandering this loan on a prostitute and wrestles with himself over when he might repay the debt (keep in mind he has a pocketful of money at this moment). Then, Stephen ponders the fluidity of identity as he rationalizes not paying the debt: "Wait. Five months. Molecules all change. I am other I now. Other I got pound" (9.205–06). As he contemplates past versions of himself in moments from his own history, he elegantly expresses the conundrum of a linked progression of identity versus a series of finite selves in terms of punctuation: "I, I and I. I." (9.212). This formulation echoes Mr. Bloom's "Me. And me now" (8.917) from the previous episode. Further linking Bloom and Stephen's thoughts in these two moments, two "flies buzzed" (8.918) on the windowpane of Davy Byrne's pub, while Stephen's inner monologue here thinks, "Buzz. Buzz" (9.207) in allusion to *Hamlet* (2.2.402). In this way, the text knits together thematically concordant passages about the relationship of memory, the soul, and change over time, signaling the importance of this idea to both the novel's investigation of the human experience and the book's own stylistic progression in the episodes ahead.

Stephen continues his lecture, interrupted first by his own haunted thoughts of his dead mother, then by Eglinton, and later by Russell's departure for the offices of the *Homestead*. Eglinton suggests that in marrying Anne Hathaway, "Shakespeare made a mistake . . . and got out of it as quickly and as best he could" (9.226–27), to which Stephen retorts, "A man of genius makes no mistakes. His errors are volitional and are the portals of discovery" (9.228–29). As A. E. prepares to leave, Eglinton asks if he will attend the literary soiree at George "Moore's tonight" (9.274); Lyster then notes that "Mr. Russell, rumour has it, is gathering together a sheaf of our younger poets' verses" (9.290–91). Stephen is stung to have been excluded from both the event tonight and this collection of poetry. As Russell departs, Stephen passes along to him the second copy of Deasy's letter for the *Irish Homestead*'s consideration. Russell makes no promises, but Stephen has fulfilled his promise to Mr. Deasy.

The discussion of *Hamlet* and Shakespeare continues. Lyster notes "the spirit of reconciliation" (9.396) in Shakespeare's later plays, and Stephen notes for the second time that "there can be no reconciliation . . . if there has not been a sundering" (9.397–98), which implies turbulence within William and Anne's marriage. The men in the office cite and discuss other critics of Shakespeare. Stephen's "enemy" (9.483) Buck Mulligan arrives and receives a convivial welcome from the other men. Stephen is silent for two pages. The others discuss the theory that Hamlet was a woman (which Bloom also considered; see 5.196) and a story by Oscar Wilde. Stephen silently counts the drinks he shared with the pressmen: he is already three beers deep. Mulligan "eye[s] Stephen" (9.545) and produces the cryptic telegram Stephen sent to The Ship that effectively canceled the drinking session with Buck and Haines. Buck exaggerates that they spent three hours waiting for Stephen to show up and buy them pints and claims that the playwright Synge is out to murder Stephen for peeing on his door late one night; Stephen retorts that "that was [Mulligan's] contribution to literature" (9.572). Mr. Lyster is then called away to assist a gentleman from the *Freeman* who has come to the library "to see the files of the *Kilkenny People* for last year" (9.586–87); this is Mr. Bloom working on the Keyes ad. We catch shadowy glimpses of him: "a patient silhouette waited, listening" (9.597) and "a bowing dark figure following" (9.602–03). Buck tells the others that he saw Bloom staring at the statue of Aphrodite; we know from the previous episode that Bloom had planned to examine the statue's backside to evaluate its anatomical accuracy. It seems he was caught in this uniquely Bloomish act. Mulligan mocks Bloom as "Ikey Moses" (9.607), meaning a middle-class Jew attempting to ingratiate himself into bourgeoise gentile society, and suggests to Stephen that Bloom has a homoerotic attraction to him.

Stephen's theory returns to Shakespeare's wife, Anne Hathaway, and her connection to Queen Gertrude. Stephen suggests that the Ghost of King Hamlet/Shakespeare expresses anger for "a broken vow and the dullbrained yokel on whom her favour has declined, deceased husband's brother" (9.667–68), setting up the idea that "Sweet Ann . . . was hot in the blood" (9.668–69) for more than one of the Shakespeare brothers. Stephen argues that Anne had an incestuous affair with her brother-in-law and cites as circumstantial evidence that she was forced "to borrow forty shillings from her father's shepherd" (9.681) in order to pay a debt even as her husband was "living richly in royal London" (9.680) at the height of fame and fortune. Then, in Shakespeare's will, he left Anne his second-best bed, further evidence of a broken marriage. Why else would a financially successful husband refuse to pay his wife's debt? And why not "leave her his best bed if he wished her to snore away the rest of her nights in peace?" (9.712–13).[5] Stylistically, this passage shifts into lines of iambic pentameter (beginning with "To whom thus Eglinton: You mean the will" [9.684]) before eventually devolving into the arranger's wordplay:

Leftherhis
Bestabed
Secabest
Leftabed. (9.703–06)

The "Woa!" (9.707) that follows suggests a pulling back on the reins of the arranger's freedom; the novel is not yet ready to cede full control to this playful, disruptive force. Thematically, Stephen's notion that Shakespeare was a cuckhold suffering a deep emotional wound resonates with readers of *Ulysses* more deeply than Stephen can know; we've just been with Mr. Bloom and his melancholic thoughts as the hour of Molly's adulterous meeting with Boylan approaches.

Eglinton "dare[s]" Stephen to "prove that [Shakespeare] was a jew" (9.763), which leads Stephen down a slight detour that he manages to reconnect to the main argument. Eglinton's increasingly pointed engagement in the lecture betrays a grudging acknowledgment that Stephen's theory has a measure of validity. Stephen then thrusts his theory into the "mystical estate" (9.838) of fatherhood, explaining that Shakespeare wrote *Hamlet* "in the months that followed his father's death" (9.829), so "being no more a son, he was and felt himself the father of all his race, the father of his own grandfather" (9.868–69). As Stanley Sultan explains, there is a "personal dimension" to Stephen's theory if we understand Stephen to have been speaking of himself, "no more a son" owing to Simon's ineffectuality yet aspiring to become "the father of all his race" through his art.[6] If Stephen succeeds in "forg[ing] in the smithy of his soul the uncreated conscience of [his] race" (*P* 235), he could become his own creator, his own father. This idea of father-son consubstantiality also reprises Stephen's fixation on heresies related to the Trinity back in "Telemachus."

In any event, Shakespeare is not Prince Hamlet, as most assume, because that would mean "his seventyyear old mother is the lustful queen. No" (9.833). Rather, Shakespeare was the Ghost of King Hamlet, telling his son, Hamnet Shakespeare (who died at eleven years old) about the incestuous adultery of Anne Hathaway with Shakespeare's brother, Richard. Stephen is getting "tired of [his] own voice" and wants "a drink" (9.981), but he continues "on" (9.982). The focus of his argument pivots toward Shakespeare's brothers, Edmund and Richard, names he provided to two of his plays' most infamous villains; Stephen also highlights the recurrence of "the theme of the false or the usurping or the adulterous brother" (9.997–98) in Shakespeare's work.

Eglinton reduces Stephen's theory simply to "he is the ghost and the prince. He is all in all" (9.1018–19), which Stephen accepts before eloquently delivering his conclusion that Shakespeare "found in the world without as actual what was in his world within as possible" (9.1041–42), that he saw everything in the external world as a source for and reflection of his art, "always meeting ourselves" (9.1046) in both reality and fiction. Buck Mulligan composes his own creative work on slips of paper in the background. Eglinton calls Stephen "a delusion" (9.1064) and asks if he believes his own theory: "No, Stephen said promptly" (9.1065–66). Mr. Best suggests Stephen compose the lecture as a dialogue, and Stephen, ever graceless in money matters, says that they can "publish this interview" (9.1085) for a guinea (slightly more than US$300 in today's money). Eglinton notes that Stephen is the only contributor to the literary magazine *Dana* who asks for compensation for the publication of his work. These middle-class intellectuals deem Stephen impolite for seeking payment for his ideas, but we know that Stephen is poor—deeply indebted, from a destitute family, and soon-to-be unemployed. Buck Mulligan adds to this embarrassment by referring to Stephen's "summer residence in upper Mecklenburgh street" (9.1088–89), located in Dublin's brothel district, and then asks Stephen, "Can you walk straight?" (9.1102–03). In short, Buck loudly exposes Stephen as a drunk who visits prostitutes. Stephen endures this pummeling, thinking, "Life is many days. This will end" (9.1097). He is unhappy, disesteemed, and unproductive here in Dublin. He must fly.

Eglinton entreats Mulligan to attend tonight's literary gathering at Moore's; Stephen is not invited. Mulligan leaves with Stephen, knowing that he has been paid this morning and owes him a few rounds. In addition to Stephen standing him up at The Ship, recall that Stephen owes Buck "nine pounds, three pairs of socks, one pair brogues, ties" (2.255). As they leave the library, Stephen notices a woman wearing a "blueribboned hat" (9.1123) and writing in the reading room of the library; this might be Emma Clery, his romantic interest in *A Portrait*. Stephen thinks of a few points to add to his lecture. Buck recites an off-color poem and tells Stephen that folks are upset with him over an unfavorable review he wrote. Buck reads to Stephen what he wrote in the office: a bawdy play title and character list. Stephen wants to "part" (9.1199) from Buck but wonders "where then" (9.1199) he might sleep tonight. We see more Scylla and Charybdis imagery as Stephen thinks,

"My will: his will that fronts me. Seas between" (9.1202). As they depart the library, "a man passed out between them, bowing, greeting" (9.1204); this is Mr. Bloom, slipping between Stephen and Mulligan (another Odysseus navigating between Scylla and Charybdis), triggering Stephen to recall the dream from the previous night he almost remembered back in "Proteus," which prophesies his encounter with Bloom later that night. The arranger directly addresses the reader again (see 3.369) to promise that "you will see" (9.1208) the two characters unite.

Buck makes a joke that Bloom "looked upon [Stephen] to lust after [him]" (9.1210). Mr. Bloom's "dark back" leaves the library ahead of Stephen and Buck with the quiet "step of a pard" (9.1214). All three characters launch out as wandering rocks into the sea of Dublin's city streets.

## Further Reading

Rasmussen, Irina D. "Riffing on Shakespeare: James Joyce, Stephen Dedalus, and the Avant-Garde Theory of Literary Creation." *Joyce Studies Annual* (2019): 33–73.

This essay establishes the avant-garde intentions of Stephen's Shakespeare theory, focusing on its modernist aesthetic principles and its departure from standard turn-of-the-century literary critical modes.

Sharpe, Garold. "The Philosophy of James Joyce." *Modern Fiction Studies* 9, no. 2 (Summer 1963): 120–26.

This essay presents an explication of the philosophical underpinnings of Stephen's *Hamlet* theory.

Steinberg, Erwin R. "Author! Author!" *James Joyce Quarterly* 22, no. 4 (Summer 1985): 419–25.

Steinberg surveys various scholarly concepts as applied to the study of Joyce's style before making the case against the existence of the arranger. Steinberg attributes the stylistic flourishes that become increasingly prominent in "Scylla and Charybdis" to James Joyce, citing the nineteenth-century tradition of authors directly addressing the reader.

# Chapter 10

# "WANDERING ROCKS" GUIDE

As the anxiety of navigating "Scylla and Charybdis" dissipates, Joyce offers "Wandering Rocks" as an interlude to mark the midway point in the novel (if not by pages, at least by episodes). Written as eighteen mini-episodes (plus a concluding coda) that occur across the city of Dublin between 2:55 and 4:00 p.m., "Wandering Rocks" was initially described by Stuart Gilbert as a "small-scale model of *Ulysses*,"[1] although a comparison to the *Dubliners* collection might be more apt. With its population of diverse and engaging characters, ingeniously interlocking parts, and obsessive attention to time and place, this episode deserves much the same awe and appreciation as does the novel as a whole. Just as Joyce has sought to depict in detail and with fidelity the inner workings of Stephen and Mr. Bloom, he was painstaking in his efforts to accurately present the city of Dublin. Indeed, Joyce claimed (hyperbolically) that *Ulysses* would "give a picture of Dublin so complete that if the city one day suddenly disappeared from the earth it could be reconstructed out of my book."[2] Frank Budgen explains that "Joyce wrote the 'Wandering Rocks' with a map of Dublin before him [and] calculated to a minute the time necessary for his characters to cover a given distance of the city."[3] Building on the "Aeolus" episode's city-scaping opening paragraphs, "Wandering Rocks" creates a composite portrait of the city of Dublin.

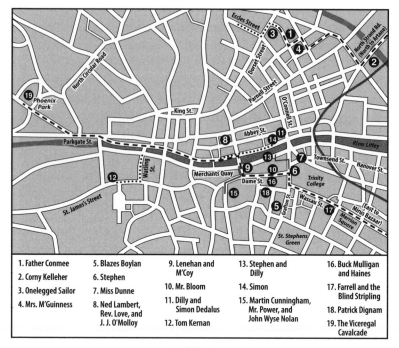

| 1. Father Conmee | 5. Blazes Boylan | 9. Lenehan and M'Coy | 13. Stephen and Dilly | 16. Buck Mulligan and Haines |
| 2. Corny Kelleher | 6. Stephen | 10. Mr. Bloom | 14. Simon | 17. Farrell and the Blind Stripling |
| 3. Onelegged Sailor | 7. Miss Dunne | 11. Dilly and Simon Dedalus | 15. Martin Cunningham, Mr. Power, and John Wyse Nolan | 18. Patrick Dignam |
| 4. Mrs. M'Guinness | 8. Ned Lambert, Rev. Love, and J. J. O'Molloy | 12. Tom Kernan | | 19. The Viceregal Cavalcade |

Dublin City

The schema lists "mechanics" as the art for this episode, and we can think of each of the nineteen sections as gears of various sizes in the Dublin machine. Simultaneous events from one section might reappear (or pre-appear) in other sections through an interpolation technique that creates what Hugh Kenner calls "mechanical linkages" across the episode.[4] Think of these interpolations as teeth from one gear momentarily interlocking with another gear in the turning apparatus of Dublin city. For example, at the end of the first section, Father Conmee encounters a blushing young couple emerging from a hedge, and the "young woman abruptly bent and with slow care detached from her light skirt a clinging twig" (10.201–02). Later, this scene reappears as an interpolation in the episode's eighth section as Ned Lambert and J. J. O'Molloy are talking:

He stood to read the card in his hand.

—The reverend Hugh C. Love, Rathcoffey. Present address: Saint Michael's, Sallins. Nice young chap he is. He's writing a book about the Fitzgeralds he told me. He's well up in history, faith.

The young woman with slow care detached from her light skirt a clinging twig.

—I thought you were at a new gunpowder plot, J. J. O'Molloy said.

Ned Lambert cracked his fingers in the air. (10.436–443)

The young woman from section 1 is interpolated into section 8, interrupting the narration of events occurring more than two miles away. Although she is physically distant from J. J. O'Molloy and Ned Lambert, her appearance links these two sections in time; the woman removes the twig from her skirt at exactly 3:29 p.m. in both sections.[5] Further knitting these synchronous moments together, Father Conmee in section 1 has just remembered the clouds over Rathcoffey, north of Clongowes Wood College, where he served as rector, while Ned Lambert in section 8 reads the card of Hugh C. Love, a priest/historian from Rathcoffey. The arranger, the omniscient architect of the novel whose influence is increasingly pronounced in the second half of the book, sees everything and knows how it all fits together. The interpolations that link the sections of "Wandering Rocks" evidence the arranger's creative disruptions. As you read this episode, you can imagine the novel's godlike arranger peering over the entire city in panorama, zooming into the space (and sometimes into the consciousness) of various Dubliners. Even while zoomed in, the arranger uses the interpolations to demonstrate awareness of events taking place simultaneously elsewhere in the city.

## Section 1: Father Conmee

The first section of "Wandering Rocks" follows Father John Conmee, known to readers of *A Portrait* as the rector of Clongowes Wood College to whom young Stephen appealed for help after Father Dolan unjustly punished him. Father Conmee moves easily through the world, self-assured and "mild" (10.188). We access his thoughts through the technique of reported speech, keeping a respectful (or mocking) distance between the reader and the gentlemanly priest.

In the opening paragraph, Father Conmee thinks about Martin Cunningham's letter requesting help in securing a school place for the late Paddy Dignam's child; later in the episode (section 15), we will hear Cunningham reference this letter and his efforts on behalf of the Dignams; later still (section 18), we will see one of Dignam's children. This sort of interconnectedness spans "Wandering Rocks" and relates to the parallax concept that appears elsewhere in *Ulysses*. In section 1, Conmee, a transactional man, shrewdly recognizes that Martin Cunningham can be "useful at mission time" (10.6), so he is on his way north to the Catholic orphanage at Artane to assist in the enrollment of the Dignam child.

As Conmee's walk continues, he encounters a panhandling amputee sailor (whom he blesses), a well-to-do wife of a politician (whom he lauds with friendly politeness), three boys who are students at Belvedere (whom he dispatches to mail a letter for him), a flamboyant dancing master named Denis Maginni, and the upright pawnshop owner Mrs. M'Guinness (whom he salutes). Readers often want to condemn Father Conmee as a hypocrite for not giving money to the beggar, which is reasonable, but Conmee has only a crown (a 5 shilling piece) in his pocket, roughly equivalent to a $100 bill, and it's not like he can ask the one-legged sailor for change. Judge him as you wish.

Similar to Bloom's idea back in "Hades," Conmee notes the need for a tramline, further revealing that he is a man of the world as much as of the cloth. As he continues his walk, he salutes and is saluted by boys, men (sober and otherwise), and a policeman. He passes by a bargeman working the Royal Canal (perhaps the same man we saw in the "Hades" episode; see 6.439–40) and then takes a tram to avoid walking through an unpleasant neighborhood. Aboard the tram, Conmee perceives his fellow passengers with patronizing interest. Father Conmee notices an advertisement posted in the tram for a minstrel show, which prompts him to think of missionary work and the doomed souls of people living in the unfortunate corners of the earth where Christianity has not yet spread. As he leaves the tram, he is saluted by its conductor and salutes in return. Father Conmee, secure in his place and pleased with himself, loves a good exchange of salutes.

Now on Malahide Road, Father Conmee muses on an idealized past where men of his ilk were truly honored, where priests of his esteem confidentially held knowledge of the sins of the aristocratic elite. In an episode so focused on time and place, Father Conmee, ironically, is an anachronism. His attention returns to the present long enough for him to observe the fleecy clouds above, which sends his mind into a reverie of his time as rector of Clongowes Wood College—walking in the fields near the playing students, reading his daily prayers, and watching the clouds over Rathcoffey to the north. Back again in the here and now, Father Conmee takes out his book of prayers and catches up on his daily office before being interrupted by the emergence of two young lovers from a hedge (they are later revealed to be Stephen's friend Lynch and a woman called Kitty). Father Conmee blesses them even as he judges them as sinners.

## Section 2: Corny Kelleher

Back in section 1, Father Conmee "passed H. J. O'Neill's funeral establishment where Corny Kelleher totted figures in the daybook while he chewed a blade of hay" (10.97–98). Now, in section 2, we join Corny Kelleher a few minutes later. He is still "chewing his blade of hay" (10.210), and he is closing his daybook after having entered his figures. He ambles over to the doorway and looks out on the street. The text then tells us that "Father John Conmee stepped into the Dollymount Tram on Newcomen bridge" (10.213), and we might be tempted to assume that this event, appearing out of narrative sequence, is an interpolation. But, no! This is a trick, one of many such wandering rocks that Joyce has laid in the waters of this episode to bring us down. When you look at the map, you notice that Corny Kelleher could easily have perceived Father Conmee on Newcomen Bridge from the doorway of O'Neill's.

A constable of the Dublin Metropolitan Police, an arm of British colonial rule, checks in with Corny Kelleher. We catch the beginning snippet of their conversation about "that particular party" (10.225), perhaps confirming that Kelleher is an informant against Irish revolutionaries, as other Dubliners suspect.

## Section 3: The Onelegged Sailor

A handicapped veteran of the British navy, previously seen (and blessed) by Father Conmee in section 1, lurches grumpily through the streets of north Dublin, grunting a patriotic song and begging for money. A woman on the street offers a penny. Children gawk. Molly Bloom's disembodied "plump bare generous arm" (10.251) tosses down a coin from a window of 7 Eccles Street. We see that the Blooms are advertising "*Unfurnished Apartments*" for rent in their home; the top floor of their Georgian row house is unused.

## Section 4: The Dedalus Sisters

In the Dedalus home, Katey and Boody return from school and join Maggy, who is cleaning shirts in a pot of boiling, sudsy water. Their address is notably unspecified to suggest the Dedalus family's instability. Stephen's younger sisters reveal the family's current level of destitution: they have unsuccessfully attempted to pawn Stephen's books at M'Guinness's shop (recall that Conmee saluted stately Mrs. M'Guinness in section 1), and they have something to eat thanks only to charity. Dilly, another Dedalus sister, has gone downtown to find Simon. Boody, at the mention of her father, curses him: "our father who art not in heaven" (10.291). At this same time elsewhere in the city, Father Conmee reads the "Our Father" in his prayer book. These sorts of ironic echoes appear across the sections of the episode.

Section 4 closes with a glimpse of the evangelical flyer Mr. Bloom tossed into the Liffey back in "Lestrygonians" as it wanders its own way through the city by water. Clive Hart notes that Joyce's attention to detail accounted even for "the throwaway, Elijah, to move at a speed which, according to the Dublin Port and Docks Board, is consistent with the probable rate of flow of the Liffey two and a half hours after high tide on that June day."[6]

## Section 5: Blazes Boylan

We've caught flashes of Blazes Boylan earlier in the novel, but this section represents our most intimate view of the slick seducer. He is shopping in Thornton's fruit and flower shop on Grafton Street, purchasing a fruit basket to be delivered to Molly Bloom prior to his arrival this afternoon. Dapper and sensuous, Boylan helps the young female attendant arrange the items in the basket and smell-browses the other fruits in the shop. In an application of the Uncle Charles Principle, the language of the narration acquires the tastes of Boylan in this section: "shamefaced peaches" (10.306), "plump red tomatoes" (10.308), "fat pears" (10.305, 333), and "blushing peaches" (10.333) all reveal Blazes Boylan's fixations on this day.

As Boylan requests that the basket be delivered immediately, we have an interpolation of "a darkbacked figure" (10.315) perusing used books; this is Mr. Bloom fulfilling the commitment he made to Molly to get her a new book, a scene that contrasts sharply with Boylan, here preparing to violate the most essential of the Blooms' marital commitments.

In the second half of the short time we spend with Boylan, we see him lie ("It's for an invalid" [10.322]) and letch ("Blazes Boylan looked into the cut of her blouse" [10.327]). He speaks "gallantly" (10.329) and "roguishly" (10.336) to the young woman, and she seems charmed by him. While we may be predisposed to dislike Boylan out of a sense of protectiveness for Mr. Bloom, we must admit that the man has game.

## Section 6: Stephen and Artifoni

At the center of town, Stephen encounters his Italian voice instructor, Almidano Artifoni, who expresses fatherly concern for his wayward pupil, saying (in Italian), "I, too, was convinced the world was a place of beastliness and sin when I was young. But your voice . . . it could be a source of income for you. Instead, you sacrifice yourself."

"Bloodless sacrifice," Stephen replies with the shy smile of a favored student.

"Let's hope so," Artifoni responds. He then says something to the effect of "but listen, be straight with me, think about it." Stephen replies that he will think about it. The two men shake hands warmly, Artifoni invites Stephen to come see him, and they exchange tender farewells. Then Artifoni realizes that he has missed his tram.

## Section 7: Miss Dunne

Blazes Boylan's secretary, Miss Dunne, sits in her office. She has been reading a romance novel while the boss (Boylan) is out, but she inserts a piece of paper into the typewriter and types out the date. This brief moment reveals that June 16, 1904, is indeed the day on which *Ulysses* is set. The five Hely's sandwich-board men (H-E-L-Y-S), seen previously by Boylan in the fruit shop and by Bloom in "Lestrygonians" (see 8.123–26), appear again here.

Miss Dunne thinks about her evening plans, recalls a man who has caught her attention, and mentally shops for a skirt she wants. She hopes Boylan won't hold her in the office too late. Then the phone rings; it is the call Boylan was about to make at the end of section 5. We hear Miss Dunne's side of the conversation with her boss. She receives his directions to book travel for two to Belfast and Liverpool (for Molly and himself during the upcoming concert tour), and he gives her permission to leave work at 6:15 (more or less a win for Miss Dunne). Then, she informs Boylan that Lenehan has been looking for him and will be at the Ormond Hotel bar at 4:00. We will see Boylan, Lenehan, and other notable characters convene at the Ormond in the next episode, "Sirens."

## Section 8: Ned Lambert, Reverend Love, and J. J. O'Molloy

The eighth section takes place in the remaining room of a tenth-century abbey that now serves as a seed and grain warehouse where Ned Lambert (seen at Dignam's funeral in "Hades" and in the newspaper offices in "Aeolus") now works. J. J. O'Molloy enters the dimly lit room to find Ned showing the building to a priest named Hugh C. Love, who is writing a book about the Fitzgeralds. Love is interested in St. Mary's Abbey because Lord Thomas Fitzgerald (Silken Thomas) "proclaimed himself a rebel" (10.408–09) against the English here in 1534.

This section includes two interpolations. First, "from a long face a beard and gaze hung on a chessboard" (10.425); this is John Howard Parnell, brother to the late politician Charles Stewart Parnell. We will see this man at his chessboard more fully in section 16. Second, we see again the young woman from section 1 emerging from the bushes.

Reverend Love exchanges niceties with Ned Lambert before departing. Lambert, who himself seems to know quite a bit of history, explains to J. J. O'Molloy about the priest. J. J. O'Molloy is there to ask Ned Lambert for money. Bloom noted back in "Aeolus" that O'Molloy is a "mighthavebeen" lawyer with a gambling problem (7.303), and toward the end of that episode, Myles Crawford denies J. J.'s request for a loan. Here, Ned Lambert seems to anticipate why O'Molloy has come calling, as he says, "Well, Jack. What is it? What's the trouble?" (10.454) before sneezing.

## Section 9: Tom Rochford's Invention, Then Lenehan and M'Coy

Tom Rochford, speaking to Nosey Flynn, Lenehan, and M'Coy, explains his invention that displays the musical act currently onstage during a program involving multiple performers. Lenehan, who we know is planning to meet Blazes Boylan in the Ormond at 4:00, pledges to pitch Rochford's invention to his friend the music concert producer.

M'Coy and Lenehan leave together, and Lenehan tells M'Coy the story of Tom Rochford's heroism in saving a man who had fallen down a manhole. Lenehan pops into Lynam's to find out the final odds on Sceptre, the horse he backed in the Ascot Gold Cup. While waiting in the street, M'Coy uses his foot to sweep a banana peel from the street into the gutter. We have access to his inner monologue as he thinks, "Fellow might damn easy get a nasty fall there" (10.513–14), revealing his concern for the well-being of others.

We then have our first of three interpolations: first, in Phoenix Park, the viceregal cavalcade begins its journey across the city; elsewhere, young Patrick Dignam leaves a butcher shop; up north, Molly replaces the *Unfurnished Apartments* card that fell in section 3. We might be tempted to think that the sight of Bloom, the "darkbacked figure scann[ing] books" (10.520–21), is an interpolation, especially since the same description appears as an interpolation back in section 5, but no: M'Coy and Lenehan actually see Bloom perusing books.

Before that, Lenehan returns from Lynam's to note that Sceptre is running at even money. He also reports that he saw Bantam Lyons on the verge of placing a wager on Throwaway (the horse Bloom unwittingly tipped back at the end of "Lotus-Eaters"), but Lenehan dissuades Lyons from making that bet. In a moment of coincidence, Lenehan and M'Coy see Bloom just as they are discussing his unintentional horse-racing tip. The men discuss Bloom and his knack for finding bargains; they base this assertion on an astronomy book he purchased at well below value, but we might wonder if they are influenced by stereotypes here.

Lenehan then launches out on a story about the Glencree dinner: after a night of music, heavy drinking, and rich foods, Lenehan sat beside Molly in a carriage. He describes her as bouncing up against him, and he claims to have gotten handsy with her ample body. Bloom, meanwhile, looked out the window, identifying constellations to Chris Callinan (another friend in the carriage). Telling this story leaves Lenehan gasping in laughter. M'Coy, a married man himself, "grew grave" (10.578) in silent rebuke of Lenehan's tale of infidelity. Lenehan takes the hint, changes his tack, and compliments Mr. Bloom, saying, "There's a touch of the artist about old Bloom" (10.582–83).

## Section 10: Mr. Bloom

In *The Odyssey*, Odysseus elects to avoid the wandering rocks, making them peripheral to his story. Conversely, Mr. Bloom, our Odysseus, is largely peripheral to the "Wandering Rocks" episode of *Ulysses*. That said, we join Bloom in section 10 as he shops for Molly's next book. Characteristically thinking of others, his thoughts turn to Mrs. Purefoy, who has been in labor for three days. The bookseller brings a few options for Mr. Bloom to consider, and Bloom notes the scent of onions on the man's breath. Lovely.

After an interpolation featuring the dancing instructor Denis Maginni, Mr. Bloom peruses a few books and evaluates their suitedness to Molly's erotic tastes. Thinking *Sweets of Sin* looks promising, he opens it at random to a few different pages and reads. Feeling himself getting aroused, he decides it's a winner.

After an interpolation shows the viceregal cavalcade, the bookseller returns, hocks a loogey on the floor, and approves of Mr. Bloom's selection. Overall, pretty unsavory. We might have hoped for a more warm and wholesome reunion with Mr. Bloom.

## Section 11: Dilly and Simon Dedalus

Dilly seems to have been waiting on her father all afternoon. You might recall that Mr. Bloom, back at the outset of "Lestrygonians," spotted Dilly Dedalus outside of Dillon's auctionrooms on Bachelor's Walk; furthermore, Bloom noted at 1:00 that she is "still" (8.28) there, implying that he first saw her when he popped down there looking for Mr. Keyes during the "Aeolus" episode. So, Dilly has been here since just after twelve noon, and now, around 3:30, she finally meets her father. Simon, as we know, has been drinking with the newspapermen in The Oval, located just up O'Connell Street and around the corner. Defensive, he immediately rebukes Dilly for her posture. Undeterred, Dilly presses her father for money. He gives her a shilling, and Dilly correctly supposes he's got more than that and presses him further. Simon blasphemes and curses his daughters as "an insolent pack of little bitches since [their] poor mother died" (10.682).

In an example of how "Wandering Rocks" (and, really, all of *Ulysses*) expects the reader to have read it before reading it, this section contains the lacquey ringing his bell "barang!" (10.689), which first appeared as an interpolation back in section 4 (see 10.281–82) in the midst of Katey, Boody, and Maggy Dedalus's conversation about Simon, Dilly, and the Dedalus family's poverty. By drawing our attention back to that scene of destitution, the arranger provokes indignation on behalf of the family that Simon has failed. Still, he is a colorful and charismatic man: he wins a grin from Dilly when he offers to look along the gutters of Dublin for spare change.

## Section 12: Tom Kernan

Mr. Kernan, whom we saw at the funeral earlier in the day, has just left a pub where he enjoyed a "thimbleful" (10.724) of gin as an afternoon pick-me-up. The prose of this section provides closer and more sustained access to Kernan's inner monologue than appears in other sections of "Wandering Rocks"; it actually feels like we have a proximity to Kernan's thoughts similar to our access to Bloom's in, say, "Lotus-Eaters." Kernan mentally replays the conversation he's just shared with Mr. Crimmins, a publican, about the ship accident in New York City. He sneaks in a bit of anti-Americanism before taking a moment to admire his own attire—a fancy coat he purchased secondhand at roughly 25 percent of its estimated original cost. *Ulysses* is a novel of the middle class.

Interpolations in this section show part of a conversation between Simon Dedalus and Father Cowley, the continued water-bound journey of the YMCA flyer, and Josie and Denis Breen in their ongoing pursuit of legal action over the U. p: up postcard.

Tom Kernan mistakes a man in a car for Ned Lambert's brother. He recalls political violence and then drops the second of the novel's seven usages of the phrase "retrospective arrangement" (10.783). At the end of the section, Kernan, a West Briton (an Anglophilic Irishman), just misses the opportunity to see the Lord Governor pass by in the viceregal cavalcade, and he is disappointed by his near miss.

## Section 13: Stephen and Dilly Dedalus

Another thread to the Dedalus family web woven in "Wandering Rocks," section 13 begins with Stephen alone, thinking abstrusely as he peers through shop windows. He stops at a book cart, wondering if perhaps one of his old books might have been pawned there by his younger siblings, and examines pages in a book of magical charms, including a spell "to win a woman's love" (10.847). Dilly surprises Stephen, who sheepishly closes and tries to hide what he's reading. Dilly has just spent half of the two pence Simon gave her in section 11 on a book to learn French.

Stephen recognizes that his sister is "drowning" and wrestles with the guilt he feels for abandoning his family, reprising the "agenbite of inwit" (10.879) he earlier ascribed to the English in their guilt over the treatment of the Irish. He knows, however, that should he try to save Dilly and his other siblings, he would only be assured of drowning with them. Stephen's silent call of "Misery! Misery!" (10.880) is truly haunting.

## Section 14: Simon Dedalus, Father Bob Cowley, and Ben Dollard

Right on the heels of the heartbreaking scene between Stephen and Dilly Dedalus, we see their father greeting Father Cowley (we first saw this exchange as an interpolation in section 12), who explains that he owes money to Reuben J. Dodd (seen and cursed by the men in the funeral carriage back in "Hades"). Dodd has staked two men at Cowley's home to collect the debt. Cowley has asked a friend, Ben Dollard, to ask "long John" Fanning, a subsheriff, to intervene. Dollard approaches and exchanges banter with Simon and Cowley. Dollard has been to see John Henry Menton (a busy man this day) for legal advice on Cowley's situation. Apparently, Cowley also owes rent to his landlord (who happens to be Reverend Love, seen in section 8), thus giving Love the prior claim over Dodd. So, while clearly not in great financial shape, Cowley at least has the legal grounds on which to get Dodd off his back.

## Section 15: Martin Cunningham, Mr. Power, and John Wyse Nolan

Martin Cunningham has been working to make arrangements on behalf of the Dignam family. He mentions that he has appealed to Father Conmee for assistance in placing one of the Dignam boys in school, and we know from section 1 that Conmee intends to help. Cunningham has also been fundraising to support the Dignams between now and when the insurance policy pays out (although Cunningham has work to do before securing that payout, as we will see). John Wyse Nolan, looking at the ledger, notes that Bloom "put his name down for five shillings" (10.974), roughly US$75 today. Martin Cunningham adds that Bloom already gave the 5 shillings; there's a big difference between pledging to give money at a graveside and actually ponying up. Bloom's generosity is met with some measure of incredulity shaded with anti-Semitism. An interpolation shows Blazes Boylan stopping drunk Bob Doran for a word.

The men find long John Fanning, referenced in the previous section, and the men shoot the breeze about local social and political circles, then Cunningham turns their focus back to Dignam. Cunningham seems to be feeling out Fanning on his willingness to contribute to the fund, but Fanning apparently did not know Paddy Dignam. Then, the viceregal cavalcade passes by.

## Section 16: Buck Mulligan and Haines

Buck Mulligan left the National Library with Stephen, but he has rejoined Haines for an afternoon snack at the Dublin Bread Co. (D. B. C.). As they enter the restaurant, Mulligan points out John Howard Parnell playing chess at another table. We saw this scene of Parnell as an interpolation back in section 8. Buck and Haines each order a *mélange* (a drink like a cappuccino), as well as scones and cakes, before turning their conversation to the topic of Stephen and his *Hamlet* lecture. Haines claims that "Shakespeare is the happy huntingground of all minds that have lost their balance" (10.1061–62). We could easily replace "Shakespeare" with *Ulysses* in that statement: anyone reading this thing must be a little crazy! Buck makes fun of Stephen's unbalanced gait when he's drunk and proceeds to claim that the Jesuits made Stephen crazy with fear of hell. If you've read *A Portrait*, you might agree with Buck's theory. Indeed, a secular artist might find little "joy" in the act of creation when s/he believes that the very act is defiant to God and therefore promising of damnation. Haines notes that ancient Irish mythology lacks any notion of hell.

The food and drinks arrive, and Buck indulges gluttonously as the two men ponder Stephen's potential as an author. Buck suggests that Stephen will "write something in ten years" (10.1089–90). I don't mean to conflate Stephen with Joyce, but in 1914, ten years after Buck's prediction, Joyce published *Dubliners*, *A Portrait* began its serialized publication in *The Egoist*, and he began writing *Ulysses*.

The section closes with our last glimpse of the "Elijah is coming" flyer's voyage out to sea. In the schema, Joyce listed "labyrinth" as the technique of "Wandering Rocks," and Richard Ellmann writes that "the successful passage through the labyrinth is signalized, as Joyce intimated to Gilbert, by the 'Elijah' throwaway" making it to the bay.[7] On its way, it passes "by the threemasted schooner *Rosevean*" (10.1098) that Stephen saw at the end of "Proteus" (see 3.504).

## Section 17: Cashel Boyle O'Connor Fitzmaurice Tisdall Farrell

Noted by Bloom as a curiosity in the "Lestrygonians" episode, Cashel Boyle O'Connor Fitzmaurice Tisdall Farrell flashes across section 17 with frowns and rudeness. He walks past Mr. Bloom's dental offices (no relation), and brushes into the blind stripling's cane (the same blind stripling Bloom helped cross that street at the end of "Lestrygonians"). Upset at being bumped off course, the blind young man curses Farrell.

### Section 18: Patrick Dignam

Young Patrick Dignam has escaped the "dull" (10.1125), mournful atmosphere of his home in order to buy porksteaks. He stops to look at a poster advertising a boxing match (he's a fan of the sweet science), and then catches a glimpse of himself in the mirror. He notes that he is a bit disheveled in his black mourning clothes and tries to tidy himself.

He sees dapper Blazes Boylan speaking with drunk Bob Doran (seen as an interpolation in section 15) and then wonders if the other schoolboys on the street notice that he's in mourning clothes. He continues with this line of thought as he imagines his friends tonight seeing his and his father's name in the newspaper. Patrick recalls the rather horrifying image from earlier in the day of a fly walking up his dead father's gray face toward the eyeball; he recalls the thumps of his father's body in the coffin; he remembers his father's most recent drunken behavior; and he thinks of his dad's deathbed request that he "be a good son to ma" (10.1170–71). He tries to acclimate himself to the finality of his father's death—"Pa is dead. My father is dead" (10.1170)—and hopes that his father is in purgatory because he went to confession just a few days before his passing.

### Section 19: The Viceregal Cavalcade

Joyce bookends "Wandering Rocks" with representatives of the church (Father Conmee) and state (the Earl of Dudley, General Governor of Ireland). In the first section, Father Conmee represents the Roman Catholic Church, and the viceregal cavalcade here represents the imperial British state, the second of "two masters" (1.638) under which Ireland is subjugated. The two form something like a cross of peace and order over the city: Conmee's movement is largely south to north, and the viceregal cavalcade progresses from Phoenix Park in the west through the center of the city to Sandymount in the east where the governor will "inaugurate the Mirus bazaar in aid of funds for Mercer's hospital" (10.1268–69). Although representative of imposing powers, both are on benevolent errands.

In section 19, we see a panoply of the novel's characters as they all watch the procession cut through the city. I've heard or read somewhere that the wandering rocks referenced in *The Odyssey* actually represented the rocky straight of the Black Sea—the rocks seemed to move based on the tide level. A student of mine once suggested that section 19 represents low tide in the "Wandering Rocks" episode: all of the characters are visible. In a city of fewer than three hundred thousand people,[8] the viceregal cavalcade passes forty-eight characters, most of whom we have encountered before, some of whom we have yet to meet (such as Miss Kennedy, Miss Douce, and Gerty MacDowell), plus the mysterious man in the brown macintosh.

## Further Reading

Gibbons, Luke. "Spaces of Time through Times of Space: Joyce, Ireland and Colonial Modernity." *Field Day Review* 1 (2005): 71–86.

This article positions *Ulysses* in its historical context, wherein notions of time and space were changing. The "Wandering Rocks" episode is explained as a paragon of simultaneity and spatial interrelatedness in modernist literature.

Hegglund, Jon. "*Ulysses* and the Rhetoric of Cartography." *Twentieth Century Literature* 49, no. 2 (Summer 2003): 164–92.

By examining the maps and geography associated with *Ulysses*, Hegglund argues that Joyce's Dublin exists in a liminal space between fact and fiction, between the imperial and postcolonial power structures.

Huang, Shan-Yun. "'Wandering Temporalities': Rethinking *Imagined Communities* through 'Wandering Rocks.'" *James Joyce Quarterly* 49, no. 3/4 (2012): 589–610.

This essay understands the many sections and nonlinear timeline of "Wandering Rocks" to represent the fragmentation of Irish community and the lack of a coherent national narrative as a result of the country's colonial history. Huang does, however, perceive the potential for a heterogeneous Ireland in the many connections that link the various sections of the episode.

Sherry, Vincent. "Distant Music: 'Wandering Rocks' and the Art of Gratuity." *James Joyce Quarterly* 31, no. 2 (Winter 1994): 31–40.

Sherry traces the theme of gratuity through the network of interpolations across this episode.

Williams, Trevor. "'Conmeeism' and the Universe of Discourse in 'Wandering Rocks.'" *James Joyce Quarterly* 29, no. 2 (Winter 1992): 267–79.

This essay examines the forces of oppression—Catholicism, colonialism, and capitalism—highlighted in the "Wandering Rocks" episode. Williams then interprets the use of reported speech in the episode's first section to reflect Father Conmee's unoppressed and therefore unfragmented consciousness.

# Chapter 11

# "SIRENS" GUIDE

Whereas most episodes in *Ulysses* begin *in medias res* and at a remove (temporally, spatially, or both) from the previous episode's conclusion, characters in episode 11 pick up almost exactly where they left off in episode 10. You'll recall that the final section of the "Wandering Rocks" episode depicts the procession of the viceregal cavalcade through the heart of the city and shows various Dubliners as they watch and react to the grandeur of this event. The "Sirens" episode opens its action by repeating nearly verbatim the description of two barmaids, Miss Douce (bronze) and Miss Kennedy (gold), peering through the windows of the Ormond Hotel bar to catch a glimpse of the procession as it rolls along the north bank of the Liffey at 3:38 p.m.[1]

The sirens correspondence refers to two birdwomen whose beautiful singing tempts sailors off course, luring their ships to wreck on a craggy island. In *The Odyssey*, Odysseus plugs his crewmates' ears with wax to prevent them from hearing the sirens' song; Odysseus, clever enough to have his cake and eat it too, ties himself to his mast so that he can enjoy the sirens' song while preventing himself from steering the ship toward the temptresses. We can apply this correspondence in various ways; Jackson I. Cope argues that Miss Douce and Miss Kennedy are the sirens, trying to tempt Boylan from his imminent adultery with Molly. The 4:00 hour of Molly's meeting with Boylan has arrived, and Cope additionally considers that Bloom's

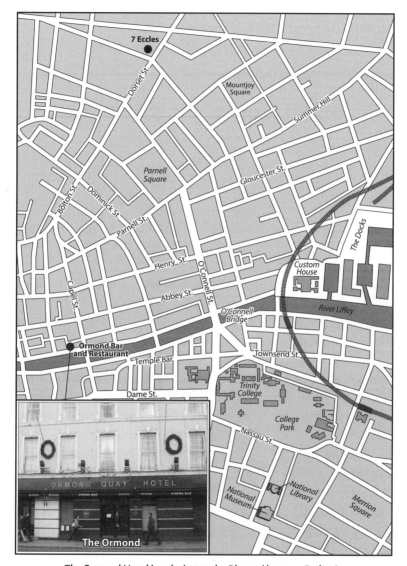

The Ormond Hotel in relation to the Blooms' home, 7 Eccles St

"impulse to interfere in their affair is a siren-song that would destroy them all."[2]

Stylistically, with this episode's musical prose elements (such as on-omatopoeia, linguistic refrains, and syncopated syntax), along with its depiction of singing performances, "Sirens" directly engages and seeks to replicate the qualities of music, which the schema lists as the art for this episode. The prominence of the musical style in this episode's discourse signals a clear departure from what we have come to regard as the initial style of the novel. When Joyce shared a manuscript of the "Sirens" episode with Ezra Pound and Harriet Shaw Weaver in July of 1919, they disliked the change. In reply to their critique, Joyce explained that the episode replicates "the eight regular parts of a *fuga per canonem* . . . to describe the seductions of music" and defended the radical stylistic departures here and in subsequent episodes as essential to *Ulysses*; he explained that the realization of his plan for the novel was "only possible by such variation which, I beg you to believe, is not capricious" (*Letters* 129). Indeed, the musicality of this episode represents its own sirens' song, a temptation away from the plot of *Ulysses* and toward a playfulness with the sound of language without much regard for a coherent narrative.[3] (If that idea sounds interesting, you should check out *Finnegans Wake*.) The "Sirens" episode, though, like Odysseus, indulges this interest in music and the expressiveness of words without running the whole ship aground; the story of the novel stays afloat. From this point on, each episode's new mode of writing serves its content in meaningful ways, making literary style as central to *Ulysses* as Stephen and Bloom.

Still, Joyce himself conceded that his fixation on style makes *Ulysses* "an extremely tiresome book" (*Letters* 128), an assessment with which first-time readers might agree, especially when encountering the baffling first sixty-three lines of "Sirens." Scholars equate this opening section to a musical "prelude" or "overture" that introduces the major notes of the chapter's language and plot.[4] While these labels are apt and instructive, I also like to think of this section as an orchestra warming up prior to a performance; the reader is like an audience listening to musicians practicing trills and phrases of the composition to be performed. It is a cacophony here, but each snatch of language will make sense when properly arranged and elaborated upon in the chapter/performance ahead. The device of this "overture" therefore signifies the kind of loop rereading that allows for maximum enjoyment and understanding of *Ulysses* while also creating tension between the past and the present: those opening lines constantly draw the reader back to the beginning of the episode. Similarly, many passages in "Sirens" recall details from "Calypso," pulling from the text's past to illuminate the present 4:00 hour and Molly's scheduled meeting with Boylan. Of course, music itself is powerfully evocative of memories, and many of the recollections conjured in this episode warble with sentimentality; such overwrought emotion is another sirens' song that threatens to lure characters toward destruction.

"Sirens" begins with the barmaids watching the passing cavalcade and laughing at a man in one of the carriages craning his neck to admire them in the window. Miss Douce's statement "he's killed looking back" (11.77) suggests the kind of "looking back" we must do as we read "Sirens" to appreciate the opening sixty-three lines. An interpolation (the same technique employed throughout "Wandering Rocks") shows Bloom carrying *The Sweets of Sin*, the erotic novel he just purchased for Molly. A barback, identified with the synecdoche of "the boots" (11.89), brings the barmaids their afternoon tea and loudly drops the tray on the counter. He gives Miss Douce some attitude, and she threatens to tell their boss about his "impertinent insolence" (11.99). The young man mocks her, saying "imperthnthn thnthnthn" (11.100), a phrase that first appeared in the opening overture (see 11.2) and was nonsensical there; it now has meaning in its proper context.

Miss Douce, recently returned from vacation, asks Miss Kennedy to check her sunburn. They discuss home remedies and laugh about an old-man druggist they both know. Mr. Bloom appears in another interpolation as "Bloowhose dark eye read" (11.149) the text of shopfronts: first Figatner's jewelers, then Lore's hat store, then Bassi's framing shop. He thinks of goddesses and remarks that he "could not see" (11.153) whether the goddess statues in the National Museum were anatomically accurate. He recalls leaving the National Library alongside Stephen about an hour earlier and deduces that Mulligan must have been the fellow exiting with him. The narrative then returns to the Ormond for about twenty-five lines, where the women are wrapping up their fit of laughter as they resume drinking tea. Miss Douce is a bit indecorous.

Another interpolation pops the narrative back to Bloom as he walks along Wellington Quay (across the river from the Ormond), passing Cantwell's wine and whiskey merchants and Ceppi & Sons framers and statuary manufacturers. His inner monologue here makes the kind of mental jumps we enjoyed following in the earlier episodes: the wares displayed in the window of one of these shops remind him of Nannetti's father selling Catholic devotional statues, which leads Bloom to think succinctly that "religion pays" (11.187), an echo of his previous pragmatic assessments of faith. You'll remember that Bloom is waiting on Nannetti's go-ahead to finalize the sale of the Keyes ad, and he again notes his need to "see him for that par" (11.187). Then other concerns return to his mind: he is hungry (that gorgonzola cheese sandwich around 1:30 was barely enough to tide him over on this busy day), and, oh yeah, his wife is going to have sex with Blazes Boylan "at four" (11.188), only about a quarter hour from now as the "clockhands turn" (11.188). Then, following immediately after this contemplation of the imminent affair, he assesses his pipeline of advertisement business and his plans to buy Molly "violet silk petticoats" (11.190) for her birthday (see 8.1059–61 in "Lestrygonians" for the first instance of this stream of thought). Bloom's generosity may strike you as extreme, but it is worth noting that he is planning on giving Molly undergarments, a particular fetish of his . . . and isn't lingerie always also a gift to the giver? Bloom then mentally alludes to the title of the book he has just bought for Molly to summarize his marital situation: "the sweets of sin" (11.190).

The narrative returns to the Ormond, where Simon Dedalus enters the bar and welcomes Miss Douce back from her vacation in Rostrevor, a seaside town about seventy-five miles north of Dublin. Simon, a talented tenor, is clearly a regular here at the Ormond bar, which is known around town as a casual place to hear and perform good music. He flirts with Miss Douce and orders a "water and a half glass of whisky" (11.211). The word "Jingle" appears, our first interpolated note of Boylan's approach to the Ormond in the jaunting car. Simon prepares his pipe for a smoke while Miss Douce pours his drink. Lenehan enters the bar, looking for Boylan.

In another interpolation, we hear all three of the novel's primary modes of voice: first, the narrator reports: "Mr. Bloom reached Essex bridge" (11.228–29). Then, the arranger echoes (or mocks) the narrator with stylish flair in the manner of a fugal counterpoint: "Yes, Mr. Bloom crossed bridge of Yessex" (11.229). Next, we hear Bloom's inner monologue: "To Martha I must write. Buy paper. Daly's. Girl there civil" (11.229–30). Finally, the arranger pipes up again: "Bloom. Old Bloom. Blue bloom is on the rye" (11.230–31). You might notice that the narrator refers to him as "Mr. Bloom" here and throughout the first half of the novel, whereas the arranger begins calling him just "Bloom," revealing a less respectful attitude.

Lenehan tries to flirt with Miss Kennedy, but she's not giving him the time of day. He then tries to engage Simon in a conversation, telling the "famous father" (11.254) that he's just "quaffed the nectarbowl" (11.263) with his "famous son" (11.254) (you'll remember Stephen, Lenehan, and the others leaving the newspaper offices and heading for drinks at Mooney's at the end of "Aeolus"). Simon notices that the piano has been moved, and Miss Douce informs him that the piano tuner had just serviced the instrument. Remember at the end of "Lestrygonians" when Bloom helps the blind stripling cross the street? Same guy. The blind stripling is the piano tuner.

Bald Pat, the waiter working in the dining room adjoining the bar, places a drink order for a diner. Simon tests the piano keys. An interpolation shows Bloom buying the paper and envelopes for his letter in reply to Martha Clifford. Through the window of the shop, Bloom spots Boylan in his distinctive bright straw hat riding a jaunting car toward the Ormond. Seeing Blazes Boylan alarms Mr. Bloom, making his inner monologue short and choppy, similar to his jumpy thoughts when he saw Boylan at the end of "Lestrygonians." His reaction here, however, differs from his panicked avoidance there: an emboldened Bloom now decides to "Follow. Risk it. Go quick" (11.305). In fact, he goes *too* quick; as Mr. Bloom starts to leave the stationer's shop in pursuit of Boylan, the shopgirl has to call him back and remind him to pay for his paper. We can assume he pays with a tanner (a sixpence coin) because she gives him his change, saying "and four" (11.308), echoing Bloom's recognition three lines earlier that Molly had informed him that Boylan was coming to meet her "at four" (11.305).

Back in the Ormond, Simon sounds the tuning fork that the blind stripling accidentally left behind. The waiter, Pat, takes a bottle to his table in the dining room. Simon begins singing and playing the piano. The language here (and elsewhere in the episode) replicates the experience and effect of music and is nothing short of astonishingly beautiful. Lenehan again seeks to gain the favor of Miss Kennedy's attention and is again rebuffed. Boylan's jaunting car arrives at the Ormond, and he enters the bar. Lenehan greets Boylan as "the conquering hero" (11.340), and the arranger counters by giving Bloom the epitaph "unconquered hero" (11.342). In this way, *Ulysses* presents Mr. Bloom as a new type of hero worthy of celebration in the modern world: assailed but enduring; not a conqueror but unconquered.

Boylan unenthusiastically returns Lenehan's greeting: "I heard you were round" (11.345). Doesn't exactly ring with excitement, does it? He tips his hat to Miss Kennedy, who offers him a smile only to be "outsmiled" (11.347) by Miss Douce. Boylan is popular. He orders a round of drinks for Lenehan and himself. Meanwhile, an interpolation shows Mr. Bloom meeting Richie Goulding (Stephen's maternal uncle, whose home Stephen considered visiting in "Proteus"). We hear bits of Bloom's conversation with Goulding as they decide to have dinner together in the Ormond dining room. This spot, Goulding says, is good to "see, not be seen" (11.358–59)—perfectly suited to Bloom's interest in spying on Boylan and allowing him to continue avoiding a direct confrontation. Also intermixed in this exchange is Bloom's inner monologue, fixated on the approaching rendezvous "at four" (11.352). The arranger, however, creates another kind of mischief, breaking the fourth wall to ask us "who said four?" (11.352), regarding the time of Molly's meeting with Boylan; this question may prompt you to flip back to "Calypso," where you'll find no mention of time for the appointment. Molly must have told Bloom that Boylan was coming at four o'clock in Mr. Bloom and Molly's off-page conversation between the end of "Calypso" and the beginning of "Lotus-Eaters." The arranger plays a prank by sending us to look for something that isn't there.

Lenehan and Boylan flirt with Miss Douce as she prepares their drinks. We hear a snippet of her inner monologue as she notices that Boylan has a flower in his coat and jealously wonders who might have given it to him. We know from "Wandering Rocks" that, in fact, Boylan "*took*" (10.328, my emphasis) the flower for himself at the shop where he bought the fruit basket for Molly. Readers keeping score between Boylan and Bloom will note that Henry Flower was *given* a flower by Martha Clifford. Point Bloom.

The men mention the Gold Cup, Boylan reveals that he has wagered some money (on Molly's behalf), and Lenehan predicts that Sceptre will win. Miss Kennedy walks by and also wonders who gave Boylan the flower. The clock strikes four. Bloom and Goulding enter the dining room,[5] and Bloom wonders why Boylan is here in the bar rather than keeping his appointment with Molly at 7 Eccles Street: "Has he forgotten? Perhaps a trick. Not come: whet appetite" (11.392–93). Maybe Boylan is playing Molly. Mr. Bloom couldn't imagine himself doing the same.

Lenehan pleads with Miss Douce to "*sonnez la cloche*" (11.404); she abides, sexily bending, lifting her skirt, and pulling her elastic garter to smack her thigh. Lenehan erupts in glee, and Douce looks down on this vulgar lout as she "smilesmirked supercilious" (11.416) on him. However, "mild she smiled on Boylan" (11.417)—she clearly seeks his favor. Boylan, resisting the temptation of this siren, declares "I'm off" (11.426) and moves to leave the bar for his appointment with Molly. As he departs, the bass singer Ben Dollard enters with Father Cowley; the two men are continuing their conversation from "Wandering Rocks"—remember that Reuben J. Dodd is aggressively seeking to collect a debt from Cowley, and Dollard has enlisted the subsheriff "long John" Fanning to intervene. Dollard asks Simon for a song. In the other room, Bloom and Goulding order drinks from Bald Pat, the waiter. Bloom hears Boylan's jaunting car jingle as it pulls from the curb en route to 7 Eccles Street. The musicality of the prose underscores Bloom's mournful resignation: "light sob of breath Bloom sighed on the silent bluehued flowers" (11.457–58).

Miss Douce also mourns Boylan's departure and wonders why he left so soon after her little exhibition. Ben Dollard and Simon reminisce about a concert years ago when Dollard borrowed a tux from Mr. Bloom, who, with Molly, was running a secondhand clothing and costume business when he was between jobs during the years 1894 to 1896. The men discuss Molly while, in the next room, Bloom is served his dinner. An interpolation shows Boylan's carriage at Bachelor's Walk, about half a mile east along the river. Back in the Ormond, singing resumes; Mr. Bloom continues to eat and, like Simon and Ben Dollard two pages before, recalls the night Dollard borrowed a tuxedo. This is another instance of parallax, the novel's recurring technique whereby we see the same thing from a different perspective. Then, Mr. Lidwell enters the bar.

The men implore Simon to sing "M'appari," and Cowley offers to accompany him on the piano.[6] Bloom mingles his memory of the opera *Martha*, from which "M'appari" comes, as he wrestles with Molly's affair, resigning himself to his reality: "Too late. She longed to go. That's why. Woman. As easy stop the sea. Yes: all is lost" (11.640–41). These thoughts echo Bloom's inner monologue in "Calypso," where he thought, "Will happen, yes. Prevent. Useless" (4.447–48). True, if Molly "longed to go" to another man, it would be "useless" for him to try to "prevent" the affair; if he interferes today, she will find a way around him tomorrow or the day after: "as easy stop the sea." That said, Bloom's recognition of the futility of intervention is only half of the reason why he remains passive in the face of Molly's affair: he also craves punishment. Mr. Bloom has already blamed himself once today for Rudy's death (see 6.329), and he will later in "Sirens" consider the poor health of their infant son to be "my fault" (11.1066); plus, he knows that he has been unsatisfactory in fulfilling other husbandly duties, so he may consider his suffering here to be a just penalty for his failures. In fact, he may desire this punishment so that he can experience contrition and then permit himself to move on from his state of passivity and paralysis. For these reasons, Bloom's heart, like Lionel's in *Martha*, "bowed down" (11.659).

As Simon begins singing "M'appari," the text brilliantly replicates the experience of music: "braintipped, cheek touched with flame, they listened feeling that flow endearing flow over skin limbs human heart soul spine" (11.668–69). I highly encourage you to find and listen to a recording of "M'appari" as you follow along with Simon's singing and the text between the song's lines.[7] It is a triumph of ekphrastic writing. Pay particular attention to the paragraph describing the longest note in the song: "*Come* . . . ! / It soared . . . endlessnessnessness . . . . . . ." (11.743–49). Listen, read, and be dazzled.

While listening to the song, Bloom's mind hops around from his own Martha (Clifford), to imagining Boylan's arrival at 7 Eccles, to the tragedy of Simon's wasted talent, to the night he first met Molly, to wondering why they became a couple: "why did she me? Fate" (11.732). At the song's conclusion, everyone applauds Simon. Tom Kernan arrives in the bar. Richie Goulding speaks a bit about Simon, his brother-in-law, and Bloom silently notes that Simon "treats [Goulding] with scorn" (11.790). Bloom unties his hands from the cat's cradle in which he has bound himself (a correspondence to Odysseus tying himself to the mast). He laments the cruelty of lost love as a ubiquitous aspect of the human condition. He reflects on the mathematical aspects of music, thinks a bit about Dignam, notes that he gave "five bob" (11.805) to the collection for the Dignam family, which we learned in "Wandering Rocks" (see 10.974–79). He begins writing his reply to Martha Clifford. As he writes, his mind wanders to some mental accounting and betrays his guilt over this illicit correspondence as he contemplates how he'd react "if [Molly] found out" (11.876). An interpolation shows Boylan arriving at Eccles Street. Mr. Bloom's mind briefly reprises many notes from earlier in the novel. When he thinks of Shakespeare, a line fuses Bloom's inner monologue with Stephen's thoughts in "Scylla and Charybdis" (see 9.651–53): "In Gerard's rosery of Fetter lane he walks, greyedauburn. One life is all. One body. Do. But do" (11.907–08). As Hugh Kenner explains, the arranger "enjoys a seemingly total recall for exact forms of words used hundreds of pages earlier."[8]

Mr. Bloom prepares to leave the Ormond; he has plans to meet Martin Cunningham in Barney Kiernan's pub, the site of the next episode, "Cyclops," to discuss Dignam's insurance situation. In the bar, Miss Douce tells the men "she had a gorgeous, simply gorgeous time" (11.921) on her vacation and shows off a seashell she brought back from the shore. A new sound, "Tap" (11.933), appears on the page; this interpolated note represents the blind stripling tapping with his cane through the streets of Dublin as he returns to the Ormond to retrieve the tuning fork he left behind. We hear a bit of the music of normal conversations taking place in various groups hanging out in the bar. Boylan knocks on the door of 7 Eccles "with a loud proud knocker" (11.987). The people in the bar request that Ben Dollard sing "The Croppy Boy," an Irish ballad telling the story of a young man who, on his way to fight for Irish independence, stops into a church to confess his sins; the priest hearing his confession is a disguised British soldier who arrests and kills the Croppy Boy.

Bloom's mind wanders (as does his eye . . . toward Miss Douce). He thinks of Molly all dressed up for a performance. He notes the end of his family line owing to his not having a son, then, in a glimmer of hope for the future, wonders "if still" (11.1067) he might have a son and heir. Dollard continues to sing "The Croppy Boy," and Bloom's inner monologue riffs on the song's lyrics. Miss Douce strokes the beer-pull suggestively, and Mr. Bloom exits the Ormond just as the song ends. As he walks away from the bar and toward a post office to mail his letter to Martha, Bloom contributes a "Pwee!" (11.1203) to the music of "Sirens"; further gaseous excretions will continue intermittently through the end of the episode. Back in the bar, the men realize that Bloom just left and was in the dining room the whole time. Lidwell, who came in after the other men had discussed Molly, talks about her "fine voice" (11.1209). Bloom seems to be principally identified around town as her husband. In an interpolation, the "stripling, blind" (11.1234), is revealed to be the source of the tapping. Bloom humorously questions the intelligence of the Croppy Boy for not noticing that the priest was a British soldier and then wonders again about the man in the brown macintosh from the funeral.

A shabby-looking "whore of the lane" (11.1250–51) approaches, and Bloom recognizes her. Because Bloom "hope[s] she" (11.1255) doesn't recognize him, we might infer that this woman is Bridie Kelly, the prostitute to whom Bloom lost his virginity many years ago. He stops to look in a shop window so that she might pass without seeing him. Back at the Ormond, the men toast Dollard's performance, and the blind stripling arrives. The whore has passed behind Bloom without incident. Bloom's rumbling fart, "Pprrpffrrpffff" (11.1293), is the episode's final note. As the text says, the "Sirens" song is "*Done*" (11.1294).

### Further Reading

Brown, Susan Sutliff. "The Mystery of the *Fuga per Canonem* Solved." *European Joyce Studies* 22 (2013): 173–93.

    After surveying the problems of Joyce's description of "Sirens" as a "*fuga per canonem*," this essay uses a page from the newly discovered NLI manuscripts to outline Joyce's (mis)conception of this musical form as he applied it to the episode. This moment in the composition represents the impetus for Joyce's departure from the initial style of *Ulysses* to the "counterpointed voices" of a new style of literature.

French, Marilyn. "The Voices of the Sirens in Joyce's *Ulysses*." *Journal of Narrative Technique* 8, no. 1 (Winter 1978): 1–10.

French first offers a clear approach to the changes in voice and tone that will dominate the second half of the novel before focusing her analysis on the stylistic techniques in the "Sirens" episode and their relationship to Bloom and narrative effect.

Howes, Marjorie. "Memory: 'Sirens.'" In *The Cambridge Companion to "Ulysses,"* edited by Sean Latham, 128–39. New York: Cambridge University Press, 2014.

As *Ulysses* departs from the initial style, this essay offers clear ideas regarding the way the novel refers to itself, the way details accumulate across the text, and how the reliance on the reader's memory and anticipation reflects the memories and anticipations of the characters.

Warren, Andrew. "How to Listen to 'Sirens': Narrative Distraction at the Ormond Hotel." *James Joyce Quarterly* 50, no. 3 (Spring 2013): 655–73.

This essay presents a more nuanced and multidimensional correspondence between the "Sirens" episode and *The Odyssey*.

# Chapter 12

# "CYCLOPS" GUIDE

The "Cyclops" episode of *Ulysses* tells the story of what occurred in Barney Kiernan's pub between the hours of 5:00 and 6:00 p.m. from the perspective of a working-class Dubliner. I use the past tense "occurred" here because the nameless narrator (referred to as the Nameless One, or "I," or "the dun") is probably telling this story in a pub at some later point in hopes of cadging drinks off those listening (though this understanding of the narrative perspective is the subject of debate).[1] Perhaps the nearest the novel approaches to moralizing, the "Cyclops" episode directly engages questions of nationalism and prejudice, love and hate, violence and injustice, but Joyce only provides the explicit opportunity to engage these central topics while viewing Mr. Bloom through the eyes of someone antagonistic toward him.

If not the climax of the novel, the "Cyclops" episode certainly represents a significant flashpoint in the events of Bloomsday. The anti-Semitism that has loomed in the background of many of Bloom's social interactions throughout the day emerges as an overt and aggressive force, principally represented in the character of the Citizen, an Irish nationalist with an eyepatch and a myopic view of who qualifies as truly Irish. This man, in the cave of Barney Kiernan's pub, is the cyclops that our Odysseus must overcome. During this hour, rumors about Bloom are hashed out, and misunderstandings lead to seething resentment. Bloom advocates for a more enlightened worldview and

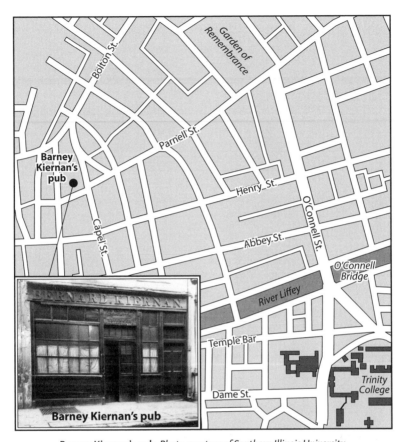

Barney Kiernan's pub. *Photo courtesy of Southern Illinois University.*

exhibits courage in standing up for himself against a pub full of bigoted men. You might even think that he is heroic in this episode.

In *The Odyssey*, Odysseus and his crew land on an island and decide to explore a cave and discover whether its inhabitants are civilized and generous to guests. The cyclops, named Polyphemus, reacts to this intrusion by eating some of Odysseus's men and trapping the rest of them in his cave. Odysseus tells the cyclops his name is "Nobody," then devises a plan to get Polyphemus drunk before stabbing out his eye with the hot point of a stick. Polyphemus calls for help from his fellow cyclops on the island, shouting that "Nobody is killing me," to which the other cyclops holler back, "Well, if nobody is killing you, then it must be a plague. You're on your own. Sorry." As he sails away, Odysseus, overly impressed by his own cleverness, calls back to taunt Polyphemus and reveals his true identity. Enraged, the cyclops hurls a boulder at Odysseus as he sails away; he misses, but Polyphemus then prays to his father, Poseidon, to hound Odysseus for the rest of his journey.

Polyphemus translates literally as "many voiced,"[2] and the Nameless One's narrative is frequently interrupted and undercut by the many voices of lengthy parodies. These interruptions—sometimes mythologizing, sometimes using formal language to mask violence, sometimes elevating the events to an ethereal plane—employ irony to reveal just how commonplace the narrated story really is. The arranger's insertion of these parodies in various literary styles (court proceedings, mythical fantasy, biblical passages, etc.) mock the events taking place in the foregrounded narration. While the Nameless One cynically tears everything down, these interruptions artificially inflate the events. They ridicule through exaggeration. The scholar Sean Latham notes the similarities between the "Cyclops" interruptions and the headlines in "Aeolus," explaining that both devices are satiric disruptions in the narrative that offer commentary on the main story.[3]

Joyce's friend Frank Budgen, a painter by trade, described the interruptions as "cubist," suggesting in a conversation with Joyce that "every event is a many-sided object. You first state one view of it and then you draw it from another angle to another scale, and both aspects lie side by side in the same picture."[4] Although appearing side by side, the tonal incongruity between the interruptions and the plot allows the text to mock the men who mock Mr. Bloom, exposing the specious self-aggrandizement of chauvinism. In this way, Joyce ironically uses the technique of "gigantism" to swat these barflies down. While the interruptions are simultaneously fanciful, funny, and frustrating, they might not be of immediate necessity to the first-time reader. Because they more or less use a different writing style to embellish or repackage what occurs in the foregrounded narration, you might allow yourself to skim the longer ones, appreciating their ironic effects without getting too bogged down.

The Nameless One begins his story by describing his close brush with a chimney sweep's gear and then his meeting of Joe Hynes (whom we saw in "Hades" and "Aeolus" and who owes Bloom 3 shillings). The Nameless One reveals that he is employed in the ignominious profession of "a collector of bad and doubtful debts" (12.24–25) and that he's currently working a job on behalf of a Jewish tea merchant (Herzog) who is owed money by a man called Geraghty. The arranger interrupts the story with the insertion of a parody of legal proceedings related to the Herzog-Geraghty dispute. The primary narrative resumes with Hynes inviting the Nameless One to accompany him to Barney Kiernan's pub so that he can tell the Citizen about a meeting he has just attended on foot-and-mouth disease. The narrator notes that Hynes is generous when he has money, but he rarely has money. The narrative is interrupted by a mock-heroic description of the city, wherein a meat-and-produce market is recast as a "shining palace" (12.87). In these sorts of moments, Sean Latham detects "a broad parody of the work of Revivalists like Yeats, O'Grady, and Lady Gregory, who sought to reconstruct an ancient Irish past by editing collections of myths and folktales."[5] Joyce was skeptical of such romanticized ideals, and he pokes fun at them here.

The two men enter Barney Kiernan's, where the Citizen is passing time with a mangy dog called Garryowen, "waiting for what the sky would drop in the way of drink" (12.120–21). The Citizen and the Nameless One are both spongers, people without money who'll soak up whatever drinks someone else will buy for them. Hynes, flush with cash on payday (see 7.113–18), offers to buy a round, and the men place their orders.

In an interruption, the Citizen is described in mythological terms: this middle-aged former shot-putter becomes a "broadshouldered deepchested stronglimbed frankeyed redhaired freelyfreckled shaggybearded widemouthed largenosed longheaded deepvoiced barekneed brawnyhanded hairylegged ruddyfaced sinewyarmed hero" with "rocklike mountainous knees" whose "heart thundered rumblingly causing the ground, the summit of the lofty tower and the still loftier walls of the cave to vibrate and tremble" (12.151–67). Regarding this parody, Marilyn French argues that "the style builds up the size and prominence of the citizen, reminding the reader of how times past would have seen this hero. At the same time it suggests the ludicrousness of such traits within our world."[6] Indeed, as the episode unfolds, the Citizen's archaic sort of masculine heroism is pitted against a more modern form of hero represented by Mr. Bloom.

Terry, the publican, brings the three pints, and Joe Hynes puts down "a goodlooking sovereign" (12.208), a £1 coin, to the amazement of the Nameless One. The Citizen then reads the marriage announcements and obituaries from the newspaper. As the narrator takes his first sip, he describes the satisfaction of his thirst: "Ah! Ow! Don't be talking! I was blue mouldy for the want of that pint. Declare to God I could hear it hit the pit of my stomach with a click" (12.242–43). We can delight in the Nameless One's vernacular expressiveness—yet another mode of language over which Joyce demonstrates mastery. The Nameless One notices Bob Doran passed out and snoring in the corner of the pub; we know that he is on a bender (see 5.107) and has been hanging out in pubs since at least 9:30 this morning. Alf Bergan is amused to see Denis and Josie Breen walk past the pub; he shares the gossip about the U. p: up postcard and Denis Breen's pursuit of legal recourse. Bob Doran rouses from his stupor and tries to join the conversation.

In a parody, Alf Bergan pays for a round of drinks: he "could ill brook to be outdone in generous deeds" (12.290–91). Dublin pub culture's social practice of generously standing rounds is explained by Mark Osteen in *The Economy of "Ulysses"* as a type of potlatch whereby men project their social and economic strength by treating other men to drinks. Osteen explains:

> Power and prestige accrue not through investing, saving money or acquiring goods, as in bourgeois economies, but through expenditures and loss of goods. But the gifts in a potlatch only seem voluntary; actually there are three intersecting obligations—to give, to receive, and to reciprocate. To fail in any of the three is to suffer social humiliation and loss of honor. The potlatch constructs the boundaries of the social group and solidifies its hierarchies: those who give or destroy wealth are included, and those who do not are cast out; those who cannot reciprocate by giving back a larger gift than the one they have received lose social status. The greater the loss, the greater the prestige.[7]

In short, men project power and imply a comfortable financial situation by cavalierly treating others to drinks. Of course, if one man stands a round, then others (like Alf Bergan here) are compelled to reciprocate the act, leading to a tit-for-tat competition of strength, wealth, generosity, and, ultimately, masculinity. The yield of this practice: everyone ends up drunker and poorer than if they simply paid for their own drinks (as promoted by the antitreating league).

Outside the pub, Mr. Bloom is pacing as he waits on Martin Cunningham to arrive for their meeting to discuss Dignam's finances. Eager to label and delineate, the Citizen growlingly identifies Bloom as a Freemason. Alf Bergan claims that he just saw Paddy Dignam; Joe Hynes shares with him the bad news that Dignam is dead. Alf is shocked and is certain he just saw Dignam "not five minutes ago" (12.323), prompting us to wonder how well these men really know each other. Bob Doran, hammered drunk, is trailing the conversation by a few beats and tries to catch up with the news of Dignam's death. We have an interruption of a parodied theosophical seance raising Dignam from the dead. The Citizen then sees Bloom again. Bob Doran disparages Christ, gets told off by the publican for that kind of blasphemous talk, and then weeps over "poor little Willy [*sic*] Dignam" (12.392). The men in Barney Kiernan's pub (which is decorated with various hangman's photographs) read a letter written by a hangman, H. Rumbold.

After lingering outside for a time, Mr. Bloom enters the pub and is immediately pressed to order a drink (and thus to join the potlatch already under way). Bloom, ever the "prudent member" (12.437), ducks this pressure by asking for a cigar. This is a deft move by Bloom, politely accepting Hynes's offer of a gift while avoiding the obligation to reciprocate by standing the next round of drinks for everyone in the pub. As the men continue their conversation, Bloom is quick to interject with his opinion and erudition. Or at least that's how the Nameless One tells the story; we might be shrewd to question his reliability: When and to whom is he telling this story? What are his audience's prejudices? Might the Nameless One be shading his narrative against Bloom to best position himself for free drinks from his listeners? In any event, Bloom wants to talk "about phenomenon and science" (12.466–67), as parodied by a paragraph of medical writing about erections induced by hanging, and the Citizen wants to talk about Irish nationalist heroes. Bob Doran clumsily plays with Garryowen.

Bloom and the Citizen get into a bit of an argument, and the Nameless One veers to mention Molly, "a nice old phenomenon" (12.503), and recounts a few rumors about the Blooms from their time in the City Arms Hotel years ago. One has to do with Bloom angling for an inheritance in the will of Mrs. Riordan (Molly will also comment on this in "Penelope"), and a few have to do with drinking. None of these rumors are flattering to the Blooms. The narrative returns to the simmering animosity between the Citizen (who is becoming belligerent) and Bloom (who seems oblivious to the danger he's tempting). Because we have seen Bloom be rather reserved in other tense moments earlier in the day, it seems strange for him to emerge as willfully argumentative here. The lengthy newspaper parody that spans lines 525 to 678 represents an opportunity for the first-time reader to skim.

When we return to the narrative, the Citizen and Bloom are trading points about the factors limiting Ireland: the Citizen feels that the Irish aren't Irish enough, and Bloom suggests that the nation is hampered by widespread alcoholism, "the curse of Ireland" (12.684). Bloom mentions the antitreating league, and the Nameless One faults Bloom for drinking off others and not standing rounds; of course, Bloom has just declined a drink, and the Nameless One himself has already leeched multiple beers off Joe, so we again must question the reliability and biases of this narrator. Garryowen noses over toward the Nameless One, and the Citizen senses that the dog makes him anxious. An interruption parodies a newspaper advertisement paragraph for an exhibition of Garryowen as a dog who can speak. Pretty funny. Funnier still, in my mind, is the Nameless One's unintentional joke: when asked if he'd like another pint, the Nameless One replies, "Could a swim duck?" (12.757). Alcohol-induced anthimeria. Pure gold.

Joe again asks Bloom if he'd like a drink, Bloom again declines and explains that he's waiting on Martin Cunningham to work through the Dignams' insurance situation. Apparently, Paddy Dignam had mortgaged the policy, so now there are complications in his widow recovering the payout. As Bloom muddles through his explanation of these technicalities, the Nameless One remembers Bloom getting into some legal hot water over selling Hungarian lottery tickets.[8] Again, suspicion and rumor cloud Bloom's reputation in this city. Also, Bloom has a bit of a Freudian slip, saying "wife's admirers" rather than "wife's advisors" (12.767, 769). Obviously, his own wife's admirer is on his mind today despite Bloom's best efforts to suppress thoughts of him.

Bob Doran continues his "bloody foolery," bewailing the passing of "poor little Willy" Dignam and imploring Bloom to pass along his condolences to Mrs. Dignam (12.783–84). The text then repeats this conversation in high formality ("Let me so far presume upon our acquaintance . . ." [12.786]) before returning to the Nameless One's narration of these rather low events ("And off with him and out trying to walk straight. Boosed at five o'clock" [12.800]). He offers some gossip about Bob Doran's prior benders and how his brother-in-law (Jack Mooney) promised violence if Bob didn't marry his sister, Polly. If you've read "The Boarding House" in *Dubliners*, you remember Jack's menacing glare down the staircase, but you also know that Jack didn't overtly threaten to "kick the shite out of" (12.816) Bob Doran if he didn't marry Polly, as the Nameless One reports. Again, we should be skeptical of the storyteller in this episode; his version of events is proximate to the truth, but he's trading almost exclusively in gossip and rumor.

The spongers drink another pint on Joe's tab. We have a moment of parallax with Joe's discussion of foot-and-mouth disease and its effect on the cattle trade, and then the Nameless One reports another rumor about Bloom getting fired from a previous job in the cattle trade with Cuffe's for talking too much and "giving lip" (12.837) to a rancher. Indeed, the Nameless One has characterized Bloom as "Mister Know-all" (12.838). We learn that Councilor Nannetti is currently on his way to London to speak before Parliament on the problem of foot-and-mouth disease. For Bloom, Nannetti leaving town presents a problem: he is still trying to nail down the Keyes ad and will ultimately need Nannetti's approval to seal the deal.

The men raise the topic of Irish games (Gaelic football, hurling, etc.) being banned by the British, who wanted the Irish to play English games like rugby and cricket. This topic turns attention back to the Citizen, who led a revival of Gaelic sports as part of the Irish nationalist movement and who himself was a champion shot-putter.

The men debate health and athletics, and Bloom is again portrayed as a loquacious contrarian. An interruption parodies the discussion in the style of formal minutes from a meeting. The men then discuss the Keogh-Bennett boxing match on which Blazes Boylan is rumored to have won £100 (and the same fight for which young Patrick Dignam saw a poster back in "Wandering Rocks"); Bloom tries to turn the topic back to lawn tennis and its benefits of "agility and training the eye" (12.944–45). Notice the many subtle references to eyes and sight in the "Cyclops" episode. There's a brief allusion to a rumor about Boylan's father gaining wealth by cooperating with the English. Anyhow, the men discuss the boxing match, and an interruption parodies sports journalism.

The discussion returns to Boylan and the concert tour he is planning. Joe Hynes, already knowing that Molly is part of Boylan's plans (musical and otherwise), prods Bloom to discuss the tour. We've previously seen other men around town insinuate about Molly and Boylan, but this gossip was previously unknown to the Nameless One: "Hoho begob . . . Blazes doing the tootle on the flute" (12.996–98). Safe to say that he is amused by this revelation.

In walk Ned Lambert and J. J. O'Molloy; they order drinks, and the Nameless One wonders what they have been up to together. You might recall that J. J. O'Molloy visited Ned back in "Wandering Rocks" to ask for money, and the Nameless One suggests that a *quid pro quo* was agreed; in exchange for a loan, J. J. O'Molloy will use his access to the legal apparatus to get Lambert "off the grand jury list" (12.1022). Who doesn't want to get out of jury duty? Denis Breen and the U. p: up postcard are discussed, and Joe asks Alf Bergan if he wrote it. J. J. supplies some legal knowledge to the conversation, but all seem to agree that Mr. Breen is crazy. Bloom clearly has a soft spot for Josie Breen and expresses his pity for her in being married to a nut. The Nameless One shares some gossip about the Breens. The men drink. Breen walks past again. J. J. gives some updates on other legal cases, mentions Reuben J. Dodd, and mocks an overly merciful judge.

After an interruption, the Citizen ramps up his racism and xenophobia, referring to foreigners (specifically Jews) as "bugs" (12.1142). Bloom pretends not to have heard and starts talking to Joe Hynes, reminding him of the money he owes him, even while excusing Hynes from repaying the debt "till the first" (12.1144). For this leniency as a creditor, Bloom exacts a bit of usurious interest by asking Joe to "say a word to Mr. Crawford" (12.1144) back at the newspaper office about the Keyes ad. Hynes promises to help. By working this new angle, Mr. Bloom might be able to close the deal without Nannetti after all. He is deft and persistent in his business dealings.

John Wyse Nolan and Lenehan enter the pub in a huff, disappointed by the result of the Gold Cup (the dark horse Throwaway won the race; the men had all wagered on either Sceptre or Zinfandel—more on that in a bit). The Citizen continues to rail against immigrants and the English strangers in the Irish house, directing his nasty speech toward Bloom, who is doing his best to ignore these provocations by "letting on to be awfully deeply interested in nothing, a spider's web in the corner behind the barrel" (12.1160–61). Nationalism and colonialism are discussed, and the Citizen continues to berate the English for cultural deficiencies. The men worry about the effects of deforestation "for the future men of Ireland" (12.1264). They hope for a return to direct trade with Europe, order more drinks, and discuss the hazing and "flogging on the training ships" (12.1331) in the British navy. The topic turns to Irish revolt and the French's unfulfilled promises to support the Irish cause, followed by comments on the English monarchy. The men order yet another round; the drinks are adding up, and the men are all surely buzzed by this point.

Bloom and John Wyse Nolan debate nationalism, persecution, and hatred, and Bloom defines a nation: "the same people living in the same place" (12.1422–23). The men poke holes in this definition and laugh. The Citizen's seething hatred for Bloom takes center stage as he asks Bloom directly, "What is your nation if I may ask?" Bloom responds, "Ireland. I was born here. Ireland" (12.1430–31). The Citizen spits with disgust at Bloom's answer. Drinks are served and an interruption describes the Citizen's handkerchief in elevated detail. Bloom continues, identifying himself with the Jewish race in addition to his Irish nationality. He states that his race suffers from hate, persecution, and injustice. John Wyse Nolan suggests that the Jews should stand up for themselves with force, but Bloom rejects this solution on very simple yet profound grounds: "Force, hatred, history, all that. That's not life for men and women, insult and hatred. And everybody knows

144 ***  THE GUIDE TO JAMES JOYCE'S *ULYSSES*

that it's the very opposite of that that is really life.... Love, the opposite of hatred" (12.1481–85). The text responds spastically to the mention of love. Bloom then leaves abruptly to search for Martin Cunningham back at the courthouse. The men debate Bloom's treatise on love and have another drink. David Hayman suggests that as the men in Barney Kiernan's turn toward civility, they gradually and subtly ostracize the Citizen, who will ultimately redirect his frustration over this exclusion toward Bloom.[9]

Lenehan claims that Bloom is in fact out to collect his winnings from the Gold Cup—remember the unwitting tip ("I was just going to throw it away" [5.534]) that Bloom gave Bantam Lyons at the end of "Lotus-Eaters"? And remember in "Lestrygonians" that Bantam Lyons told the other men in Davy Byrne's pub that Bloom had tipped him off on Throwaway? Lyons also told Lenehan, and Lenehan now tells the men in Barney Kiernan's that he supposes Bloom "had a few bob on *Throwaway* and he's gone to gather in the shekels" (12.1550–51), suggesting that Bloom won "a hundred shillings to five on. He's the only man in Dublin has it" (12.1556). The odds on Throwaway were twenty to one.

The Nameless One goes "round the back of the yard" (12.1561–62) to urinate (one of the moments that complicate a reading of the episode as a retelling of these events later in the day). When he returns, rumors about Bloom are swirling regarding his involvement with Sinn Fein (the Irish independence party). Martin Cunningham finally arrives, "asking where was Bloom" (12.1621). The men ask Cunningham about Bloom and Sinn Fein, and he confirms Bloom's role in introducing "the Hungarian system" of subverting colonial institutions (whereby Hungary successfully achieved independence from Austrian rule) into the practices of Sinn Fein.[10] This exchange also contains another of my favorite jokes in the novel: "Who made those allegations? says Alf. / I, says Joe. I'm the alligator" (12.1625–26).

Anti-Semitic comments fly, and then Ned Lambert tells a story, making fun of Bloom for "buying a tin of Neave's [baby] food six weeks before the wife was delivered" (12.1651–52). The Citizen uses this story to challenge Bloom's masculinity. Joe Hynes wonders if Bloom has ever had sex. The Citizen questions the legitimacy of Bloom's children.

The Nameless One suggests killing Bloom would be "justifiable hom-
icide" (12.1662). Barney Kiernan's pub has become a sharply hostile
environment now that the men think Bloom has made money on the
horse race. They order more drinks. There's a long interruption with
a list of names.

Bloom returns in a hurry seeking Martin Cunningham. Everyone
in the pub assumes he has just collected his windfall from the Gold
Cup, making Bloom's unwillingness to "stand us a drink" (12.1760)
all the more infuriating. The Citizen begins to confront Bloom, and
Martin Cunningham, seeing trouble coming, starts to shuffle Bloom
out of the pub "quick as he could" (12.1768). As they leave, the Citizen
gets up and pursues Bloom with a mocking cheer for Israel. Here, the
Nameless One starts to condemn the Citizen's belligerence, or he at
least expresses exasperation: "there's always some bloody clown or other kicking up a bloody murder about bloody nothing" (12.1793–95). It
seems the Citizen's "fly is open" (12.1802). Bloom retorts back to the
Citizen by naming famous Jewish philosophers and artists, including
Jesus. This sends the Citizen over the edge: he goes back inside the
pub, grabs the biscuit tin, and hurls it at Bloom as the carriage drives
away. An interruption describes the event in seismic terms, and the
episode concludes with a description of Bloom's safe departure with
imagery of biblical rapture.

## Further Reading

Groden, Michael. "Joyce at Work on 'Cyclops': Toward a Biography of
  *Ulysses.*" *James Joyce Quarterly* 44, no. 2 (Winter 2007): 217–45.
  Groden examines the early manuscript of the "Cyclops" episode acquired
  by the National Library of Ireland in 2002 and situates this episode in
  Joyce's biography, including Joyce's attitudes toward nationalism in the
  era of World War I and the Irish War of Independence.

Norris, Margot. "Fact, Fiction, and Anti-Semitism in the 'Cyclops' Episode
  of Joyce's *Ulysses.*" *Journal of Narrative Theory* 36, no. 2 (Summer 2006):
  163–89.
  This essay engages the debate between David Hayman and Herbert
  Schneidau over when/where the storytelling presented in the "Cyclops"
  episode actually occurs. Norris guides the reader through the episode,

evaluating the trustworthiness of the Nameless One and the anti-Semitism that pervades his narration.

Pringle, Mary Beth. "Funfersum: Dialogue as Metafictional Technique in the 'Cyclops' Episode of *Ulysses.*" *James Joyce Quarterly* 18, no. 4 (Summer 1981): 397–416.

After commenting on the disputed narrative perspective of this episode, Pringle presents the relationship underlying the "I-narration" of the Nameless One, the parodies that interrupt that narration, and the mediating device of dialogue.

Senn, Fritz. "Ovidian Roots of Gigantism in Joyce's *Ulysses.*" *Journal of Modern Literature* 15, no. 4 (Spring 1989): 561–77.

By identifying the extensive lists that appear in the "Cyclops" episode with the portrayal of Polyphemus in Ovid's *Metamorphosis*, Senn situates the stylistic interruptions or "insertions" of this episode in the context of one of Joyce's forebears in recycling Homeric content.

# Chapter 13

# "NAUSICAA" GUIDE

The "Nausicaa" episode takes place at twilight on Sandymount Strand, where Mr. Bloom is taking a rest from a long and draining day. After escaping the Citizen at the end of the "Cyclops" episode, Mr. Bloom and Martin Cunningham visited Mrs. Dignam to review her late husband's insurance policy. Afterward, Mr. Bloom walked a few minutes east from the Dignam home at 9 Newbridge Avenue to watch the sunset on the same shoreline Stephen walked along in "Proteus" this morning. There, Bloom encounters three young women, two little boys, and a baby. We don't hear from Mr. Bloom, however, until midway through "Nausicaa"; the first half of the episode's narration is focalized around a woman named Gerty MacDowell.

As *Ulysses* ventures into ever stranger and more disparate literary territories, its styles and voices will continue to shift, meaningfully shaping our experience of the plot. We might read the style of "Nausicaa" as the arranger's pastiche of a bad Victorian novelette, like an extended version of the interruptions that appear in the "Cyclops" episode. If this is the case, the "namby-pamby" (*Letters* 135) style of the first half of the episode is making fun of the encounter that occurs between Bloom and Gerty MacDowell. Or, we could read "Nausicaa" as using the technique of free indirect discourse to voice Gerty Mac-Dowell's consciousness: a third-person narrator presents Gerty's interiority in her own idiom, influenced as it is by her reading of cheap

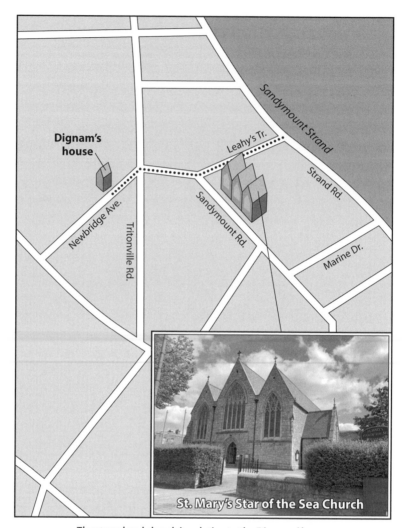

The strand and church in relation to the Dignams' home

romance novels and beauty magazines. Gerty's characterization is therefore heavily adorned with references to beauty products, fashion trends, and efforts at physical self-improvement. By the Uncle Charles Principle, the narrator adopts the sugary sort of language that Gerty MacDowell would herself most naturally use. Together, these elements of the episode's narrative style allow for the reporting of both external and internal events, suggesting that the performance of female stereotypes is influenced by both the male gaze and Gerty's own internalized notions of femininity.[1] Heather Cook Callow explains that "Gerty, in her words and thoughts, merely uses the discourse in which she has been schooled to express herself, but that discourse has been coded so that the normative male or male-oriented reader will smile and dismiss its content."[2] So, Joyce might be using the style of "Nausicaa" to expose the limitations placed on most women in this society. Because the episode also includes interpolations from a temperance retreat at a nearby church where men offer prayers to the Blessed Virgin Mary, the "Nausicaa" episode presents multiple patriarchal ideals of femininity: a beautiful object, a pure virgin, and a refuge "to the stormtossed heart of man" (13.7–8).

The "Nausicaa" episode opens on the beach at around 8:15 p.m. with three young women (Gerty MacDowell, Cissy Caffrey, and Edy Boardman) watching over three little boys. We might read Tommy and Jacky Caffrey's squabble over a sandcastle as a retelling of the quarrel between "headstrong" (13.45) Buck Mulligan and "selfwilled" (13.46) Stephen for control over the Martello tower in the "Telemachus" episode. Cissy Caffrey referees her little brothers before the text trains its attention on Gerty MacDowell, whose physique, attitudes, and desires emerge as the narrative's central focus. Joyce's schema lists "the projected mirage" as the meaning for this episode, implying that the media consumed by Gerty projects the illusion of a certain type of feminine ideal that she feels compelled to embody. Joyce stated to Arthur Power that "Bloom's encounter with Gerty MacDowell . . . took place in Bloom's imagination," so we might read Gerty as the fantasy of a male advertising agent: a woman whose deepest desires are linked to the products he aims to sell her (and who happens to find him attractive).[3] Along these lines, David Hayman describes the first half of "Nausicaa" as "an artificial voice in . . . a stereotyped world. . . . Gerty is a figment of the male imagination even in her own eyes: a product."[4]

Indeed, the initial description of Gerty MacDowell is dominated by her physical features: "her figure was slight and graceful" (13.83), "the waxen pallor of her face was almost spiritual in its ivorylike purity" (13.87–88), "her rosebud mouth was a genuine Cupid's bow" (13.88), "her hands were of finely veined alabaster with tapering fingers" (13.89–90), she has a "higharched instep" (13.98) on her petite size-five foot with "wellturned ankles" (13.168), her eyes are "bluest Irish blue" (13.108), her hair is "dark brown with a natural wave in it" (13.116–17), and she has a "slim graceful figure" (13.155). These physical descriptions are augmented with references to a catalogue of beauty products and advice: take "iron jelloids" rather "than the Widow Welch's female pills" (13.84–86), use "lemonjuice and queen of ointments" (13.90), "wear kid gloves in bed" (13.91), "take a milk footbath" (13.91–92), apply "eyebrowleine" (13.111). And then there's the exhaustive description of her fashionable attire: "a neat blouse of electric blue" (13.150), "a navy threequarter skirt" (13.154), "a coquettish little love of a hat" (13.156), shoes "with patent toecaps and just one smart buckle" (13.167), "finespun hose" (13.170), and blue undies with "awfully pretty stitchery" (13.174). She is presented as an amalgamation of advertisements from a beauty magazine. It may be worthwhile to note that Gerty's interest in women's fashion was subtly established earlier in the novel; when we briefly saw her as the cavalcade passes in the final section of the "Wandering Rocks" episode, she tries to see "what Her Excellency had on" (10.1209).

Gerty is also initially defined by her "sorrow" (13.188) over what seems to be a disintegrating romance with Reggy Wylie; we know from "Cyclops" that "Gerty MacDowell loves the boy that has the bicycle" (12.1494). In addition to this unrequited love, she is further characterized by the description of her ideal husband: "a manly man with a strong quiet face . . . , perhaps his hair slightly flecked with grey" (13.210–11). While all this information may feel like a lot to consider, keep in mind that Gerty is the first new character to take center stage since we met Mr. Bloom back at the beginning of "Calypso." Plus, she is the novel's most prominent focalized female prior to Molly's soliloquy in "Penelope."

On the beach, Cissy Caffrey uses a mildly inappropriate word, "beeoteetom" (13.263), and the other women worry that "the gentleman opposite" (13.267) has heard her. This man will later be revealed to be Mr. Bloom. While his business for the day is done, he is delaying his return home, not yet ready to face Molly. The sound of praying voices and a church organ fills the air as a men's temperance retreat (like a Catholic mass combined with an AA meeting) has convened at the St. Mary's Star of the Sea Church nearby, just off the strand.

Gerty blames her father's being "in the clutches of the demon drink" (13.290) for the fact that her marriage to a proper gentleman has not yet been arranged, and it seems that Mr. MacDowell's alcoholism has also resulted in "deeds of violence" (13.298) in her home. Gerty blames alcohol for the death of Mr. Dignam, who happens to be a friend of her father's and whose funeral Mr. MacDowell could not attend because of a flare-up of gout, a symptom of his own alcoholism. His being laid up required Gerty to run a business errand in the city for her father, which we saw her doing in "Wandering Rocks" (see 10.1206–07). Gerty is "a sterling good daughter" (13.325) to a flawed and abusive father. Perhaps her ideal husband being an older man is rooted in her father's dysfunction.

We learn that Garryowen, the dog with the Citizen in Barney Kiernan's, belongs to Gerty's "grandpapa Giltrap" (13.232). We hear more about Gerty's dream marriage. Jacky Caffrey kicks the ball down the beach, and Bloom retrieves it. He "aimed the ball once or twice and then threw it up the strand towards Cissy Caffrey but it rolled down the slope" (13.353–54). A quarterback Bloom is not. The ball, having missed its target, sweeps down to Gerty, who tries to kick it. She misses on first try, embarrassing her in front "of the gentleman opposite looking" (13.365), but she makes solid contact on her second effort. Speaking of making contact, Gerty and Mr. Bloom lock eyes, and his face "seemed to her the saddest she had ever seen" (13.369–70).

The girls work on teaching the baby to "say papa" (13.387) before realizing he has a wet diaper; the baby fusses about getting changed but is pacified by sucking on an empty bottle. In a sharp moment that stands out from the prevailing tone of the episode, Gerty silently expresses her frustration that Cissy and Edy won't "take their squalling baby home out of that and not get on her nerves, no hour to be out, and the little brats of twins" (13.404–06). This spike of free expression pierces through the idiomatic and social constraints that define Gerty's character, suggesting that behind the Victorian facade is a modern consciousness on the verge of liberation.[5] Perhaps emboldened by this pop of freedom, Gerty looks back toward Bloom and welcomes the intensity of his gaze, but her discourse then returns to the idealized norm, imagining the man as her "dreamhusband" (13.431), whom she loves unconditionally and whose wounds she seeks to heal.

In *The Odyssey*, a shipwrecked, storm-tossed, and exhausted Odysseus washes ashore in Phaeacia, where Princess Nausicaa finds him naked and brackish. Other women run away from him in a mix of disgust and fear, but Nausicaa, perceiving the nobility beneath Odysseus's ragged surface, remains behind and helps him, providing respite from his arduous journey. Gerty is the sympathetic Nausicaa to Bloom's shipwrecked Odysseus.

The text presents language from the mass, and Gerty "could picture the whole scene in the church" (13.446). The twins start squabbling again, and Gerty's unrestrained inner voice angrily calls them "little monkeys common as ditchwater" (13.467–68). Gerty then turns her ire toward Cissy's flaunting of her running skills, wishing Cissy would "trip up over something" (13.485) and embarrass herself in front of the gentleman/Bloom. But Bloom isn't watching Cissy; "he never took his eyes off [Gerty]" (13.495–96).

The text dips back into the interpolation technique and shows us a glimpse of the church service. Then Gerty bobs her foot up and down and thinks about her stockings, when and where she bought them; she notices that Bloom is eying them with appreciation for their... quality. She takes off her hat to show off her lustrous hair and resets it at just such an angle that will allow her to surreptitiously see from under the brim. Gerty knows that she is arousing Bloom, that "he was eying her as a snake eyes its prey" (13.517), and she likes it: "a burning scarlet swept from throat to brow till the lovely colour of her face became a glorious rose" (13.518–20). She is turned on by her ability to turn him on. Edy Boardman senses what is going on here and asks what's on Gerty's mind. After sharply thinking that Edy is an "irritable little gnat" (13.523) for interrupting her connection with Bloom, Gerty deflects, saying she was wondering what time it was. Cissy volunteers to go ask Bloom if he has the time. At her approach, Bloom nervously takes his hand out of his pocket. The text celebrates his "selfcontrol" (13.542), which is ironic (just wait). Bloom's watch has died, he tells Cissy, but he guesses that it is "after eight because the sun was set" (13.547–48). An interpolation shows the goings-on in the church. Bloom winds his watch and returns his gaze to Gerty, "worshipping at her shrine" (13.564).

It is worth noting the echoes between the Bloom/Gerty encounter and the Stephen/birdgirl scene in *A Portrait*. At the end of chapter 4 of Joyce's first novel, Stephen is walking along the beach alone when he comes across a young woman standing in the water: "She was alone and still, gazing out to sea; and when she felt his presence and the worship of his gaze her eyes turned to him in quiet sufferance of his gaze, without shame or wantonness . . . and a faint flame trembled on her cheek" (*P* 186). At the risk of belaboring the point, both Stephen and Bloom stare worshipfully at girls on the beach, both Gerty and the birdgirl blush and allow them to stare; both women are described in terms of delicacy and "ivorylike purity," and they both wear blue; both scenes feature the "lightclad figures of children and girls and voices childish and girlish in the air" (*P* 185). Other echoes will appear later in the episode, including the words "hither, thither," as well as skirts "bared almost to the hips."⁶ Joyce here seems to be mocking Stephen as well as his younger authorial self while drawing ironic parallels that highlight the two protagonists' differing reactions to these similar encounters. Whereas Stephen's encounter with the birdgirl releases his euphoric acceptance of a calling to artistic creation, Bloom's parallel experience brings about a more physical sort of release.

As Cissy and Edy depart, Edy gratuitously jabs Gerty over Reggy Wylie's fleeting affections. Gerty is "cut deep" (13.579) but "fought back the sob that rose to her throat" (13.582) before parrying. The women and boys leave, a bell rings, and a bat flies through the air. We get an inventory of Gerty's private drawer (we will get a similar inventory of Bloom's private drawer in the "Ithaca" episode). She wonders if Bloom is "a married man or a widower who had lost his wife" (13.656–57). She wrestles with social pressures for women in romantic relationships. Another interpolation shows the interior of the church.

Fireworks from the Mercer's hospital bazaar begin to explode in the sky. The girls call for Gerty to join them in running down the beach for a better view, but she can see well enough from her current spot—and she wants to stay close to Bloom, especially now that they will be "left alone" (13.692). Gerty leans back under the pretense of seeing the fireworks, revealing her legs to Bloom, and "she saw that he saw" (13.726). Similar to the way that the inflated language of the interruptions in "Cyclops" puffs up the commonplace events at Barney Kiernan's pub, the language of "Nausicaa" trickles sweet syrup on objectionable behavior. In long, flowing sentences that predict Molly's stream of consciousness in "Penelope," Gerty advertises her undergarments and expresses her desires. She leans further back, revealing more of herself. Bloom, whose hand has been in his pocket, ejaculates. His climax is comically stylized with puns related to the fireworks, but this scene places the reader in a position of moral conflict: if you condemn Bloom's behavior outright as a gross affront, then you risk condescension toward Gerty specifically and women generally "as innocent (and therefore childlike) victim[s] of brutal male desire," which the scholar Vicki Mahaffey warns against because "Gerty solicits [Bloom's] gaze."[7] Gerty exercises her own agency (limited though it may be in this society) and enjoys the flirtation. But if you excuse Bloom based on his and Gerty's mutual attraction, then you are assuming that Gerty has given unspoken consent; she may be gratified by Bloom's attraction to her, but that doesn't mean that she would permit him to masturbate while looking at her. Every reader will have a reaction to this moment in the novel, and it is sure to elicit spirited discussion and careful consideration (and then reconsideration). In any event, you might now better understand why the "Nausicaa" episode was cited as evidence of the novel's obscenity in the court case that led to the banning of *Ulysses* in most of the English-speaking world.[8]

In terms of the technique listed in the schema for this episode, the "tumescence" is now complete, and the "detumescence" begins. Gerty eyes Bloom with "shy reproach" (13.743), but she pledges to keep the encounter "their secret" (13.750) with a "sweet forgiving smile" (13.765). Here, she does not seem to feel violated. Perhaps Bloom's attraction to her provides a welcome boost of confidence. Or, maybe her "pathetic little glance of piteous protest" (13.742–43) is further evidence of the limited vocabulary with which Victorian society has provided Gerty to label what has just occurred and to process her life in general. Either way, when she walks away, we get a surprise: Gerty MacDowell is "lame! O!" (13.771) and walks with a limp. At this revelation, the voice and focalization of the episode shifts to Bloom, who maintains his attraction to Gerty and is perhaps even further aroused by the taboo of this physical "defect" (13.774). He does not seem to feel guilty or ashamed at all.

We now have sustained access to Bloom's inner monologue for the first time since "Lestrygonians" (not counting Bloom's short section in "Wandering Rocks"). He contemplates Martha, the nature of menstruation, recalls the events from "Lotus-Eaters," thinks about attire and attraction, and parodies what he considers to be women's false kindness to one another. He examines his own attractiveness and is glad that he "didn't let [Gerty] see me in profile" (13.836), perhaps betraying some body image issues (or maybe self-consciousness over his Jewish nose?). He decides he must be at least fairly handsome to have married Molly. He wonders about Molly's value: "suppose [Boylan] gave [Molly] money. Why not? All a prejudice. She's worth ten, fifteen, more, a pound. What? I think so. All that for nothing. Bold hand: Mrs Marion" (13.841–43). While assigning a price to your spouse's sexual favors is certainly cringeworthy, Bloom also seems to be weighing the cost of her infidelity. When he checked his watch for Cissy, he noticed that it had stopped at 4:30, which makes him wonder, "was that just when he, she" (13.848) consummated the affair?

He deals with the mess on his "wet shirt" (13.851), offers some further ideas and observations about women (misguided, insightful, and otherwise), and recalls an experience with a prostitute. In a moment that typifies Mr. Bloom's conflicting characteristics—his admirable empathy and his more problematic traits—he feels badly for prostitutes who solicit and don't sell. He thinks about Molly's first kiss at age fifteen to Lieutenant Mulvey in Gibraltar (we will hear more about this kiss from Molly in "Penelope"). Exhausted from a long day and drowsy from his ejaculation, Bloom's sentences fade without completion; his ideas ebb and flow and mingle together in the rocking sea of his mind. It is also worth noting that these pages offer the novel's most uninterrupted stream of Bloom's consciousness: there are minimal external stimuli, no other characters to interact with, and he is stationary rather than moving through the world and mentally reacting to what he encounters. Here, we are privy to his thoughts when his guard is down and his mind is tired but relaxed.

His thoughts return to Gerty; he assumes that she knew what he was doing to himself. He thinks of Milly, her maturation, and her reference to the "young student" (13.928) [Bannon], who is flirting with her. He shifts his thinking back to Gerty and admires her stockings. A firework goes off, and he sees Gerty, far down the beach, look back at him one last time. Quoting from the first scene of *Hamlet* ("for this relief much

thanks" [13.940]), he feels better for his encounter with Gerty, rejuvenated after the darkness of the Dignam situation and his conflict with
the Citizen. He notes the immediate connection that formed between
himself and Gerty and wonders whether she might be his erotic pen
pal—perhaps Gerty is using Martha Clifford as a pen name in the same
way that Bloom is using Henry Flower. It's a long shot.

He thinks about his poor throwing arm, criticizes Cissy for giving
the baby an empty bottle to suck as a pacifier (because it makes the
baby gassy—which is true. A babysitter did exactly this to my first
son at four months old, and he was miserable for the rest of the day).
Bloom thinks of Mina Purefoy (13.959) and plans to visit her in the
Holles Street Maternity Hospital (which foreshadows the setting of
the next episode, "Oxen of the Sun"). He thinks about drunk hus-
bands, romantic destiny, and marriages between unlikely pairs. He
also continues to deal with the mess he made in his pants. He thinks
again about the coincidence of his watch stopping at the exact time he
imagines Boylan and Molly consummated their affair and engages in
some shaky scientific conjecture regarding magnetism.

He catches a whiff of Gerty's perfume (from the handkerchief she
waved at him as she left) and begins contemplating olfactory matters
and the bodily origins of human scent. He takes a sample of his own
smell, which is at this moment dominated by a lemon scent from
the bar of soap in his pocket. Thinking of the lemon soap makes him
remember that he has forgotten to circle back to Sweny's to pick up
Molly's lotion (13.1044); because he was planning to return later, he
did not pay for the soap, which bothers him. He contemplates the
psychology of credit and business—how much of a tab should a business owner allow a customer to build before calling it due? Ironically,
if you give too much credit, you'll lose the customer (they will avoid
returning and being asked to pay down the debt). He also thinks again
of the 3 shillings Hynes owes him but is willing to forgive the debt if
Hynes can assist him in finalizing the Keyes ad, as they discussed in
the "Cyclops" episode.

A man walking on the beach passes by, and Bloom wonders who he
is, thinks of writing a short story about this "mystery man" (13.1060),
referring back to the idea that he might "invent a story" (4.518) for

publication in *Tit-Bits*. He then reprises the mystery of the man in the brown macintosh and anticipates rain (it will pour in the next episode). The sun now down, Bloom notices the Bailey lighthouse at Howth and thinks about light and optical effects. After worrying about Gerty getting "fluxions" (13.1082) (a type of skin irritation, from what I can tell) and himself getting "piles" (13.1083) (hemorrhoids) from sitting on the chilly beach for a prolonged period of time, he recognizes that he finds himself attracted to younger women these days, which brings him back to memories of Molly and the early days of their relationship. He looks again toward Howth, remembering his picnic proposal to Molly there, and seems to question his strategy of yielding to Boylan, thinking, "I am a fool perhaps. He gets the plums, and I the plumstones" (13.1098–99).

He sees a bat that he suspects flew from the belfry of St. Mary's Star of the Sea Church when the bells rang and notices that the mass must have ended. In another of his observations regarding the practicalities of religion, he identifies similarities between the use of repetition in the liturgy and in advertisements. He ponders various animals. In a wonderful moment that replicates the way our minds work, Bloom fills in a gap from his thinking back in the "Lotus-Eaters" episode where he couldn't recall the name of Archimedes' Principle (see 5.39–42); here, nearly eleven hours later, Bloom has a moment of recall: "Archimedes. I have it! My memory's not so bad" (13.1142). Hooray Bloom!

After some thoughts regarding birds and insects (and another reference to the bee sting he suffered), he ponders the life of sailors and superstitions. Bloom's inner monologue, which has been going strong with minimal interruptions by the narrator, withdraws for a full paragraph of narrative description of the end of the fireworks and interpolations of other events taking place in Sandymount. We also get a fanciful image of Howth anthropomorphized, nestling into bed for sleep and winking at Mr. Bloom (13.1177–81). Bloom's inner monologue returns, and he's still thinking about sailors and the sea. He thinks of children generally and then Milly specifically, recalling different stages of his daughter's maturation. He remembers Molly telling him she chose to marry him because he was "so foreign from the others" (13.1210).

As the 9:00 hour approaches, Bloom decides to get moving, realizes he has missed the performance of *Leah* at the Gaiety Theater, and considers going home but decides not to; he is still not ready to see Molly. He decides to visit the Maternity Hospital on Holles Street to check on Mina Purefoy, hoping that she has finally delivered the baby. He recaps Bloomsday's main events with some commentary. He reminds himself to fulfill his promise to Mrs. Dignam regarding her insurance policy with Scottish Widows, which makes him think of widows generally. Like Stephen on this same beach ten hours prior (see 3.365), he half-recalls a dream from the previous night. Bloom's dream involves Molly wearing red slippers and "Turkish" (13.1241) pants. He plots success for the Keyes ad and plans to use the income to buy Molly's birthday present.

Bloom finds "a piece of paper on the strand" (13.1246) but can't make out what is written on it. Just as Gerty indicated her intention to return to this same place tomorrow in hopes of seeing Bloom again, he wonders, "Will she come back here tomorrow?" (13.1253–54). He picks up a stick to write a message for her in the sand. He writes "I. AM. A." (13.1258, 1264) and then runs out of space for the final word(s), and we are left to guess: Cuckold? Jew? Father? Onanist? How does Bloom define himself?

He thinks about Molly's upcoming concerts in Belfast and Liverpool and reconfirms that he "won't go" (13.1276) with Molly and Boylan on the tour. He closes his eyes for a "short snooze" (13.1274); and, to conclude Bloom's inner monologue, we have a paragraph of thoughts in his fading consciousness that hop from topic to topic. The close reader of the novel can follow each jump and discern the references. Test yourself.

The narrator closes the episode with the bat flying to and fro, bells chiming 9:00, an interpolation of the priests having dinner after the mass, and an interpolation of Gerty MacDowell thinking of Bloom. Just as the "Telemachus" and "Calypso" episodes ended with bell chimes translated by Stephen and Bloom at 8:45 a.m., the text offers nine "Cuckoo"s here. As we've seen, Mr. Bloom is many things, but the novel here seems to insist that he is now a cuckold and will be forever more.

## Further Reading

Bednarska, Dominika. "A Cripped Erotic: Gender and Disability in James Joyce's 'Nausicaa.'" *James Joyce Quarterly* 49, no. 1 (2011): 73–89.

This essay argues that Joyce disputes traditional ideas of beauty through Bloom's attraction to Gerty despite her disability.

Callow, Heather Cook. "Joyce's Female Voices in *Ulysses.*" *Journal of Narrative Technique* 22, no. 3 (Fall 1992): 151–63.

This essay presents the varied opinions on Joyce's gender politics before arguing that Joyce's technique of narrative reversal serves to undermine patriarchal authority. By comparing our initial conception of Bloom as meek and unattractive (formed largely from the opinions of men) with female assessments (including Gerty's) of his appeal, the reader is compelled to question ideas and expectations received from patriarchal sources.

Mahaffey, Vicki. "*Ulysses* and the End of Gender." In *A Companion to James Joyce's "Ulysses,"* edited by Margot Norris, 151–68. New York: Bedford, 1998.

This essay focuses on Stephen Dedalus, Gerty MacDowell, and Molly Bloom to demonstrate the ways that Joyce complicates, subverts, and ultimately rejects gender norms in *Ulysses.*

McGee, Patrick. "Joyce's Nausea: Style and Representation in 'Nausicaa.'" *James Joyce Quarterly* 24, no. 3 (Spring 1987): 305–18.

This essay examines various interpretations of the style associated with Gerty MacDowell and the effect of its inclusion in *Ulysses.* McGee then applies the notion of desire to explain Gerty, Bloom, and Joyce's stylistic change midway through the episode.

Norris, Margot. "Modernism, Myth, and Desire in 'Nausicaa.'" *James Joyce Quarterly* 26, no. 1 (Fall 1988): 37–50.

By identifying multiple layers of classical allusion in the "Nausicaa" episode, Norris explains the contradictory intentions of high modernism in terms of the preservation, reinvention, and subversion of cultural symbols and traditions of prestige.

# Chapter 14

# "OXEN OF THE SUN" GUIDE

The "Oxen of the Sun" episode takes place between 10:00 and 11:00 p.m. at the Holles Street Maternity Hospital, where Stephen is drinking with three medical students (Dixon, Lynch, and Madden) and a few other miscellaneous Dubliners (Lenehan, Punch Costello, and Crotthers). Mr. Bloom will soon join this group, having taken a tram from Sandymount to Merrion Square in order to check on Mrs. Purefoy, who has been in labor at the hospital for three days.

In *The Odyssey*, Odysseus and his crew land on the island of Thrinacia, home of the sun god's immortal sheep and longhorn cattle. Both Circe and Tiresias have warned Odysseus to avoid this island entirely; at the very least, they mustn't harm Helios's oxen—sacred symbols of fertility—lest the gods punish the offenders with annihilation. After making his crew swear that they will leave the cattle alone, Odysseus hikes inland, prays to the gods for help getting home, and falls asleep. Meanwhile, his irresponsible men feast on the oxen of the sun. Odysseus returns and is dismayed. As the ships leave the island, Zeus strikes them with a devastating lightning storm, killing everyone except Odysseus, the only member of the crew innocent of violating sacred fertility.

In "Oxen of the Sun," Joyce uses a series of thirty-two parodies to represent the "embryonic development" he identified in the schema as his technique for this episode. These parodies chart the growth of literary style from preliterate pagan incantations into Middle English,

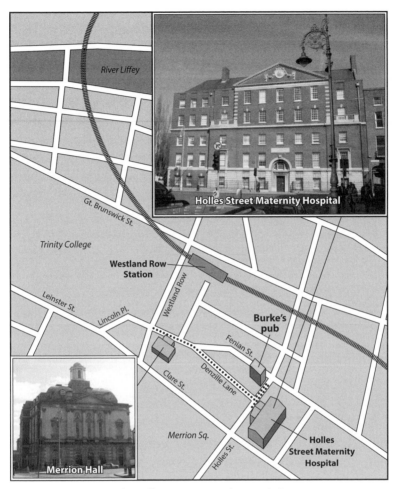

The Holles Street Maternity Hospital

followed by the Latinate styles of Milton, imitations of satirists such as Swift, and eventually up to nineteenth-century novelists such as Dickens. This episode, then, is the ultimate authorial powerflex: Joyce continues the plot of his own story while demonstrating mastery of every style of writing that led to the birth of *Ulysses*. Exhibiting Joyce's unparalleled literary dexterity and depth of knowledge, this episode is an impressive execution of an audacious idea; Joyce estimated that he spent one thousand hours writing it (*Letters* 141). Yet none of that makes it particularly fun to read.

Because these parodies of various styles dominate the surface of the narrative, "Oxen" is perhaps the most challenging episode to get through. Some might even call it tedious. Joyce himself described it as "the most difficult episode . . . both to interpret and to execute" (*Letters* 137). Harriet Shaw Weaver, Joyce's benefactor, wrote with some bite that "Oxen" "might also have been called 'Hades,' for the reading of it is like being taken the rounds of hell" (*JJ* 476). But having come this far in your reading of *Ulysses*, you'll go a little further, even if that means spending a few hours in hell. When you reread the novel in a few years, you might skim or even skip it. For now, though, let's do our best to get through it together, because there are certainly some clever moments to enjoy and many important details to gather. At the very least, we can appreciate the episode's ingenuity.

"Oxen" entirely abandons the elements of narrative style we've come to associate with *Ulysses*—inner monologue, realism, intimacy with the characters, dialogue, etc.—and instead presents the happenings of the ten o'clock hour in a series of adopted prose styles. The parodies that interrupted the narration of "Cyclops" have become the dominant mode here in "Oxen." In effect, the style forces us to translate rather than read this episode.[1] The identification of the specific source for each of the episode's thirty-two parodies is interesting, though perhaps unnecessary for the first-time reader. Indeed, William Tindall warns against labeling each imitation because "there is danger that, attempting identification and distracted by surface, we may lose track of story and underlying idea."[2] So, while we won't dwell on the individual styles Joyce imitates, I have included at the end of this Episode Guide a list identifying each parody—per Joyce's letter to Frank Budgen (*Letters* 139)—with its first line number (per Gifford) along with each parody's initial passage. Sophisticated alignments can be discerned between what occurs in the plot and the prose styles used to represent those events, and the characters' actions are often influenced by the values associated with the style. For example, Bloom behaves differently in the role of Arthurian "Sir Leopold" (14.169–70) than when he is cast as a preacher's "Mr Cautious Calmer" (14.469–70).[3] Despite these subtle associations between style and plot, most readers will feel that the text operates at a remove from the characters and the action, challenging the conventional aspirations of literature to represent a reality.[4] So, this grand literary experiment may ultimately reveal the absence of objective reality in the novel / the world, or "Oxen" at least exposes the limited ability of language—no matter the style—to express any such reality. As Marilyn French explains, "Each style shows us a piece of truth, but none bears the final truth, certitude."[5] The "Oxen of the Sun" episode, then, is largely a text about text, a work of literature about literature, and the plot operates somewhere beneath that lofty level of metatextual discourse.

The discourse, though, is intricately and deliberately designed to replicate, celebrate, and perhaps rival the awesome power of a mother's creation of life. Joyce wrote "Oxen" with a medical diagram of embryonic development on his desk, and he drafted the episode in nine notebooks, each containing its own section of the chapter with notes corresponding to the nine months of gestation (I have subdivided this Episode Guide based on the months of embryonic development as indicated in Joyce's notebooks).[6] Hugh Kenner has pointed out that the episode consists of forty paragraphs, corresponding to the forty weeks of pregnancy.[7] Building on the meaning of this correspondence to pregnancy, Richard Ellmann explains that "Joyce's scheme for the episode included minor as well as major imitations of the birth process. One of these was the idea, communicated in a letter to Budgen, that Bloom is the spermatozoon, the nurse the ovum, the hospital the womb, and Stephen the embryo."[8] Tindall takes that notion one step further, claiming that once "fertilized by Bloom, embryonic Stephen may develop to the point of rebirth."[9] Indeed, we have spent the first two-thirds of this novel learning what Bloom has to offer and what Stephen needs; the last third of *Ulysses* will present the cross-fertilization between this lost son with this sonless father.

Buried beneath all of these parodied styles and the literary attempt to replicate embryonic development, "Oxen" means to condemn violations against sacred fertility. The theme of this episode might be the impropriety of waste—the waste of fertility through contraception and fornication, the waste of time and talent, and, as David Hayman writes, "youthful potential wasted through the labored wit of intellectuals."[10] Just as the living have a sacred duty to create life, the artist, in Joyce's view, has a sacred duty to create art. To fail in fulfilling either creative duty is an abomination. The raucous and bawdy behavior of the young men gathered in the Maternity Hospital represents a sacrilege against the women birthing new life upstairs. The novel holds these mothers aloft as sacred symbols of fertility, like the oxen of the sun god Helios.

The episode opens with pagan incantations, which translate to "let us go south to Holles Street," followed by a prayer to the sun god / Dr. Horne (one of the two doctors at the Maternity Hospital), and ending with a midwife's celebratory announcement, "It's a boy!" The second paragraph is linguistic chaos, a direct translation of Latin without Anglicized diction or syntax. Still, you might pull from this hodgepodge a few phrases that establish the central importance of procreation: "by no exterior splendour is the prosperity of a nation more efficaciously asserted than by the measure of how far forward may have progressed the tribute of its solicitude for that proliferent continuance" (14.12–15), as well as "that exalted of reiteratedly procreating function" (14.31–32). The following paragraph celebrates the history of Irish medicine, gradually focusing on pregnancy and labor, "that allhardest of woman hour" (14.46).

## First Month of Embryonic Gestation

That focus continues until Mr. Bloom enters the hospital at line 71, presented with tropes of the Wandering Jew. He visits out of pity and concern for Mina Purefoy: "Stark ruth of man his errand that him lone led till that house" (14.73). Standing in the hall holding his hat, Bloom is met by Nurse Callan, a former neighbor of the Blooms from when they lived on Holles Street about nine years ago. Seeing her here, Mr. Bloom apologizes for not tipping his hat in greeting to her when he last saw her in town. Nurse Callan "blushes" (14.91) at Bloom's gentlemanly attention—in the "Ithaca" episode, she will be counted among the women charmed by Bloom's "magnetic face, form, and address" (17.1844–45). In other words, Bloom's still got it.

Bloom asks Nurse Callan about a previous acquaintance, Dr. O'Hare, and is saddened to learn that he died three years ago of "bellycrab" (14.102) (perhaps some sort of stomach issue). They share a moment "in wanhope sorrowing one with other" (14.106–07) over this loss. The text then echoes the opening of the Middle English morality play *Everyman*, warning of our mortality. Bloom asks about Mina Purefoy's condition, and Nurse Callan tells him that she has "seen many births of women but never was none so hard as was that woman's birth" (14.116–17). Empathetic Mr. Bloom "felt with wonder woman's woe in the travail they have of motherhood" (14.119–20). He also admires Nurse Callan's "fair face" (14.120) and wonders why she does not have children herself.

## Second Month of Embryonic Gestation

The door to the waiting room opens, emitting the noise of the young men carousing there. Bloom greets Dixon, a medical student, as he passes on his way into the waiting room; Dixon recently treated Bloom's bee sting, described here hilariously as "a spear wherewith a horrible and dreadful dragon was smitten him for which he did do make a salve of volatile salt and chrism" (14.129–31). Dixon invites Bloom to join the men gathering in the waiting room, Bloom politely declines, Dixon insists, and Bloom eventually accepts the opportunity to rest his legs after the day's "many marches" (14.139). Keep in mind Bloom has been out and about for thirteen hours at this point. By the end of the day, he will have walked around nine miles.[11]

The waiting room's large central table, cutlery, glasses, and a tin of sardines are described in fantastical terms. The twisting vines of hops, for instance, are described as entwined serpents, from which scales are plucked to brew mead (14.159). Dixon pours Bloom a beer. Cautiously sober, Bloom takes a polite sip before stealthily emptying most of his glass into the cup beside his. The young men are getting rowdy, and a nurse comes to the door of the waiting room and "begged them . . . to leave their wassailing for there was one quick with child, a gentle dame, whose time hied fast" (14.167–69). Clearly, their raucous behavior is inappropriate for this sacred time and place. Just as Odysseus's crew were warned not to slaughter the sacred oxen, these young men are being warned not to violate the sanctity of childbirth. Like Odysseus's crew, these young men will ignore this warning.

Bloom hears a cry in one of the delivery rooms and wonders whether it was from a mother or a baby. Recognizing Lenehan as the other older man at the table, Bloom addresses him with his hopes that Mina

Purefoy won't be too much longer in labor. Lenehan replies with a twisted quotation (whether out of drunkenness or cheek, we can only guess): "expecting each moment to be her next" (14.178). Regardless, Lenehan takes the opportunity to drink to the health of Mrs. Purefoy and the baby. The text celebrates Bloom's favorable qualities (good, meek, kind, and true) as he again pities Mina Purefoy and all mothers: "woman's woe with wonder pondering" (14.186).

We get a roll call of who, besides Bloom, is at the table—Dixon, Lynch, Madden, Lenehan, Crotthers, Stephen, and Punch Costello. Stephen is the drunkest of the bunch. They are waiting on Buck Mulligan to arrive (he is attending A. E.'s literary gathering to which Stephen wasn't invited). The text exaggerates Bloom's "fast friendship" (14.198) with Simon Dedalus, using that as a pretext for his concern over Stephen's drunkenness. The men debate the question of whether to prioritize saving the mother or the baby in a dangerous childbirth. The Catholic Church says to save the baby, but the law offers no guidance. Stephen blasphemes. They ask Bloom his opinion, and he ducks the question by deftly pointing out that the church makes money through both a funeral and a baptism.

Bloom's mind returns to Molly and Rudy, who was buried in "a fair corselet of lamb's wool" (14.269) knitted by Molly. He mourns his lack of a son and "so grieved he also in no less measure for young Stephen for that he lived riotously with those wastrels and murdered his goods with whores" (14.275–76). Over the course of the episode, the focus of Bloom's pity and concern will shift from Mina Purefoy toward Stephen.

## Third Month of Embryonic Gestation

Stephen fills everyone's glass and parodies the celebration of the Eucharist. He shows the other men that he has £2 19s., claiming it is payment for a poem (a lie). Stephen has already spent 13 shillings (nearly US$200 in today's money) since being paid by Mr. Deasy this morning. Stephen claims that the artist rivals the creative act of motherhood, saying "in woman's womb word is made flesh but in the spirit of the maker all flesh that passes becomes the word that shall not pass away" (14.292–94). He goes on to argue that either Mary did not know that her son Jesus was God, which makes her a denier alongside Peter, or else Mary knew that her son was God, therefore making her the "creature of her creature" (14.302)—as a child of God, she is child of her child; she is the creation of God, who she in turn created. This paradox echoes Stephen's *Hamlet* theory that Shakespeare "felt himself the father of all his race, the father of his own grandfather" (9.868–69).

All of Stephen's pontification seems a bit above the heads of the other men at the table, so Punch Costello begins to sing a bawdy song. Nurse Quigley, an older woman, enters the room and angrily rebukes the men for their shameful behavior. This is their second warning against the slaughter of sacred fertility (remember that Odysseus also had two warnings—one from Circe and one from Tiresias). Nurse Quigley leaves, and Costello curses her. Bloom advises the men to calm down, citing "the time's occasion as most sacred" (14.331–32). While Bloom is upright in rejecting the violation of sacred fertility and procreation, Stanley Sultan points out that, among the men carousing inappropriately in a maternity hospital,

> [Bloom] is the cardinal sinner among them. Not only has he just come from his "spilling" [in "Nausicaa"], but it is more significant than any mere sexual escapade of some of the others: it represents surrender of his responsibility to maintain "that proliferent continuance," of his identity as husband and potential father. . . . He sins while exalting maternity and fecundity. Odysseus regards the sacred cattle of the sun with the proper reverence and is innocent of their slaughter. Bloom shares Odysseus' reverent attitude, but acts like the Achaean's sinful, and, consequently, destroyed, crew.[12]

In short, Bloom is a hypocrite.

Dixon teasingly asks Stephen why he didn't become a priest. Stephen offers a witty retort, but Lenehan turns up the heat, voicing a rumor he heard about Stephen's dalliances. The men discuss outlandish sexual wedding ceremonies performed in Madagascar. Stephen recites a sexual poem and offers a long monologue filled with bawdy puns and blasphemies. Punch Costello tops it off with more loud, improper singing.

At this impropriety, "a black crack of noise in the street here, alack, bawled back. Loud on left Thor thundered: in anger the hammer-hurler. Came now the storm that hist his heart" (14.408–09). Remember that in *The Odyssey*, Odysseus's crew and ship are destroyed by a thunderstorm at sea, Zeus's punishment for their sacrilege. Lynch explains that "the god self was angered for [Stephen's] hellprate and paganry" (14.411). Nobody is destroyed here, but Stephen is scared of thunder, and he cowers. Mr. Bloom seeks to soothe him with "calming words to slumber his great fear" (14.425), explaining that thunder is simply a "natural phenomenon" (14.428).

## Fourth Month of Embryonic Gestation

Despite Bloom's efforts to calm him, Stephen is disconsolate; he wrestles with his mortality, questions of heaven, and his sinful whoring. He recognizes in the thunderclap "the voice of the god that was in a very grievous rage that he would presently lift his arm up and spill their souls for their abuses and their spillings done" (14.471–72). The "spillings" here referenced are these men's wasteful acts of fornication that violate the sacred duty to procreate legitimately.

## Fifth Month of Embryonic Gestation

The text records the thunderstorm in the manner of a seventeenth-century English diarist, and an interpolation shifts the perspective outside of the hospital, where we see Buck Mulligan making his way through the downpour. He bumps into Alec Bannon, who has just arrived in town from Mullingar. Bannon agrees to accompany Buck to the hospital for a drink, eager to share that he has a new romantic/sexual interest (Milly Bloom), described as a "skittish heifer, big of her age and beef to the heel" (14.502–03). This episode includes a plethora of offensive comments featuring cows, emphasizing the link between these men's impiety and the allusion to *The Odyssey*.

## Sixth Month of Embryonic Gestation

Lenehan, whom the text frames as something of a lowlife, raises the topic of foot-and-mouth disease; he perhaps read Deasy's letter in the evening newspaper. Bloom worries that all of the cattle he saw on the carriage ride to Glasnevin Cemetery must be slaughtered, but Stephen allays his concerns, explaining that Dr. Rinderpest is coming over from Russia to cure the beasts. The men then launch into a telling of "The Parable of the Bulls," an elaborate, Swiftian history of Ireland that depicts the Irish people as pawns in a power struggle between the Roman Catholic Church (farmer Nicholas) and the English monarchy (Lord Harry). The parable culminates in the Irish emigration to America.

## Seventh Month of Embryonic Gestation

Mulligan and Bannon arrive at the hospital. Buck boldly takes center stage of the gathering in the waiting room, handing around mock business cards that he has had printed that read: *"Mr Malachi Mulligan. Fertiliser and Incubator. Lambay Island"* (14.660). Overwhelmed with sadness that so many attractive women are not pregnant, he plans to solve this problem by setting up a "national fertilising farm" and "to offer his dutiful yeoman services for the fecundation of any female" (14.684–87). A true humanitarian. With Buck's entrance, Stephen recedes into the background for the remainder of the episode.

Bannon begins to tell the person sitting beside him (Crotthers) about Milly. Buck notices Bloom and asks if he is in need of medical assistance. Bloom, prudently "preserving his proper distance" (14.723), explains that he has come only to check on Mrs. Purefoy. (Minor question: just why exactly is Mr. Bloom checking on Mina Purefoy? Are they good enough friends for him to be in the waiting room at the hospital while she is in labor? More likely, Bloom is using this detour as a way to kill a little more time so that Molly will be asleep when he gets home. He's still not ready to see her.)

Using medical terminology, Dixon teases Buck about being fat—is he pregnant? Buck laughs it off and offers a witty reply, mimicking Mother Grogan, sending the room into "violent agitations of delight" (14.735). Crotthers, "the listener" (14.738) to Bannon's stories about Milly, congratulates Bannon and gets some beer passed to their end of the table in order to toast his friend's good fortune. Bannon pulls out a photo of Milly, and the text gets dewy with sentimentality. He mentions her "new coquette cap" (14.758), which we know was a birthday present from Bloom; remember Milly's letter to her Papli: "Thanks ever so much for the lovely birthday present. It suits me splendid. Everyone says I am quite the belle in my new tam" (4.398–99). In coded language, the men discuss the procurement of a condom—"as snug a cloak of the French fashion as ever kept a lady from wetting" (14.777–78). Lynch reveals that he was with Kitty this afternoon—more on that in a bit.

A bell rings and Nurse Callan enters, calling Dixon over for a private word. When she leaves, Punch Costello spews unpleasant remarks about her, calling her "a monstrous fine bit of cowflesh!" (14.807), and insinuates that Dixon has practiced his "bedside manner" (14.809) with her. Before rebuking Costello, Dixon informs the room that he is needed in the delivery ward—Mina Purefoy has "given birth to a bouncing boy" (14.822–23). Hoopsa boyaboy hoopsa!

## Eighth Month of Embryonic Gestation

We "revert to Mr Bloom" (14.845) and gather that he has quietly endured the misbehavior of these young men, attributing most of their indecency to the immaturity of "overgrown children" (14.848–49); however, the text unloads his low opinion of Punch Costello. Bloom is "nauseated" by this grotesque "creature," this "missing link" between ape and man (14.854, 858). He asserts that "those who create themselves wits at the cost of feminine delicacy" are beneath "proper breeding" (14.865–68). Indeed.

The young men have a laugh at the expense of Mina Purefoy's husband, "the old bucko that could still knock another child out of her" (14.892–93)—this new baby is Mina's ninth living child, twelfth overall. Then, in the style of the eighteenth-century satirist Junius, the text claps back at Bloom after his rebuke of Costello: on what grounds can this immigrant judge an Irishman? He should be grateful for all the benefits and blessings he has received in this country! And, what about hypocritical Bloom's own misbehaviors? Didn't he "attempt illicit intercourse with a female domestic" (14.922–23) (this is a reference to the Blooms' former housekeeper, Mary Driscoll, who will appear in the upcoming "Circe" episode). Didn't he get fired by Mr. Cuffe for his "peevish asperity" (14.926) toward a rancher? Is he not failing in his most basic duty as a husband? Has he not as recently as this very evening committed the reprehensible act of masturbation? Quite a piling on.

Various topics related to pregnancy are engaged (in rather tedious fashion), but Mulligan breaks the dullness with his statement that "the supremest object of desire" is "a nice clean old man" (14.999–1000). Buck is absurd, but he is funny. His statement here also promotes sterility, even if ironically, thus further contributing to the mounting violations against fertility. An argument arises about the "theological dilemma created in the event of one Siamese twin predeceasing the other" (14.1002–03), and the question is put to Bloom, who defers to Stephen, who we realize has been "hitherto silent" (14.1005); the text hasn't recorded him speaking since Mulligan arrived. Stephen's response to the Siamese twin debate repeats a line from his *Hamlet* lecture in the library: what God has joined, let no man put asunder.

The next parody is surely among the funniest parts of the episode. In the style of a gothic novel, Buck Mulligan "freeze[s] them with horror" (14.1010) as he speaks about Haines, who appears from behind a hidden sliding panel holding a book of Celtic literature and a vial of poison. The other men receive this apparition (Haines is not actually there) as a villain, and he confesses to the murder of Samuel Childs (the Childs murder case has been a recurrent topic throughout the novel). Haines vanishes . . . and then his head pops back in to tell Buck to meet him at Westland Row Station at ten past eleven (they plan to take the last train to Sandycove together; Stephen is excluded from this return to the Martello tower).

The tone shifts to nostalgia in the next paragraph as Bloom remembers himself at various stages of his own growth and development: first as an eighteen-year-old high school student, then as a door-to-door salesman for his father's jewelry business, then as a twentysomething having his first sexual experience with a prostitute named Bridie Kelly. Within this paragraph, we also see the most explicit unveiling of the way this novel works: "a retrospective arrangement, a mirror within a mirror (hey, presto!)" (14.1044–45). The arranger functions as a mirror looking back self-reflexively with an "ideal memory" of *Ulysses*,[13] and the novel itself is a mirror reflecting the essence of human experience. And yes, Bloom lost his virginity to a whore; reread the novel with that fact in mind for some retrospective arrangement.

A note of melancholy, beginning with the reminder of Bloom's son-lessness, sustains itself through the next few paragraphs.

### Ninth Month of Embryonic Gestation

Francis "Punch" Costello reminisces with Stephen about their time together in school. Stephen, in a moment of rejuvenated spirit and confidence in his ability to create art, claims to be "lord and giver of their life" (14.1115–16) and mimes the placement of laurels on his head. Costello questions Stephen's self-identification as an artist, saying that he will deserve that title "when something more, and greatly more, than a capful of light odes can call your genius father" (14.1118–19). Simply and harshly put, Stephen hasn't created enough yet. Costello softens the blow somewhat, affirming that his friends are rooting for him: "all desire to see you bring forth the work you meditate" (14.1120–21). Already stung by this questioning of his identity as an artist, Stephen then suffers a gut-punch when Lenehan references his mother. These are painful moments for Stephen, who has already been brooding in Buck Mulligan's shadow. He is on the verge of leaving.

But discussion of the Gold Cup pulls attention away from Stephen, so he stays. Lenehan recaps the race. Lynch then reports his afternoon hookup with Kitty and their ensuing encounter with Father Conmee. We previously saw this scene from Father Conmee's perspective in the first section of "Wandering Rocks," so we can now identify Lynch as the "flushed young man" and Kitty as the "young woman [who] abruptly bent and with slow care detached from her light skirt a clinging twig" as they emerged from the field through a hedge (10.199–202). Cheered by this story, Lynch and Lenehan reach for a bottle of beer, but Buck halts them from disturbing Bloom, who is lost in thought, mesmerized by the red triangle logo on the Bass Ale bottle. "During the past four minutes or thereabouts he had been staring hard at a certain amount of number one Bass" (14.1181–82), thinking first about his younger days (which we saw three pages earlier) and now considering "two or three private transactions" (14.1189). Bloom realizes that the others are watching him stare, picks up the bottle, and fills their glasses. We get a somewhat confusing description of the seating arrangement around the table; Hart and Gunn sort out the confusion and produce a diagram of the table and chairs in their book *James Joyce's Dublin*.[14]

The men enter a discussion of science and its limitations, particularly in predetermining the gender of a baby. Topics related to the health and wellness of a pregnant woman and her child are covered. The phenomenon of seemingly healthy babies born of healthy parents dying in early childhood confounds scientific explanation, but we must assume this mystery is related to "the survival of the fittest" (14.1285). Bloom, quirky as ever, describes the relationship of sex, pregnancy, and delivery: "once a woman has let the cat into the bag . . . she must let it out again or give it life . . . to save her own" (14.1304–07). Exactly.

A parody of Charles Dickens focuses on Mina Purefoy, lauding her strength of spirit and depicting her bliss at cuddling her new baby boy. Happy and thankful, Mina only wishes for her husband, called Doady here, to be present to "share her joy" (14.1321). I guess when you have eight other kids at home, you can't come to the hospital for the birth of your ninth. She praises her husband's dignified responsibility and faithfulness to their twelve babies. Her gracious sharing of the credit with him, after she has just endured three days of excruciating, exhausting labor, might feel a bit over the top, but remember that this episode holds procreation as sacred, and old Doady has "played loyally [the] man's part" (14.1342), in sharp contrast to each of the men carousing in the waiting room.

A parody of Cardinal Newman offers a sermon on sins buried deep in the subconscious, warning that they will eventually emerge to confront the sinner. This predicts the upcoming "Circe" episode, where "the sins of the past" (15.3027) return to haunt both Stephen and Bloom. Bloom, looking at Stephen, recalls his first encounter with the young man at one of Matthew Dillon's garden parties some seventeen years ago. In this memory, young Stephen is a frowning lad of five years old surrounded by four adoring young women; he glances to his mother for reassurance. We will revisit this scene in the "Ithaca" episode, where we will learn that shy Stephen was "reluctant to give his hand in salutation" (17.469–70) to Mr. Bloom that day. A parody of the art critic Ruskin provides imagery of the thunderstorm that just passed through.

## Birth and Afterbirth

Stephen rallies, proclaiming Burke's pub a block north as their next destination. In a riotous flurry of activity, the men gather their belongings and, in keeping with the fertility theme, they ejaculate themselves out of the hospital and into the street. Bloom lingers behind to say goodbye to Nurse Callan, asking her to please "send a kind word" (14.1401) to Mrs. Purefoy for him. Then, endearingly awkward, "he whispers close in going: Madam, when comes the storkbird for thee?" (14.1405–06). Smooth.

In the next paragraph, Mr. Purefoy gets a pep talk from the novel. Then, in the closing 150 lines of the episode, the prose disintegrates into muddled snatches of slang and drunken dialect as the men move through the street, enter Burke's pub ten minutes before closing, order two rounds of drinks (Stephen sets the pace), and get booted back into the street at 11:00. Serving as a bookend to the dense and difficult Latinate passage at the beginning of the episode, this final explosion of grammatically ungoverned slang is a chaotic reading experience, but it is capable of being sensibly understood. As John Noel Turner has demonstrated, "the entire passage is essentially dialogue" and "makes sense, if conversations are allowed to drift in and then out like radio frequencies."[15] This concluding section of the episode completes Joyce's demonstration of virtually every sort of linguistic expression, ranging from Swiftian satire to the coded slang of drunk young men.

Within this final scrum, there are a few highlights: Stephen is mistaken in his Latin Quarter hat for a "drunken minister" (14.1444–45). And Buck Mulligan says his aunt is going to write to Simon Dedalus because "baddybad Stephen lead [*sic*] astray goodygood Malachi" (14.1487–88), reciprocal to Simon's threat to write Buck's aunt back in the "Hades" episode. Bannon finally realizes that Bloom is "Photo's papli, by all that's gorgeous" (14.1535–36). We again see the man in the brown macintosh and gather a few ineffectual clues related to his identity. Stephen and Lynch make plans to go to the brothel/"Bawdyhouse" (14.1573). And somebody pukes his guts out: "yooka . . . yook . . . ook" (14.1567–68).

As Joyce himself summarized this episode, "How's that for high?" (*SL* 252).

## List of Parodies with Opening Passages and Line Numbers (per Gifford)

1. Roman incantatory prayer to fertility goddess: "Deshil Holles Eamus. Deshil Holles Eamus. Deshil Holles Eamus" (1).

2. Latin prose style of historians Sallust and Tacitus: "Universally that person's acumen is esteemed very little perceptive" (7).

3. Medieval Latin prose: "It is not why therefore we shall wonder if, as the best historians relate" (33).

4. Anglo-Saxon alliterative prose of Aelfric: "Before born babe bliss had. Within womb won he worship" (60).

5. Middle English: "Therefore, everyman, look to that last end that is thy death" (107).

6. Medieval travel stories from the 1400s: "And whiles they spake the door of the castle was opened" (123).

7. Arthurian legend from the 1400s: "This meanwhile this good sister stood by the door and begged them" (167).

8. Elizabethan history chronicles: "About that present time young Stephen filled all cups that stood empty" (277).

9. Miltonian Latinate prose from the 1600s: "To be short this passage was scarce by when Master Dixon" (334).

10. Religious allegorical prose of John Bunyan: "But was Boasthard's fear vanquished by Calmer's words?" (429).

11. Seventeenth-century English diarists such as Pepys: "So Thursday sixteenth June Patk. Dignam laid in clay" (474).

12. English journalist Daniel Defoe: "With this came up Lenehan to the feet of the table" (529).

13. Irish satirist Jonathan Swift: "an Irish bull in an English chinashop" (581).

14. Early 1700s periodical essays in *Tatler* and *Spectator*: "Our worthy acquaintance Mr Malachi Mulligan now appeared" (651).

15. Eighteenth-century Irish novelist and clergyman Laurence Sterne: "Here the listener who was none other than the Scotch student" (738).

16. Eighteenth-century Irish novelist, poet, and playwright Oliver Goldsmith: "Amid the general vacant hilarity of the assembly" (799).

17. Eighteenth-century Anglo-Irish philosopher Edmund Burke: "To revert to Mr Bloom" (845).

18. Dublin-born politician and playwright Richard Brinsley Sheridan: "Accordingly he broke his mind to his neighbor" (880).

19. Eighteenth-century satirist Junius: "But with what fitness, lest it be asked of the noble lord" (905).

20. Philosophical historian Edward Gibbon: "The news was imparted with a circumspection recalling the ceremonial usage" (942).

21. Gothic novelist Horace Walpole: "But Malachias' tale began to freeze them with horror" (1010).

22. Nostalgic essayist Charles Lamb: "What is the age of the soul of man?" (1038).

23. Nineteenth-century English Romantic Thomas De Quincey: "The voices blend and fuse in clouded silence" (1078).

24. Landor's "Imaginary Conversations" essays: "Francis was reminding Stephen of years before when they had been at school" (1110).

25. English essayist and historian Macaulay: "However, as a matter of fact though, the preposterous surmise" (1174).

26. Nineteenth-century English naturalist and evolutionist Thomas Henry Huxley: "It had better be stated here and now" (1223).

27. English novelist Charles Dickens: "Meanwhile the skill and patience of the physician had brought about" (1310).

28. English convert to Catholicism Cardinal Newman: "There are sins or (let us call them as the world calls them)" (1344).

29. English essayist Pater: "The stranger still regarded on the face before him a slow recession" (1356).

30. Art critic Ruskin: "Mark this farther and remember. The end comes suddenly" (1379).

31. Nineteenth-century Scottish essayist and satirist Thomas Carlyle: "Burke's! outflings my lord Stephen" (1391).

32. The prose disintegrates into dialect and slang: "All off for a buster, armstrong, hollering down the street" (1440).

## Further Reading

Bazargan, Susan. "'Oxen of the Sun': Maternity, Language, and History." *James Joyce Quarterly* 22, no. 3 (Spring 1985): 271–80.

Bazargan explains how the parodies of this episode regenerate the literary styles of the past and how they demonstrate the relationship between language, mental state, and history.

Gordon, John. "The Multiple Journeys of 'Oxen of the Sun.'" *ELH* 46, no. 1 (Spring 1979): 158–72.

This essay traces the progression of the parodies and the relationships between discourse and meaning in terms of linguistics, literary effect, history, and politics.

Janusko, Robert. "Grave Beauty: Newman in 'Oxen.'" *James Joyce Quarterly* 28, no. 3 (Spring 1991): 617–21.

This piece compares the text of "Oxen," Joyce's drafting note sheets, and the source material for the parody of Newman. Janusko here and elsewhere is helpful to our understanding Joyce's process in composing this episode.

Lee Moore, John. "'With a Glance of Motherwit Helping': Empathy and Laughter in 'Oxen of the Sun.'" *Joyce Studies Annual* (2014): 143–63.

This essay examines the various forms of humor employed by the characters in "Oxen" and the dissonance between the raucous laughter evoked by these jokes and the screams of labor heard in the hospital. Mr. Bloom's empathetic concerns serve a mediating role between these two noises in the text.

# Chapter 15

# "CIRCE" GUIDE

Beginning shortly before midnight, the "Circe" episode uses the form of a play to portray a kaleidoscopic blend of real and imaginary happenings over the course of an hour in Dublin's brothel district. "Circe" takes up nearly 150 pages in the Gabler edition of *Ulysses*, making it about as long as the first eight episodes of the novel combined.

Worried over Stephen's drunken condition, Bloom has followed him into Nighttown in hopes of taking care of him. Between the end of "Oxen" and the start of "Circe," a conflict occurred between Stephen and Buck Mulligan in Westland Row Station; perhaps Buck simply abandoned Stephen, or maybe there was a physical altercation. Regardless, Buck and Haines have departed without Stephen on the last train toward Sandycove. Just as Stephen anticipated all the way back in "Telemachus," Buck has usurped his place at the tower, and Stephen will not sleep there tonight. Instead, he has taken the train from Westland Row to Amiens Street and is now on his way to a brothel, accompanied by Lynch. Bloom missed the Amiens Street train stop and had to double back, so he is trailing Stephen by about fifteen minutes, hustling to catch up.

In *The Odyssey*, Odysseus and his crew land on Aeaea, and a team of scouts discover the palace of Circe, a witch goddess. Circe invites Odysseus's men inside for a drink and then magically turns them into pigs. One man escapes to tell Odysseus about their comrades' situation under the power of Circe's magical trickery. Odysseus bravely hopes

178

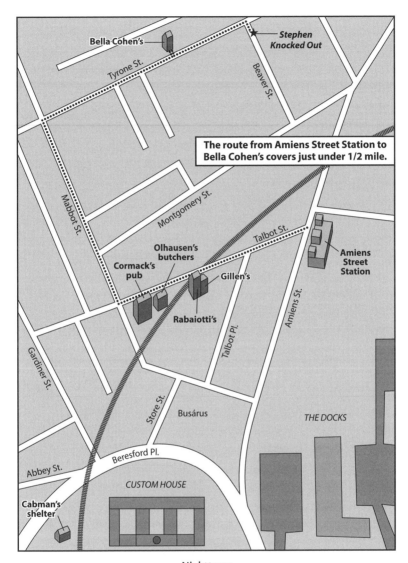

Nighttown

to rescue his men from Circe's enchantment; on the way to her house, he receives help from Hermes, who provides him with a plan and with moly, an herb that will protect him from Circe's witchcraft. The plan works: the moly counters Circe's magic, and she swoons for Odysseus and transforms his crew from pigs back into men. Odysseus and Circe then make love. For a year. Eventually, some of Odysseus's crew shake him from the madness of his long Circean interlude and compel him to resume the journey home to Ithaca.

In early spring 1920, Joyce emerged from the thousand hours he had spent writing "Oxen" and turned his attention to "Circe." He expected that this episode, like the few he had recently composed, would take him two to three months to complete. Little did he know that "Circe" would require nine drafts and take over half a year to write (*Letters* 156), much less that it would have the power to bewitch his creative process and entirely transform *Ulysses*. This episode, with its exhaustive reprises of virtually every character, object, and idea introduced in the novel thus far, would compel Joyce to revise much of what he had previously written. He estimated that he wrote a third of *Ulysses* at the proof stage of the revision process,[1] arranging codependent details all over the novel and weaving a web of intratextual puzzles that would "keep the professors busy for centuries" (*JJ* 521).

In addition to the power of "Circe" to transform Joyce's project in this novel, this episode also depicts a grotesque transformation of hundreds of its characters (dead and living), inanimate objects, and concepts. During the composition of this episode, Joyce drafted as a reference a "pair of notesheets . . . where Joyce listed all the 'characters' that had appeared thus far in *Ulysses* to assure their inclusion in 'Circe.'"[2] This list also includes concepts like parallax and topics of conversation from earlier in the novel that Joyce intended to reprise. As David Hayman puts it, "Joyce seems to have taken the whole book, jumbled it together in a giant mixer and then rearranged its elements in a monster pantomime."[3] The episode's dramatic entertainment is often hilarious in its expressiveness, wit, and hyperbole, but it also has moments of monstrous darkness.

We've seen glimpses elsewhere in *Ulysses* of each of the magical spells cast by "Circe." Consider Stephen's haunting memories in "Telemachus," Mr. Bloom's exotic reveries in "Calypso" and "Lotus-Eaters," the extensive lists and exaggerations of "Cyclops," and Buck's brief dramatic script in "Scylla and Charybdis." We have also seen the text ascribe personality to inanimate objects and animals, such as Stephen's ashplant in "Telemachus," Bloom's cat in "Calypso," and the gulls in "Lestrygonians." That said, whereas the novel largely suppresses these impulses in the previous fourteen episodes, "Circe" allows for their unrestrained expression. As Karen Lawrence explains, "'Circe' provides a stage for a libidinous release of tendencies in the language and in the characters."[4]

The performance features the subconscious in a series of seven major fantasies and a slew of shorter ones. Indeed, imaginary events dominate the episode's content, accounting for roughly 90 percent of its text.[5] These fantasies may be split-second flights of imagination in the character's mind, yet some of them require dozens of pages to be faithfully represented. Some of these daymares consume the conscious attention of Bloom or Stephen and distract them from external reality. Others may be purely textual flourishes inserted by the arranger to express the novel's own subconscious without basis in the characters' psyches. The episode's shifting among these different modes of fantastic expression is disorienting and difficult to follow. David Hayman explains that "though the major hallucinatory sequences are carefully set off . . . , the arranger makes no clear distinction between minor hallucinations and the normal surface."[6] Furthermore, as Karen Lawrence explains, "This confusion is compounded, of course, by the fact that most of the dramas in which the characters participate are *composite* dramas that recombine elements from the book's past, transgressing the boundaries of the psyches of the characters."[7] The episode's style, like a fun-house mirror, creates distorted and exaggerated reflections of Bloom, Stephen, and the text of *Ulysses* itself. In these ways, "Circe" resists rational analysis and clear explanation, but I endeavor to guide you through the dark magic of this episode.

If you thought that a visit to the brothel district was going to be fun and sexy, the "Circe" episode's opening stage directions quickly dispel that notion by establishing the unseemly setting of Joyce's Nighttown. The tracks are "skeleton," the signals warn of "danger," the houses are "grimy," the men are "stunted," and the women "squabble" (15.2, 3, 5). Indeed, this part of Dublin was labeled "the worst slum in Europe" by *Encyclopaedia Britannica* in 1885 (*JJ* 367). Located in east Dublin between Montgomery Street and Tyrone (né Mecklenburgh) Street, Nighttown is an ugly place filled with unsavory people.

You'll remember Cissy Caffrey from the "Nausicaa" episode, and you might wonder what she's doing here at this hour of night. She's hanging out with two crude British soldiers, Private Carr and Private

Compton, who will feature prominently in the episode's final scene. The redcoats mock Stephen as "the parson" (15.64)—he's still wearing his wide-brimmed hat—as he and Lynch slip past on their way to the brothel. Lynch was first introduced in *A Portrait* as a university friend of Stephen's, and you might remember Father Conmee catching this young man as he emerged from the bushes with a young woman back in "Wandering Rocks." Lynch has just been drinking and teasing Stephen in "Oxen." Here in "Circe," he is described as having "a sneer of discontent wrinkling his face" (15.75). He and Stephen ignore the solicitation of an elderly bawd with "snaggletusks" (15.78) as Stephen recites Latin from the Catholic Mass. They pass Edy Boardman (from "Nausicaa"), "bickering" (15.90) about another woman, and Lynch kicks at a stray dog. Lynch notes the absurdity of Stephen spouting "metaphysics in Mecklenburg street" (15.109) and inquires about which brothel they are going to. Stephen is hoping to see Georgina Johnson, the prostitute on whom he spent the money A. E. loaned him for food (see 9.195). A drunk navvy (a term for a manual laborer) fires a snot rocket.

The Caffrey twins from "Nausicaa" appear and climb a lamppost. You may be thinking, okay, maybe Cissy Caffrey and Edy Boardman are here, but there's no way two four-year-old boys are running around the red-light district at midnight. Probably not, but we can't be entirely sure about anything in this foggy episode. As you read, you'll be tempted to wonder whether a moment in "Circe" is imaginary or real, and I'll do my best to differentiate between the two in this guide, but I'll also suggest that you may find it more interesting and productive to inquire into the literary effect of those uncertain moments. As the style of this episode combines and warps the novel's elements in irrational ways, try to allow yourself to be affected by these absurdities rather than trying to pin them down rationally. "Circe" is a performance, after all.

Mr. Bloom emerges from amid hazy "snakes of river fog" (15.138) with snacks, "flushed, panting" (15.142–43) as he tries to catch up to Stephen. He is a few minutes behind, as we can tell from his passing "Antonio Rabaiotti's" ice-cream cart, which we first saw "halted" (15.5) as Stephen and Lynch walked past at the outset of the episode. Bloom stops again to buy some street meat and suffers from a stitch in his side.

He notes a glow south of the river and assumes that there is a fire, a "big blaze" that might engulf "his [Blazes's] house" (15.171). Realizing that he'll lose Stephen if he doesn't "Run. Quick" (15.174), he crosses the street and is nearly struck by passing cyclists. He is then nearly run over by "a dragon sandstrewer" (15.185). Bloom raises "a policeman's whitegloved hand" (15.190–91) to signal stop; we can reasonably assume that he does not instantaneously put on a white glove to direct traffic, so this is the first instance of the text augmenting reality. The motorman slams on the brake and is "thrown forward" (15.192). He curses Bloom, who nimbly "trickleaps to the curbstone" (15.196). Pretty funny stuff. It is worth noting Bloom's characteristic pragmatism in response to these close calls; he thinks he should resume Sandow's exercises and considers expanding his insurance coverage to include street accidents. Notice also that the bicycle bells and motorman's footgong have speaking parts in the play. Back in the "Aeolus" episode, Bloom remarked in his inner monologue that "everything speaks in its own way" (7.177), and the "Circe" episode pushes this thought to an extreme, giving voice to everything, including inanimate objects, dead people, animals, and characters who aren't actually present.

A brief encounter with a "sinister figure" (15.212) in a sombrero guarding the entrance to Nighttown is the first of the episode's imagination-embellished events we can locate in Bloom's subconscious. As a married man in this part of town, Bloom is clearly feeling some measure of discomfort, and he mutters that the figure is a "Gaelic league spy" (15.220) sent by the Citizen, conveying the paranoia and trauma that Bloom is carrying from the clash in Barney Kiernan's a few hours earlier. Then, Bloom's slapstick encounter with the ragsackman exemplifies how quickly the tone and register of this episode can shift. Little Jacky and Tommy Caffrey collide with Bloom, and, thinking they might be pickpockets, he quickly checks the inventory of his pockets. Discerning what actually happens in all of this, we might assume that Bloom noticed a person leaning against the wall (but he did not speak to this person—certainly not in Spanish); perhaps his path was momentarily obstructed by a man carrying a sack across his shoulders (but they don't leap left and right in unison), and maybe somebody short accidentally bumps into him (but it wasn't the Caffrey twins).

## Extended Fantasy 1:
## Bloom's Father and Molly (Marion)

The episode's first sustained fantasy occurring entirely in a character's psyche begins with the appearance of Bloom's late father, Rudolph. Rudolph scolds his son for his imprudence with money, for being in Nighttown, for leaving Judaism (which seems unfair since Rudolph himself converted to the Church of Ireland), and for running with the wrong crowd once or twice back in high school. Bloom's mother, a gentile, appears and dramatically laments the corruption of her son. Clearly, Bloom is wrestling with hefty loads of guilt here. As these fantasies reveal characters' dark, buried memories and thoughts, you may recall a passage from "Oxen of the Sun" predicting this aspect of the "Circe" episode: "There are sins or (let us call them as the world calls them) evil memories which are hidden away by man in the darkest places of the heart but they abide there and wait. . . . Yet a chance word will call them forth suddenly and they will rise up to confront him in the most various circumstances, a vision or a dream" (14.1344–50). As suggested in "Oxen," a simple word or gesture in reality can trigger a significant psychological event in this episode.

Bloom's feelings of meek shame continue as a domineering Molly appears, demanding to be called "Mrs Marion" (15.306), a reference to the way Boylan addressed his letter to her this morning (see 4.245). She is wearing the Turkish attire she wore in Bloom's dream last night, as he recalled toward the end of "Nausicaa": "She had red slippers on. Turkish. Wore the breeches" (13.1240–41). In this fantasy, Molly/Marion is clearly wearing the pants in the relationship. She is accompanied by a turbaned camel, who plucks for her a mango and bows subserviently. Bloom also "stoops his back" (15.323) and stutters deferentially before Molly/Marion, seemingly implying that she is pregnant, presumably with Boylan's child.

In an illustrative moment, the language of Molly's exclamation of "Nebrakada! Femininum!" (15.319) is taken from the book of secret prayers/spells Stephen thumbed through in the "Wandering Rocks" episode before Dilly interrupted him (see 10.849). The fact that Molly, a figure in Bloom's imagination, borrows language from Stephen's day exemplifies the impossibility of pinning "Circe" down. As Hugh

Kenner states, "however we try to rationalize 'Circe' there are elements that escape. It is the second narrator's justification and triumph, an artifact that cannot be analyzed into any save literary constituents."[8] In short, the arranger has the entire text at his disposal, and he is recycling its language into "Circe" as a new, unexpected, irrational, and evocative work of literature that is in some ways distinct from the rest of *Ulysses* while being entirely dependent upon it.

The guilt Bloom feels for not fulfilling his role as a husband continues as he explains to Molly/Marion that he failed to pick up her lotion from Sweny's. Then, the bar of lemon soap speaks a couplet in tetrameter before Sweny's face "appears in the disc of the soapsun" (15.340–41) and announces Bloom's bill from this morning. Molly/Marion speaks lines from Mozart's *Don Giovanni*, Bloom again wonders whether she is pronouncing the Italian correctly, and she "saunters away" (15.352), signaling the end of this first extended fantasy.

## Reality: Nighttown

We momentarily snap back to reality with the unpleasant image of an elderly bawd with "the bristles of her chinmole glittering" (15.357) as she peddles a virgin. This is the same "snaggletusked" woman who previously solicited Stephen and Lynch. Then, the prostitute with whom Bloom had his first sexual encounter, Bridie Kelly, briefly appears (probably only in his imagination).

## Extended Fantasy 2: Bloom and Women from His Past

The next extended fantasy begins with Gerty MacDowell expressing contempt (and then love) for Bloom and his behavior on the strand in "Nausicaa." Then Josie Breen, Bloom's ex, appears and shames him for being "down here in the haunts of sin" (15.394). Bloom offers disjointed denials, explanations, pleasantries, and flattery. Josie threatens to tell Molly that she caught him in Nighttown. The Bohee brothers appear and perform their banjo minstrel show (which is full of racist imagery and stereotypes). Bloom, "always a favourite with the ladies" (15.448), tries to charm Mrs. Breen. Costume changes and histrionics ensue. Denis Breen appears with the H-E-L-Y-S sandwich boards, and the text seems to suggest that Alf Bergan is the author of the U. p: up postcard. Josie warms to Bloom, who acts scandalized by her advances and tests out the *Leah* alibi that he will later use with Molly. His mentioning of supper introduces into the fantasy Richie Goulding and the waiter Pat from the Ormond Hotel restaurant. The navvy we saw earlier in the episode gores Goulding with his "flaming pronghorn" (15.514), and Bloom suggests that he is a spy. The fantasy returns to Bloom's conversation with Mrs. Breen, who calls B.S. on the *Leah* story, and Bloom asks her to walk on for a more confidential conversation. She agrees, and he asks her to recall in vivid detail a horse-race outing they shared fourteen some-odd years ago. It seems like Bloom and Josie had some sort of connection that day, but, after a series of seven yesses, she fades away and the fantasy ends before the memory reaches its climax.

We return to the revolting reality of Nighttown as "a standing woman, bent forward, her feet apart, pisses cowily" (15.578–79). The chorus of loiterers, whores, the navvy, and the redcoats sing and shout. A passage of Bloom's inner monologue conveys his sense that pursuing Stephen is a "wildgoose chase" (15.635), reveals that he's tipsy on only two drinks, indicates that he's hoping to look after Stephen and his money, appreciates that he was saved from the sandstrewer by his "presence of mind" (15.644),[9] and recalls that Molly once drew a penis on a frosted carriagepane. He passes by whores smoking cigarettes, and the arranger infuses the wreaths of "sicksweet weed" smoke with language from the "Sirens" episode: "Sweet are the sweets. Sweets of sin" (15.655, 11.156). Charitable Bloom gives the meat he just purchased to the stray dog that has appeared (and changed breeds) throughout the episode.

Two police approach Bloom, and in his paranoid imagination, they accuse him of committing a public nuisance. He protests that he is "doing good to others" (15.682) by feeding the dog and, presumably, by trying to take care of Stephen. The gulls he fed in "Lestrygonians" serve as character witnesses to his benevolence. Poor Bob Doran falls off his barstool into oblivion. The watchmen ask for his name and address, and he tells them he is "Dr Bloom, Leopold, dental surgeon" (15.721)—the dentist who has been referenced twice previously in the novel. The watch ask for proof, and the Henry Flower card falls out of Bloom's hatband. When pressed, he produces the yellow flower Martha Clifford sent him. He gets chummy with the watch and poses as a gallant. Martha Clifford appears and uses language heard in "Sirens" from the song "Martha." When the watch begin to arrest Bloom, he claims "mistaken identity" (15.760) and twists Martin Cunningham's statement in "Hades" that it is "better for ninetynine guilty to escape than for one innocent person to be wrongfully condemned" (6.474–75) into the self-serving "better one guilty escape than ninetynine wrongfully condemned" (15.763). When Martha accuses Bloom of being a "heartless flirt" (15.767), the fantasy becomes a trial.

Bloom first poses as a Britisher, citing his father-in-law's service and then falsely claims that he fought in the Boer War. Next, he presents himself as a writer of fiction; Myles Crawford from "Aeolus" and Philip Beaufoy, author of the story Bloom read in the outhouse in "Calypso," appear as witnesses. Beaufoy accuses Bloom of plagiarism and of "leading a quadruple existence" (15.853–54). Mary Driscoll, the Blooms' former housekeeper, then takes the witness stand against Mr. Bloom and accuses him of assault. Bloom "mumbles incoherently" (15.923). Under the direction of Professor MacHugh from the pressroom in "Aeolus," a "crossexamination proceeds re Bloom and the bucket" (15.929)—it seems that Bloom once emergency-pooped in a plasterer's bucket he found on the street.

Bloom is defended in this trial by J. J. O'Molloy, the talented but down-on-his-luck lawyer whom we've seen in "Aeolus," "Wandering Rocks," and "Cyclops." O'Molloy offers unconvincingly halting and varied defenses of Mr. Bloom's behavior toward Mary Driscoll, and we might deduce that Bloom did in fact make inappropriate advances. O'Molloy goes on to claim that Bloom is simpleminded (and Bloom performs as such). He argues that a conspiratorial "hidden hand" (15.975) is acting against Bloom. Dlugacz and the Zionist Agendath Netaim investment prospectus are recalled from "Calypso." In the end, O'Molloy pleads that the court give Bloom the "benefit of the doubt" (15.1004). Bloom cites a few former employers and landlords as references, but he lies again about his day. A parade of three high-class women then accuse Bloom of improper advances; as Kevin Dettmar points out, these "Me too" (15.1075, 1077) accusations against Bloom amount to *Ulysses*'s own #MeToo movement.[10] Mrs. Bellingham claims that Bloom once complimented her as a "Venus in furs" (15.1046), which is the title of a novel by Leopold von Sacher-Masoch, from whose name the term "masochism" is derived.[11] Along these lines, Bloom implored Mrs. Talboys "to chastise him as he richly deserves, . . . to give him a most vicious horsewhipping" (15.1070–73). More on Bloom's masochism later, but as you have likely already gathered from the two fantasies we've seen thus far, Bloom is subconsciously craving punishment for his various failures, misbehaviors, and flaws.

As the focus shifts away from Bloom's ogling and toward his cuckolding, the text gives voice to the quoits of the Blooms' bed, which we also heard as a trilling note in the musical "Sirens" episode in association with Boylan's ride in the jaunting car to 7 Eccles Street. The jury box contains a jury of Bloom's peers—men he has encountered over the course of the day, including the Nameless One who narrated the "Cyclops" episode. The Nameless One conflates Boylan and Molly's affair with the tension over Bloom's presumed winning of a "hundred shillings to five" (15.1149) by betting on Throwaway in the Gold Cup. The second watch levels a slew of other wild accusations against Bloom, and long John Fanning (the subsheriff) appears and arranges for Bloom to be hanged by H. Rumbold, whose letter we saw back in "Cyclops" (see 12.415–31).

The bells toll, signaling doom and echoing the "Heigho! Heigho!" of St. George's church bells in "Calypso." Bloom offers a final sputtering defense of his own character and appeals to Joe Hynes (who still owes him 3 shillings) for support. Hynes "coldly" (15.1195) denies him. We begin to circle back to the impetus for this fantasy (the police seeing Bloom lay down the parcel of meat for the dog) as the second watch claims it was a bomb. Bloom explains that the package contained pig's feet and that he attended a funeral. The text exhumes Paddy Dignam to validate Bloom's alibi. When Dignam "worms down" (15.1255) to the underworld, he is followed by the huge rat that caught Bloom's attention in "Hades." Tom Rochford, who we learned in "Wandering Rocks" saved a man who fell down a manhole, dives after Dignam to save him, too. The fantasy recedes as kisses materialize in the air and "flutter upon" (15.1275) Bloom.

### Reality: Arrival at Bella Cohen's Brothel

Bloom hears "a piano sound" (15.1268) inside a brothel. This "sad music" (15.1278) makes him think he's perhaps found Stephen. He's right. A prostitute named Zoe Higgins "accosts" (15.1281) Bloom and points him into the brothel run by Mrs. Cohen, who is "on the job herself tonight" (15.1288). Zoe asks if Bloom is Stephen's father on account of both men wearing black; we know that Bloom is a father in search of a son, and Stephen is a son in search of an adequate father figure, but a whorehouse is an unlikely location for this heralded union to occur. That's *Ulysses* for you. Zoe's wandering hands entice Bloom, and, searching for his nuts, she finds his mother's potato "talisman" (15.1313) in his pocket and keeps it. In another description that takes the sexy out of Nighttown, "she bites his ear gently with little goldstopped teeth, sending on him a cloying breath of stale garlic" (15.1339–40). Nevertheless, Bloom's "awkward hand" (15.1343) explores Zoe. She asks if he has a cigarette, and he lectures her about smoking before lewdly suggesting that "the mouth can be better engaged than with a cylinder of rank weed" (15.1350–51). Zoe's invitation to "make a stump speech out of it" (15.1353) sends Bloom's imagination into a prolonged fantasy of his political rise and fall. The bells of nearby churches chime midnight.

### Extended Fantasy 3: Bloomites and AntiBloomites

This third extended fantasy taps into Bloom's deep desire for approval and his closely held aspirations to distinguish himself as a social reformer and civic problem-solver. After delivering his "stump speech" on tobacco and the ills of "public life" (15.1361), Bloom is named Lord Mayor of Dublin, celebrated by a "torchlight procession" (15.1373), and congratulated by high-profile individuals. Bloom delivers a garbled yet passionate speech on machines, reprising his vacillations in "Hades" (see 6.176–79) regarding technological innovation and its impact on working people. A triumphal parade follows, and Bloom is anointed "Leopold the First" (15.1473). In a universally transmitted decree, Bloom ditches Molly for "the princess Selene" (15.1506–07), a spouse more appropriate to his high station. John Howard Parnell proclaims

Bloom the "successor to [his] famous brother" (15.1513–14), meaning Charles Stewart Parnell. Bloom announces "the new Bloomusalem" (15.1544), and construction begins on "a colossal edifice with crystal roof, built in the shape of a huge pork kidney, containing forty thousand rooms" (15.1548–49). Bloom's ascendancy is not without destruction or casualties.

The man in the brown macintosh from Dignam's funeral appears and casts doubt on Bloom, claiming "his real name is Higgins" (15.1562), which was Bloom's mother's maiden name (and Zoe's last name, coincidentally). Bloom orders that the man in the brown macintosh be shot, and he disappears. Other enemies die, including graziers—remember that Bloom was fired from his job at Cuffe's for "giving lip to a grazier" (12.837–38). Women and children shower Bloom with adoration, and he gregariously makes the rounds. Hynes finally offers to repay the 3 shillings he owes Bloom, which Bloom magnanimously refuses to accept. Even the Citizen, "choked with emotion" (15.1617), is moved to tears by his love for Bloom.

Bloom speaks what little Hebrew/Yiddish words he knows, and the gibberish is translated into an announcement of Bloom's offering of "free medical and legal advice" (15.1630). The following Q&A is pretty funny. Larry O'Rourke, the publican around the corner from the Blooms' home, offers a gift of "a dozen of stout for the missus" (15.1674–75), which Bloom refuses. Above reproach, Bloom "stand[s] for the reform of municipal morals" and for "the union of all" (15.1685–86). The text continues to play the hits, reprising Davy Byrne's yawn from "Lestrygonians": "Iiiiiiiiaaaaaaach!" (15.1697, 8.970). The statues of goddesses are carted in, presumably for Bloom's inspection (thwarted as he was by Buck Mulligan in the National Museum). As "all agree with" Bloom's "schemes for social regeneration" (15.1702–03), we see the depth of Bloom's desire for acceptance in this fantasy of widespread and enthusiastic appreciation for his ideas.

Father Farley, a Jesuit who refused to admit Molly into a church choir years ago (perhaps because of Bloom being a Freemason), condemns Bloom as "an anythingarian seeking to overthrow our holy faith" (15.1712–13). Dante Riordan curses Bloom much like she cursed Parnell in *A Portrait*. Bloom is also cursed by Mother Grogan, the bawdy Irish folk character referenced in "Telemachus." Against this upbraiding,

Bloom tells the *Rose of Castile* / Rows of Cast Steel joke Lenehan told back in "Aeolus"; Lenehan appears and accuses Bloom of being a "plagiarist" (15.1734). But Bloom had already left the newspaper offices to find Mr. Keyes (see 7.436) when Lenehan told this joke (see 7.591). This discrepancy is either a mistake by Joyce (unlikely) or a demonstration of the arranger's mischievous bending of the text in this episode.

The fantasy twists to a conflict between Bloomites and antiBloomites (pick a side!). Bloom blames Henry Flower, his "double" (15.1770), for the debauchery and hypocrisy of which he is accused. He calls on the doctors and medical students from "Oxen" to testify on his behalf. Mulligan diagnoses Bloom as "bisexually abnormal" (15.1775–76), and Dixon calls him "a finished example of the new womanly man" (15.1798–99). Joyce here seems to be playing with Otto Weininger's 1903 pseudoscientific book *Sex and Character*, which argued that all people possessed both male and female "plasms" on a cellular level, and the relative balance of these plasms within an individual contributed to a sliding scale of gender performance.[12] Along these lines, Bloom is revealed to be pregnant and "so want[s] to be a mother" (15.1817). Mrs. Thornton, the midwife who delivered Milly and Rudy, helps Bloom give birth to male octuplets who go on to be attractive, cultured, and prominent men, emphasizing his unsatisfied dream of raising a successful son. Also interesting to note: one of Bloom's sons is named Chrysostomos, the first word the text accesses in Stephen's inner monologue all the way back in "Telemachus" (see 1.26).

Challenged to perform a miracle, Bloom offers eleven amazing feats, the last of which, "eclips[ing] the sun by extending his little finger" (15.1850–51), he already performed once today in the "Lestrygonians" episode (see 8.566). Then, Bloom is renamed Emmanuel and placed at the end of an absurd messianic lineage. But Bloom is no messiah, and he clearly has some shameful moments to account for, as implied by the testimony of a crab, a female infant, and a hollybush. The tide turns against Bloom: "all the people cast soft pantomime stones at Bloom" (15.1902), and even his old friends Mastiansky and Citron "wag their beards" (15.1905) and decry Bloom as a false messiah. Two other Jews, Mesias the tailor and Reuben J. Dodd appear. Then Bloom is set on fire. The Citizen approves. Bloom becomes a martyr, and the grieving Daughters of Erin offer a Bloomian version of the Litany of Mary consisting of *Ulysses* inside jokes. The third extended fantasy concludes with "a choir of six hundred voices" (15.1953) singing Handel's "Alleluia."

## Reality: Inside Bella Cohen's Brothel

As reality returns to the foreground, we realize that Zoe is just finishing the retort she began back at line 1353: "Go on. Make a stump speech out of it. . . . Talk away till you're black in the face" (15.1353, 1958). Literally no time has passed during these seventeen pages of fantasy. Zoe brings Bloom into the brothel, and Bloom seems poised to secure her services for a "short time" (15.1985). Bloom expresses a thought of Molly, which Zoe assuages and "lur[es] him to doom" (15.2012–13). Zoe may seem unappealing with "the odour of her armpits" and "the lion reek of all the male brutes that have possessed her" (15.2015, 2017), yet these scents draw Bloom into the music room, where he finds Lynch, Kitty, Stephen, and Florry. Stephen drunkenly pontificates about music. Lynch mocks and teases Stephen. Florry suggests that "the last day is coming this summer" (15.2129), which sends Stephen's mind into an apocalyptic vision of a hideous, manic hobgoblin playing roulette with planets, revealing his conception of a callous or even malevolent force controlling the universe. In another manipulation of the text, Stephen's mind borrows language from the snippet of theosophical dialogue Bloom overheard A. E. saying to Lizzie Twigg as they passed on their bicycles in "Lestrygonians" (see 8.520). The evangelist preacher advertised in the "Elijah is coming" flyer (see 8.13) sermonizes. The time is now 12:25 a.m. The men from the Holles Street Maternity Hospital become "the eight beatitudes" (15.2237), and the men from the National Library also appear. In reality, Zoe adjusts the gasjet on the chandelier and lights a cigarette. Lynch uses a poker to lift her slip, revealing that she is naked underneath.

## Extended Fantasy 4: Grandfather Virag

Bloom's grandfather Lipoti Virag appears and leads Bloom through an enthusiastic and authoritative appraisal of the three whores. Zoe isn't wearing underwear, garments for which Bloom has a fetish; Kitty is too skinny and is feigning sadness; Florry is attractively plump, but

Bloom is put off by the stye on her eye (note the pun on "stye"—Circe transforms Odysseus's men into pigs). Virag, like Bloom, is an armchair scientist and suggests remedies for the stye. He inspires Bloom toward assertiveness and encourages him to "stop twirling your thumbs and have a good old thunk" (15.2382–83) with one of the prostitutes. He ridicules Bloom for previous plans and ambitions left unfulfilled, including his intended studies of religion and a geometry problem. Bloom expresses some musings on the paradox of his place in time, a moth circles around a light, Virag discusses aphrodisiacs, and female anatomy is worried over. Henry Flower appears and suavely sings a song while strumming a guitar.

## Reality: Stephen

The focalization returns to Stephen at the pianola, and his inner monologue first thinks of his dad and then turns to another inadequate father figure, Mr. Deasy. Stephen thinks of sending "old Deasy" a telegraph, which he mentally drafts: "Our interview of this morning has left on me a deep impression. Though our ages. Will write fully tomorrow. I'm partially drunk, by the way" (15.2497–99). Hilarious. Almidano Artifoni, Stephen's Italian voice teacher who expressed fatherly concern for Stephen in the "Wandering Rocks" episode, then appears. His words of advice and encouragement (see 10.344–51) are warped into "you ruin everything."[13] Florry asks Stephen to sing, but he refuses. Stephen's mind splits into Philip Sober, who scolds him for his drinking and money-wasting, and Philip Drunk, who tries to remember the person with whom he previously discussed Swinburne in the brothel. Stephen is too drunk to sing, and the Philips mock him.

Zoe claims that a priest recently visited Mrs. Cohen's but couldn't ejaculate. Virag, still present in Bloom's mind, offers anti-Catholic ideas regarding the corruption of priests. The text flits back and forth between fantasy and reality, and Virag becomes increasingly unhinged until he finally "unscrews his head" (15.1636) and exits. The two Philips recycle language from Stephen's inner monologue from "Proteus," and then the style of Gerty's half of "Nausicaa" is reprised in describing Kitty's head of "winsome curls" (15.1586). An animalistic Ben Dollard is described in terms reminiscent of the gigantism of the "Cyclops" episode as he sings and is adored by the virgin nurses from "Oxen." Henry Flower plucks a lute and sings the "Martha" song from "Sirens" while "caressing on his breast a severed female head" (15.2620). This section of "Circe" is particularly bonkers.

Florry, more right than she could know, calls Stephen "a spoiled priest" (15.2649). Lynch presses the joke, claiming that Stephen is "a cardinal's son" (15.2651), which brings to Stephen's mind Simon, "primate" (15.2654) of Ireland, reciting verses and being swarmed by midges. Another john comes down the stairs after a visit with the madame, Bella Cohen, and retrieves his coat and hat before leaving the brothel. Bloom passes around the chocolate he purchased prior to the start of the episode and wonders if perhaps the departing man is Boylan, paying for sex because his affair with Molly didn't come off . . . or maybe he's doing "the double event" (15.2706). He relaxes when the man departs into the night. Accepting his chocolate back from Zoe, he takes a bite and thinks about aphrodisiacs. He seems to have been convinced by his grandfather to satisfy himself with a prostitute.

Then Bella Cohen enters. She is described as a "massive whoremistress" with a "sprouting moustache" on her "olive face"; she is wearing a fringed "threequarter ivory gown" and is using a fan to cool herself from her recent exertions (15.2742–47). She vulgarly announces that she's "all of a mucksweat" (15.2750) and makes eye contact with Bloom.

## Extended Fantasy 5: Bello

In reality, Bloom doesn't seem to interact with Bella Cohen until line 3480, some twenty-two pages after she first looks at him; in fact, he doesn't really interact with Bella in the fifth extended fantasy, either: the text portrays him in conversation with The Fan, The Hoof, and Bello, but not Bella. Joyce's use of synecdoche here manipulates the basic understanding readers have about figurative language: rather than the part representing the whole, the part itself is personified and invested with agency, as demonstrated by Bloom's conversation with The Fan. The Hoof then threatens violence while Bloom laces its boot. Bella becomes Bello, and Bloom's pronoun changes to "her" (15.2847). This gender bending recalls the Weiningerian gender theory mentioned earlier. Bello grinds his heel into Bloom's neck and promises to "shame it out of [him]" (15.2868), exposing Bloom's masochistic desire to be punished for his various failures. Without moly, our Ulysses is transformed into a pig "on all fours, grunting, snuffling, rooting at [Bello's] feet" (15.2852–53).

Bloom tries to hide, and the other whores intercede on "her" behalf. Bello sits on him and smokes a cigar while reading the paper, twisting Bloom's arm and slapping "her" face. The other whores now join in Bello's domination of Bloom. The Ascot Gold Cup pops up again as Bello reads the result in the paper, curses the "outsider *Throwaway*," and "quenches his cigar angrily on Bloom's ear" (15.2936–37). Bello begins to ride Bloom like a horse, squeezes Bloom's "testicles roughly" (15.2945), and "farts stoutly" (15.2958–59) on "her." If Bloom was craving punishment, "what [he] longed for has come to pass" (15.2964–65).

The fantasy moves from physical violence to an accounting of "the sins of the past" (15.3027). Bloom twice wore Molly's undergarments and posed for himself in the mirror. He offered Molly in ads written on the walls of five public bathrooms and "presented himself indecently" (15.3031), among other things. Bloom is now in Bello's servitude, forced to drink piss. Bello plans to pimp "her" out as the brothel's "new attraction" (15.3083). Bello then speaks of Bloom like cattle at an auction.

Bello asks if Bloom can "do a man's job" (15.3132), to which Bloom begins to reply "Eccles street" (15.3134) before Bello alludes to Boylan as "a man of brawn in possession there" (15.3137). Bloom has been usurped, and Bello claims that Boylan has impregnated Molly. A disjointed series of pleading exclamations—"To drive me mad! Moll! I forgot! Forgive! Moll . . . We . . . Still . . ." (15.3151)—reflects Bloom's mental anguish, his neglectful forgetting of his duties as a husband, his desire for Molly's forgiveness, and his belief in the "still" possible redemption of their marriage. Bello "ruthlessly" (15.3153) quashes these thoughts.

Then, like the Ghost of Christmas Past, Bello prompts Bloom to return to see what he recognizes as the party at which he first met Molly, but Bello is messing with him; the woman he sees is his daughter Milly with Bannon. Bello continues to manipulate Bloom's mind, suggesting that Bloom's most treasured household items will be defiled. Bloom seems to be turning a corner from a desire for punishment to a desire to "return" (15.3191) and recover what he has lost. The Nymph from the framed picture in the Blooms' bedroom appears to comfort Bloom and thank him for rescuing her from the pages of *Photo Bits*, a softcore porn magazine. But the Nymph has also been scandalized by what she has seen and heard in the Blooms' bedroom.

The fantasy supplies somewhat hazy memories of Bloom's adolescence and a school field trip to Poulaphouca waterfall, where it seems that Bloom pleasured himself "in the open air" (15.3344). He explains it as a sacrifice "to the god of the forest" (15.3353), notes the various arousals of springtime, cites the effect of peeping on a woman in her bathroom (is that an excuse?), resorts to blaming a "demon" (15.3359), and eventually says that he was "simply satisfying a need" (15.3365) that wasn't being fulfilled by the girls his age, who apparently didn't find him attractive. As we continue to learn Bloom's most intimate secrets and plumb the depths of his subconscious, it may be worth considering that we perhaps now know Mr. Bloom more completely—good, bad, and ugly—than it might be possible to know a real person.

The scene shifts to Howth Hill, the site of Bloom's proposal to Molly, as remembered in "Lestrygonians" (see 8.900–916). Bloom borrows language from the "Sirens" episode ("Done. Prff!" [15.3390]), and the Nymph finally answers Bloom's question regarding the private parts of goddesses. The fantasy's grip begins to loosen as voices from the music room blend with the imaginary voices. As Bloom emerges from the Bello daymare, he stands more upright, representing a change in posture and in attitude. As evidence of this change and its real-world effect, the back button on his pants pops off and says, "Bip!" (15.3441). Newly assertive and "composed" (15.3483), perhaps Bloom has finally "broken the spell" (15.3449) of his guilt over Rudy's death and subsequent deficiencies. Heroically, he is able to endure and overcome this intense shame as well as these frank reckonings with his life's failures and most mortifying moments.

## Reality: Money

Back in reality and reflective of this shift in his mentality, Bloom asks Zoe to return his potato. Not a huge deal on its face, but he's standing up for himself and claiming what's rightfully his. It's a start. Bella attends to the business side of things, asking "who's paying here?" (15.3529). Each prostitute charges 10 shillings (roughly US$150 in today's money) for the pleasure of their company. Stephen is exceedingly sloppy in the transaction, initially giving Bella a £1 banknote, which would pay for him and Lynch. When Lynch calls for Dedalus to cover him, Stephen unnecessarily gives Bella a half sovereign coin (worth 10 shillings). Bella is confused by this overpayment, and Stephen apologizes and "fumbles again and takes out and hands her two crowns" (15.1545–46); a crown coin is worth 5 shillings. So, Stephen has just given Bella an additional 10 shillings for a grand total of 40 shillings, or £2. He has handed over the equivalent of roughly US$600 in today's cash. Keeping in mind that Stephen received £3 12s. from Deasy this morning (see 2.209–22) for a month's teaching salary, this level of carelessness is astounding. Stephen returns to the pianola and reprises his fox riddle from "Nestor," leaving the others to sort out the financial confusion. Clever Bloom "quietly lays a half sovereign on the table" (worth 10 shillings, bringing the total paid to 50 shillings) and then "takes up the poundnote" (worth 20 shillings, thus bringing the total paid back to 30 shillings) and states simply "three times ten. We're square" (15.3583–84). Point Bloom.

He returns the rescued poundnote to Stephen and offers "to take care of" (15.3601) Stephen's money. Bloom counts Stephen's cash and rounds up what he still owes him back by a penny. Stephen mourns that his favorite whore, Georgina Johnson, "is dead and married" (15.3620). Stephen is too drunk to light his cigarette (always a good hint to call it a night). Bloom, emboldened and fatherly, tells Stephen, "Don't smoke. You ought to eat" (15.3644). Zoe begins reading palms. Lynch slaps Kitty's bottom like a "pandybat" (15.3666), which triggers for Stephen a brief fantasy of the unjust punishment he received from Father Dolan at Clongowes (as portrayed in *A Portrait*). Mild Father Conmee from "Wandering Rocks" and *A Portrait* then appears in the fantasy and intervenes on Stephen's behalf. Back in reality, Zoe continues reading palms, and Bloom identifies a scar (see 15.274). Stephen winces and observes that he "hurt [his] hand somewhere" (15.3720–21), which might be psychosomatic pain from the fantasy of Father Dolan's flogging, or it might be related to a real scuffle with Buck Mulligan at Westland Row Station just over an hour ago. The whores giggle in the background, and the barmaids and the boots from "Sirens" appear in the book's imagination.

## Extended Fantasy 6: Boylan

The sixth sustained fantasy begins with Blazes Boylan arriving with Lenehan. These two uncouth men make lewd comments to one another before Boylan calls to Bloom, treats him like a servant, and casually cuckolds him (he even invites Bloom to watch through the keyhole). Bloom has been actively suppressing this scene all day, but it tumbles out of his subconscious here in the most disturbing and degrading way possible.

The whores continue to giggle. A crossfade occurs as Bloom and Stephen both "gaze in the mirror" (15.3821), and the image of Shakespeare appears and coexists in the reflection of both men. Bloom, like Shakespeare in Stephen's theory, is a cuckold; Stephen, like Shakespeare, is a troubled artist. Paddy Dignam's widow appears with her children. Martin Cunningham's face appears in the mirror and "refeatures Shakespeare's beardless face" (15.3854–55). Bloom previously connected Cunningham with Shakespeare during the carriage ride in "Hades" (see 6.345).

## Reality: Stephen Loses It

We return to reality with Stephen blaspheming, which Bella won't tolerate in her brothel. The whores ask him to speak some French. He speaks drunken bawdy gibberish in French syntax. The prophetic dream he remembered in "Proteus" (see 3.365–69) finally clicks: "It was here. Street of harlots. . . . Where's the red carpet spread?" (15.3930–31). Recognizing that Stephen is losing it, Bloom tries to calm him with fatherly cautioning even as Stephen proclaims that he has soared to freedom beyond any sort of paternalistic forces. At Stephen's combative cry, a fantasy begins as his real father, Simon, "swoops uncertainly through the air, wheeling . . . on buzzard wings" (15.3945–46). A scavenging vulture, Simon encourages Stephen to win for the family and "keep our flag flying" (15.3948). Stephen becomes the fox from his riddle, "having buried his grandmother" (15.3952–53), pursued by a "pack of staghounds" (15.3954). This race becomes a rerunning of the Gold Cup with Mr. Deasy riding a horse called Cock of the North.

In reality, Private Carr, Private Compton, and Cissy Caffrey discordantly sing "My Girl's a Yorkshire Girl" as they pass the window of Mrs. Cohen's; Zoe, a Yorkshire girl, goes to the pianola, puts on this song, and gets everyone dancing except for Bloom, who "stands aside" (15.4030). The dancing master Denis Maginni appears dressed to the nines and instructs the other dancers. Stephen, Lynch, Florry, Zoe, and Kitty twirl and waltz. Stephen calls for a "*pas seul*" (15.4120) (a solo dance), and busts a move: he "frogsplits in middle highkicks with skykicking mouth shut hand clasp part under thigh" (15.4124–25). Try it. I dare you.

Dizzy and lightheaded from this exertion, Stephen hallucinates the appearance of his dead mother, "her face worn and noseless, green with gravemould" (15.4159). Since the very beginning of the novel (see 1.103–10), Stephen has been haunted by the memory of her death, his guilt for refusing to pray for her on her deathbed, and her appearance to him in a nightmare. Of course, Buck Mulligan shows up to needle him. Stephen's mother implores him to pray and "repent" (15.4198) and expresses her eternal motherly love for him. This imaginary encounter has clearly affected Stephen in reality, as Florry notes that "he's white" (15.4208). Back in the hallucination, Stephen's mother warns him of "the fire of hell" (15.4212) and to "beware God's hand" (15.4219). Perhaps representative of God's hand, "a green crab with malignant red eyes sticks its grinning claws in Stephen's heart" (15.4220–21). Horror-struck and "strangled with rage," Stephen yells, "Shite!" and then "*Non serviam!*" (15.4223, 4228), echoing Lucifer's refusal to serve God. The others in the brothel are alarmed, and Florry rushes out to get Stephen some cold water. Stephen "lifts his ashplant high with both hands and smashes the chandelier" (15.4243–44) before flying from the room and out into the street.

Bella grabs Bloom and demands 10 shillings in compensation for the damage to the lamp. Bloom calmly takes a look and discerns that "there's not sixpenceworth of damage done" (15.4290–91). Bella threatens to call the police, but Bloom offers a variety of pragmatic reasons (some true, some false) to handle this situation discreetly. Finally, he deploys his knowledge that Bella's son is a student at Oxford, which he learned from Zoe when he arrived at the brothel (see 15.1289). Bella is startled. Bloom leaves a shilling "for the chimney" (15.4312–13) of the chandelier and hurries out to find Stephen. As he is leaving Mrs. Cohen's, he "averts his face" (15.4320) as he passes three other men entering the brothel, including Corny Kelleher and perhaps Blazes Boylan—more on this in a bit. Bloom, carrying Stephen's abandoned ashplant, is pursued (not really) by a large crowd of people from his past and from this day, most of whom are antagonistic toward him or at least suspicious of him.

Bloom comes upon a crowd gathering around a confrontation between Stephen and Private Carr. It seems the soldiers found Stephen speaking with Cissy Caffrey when they returned from urinating. Private Carr accuses Stephen of insulting Cissy, and Stephen seems heedless of the danger as he drunkenly pontificates. Private Compton eggs on his buddy to "biff him one" (15.4392). Carr threatens to "bash in [Stephen's] jaw" (15.4411). Stephen teaches the definition of a rhetorical device. Not only is Stephen hammered to the point of obliviousness, but he is a pacifist who "detest[s] action" (15.4414). Bloom makes his way through the crowd and attempts to extricate "professor" (15.4424) Dedalus from the dangerous situation. Stephen can barely stand up.

Gesturing toward his mind, Stephen explains to the soldiers that "here it is I must kill the priest and the king" (15.4436–37). Poor choice of words. Carr takes this statement as a direct threat against the king of England, whom the text promptly conjures to officiate the fight. Bloom tries to appeal to the redcoats, explaining that Stephen is drunk on absinthe and "a gentleman, a poet" (15.4488). The privates "don't give a bugger who he is" (15.4493); plus, they are total meatheads.

As Bloom continues to coax Stephen to leave, the text produces a slew of quick figurations of the Irish-English conflict. Carr continues his taunts, and Stephen exclaims, "O, this is too monotonous!" (15.4568) and "tries to move off" (15.4575). He has also forgotten where his money went. The privates accuse Stephen of being a pro-Boer, but Bloom retorts that the Royal Dublin Fusiliers fought for Great Britain in South Africa, which prompts a fantasy of Major Tweedy (Molly's dad) confronting the Citizen. Carr seems determined to hit Stephen, and Cissy seems excited by the prospect of being fought over. Carr offers unwitting puns about his "bleeding fucking king" (15.4645)—King Edward VII was a hemophiliac ("bleeding") and a notorious womanizer ("fucking"). Bloom implores Cissy Caffrey to intervene and pacify the situation. She tries, but it's too little, too late. After some imaginary hysteria, Bloom then pleads with Lynch to help get Stephen away from this danger. Lynch can't be bothered and slinks off with Kitty. As he leaves, Stephen calls him "Judas" (15.4730)—but isn't Lynch's refusal to help Stephen more like Peter's denial of Jesus than Judas's betrayal? Anyhow, Bloom again tries to get Stephen away; Cissy forgives Stephen for insulting her and tries again to get Carr to leave. Just as you think it might end peacefully, Private Carr "rushes towards Stephen, fist outstretched, and strikes him in the face" (15.4747–48). Stephen collapses, out cold.

The first and second watch return from the beginning of the episode to investigate the incident. Bloom gets full of himself and instructs the watch to "take [Carr's] regimental number" (15.4788–89). They don't like being bossed around. Compton realizes that Carr should leave the scene to avoid getting in trouble with his superior officer, and Bloom realizes that Stephen might get arrested. Just in time, Corny Kelleher comes upon the scene, and Bloom fills him in on what has occurred. Kelleher, known by the police to be a valuable informant, calls off the watch. Phew! Richard Ellmann explains the appearance of Corny Kelleher, who works for O'Neill's undertakers, as symbolic of "the burial of the old Stephen."[14] As we read the remaining episodes of the novel, we can judge whether, indeed, a new Stephen arises from this collapse.

Corny and Bloom now somewhat awkwardly have to explain why they are in Nighttown. Corny claims to have been drinking with two other guys who "were on for a go with the jolly girls" (15.4863), but Corny refrains from joining them in the brothel because he is married and "ha[s] it in the house" (15.4870). One of Corny's companions lost £2 on the Gold Cup, as did Boylan, so Bloom might have brushed shoulders with his rival at Mrs. Cohen's. For his part, Bloom offers a totally bogus and implausible explanation.

What to do now? Thinking Stephen lives in Cabra, Corny offers to give him a ride home in his carriage. When he learns that Stephen has been staying all the way down in Sandycove, Corny shrugs, "Ah, well, he'll get over it" (15.4896). Bloom realizes that he doesn't really have an endgame, and now he's stuck holding the bag of a knocked out, passed out twenty-two-year-old he scarcely knows. As Corny departs in the car, he "sways his head to and fro in sign of mirth at Bloom's plight"; "Bloom shakes his head in mute mirthful reply" (15.4910–13). You can only laugh.

Mr. Bloom, characteristically caring and kind, bends down to shake Stephen's shoulder, trying to rouse him. Stephen speaks a few fragments and murmur-sings a few words from "Who Goes with Fergus?"—Yeats's song is still in Stephen's mind from this morning, when he remembers singing it to his mother on her deathbed. Stephen's recollection of his mom's response—"for those words Stephen: love's bitter mystery" (1.252–53)—predicts this moment and Bloom's unexpected act of love. Because Bloom does not recognize Yeats's poem, he misunderstands "Fergus" and "white breast" to refer to "a girl" (15.4950); he thinks in a fatherly way that a stable relationship would be the "best thing [that] could happen [to Stephen]" (15.4950).

## Extended Fantasy 7: Rudy

Standing guard over Stephen, Bloom conjures a fantasy of Rudy, now eleven years old, reading Hebrew, "smiling, kissing the page" (15.4959–60). This concluding image is lovely, poignant, and emotionally affecting. You may even be moved to tears.

Scholars have lots of opinions on this concluding fantasy. Richard Ellmann claims that "here, out of love for his dead child, [Bloom] does more than remember, he reshapes Rudy's misshapen features and raises him from the grave."[15] In contrast, Hugh Kenner suggests that "Rudy, we may deduce, does not appear to Bloom at all. [He] appears to *us*, a gratuitous pantomime transformation supplied by the second narrator to resolve and terminate the episode, and to serve as notation for the empiric truth that Bloom's next thoughts are paternal ones."[16] If Kenner is correct and Bloom does not see Rudy, then our vision of Rudy allows the text "to project one of Bloom's deepest wishes at a strategic moment [and] to feel where the climax would have been in a more conventional novel,"[17] as Karen Lawrence suggests. At the very least, the novel here seems to acknowledge and reinforce that the loss of Rudy thwarted Mr. Bloom's strong paternal instincts, and he senses in Stephen an opportunity to redeem this unfulfilled element of his character.

❊❊

In the process of composing "Circe," with its hundreds of recycled parts taken from elsewhere in *Ulysses*, Joyce expanded his understanding of this novel's potential as "a kind of encyclopedia" (*SL* 271). He began revising the rest of the book accordingly, retrospectively arranging snippets of interrelated details throughout the previous episodes into an intricate network of minor motifs that accumulate and aggregate in the careful reader's awareness. "Circe" thus serves as an absurd but cathartic outpouring of *Ulysses* thus far.

Having gotten all that out of our system, we are ready for the episodes Joyce called the "Nostos," the return.

## Further Reading

Attridge, Derek. "Pararealism in 'Circe.'" *European Joyce Studies* 22 (2013): 119–25.

Using specific examples from the episode, Attridge presents the concept of pararealism to describe the shading back and forth between the realism of Nighttown and the distortions and exaggerations that augment that described reality.

Briggs, Austin. "Joyce's Drinking." *James Joyce Quarterly* 48, no. 4 (Summer 2011): 637–66.

After a comprehensive critique of various Joyce biographies in terms of their general avoidance of commentary on his drinking, this essay collates descriptions of Joyce's drinking into a devastating portrait of his alcoholism.

Earle, David M. "'Green Eyes, I See You. Fang, I Feel': The Symbol of Absinthe in *Ulysses*." *James Joyce Quarterly* 40, no. 4 (Summer 2003): 691–709.

This essay examines absinthe's history and associations before interpreting its appearance in *Ulysses* as a projection of Stephen's self-imposed exile, bohemian affectations, and artistic sensibilities. Earle also notes the appropriateness of absinthe to the stylistic disorientation of these episodes of the novel.

Steinberg, Erwin R. "The Source(s) of Joyce's Anti-Semitism in *Ulysses*." *Joyce Studies Annual* 10 (1999): 63–84.

This essay examines Joyce's treatment of Weininger's pseudoscience as it pertains to gender and Judaism. This context helps explain the gender fluidity presented in "Circe."

# Chapter 16

# "EUMAEUS" GUIDE

Picking up the action immediately after the end of "Circe," the "Eumaeus" episode covers the time between roughly 12:45 a.m. and 1:40 a.m. Mr. Bloom helps Stephen to his feet and takes him to a nearby cabman's shelter for some sustenance and recuperation.

The style of the "Eumaeus" episode, identified by Joyce in the schema as "narrative (old)," has elicited divergent critical opinions. Marilyn French considers the strained sentences to reflect the tension between overeager Bloom and disengaged Stephen; in French's reading, the tedious style of "Eumaeus" serves as "an obscurant: we have wanted to see what would happen when Bloom and Stephen finally came together, here they are, and nothing happens."[1] Richard Ellmann claims that the episode "struggles clumsily for the right expression,"[2] while Stanley Sultan describes it as "the attempt of a poorly-educated man to impress by discoursing with sophisticated eloquence."[3] David Hayman calls the episode "a tired, threadbare, flatulent narrative larded with commonplaces" whereby "the arranger conveys with surprising accuracy the drink and fatigue-dulled sentiments of both protagonists."[4]

In my opinion, the most useful understanding of the style of this episode relies on the Uncle Charles Principle, which "entails writing about someone much as that someone would choose to be written about."[5] Applying this concept to the current episode, "Eumaeus" is written in the style that Mr. Bloom would have employed if he himself had written the episode; indeed, Bloom later announces his intention

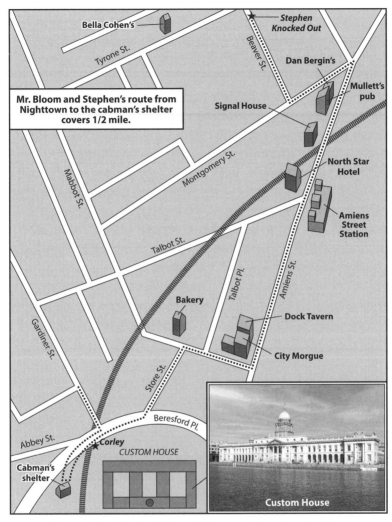

Bloom and Stephen's walk from Nighttown to the cabman's shelter

to compose exactly this piece of literature: "suppose he were to pen something out of the common groove (as he fully intended doing) at the rate of one guinea per column. *My experiences*, let us say, *in a Cabman's Shelter*" (16.1229–31). So, rather than condemning "Eumaeus" as stilted, overornamented prose with garbled syntax and imprecise diction, we might instead consider the episode's use of Bloom's own literary style (flawed as it may be) as Joyce's ultimate celebration of Bloom himself (flawed as he may be). By ceding such control to Mr. Bloom, "Eumaeus" represents "the book's most profound tribute to its hero."[6] With this gesture in mind, the episode's flabby sentences and cringeworthy clichés become endearing à la Bloom himself. The episode's inferior style, though, is also a demonstration of Joyce's extreme facility with language. Just as it takes a very good piano player to play a song really poorly—you have to know the exact wrong notes to play to make it sound truly awful—it takes an immensely talented writer to intentionally write this badly. Bearing this in mind, we can better appreciate the humor embedded in the style of this particular episode.

"Eumaeus" is the first of three episodes forming part 3 of *Ulysses*, which Joyce titled the "Nostos," the return. Appropriately, but subtly, language returns from the novel's opening scene on the rooftop of the Martello tower: the words "brush," "shaving," and "buck" (16.1–2) all reappear as Bloom rouses Stephen from his stupor. Bloom suggests that they go for some refreshments at a cabman's shelter near the Custom House, about a ten-minute walk from the site of Stephen's collapse in Nighttown.

In *The Odyssey*, Odysseus finally returns home to Ithaca and emerges from an Athena-induced haze. He disguises himself as a beggar and goes to the hut of his swineherd, Eumaeus. Rather than reveal himself immediately, Odysseus tells Eumaeus false stories about his identity and origin. After Eumaeus passes a loyalty test, Odysseus reveals his true identity. Later, in Eumaeus's hut, Odysseus is united with his son, Telemachus. Together, the three men plot an attack on the suitors plaguing Odysseus's home and besetting his wife, Penelope. As we will see, some of these correspondences are clear, but others are more nuanced.

From the very outset of "Eumaeus," we halt at the Bloomish inexactitude of the episode's language. Reading the incongruous pairing of "orthodox Samaritan" (16.3), we know what is meant by this phrase (something like, "thoroughly charitable"), but the words aren't quite right: Samaritans by definition are not Orthodox; they are distinct branches of Judaism. The wobbly prose style also strains our attention: "For the nonce he was rather nonplussed but inasmuch as the duty plainly devolved upon him to take some measures on the subject he pondered suitable ways and means during which Stephen repeatedly yawned" (16.11–14). With that kind of syntax, yawning is understandable. Next, consider that Mr. Bloom is described as "anything but a professional whistler" (16.29). These examples demonstrate the sort of quirks facing readers of this episode, but if you can see the humor in them, you'll have a much better time with these next forty pages.

As the two men make their way toward the cabman's shelter, they encounter a sandstrewer, prompting Bloom to recount his near miss at the beginning of "Circe." Stephen, meanwhile, "thought to think of Ibsen" (16.52). Throughout much of the episode and for various reasons, the two men are on different wavelengths. Shame on you for expecting Joyce to give us a wholly satisfying and unironic union between the two characters we've been waiting to see united for the entire novel. As they walk, Bloom, "disgustingly sober" (16.62), offers Stephen, disgustingly drunk, some unsolicited advice. First, he comments on visiting prostitutes: "barely permissible once in a while though not as a habitual practice" (16.64–66). Then, absurd yet prudent, Bloom recommends knowing "a little jiujitsu for every contingency" (16.67). Finally, he warns Stephen to mind "who [he] got drunk with" because it leaves you "at the tender mercy of others" (16.67, 88–89, 94). He's like your hip, nonjudgmental uncle!

As they approach "the back of the customhouse" (16.101), Stephen is hailed by Corley, whom we know from the "Two Gallants" story in *Dubliners*. He is broke and needs a job. Stephen tells Corley that there will be a position open at Mr. Deasy's school tomorrow or the next day; evidently, Stephen is quitting his teaching job. Corley is unfit for work in education (he had to repeat two grades in school himself). Stephen reaches into his pocket to lend Corley some money and is surprised to find "his cash missing" (16.185); he has forgotten that Bloom took it for safekeeping back at Bella Cohen's. Stephen is able to find two coins anyhow and gives them to Corley, thinking they are pennies. Corley tells Stephen (honorably enough) that in fact the coins are half-crowns, 2½ shilling coins—not an insignificant sum at all; you might remember that Bloom is lauded for donating exactly this amount (5 shillings) to the Dignams. Corley then inquires about Bloom, remembering that he has on previous occasion seen him with Boylan, and asks if Bloom can perhaps get him a job with Boylan's advertising firm. I wouldn't bank on it.

Stephen rejoins Bloom and explains that he gave Corley money for a place to sleep. Bloom asks Stephen where he himself plans to sleep tonight: "Walking to Sandycove is out of the question. And even supposing you did you won't get in after what occurred at Westland Row station" (16.249–51). An altercation seems to have occurred, and Bloom observed Buck Mulligan and Haines "give Stephen the slip" (16.266–67) as they caught the last train to Sandycove without him.[7] Generally, Bloom distrusts Mulligan. So, Bloom asks why Stephen left his father's house, to which Stephen replies somewhat glibly, "to seek misfortune" (16.253). Bloom tells Stephen that Simon is proud of him. Stephen mentally recalls his last visit home. Given that most of this episode's narration is focalized on Bloom, this "repicturing" of the Dedalus home is one of only a few moments where the narration accesses "Stephen's mind's eye" (16.269). They come across two Italian men in heated conversation, and Bloom notes their beautiful language; Stephen, who of course is fluent, informs him that the two men "were haggling over money" (16.348), perhaps over the price of a whore. The contrast between Bloom's ignorance and Stephen's education is comedic.

Stephen and Bloom finally reach the cabman's shelter, "an unpretentious wooden structure" (16.321) tucked under the Loopline Railway Bridge on the north bank of the Liffey, adjacent to Butt Bridge. These little huts provided a place for drivers of carriages and cabs to rest, eat some light fare, and stay sober (they did not serve alcohol). This particular cabman's shelter is patronized on this late night by a "miscellaneous collection of waifs and strays and other nondescript specimens" (16.327–28). The keeper of the cabman's shelter is understood to be James Fitzharris, a.k.a. Skin-the-goat, a member of a famous group of Irish nationalists called the Invincibles. Fitzharris drove one of the getaway carriages after the Phoenix Park murders, the sensationalized 1882 assassination of two British officials discussed back in "Aeolus." They enter the shelter and take seats in the corner, striking an odd couple at this late hour of night in their matching black suits and age gap of sixteen years. Bloom orders coffee and a bun for Stephen, and Fitzharris brings them to the table. Bloom pushes the coffee and the bun toward Stephen, and the narration regards both items with some uncertainty. Seizing on this skepticism, Stanley Sultan claims that "the narrator has gone to lengths to indicate that the 'concoction labelled coffee' and the 'so-called roll' are wine and wafer, the Eucharist in disguise—that the messianic Bloom is unwittingly urging Stephen to accept Communion with God."[8] Maybe. If not communion with God, Mr. Bloom is certainly hoping Stephen will commune with him.

Among the men already in the shelter, a redbearded sailor named D. B. Murphy asks Stephen his name. When the sailor then asks if he knows Simon Dedalus, Stephen cagily replies, "I've heard of him" (16.379); Murphy tells a story of seeing Simon Dedalus "shoot two eggs off two bottles at fifty yards over his shoulder" in Stockholm as part of Hengler's Royal Circus world tour (16.389, 411–13). He then explains that he has been away at sea for seven years and has just today returned home on the *Rosevean*, the three-masted ship we first saw entering Dublin Bay at the very end of "Proteus." This man, Murphy, corresponds to Odysseus returning in disguise to Ithaca and inventing an elaborate false identity when he first speaks with Eumaeus.

Bloom imagines the scene of Murphy returning to his wife and home. Back in the shelter, Murphy asks for a chaw of tobacco. The narrator expresses some skepticism about Murphy: he "scarcely seemed to be a Dublin resident" (16.441), and the discharge document he supposedly received this morning is "not very cleanlooking" (16.454). Murphy spins further yarns about where he has been and what he has seen in his travels; he produces a "picture postcard from his inside pocket" depicting "a group of savage women in striped loincloths" (16.472, 475–76) from his time in Bolivia. Bloom subtly "turned over the card to peruse the partially obliterated address and postmark" to reveal that the card was actually sent to a Señor A. Boudin in Chile (16.488–89), prompting Bloom to "nourish some suspicions of our friend's *bona fides*" (16.498). Richard Ellmann posits that Murphy demonstrates the difference between the artistic fiction that Joyce has created in *Ulysses* and the misleading fiction of lies. Joyce's novel has sought to depict in exacting (but ultimately false) detail a real city filled with real people on a real day, whereas "with falsisimilitude Murphy would ambush the verisimilitude that is claimed in *Ulysses*, and . . . the sailor would change the impulse of art to create into the pseudo-artistic impulse to gull."[9] Essentially, *Ulysses* uses fiction that resembles reality in order to tell truths, whereas Murphy uses fiction simply to deceive.

After considering his own plans to travel, Bloom conceives of "the Tweedy-Flower grand opera company" (16.525), a summer concert tour of English seaside towns that would essentially usurp Boylan's business relationship with Molly; indeed, he's plotting a retaliatory counterusurpation. He realizes, though, that he would need "some fellow with a bit of bounce" (16.529) to generate publicity for the venture. "But who?" (16.530). Bloom has seen Stephen earlier today with prominent newspapermen; the wheels begin to turn in the businessman's head.

Murphy continues to tell stories about China and Trieste, claiming that he witnessed a murder by stabbing, which turns attention to Skin-the-goat (the Phoenix Park murders were committed with surgical knives). Bloom asks Murphy if he has seen Gibraltar; Murphy responds with an ambiguous grimace. Bloom inquires further, but Murphy avoids the question and takes a storytelling break. He claims he wants to settle down and give up the sailor's life of wandering and mentions that his son has now gone to sea. Bloom, perhaps mischievously probing Murphy's veracity, inquires about how old his son is. Murphy guesses his son must be around eighteen (not unlike Telemachus, advancing the Murphy-Odysseus correspondence). Murphy then displays a tattoo of an anchor, a face in profile, and the number sixteen in blue ink on his chest. The facial expression on the face can be changed by manipulating the skin, which everyone in the hut admires. Murphy claims that the tattoo artist, a Greek man named Antonio, was eaten by sharks.

Then, the same woman in a black straw hat that Bloom saw (but anxiously avoided) at the end of the "Sirens" episode enters the shelter. Bloom again reacts nervously, hiding behind a newspaper, so I again suggest that she is Bridie Kelly, the prostitute to whom Bloom lost his virginity. He is relieved when Skin-the-goat "made a rude sign to take herself off" (16.722). Bloom the realist/reformer pontificates on prostitution, calling it "a necessary evil" and arguing that the women should be "licensed and medically inspected by the proper authorities" (16.742–43).

The next passage of the conversation (if you are willing to call their interaction to this point a conversation) emphasizes Bloom's misunderstanding of Stephen. First, Bloom mistakes Stephen for "a good catholic" (16.748). Then, he attempts to engage with Stephen on the topic of dualism. Stephen quotes St. Thomas Aquinas, asserting that the soul is incorruptible because it is "simple," meaning without contrariety.[10] Bloom, "a bit out of his sublunary depth" (16.762), does not grasp the philosophical context out of which Stephen uses the word "simple," thinking Stephen uses it to mean uncomplicated. Under this misunderstanding, Bloom rebuts Stephen. They then briefly debate "the existence of a supernatural God" (16.770–71), and the text tells us "on this knotty point however the views of the pair, poles apart as they were both in schooling and everything else with the marked difference in ages, clashed" (16.774–76). While perhaps ill-suited to each other, "that they are in many ways different does not prevent fusion, any more than the difference in character between Odysseus and his swineherd prevented them from standing together against the suitors' tyranny."[11] At this point in the episode, fusion has yet to occur between the two men. Bloom again encourages Stephen to drink the coffee and eat the bun, but Stephen refuses.

The text comments on cabman's shelters' services to the lower classes (promotion of the temperance movement, musical performances, lectures, and so on) and notes that Molly used to play the piano at the Coffee Palace for a small sum (presumably during the Blooms' financial rough patch, 1894–96). Bloom stirs the sugar into the coffee, pushes Stephen once more to try it, and he finally has a taste. Bloom advises Stephen to eat more often, and Stephen asks Bloom to take away the knife because it "reminds [him] of Roman history" (16.816). Naturally. Bloom asks Stephen if he believes the sailor's stories, and the text reveals Bloom's inkling that Murphy has recently been released from prison. He dabbles in racist generalizations, leading to a presentation of Molly as a "Spanish type" (16.879). He compares Irish women unfavorably to the physical "proportions" of the Greek goddess statues he examined at the National Museum earlier in the day. Bloom also explains that he is unimpressed with Irish women's fashion.

The others in the shelter discuss various shipwrecks. Murphy heads outside to drink some rum from his flask. Bloom suspects that Murphy also hopes to flag down the whore. A nationalist conversation touches on the disuse of Irish harbors, the superiority of Irish natural resources, the forthcoming fall of the British Empire, Ireland's role in that fall as England's "Achilles heel" (16.1003), anti-emigration sentiments, and the supreme effectiveness of Irish soldiers. Murphy claims the Irish to be "the backbone of our empire" (16.1022), which draws rebuke from Skin-the-goat, who "considered no Irishman worthy of his salt that served" the British Empire (16.1024–25). An argument between the two men ensues. The text offers access to Bloom's opinions on the subject of Irish nationalism and the British Empire. He expresses admiration for Fitzharris because he had "brandished a knife, cold steel, with the courage of his political convictions," although he later remembers that Skin-the-goat "merely drove the car" and had not actually used a knife (16.1059, 1066). Bloom realizes that he himself was assaulted with exactly this sort of nationalist rhetoric this afternoon and tells Stephen about his encounter with the Citizen.

Bloom offers a statement of political philosophy: "I resent violence and intolerance in any shape or form. It never reaches anything or stops anything. A revolution must come on the due installments plan" (16.1099–1101). Citing historical evidence, Bloom rejects the specious arguments of anti-Semitism. Furthermore, he blames "the money question which was at the back of everything greed and jealousy" (16.1114–15) and goes on to espouse socialist policies of a universal basic income of £300 a year and the sense that all people should "live well . . . if [they] work" (16.1139–40). Stephen says simply, "Count me out" (16.1148), and Bloom scrambles to clarify that "literary labor" (16.1153) would be included in his scheme. Stephen offers a wholesale rejection of Irish nationalism and any form of servitude: "You suspect that I may be important because I belong to Ireland. . . . But I suspect that Ireland must be important because it belongs to me" (16.1160–65). Bloom is dumbfounded by this assertion, and Stephen grumpily "shoved aside his mug of coffee or whatever you like to call it none too politely, adding: 'We can't change the country. Let us change the subject'" (16.1169–71). This much-anticipated encounter between our two heroes isn't going very well, is it?

Bloom, though, has two purposes in continuing to seek unity with Stephen: "fear for the young man" (16.1179) and "to cultivate the acquaintance of someone . . . who could provide . . . intellectual stimulation" (16.1219–21). In short, he is worried about Stephen (for good reason), and Bloom, as an isolated middle-class armchair intellectual, is lonely. He waits out the awkwardness by skimming the newspaper.

He initially misreads and is startled by the name "H. du Boyes" because it looks a bit like "Hugh Boylan"; he sees the results of the Gold Cup, and he reads the notice of Paddy Dignam's funeral. A few details amuse him in the write-up of the funeral: his name is misspelled ("L. Boom"), Stephen's name is erroneously included, the typesetter got distracted and included some nonsensical text, and the mysterious M'Intosh makes his obligatory appearance in the episode. Stephen, yawning, breaks the silence by asking if Deasy's letter on foot-and-mouth made it into the paper. It did.

The text reminds us that Stephen's hand is hurt (16.1296); as previously suggested, he seems to have suffered a mysterious injury between the end of "Oxen" and the beginning of "Circe," perhaps in the altercation with Buck. The men in the shelter offer a further mystery related to Parnell being alive on the far side of the planet, poised to return. Like Elvis. Or Tupac. Further commentary on Parnell leads to the story of Bloom's brief personal interaction with him: Bloom "handed [Parnell] his silk hat when it was knocked off and he said *Thank you*" (16.1335–36). Skin-the-goat curses Kitty O'Shea for initiating Parnell's downfall, and the men in the shelter discuss the scandalous affair. You can draw parallels to Molly's affair with Boylan: both Kitty and Molly are half Spanish, and both Boylan and Parnell are depicted as "real m[e]n arriving on the scene" (16.1381–82). Given the events of this day, there is weight behind the question "can real love, supposing there happens to be another chap in the case, exist between married folk?" (16.1385–86). This question is central to the "Nostos" episodes as Bloom prepares to finally return home to Molly.

These reminders of his predicament raise the stakes on Bloom's encounter with Stephen (more on this in a moment), so Bloom produces from his pocket a photograph of Molly "in the full bloom of womanhood in evening dress cut ostentatiously low for the occasion to give a liberal display of bosom" (16.1429–30). Bloom presents his wife as a prominent singer but notes that the photo "did not do justice to her figure" (16.1445). He leaves the picture on the table for Stephen to "drink in the beauty for himself" (16.1458–59). Maybe Bloom uses the photo of Molly to elevate his status in Stephen's mind and entice him into friendship: "the vicinity of the young man he certainly relished," and Stephen "said the picture was handsome" (16.1476–79). Or perhaps Bloom is hoping to oust Boylan by bringing Stephen into a "matrimonial tangle" (16.1482) with Molly. Taking a bit more wholesome view of the hypothetical love triangle, Richard Ellmann conceives of Bloom, Molly, and Stephen as "a new, three-in-one being, a human improvement upon the holy family as upon the divine trinity"; making the correspondence explicit, Molly and the Virgin Mother Mary share their birthday on September 8.[12] Feel free to buy or sell any or all of these notions as you wish, but the topic of an extramarital relationship involving Stephen arises again in lines 1533–52, where the text considers "*liaisons* between still attractive married women . . . and younger men" where a wife "chose to be tired of wedded life and was on for a little flutter in polite debauchery" and "the aggrieved husband would overlook the matter." Taking these passages together, we can deduce that Bloom may have more in mind than simply providing Stephen with a stale bun and a bad cup of joe.

The story of Bloom recovering Parnell's hat is repeated, and Parnell's gracious tone in thanking him is compared favorably to that of John Henry Menton, "whose headgear Bloom also set to rights earlier in the course of the day" (16.1524–25), which you'll remember from the end of the "Hades" episode. Bloom worries over the waste of Stephen's time and talent with prostitutes who might give him an STD. He continues to misunderstand Stephen's woozy singing of "Who Goes with Fergus?" at the end of "Circe" for a love interest named "Miss Ferguson" (16.1559–60). He also returns to his concern over Stephen's diet and asks when he last ate; Bloom is "literally astounded" (16.1578) to learn that Stephen has not eaten since sometime on June 15. (But didn't Stephen eat some of the breakfast Buck prepared in the tower this morning? See 1.524). The text remembers younger Bloom's aspirations to a life in public service, but he ultimately rejects politics because of the "mutual animosity and the misery and suffering it entailed" (16.1600–1601).

Bloom, realizing it is "high time to be retiring for the night" (16.1604), contemplates whether or how to invite Stephen home with him. He remembers Molly's temper when he previously brought home a gimpy stray dog, and he acknowledges that Stephen has been "a shade standoffish" with him and might not "jump at the idea" (16.1614–16).

At the same time, he knows it is "too late for the Sandymount [Gould-ing home] or Sandycove [Martello tower] suggestion" (16.1611). So, considering the need for Stephen to find a safe place to lay his head and taking up the photo of Molly, Bloom offers Stephen some cocoa back at his place. While there is genuine altruism in Bloom's offer to Stephen, he also immediately begins planning ways of capitalizing on Stephen's tenor voice alongside Molly's soprano in "duets in Italian" and "concert tours in English watering resorts" (16.1654, 55). Bloom pays the bill, and the two men begin to leave the cabman's shelter. At the door, Stephen confesses to not knowing something: "why they put . . . chairs upside down on the tables in cafes," "to which impromp-tu the neverfailing Bloom replied without a moment's hesitation, say-ing straight off: 'To sweep the floor in the morning'" (16.1709–13). Point Bloom.

At Bloom's suggestion that a walk in fresh air will do Stephen well, the two men leave together, arm in arm. Note that Stephen has pre-viously rejected Cranly's arm and Buck's arm, but he accepts Bloom's, saying "yes" (16.1723). This affirmative word, "yes," will feature prom-inently later in the "Nostos." Finally finding union in each other, Ste-phen and Bloom walk home, "chatting about music" (16.1733) and Molly. Stephen sings a few bars, and Bloom silently imagines pairing Stephen with Molly in concert and facilitating Stephen's career. Fur-thermore, Bloom imagines the stir it would cause in town for Ste-phen to be hanging out with the Blooms at Christmastime. Clearly, Mr. Bloom is aware of the social capital he would gain through as-sociation with Stephen Dedalus, yet he seems genuinely to care for the young man and advises him to "sever his connection with a cer-tain budding practitioner" (16.1868–69), meaning Buck Mulligan. It's good fatherly advice. Joyce, though, always quick to subvert any-thing approaching sentimentality, sullies the romanticized notion of a Stephen-Bloom-Molly trinity by having a horse drop its own trinity of "three smoking globes of turds" (16.1876–77).

The episode concludes with the removed perspective of a driver watching this odd couple make their way north together. The lyricism and human warmth of this final image is worth savoring before we head into the cold of interstellar space in "Ithaca."

## Further Reading

Breuer, Horst. "Henry Flower Writes a Story." *James Joyce Quarterly* 47, no. 1 (Fall 2009): 87–105.

After providing a succinct survey of various narratological modes used in *Ulysses*, Breuer argues that the writer of "Eumaeus" is Henry Flower, Bloom's literary persona. Explained as a comic persona conjured by the arranger, Henry Flower accesses Bloom's interiority through free indirect discourse and is inclined toward embellishing Bloom's stylistic quirks, including his pretention to linguistic elegance and hackneyed clichés.

Lawrence, Karen R. "'Beggaring Description': Politics and Style in Joyce's 'Eumaeus.'" *Modern Fiction Studies* 38, no. 2 (Summer 1992): 355–76.

This essay explains how the style of "Eumaeus" reflects economic concerns of bourgeois productivity and sociopolitical tension in colonial Ireland.

Levine, Jennifer. "James Joyce, Tattoo Artist: Tracing the Outlines of Homosocial Desire." *James Joyce Quarterly* 31, no. 3 (Spring 1994): 277–99.

In addition to addressing the character of Murphy and his slanted parallels to Bloom, this essay illuminates the subtle but intricate network of homosexual innuendo in this episode. Levine also explores Bloom's pursuit of homosocial attachment in his encounter with Stephen.

# Chapter 17

# "ITHACA" GUIDE

The "Ithaca" episode continues the action of the novel more or less seamlessly from the end of "Eumaeus" (which itself is continuous from the end of "Circe"). The time at the start of the present episode is roughly 1:40 a.m. Mr. Bloom and Stephen Dedalus are walking north from the cabman's shelter to the Blooms' home on Eccles Street, a 0.8-mile walk that should take them roughly twenty minutes.

In *The Odyssey*, Odysseus has finally returned to his home on the rocky island of Ithaca. After revealing himself to his son in Eumaeus's hut, the heroes plan Odysseus's recapturing of his palace and assault on the suitors; he will remain disguised as a beggar until he strings his mighty bow and shoots an arrow through a dozen axes, proving his strength and precision.

The idea of precision is useful as we orient ourselves to the style of the "Ithaca" episode. In the schema, Joyce listed the technique for this episode as "catechism (impersonal)," a multivalent reference. Most obviously, the term "catechism" applies to the Catholic texts that use a series of questions and answers to define the theological and moral beliefs of the church, and Joyce's Jesuit education would have made him intimately familiar with this form of writing. Similarly influential, a catechetical or Socratic method of question-and-answer would have been central to the classroom instruction Joyce experienced in his late nineteenth-century schooling; indeed, "critics have proposed that the form of 'Ithaca' is directly indebted to Richmal Mangnall's

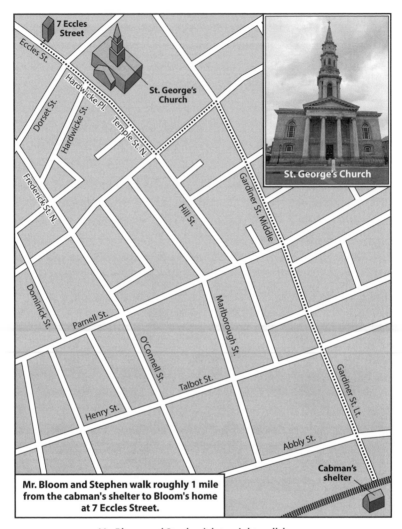

Mr. Bloom and Stephen's late-night walk home

*Historical and Miscellaneous Questions*, a textbook of encyclopedic knowledge which . . . was still in use in Joyce's day."[1] Back in the Clongowes section of *A Portrait*, young Stephen Dedalus even daydreams of being included in Mangnall's book of questions. Both of these types of catechism would have been formative to Joyce's intellectual development, and this meticulous form replicates Odysseus's precision with the bow and arrow.

But the episode also playfully pushes this precision to an absurd extreme, an over-the-top exactitude Hugh Kenner credits to Mr. Bloom's favorite weekly magazine, *Tit-Bits*: "each issue . . . contained a page called 'Tit-Bits Inquiry Column': answers to questions no one would have thought to ask."[2] More ironic than precise, the tongue-in-cheek *Tit-Bits* catechism also fits the "Ithaca" episode's intention to provide an appendix of facts, figures, and other information useful to our retrospective understanding of *Ulysses* while undercutting its own seriousness with obviously exaggerated specificity.

Like all of *Ulysses*, then, "Ithaca" elevates Bloom and Stephen into the sphere of timeless epic heroes while also exposing them as profoundly unexceptional. A. Walton Litz explains the effect of this tension well: "It is as if we were viewing Bloom and Stephen from a great height, against a vast backdrop of general human action and knowledge, while at the same time standing next to them and observing every local detail. It is this 'parallax' achieved by the macrocosmic-microcosmic point-of-view which gives the episode the grandeur and sweep that Joyce certainly intended."[3] It may be no surprise, then, that "Ithaca," which Joyce called the "ugly duckling of the book," was his "favourite episode" of the novel.[4] He felt that it had a "tranquilising spectrality" (*Letters* 176) and described it as "a mathematico-astronomico-physico-mechanico-geometrico-chemico sublimation of Bloom and Stephen" (*Letters* 164). The episode, on its face, has a cold, bare-bones feel (Joyce listed "skeleton" as the episode's organ in the schema), yet it is "supersaturated with Bloom's humanity, a humanity that is enhanced if anything by the impersonality of the prose."[5]

As we have seen in episodes such as "Oxen of the Sun," these revolutionary elements of form and style still must service the actions of plot. You may find it frustrating that the text retreats from the intimacy we once felt with Stephen and Bloom at the moment when we most desire access to their unfiltered inner monologues. What is Stephen thinking and feeling during this hour shared with Bloom? He seems to have warmed up to him enough to leave the cabman's shelter with him and head toward his home for further conversation, which is all the more remarkable given Stephen's years of self-imposed exile and rejection of any sort of union. From Bloom's perspective, after spending most of the day either alone or isolated (and, indeed, after spending many years in much the same condition), he finally has a companion. What sorts of Bloomian thoughts are running through his mind as Stephen engages with him? And, later in the episode, what does Bloom feel when forced to finally confront the reality of Molly's affair? Ever guarding against sentimentality, Joyce denies us access to these thoughts and feelings, except as filtered through the detached, academic precision of the voices of the interlocutor and the respondent. As Karen Lawrence writes, "'Circe' is the past served 'hot'; 'Ithaca' is the past served 'cold.'"[6]

Joyce conceived of "Ithaca" as a series of scenes, "and on the early typescripts he blocked out these scenes under the titles 'street', 'kitchen', 'garden', 'parlour', 'bedroom.'"[7] I will employ these same titles to orient our experience of the homecoming in "Ithaca."

## Street

Bloom and Stephen walk together and engage in a wide-ranging and apparently lively conversation. They move through the empty city streets along "parallel courses" (17.1), which means that, while they are aligned, Stephen and Bloom will never intersect.[8] We can therefore extrapolate the plot of "Ithaca" from these first few words of the episode: Bloom and Stephen are together, but their parallel trajectories make union ultimately impossible. But that subtle spoiler shouldn't stop you from relishing the opportunity to imagine the back-and-forth these two men share on the listed topics as they walk toward Bloom's home. While they don't agree on all points (both men are independent thinkers), they each admit to the "obtunding influence" (17.25–26) of attraction to women. With regard to the cause of Stephen's "collapse" a few hours earlier, Bloom blames alcohol and dancing; Stephen blames the cloud both men saw some seventeen hours earlier. I'll side with Bloom on this one. The text reveals that Bloom hasn't had this sort of friendly conversation very often in his life—and not at all since the death of Rudy in January of 1894. Bloom attributes this dearth of friendship to the simple fact that we have fewer friends as we age. He's not wrong, but this revelation of the extent and duration of Bloom's isolation only serves to illuminate his endurance of spirit and confidence.

Arriving at 7 Eccles Street, Bloom realizes that he does not have the key to his own home; however, he triumphs over the sort of paralysis that has been so thematically central to Joyce's work by devising "a stratagem" (17.84) that is both active (in solving the problem for himself) and passive (in avoiding a confrontation with Molly). He climbs over the railing at the front of the house, drops down to the basement level, and enters his home via the scullery (kitchen) door. Testifying to Joyce's careful verisimilitude, he inquired in a letter to his Aunt Josephine: "Is it possible for an ordinary person to climb over the area railings of no 7 Eccles street, either from the path or the steps, lower himself down from the lowest part of the railings till his feet are within 2 feet or 3 of the ground and drop unhurt?" (*Letters* 175). Joyce had witnessed his friend Byrne (the model for Cranly's character in *A Portrait*) accomplish this feat years before, but Byrne was an athlete. Bloom is not. That said, he isn't as pudgy as some readers might assume from earlier passages; we learn here that he is 5 feet, 9½ inches and 158 pounds. For context, the average height of men serving in the British military at the turn of the century was 5 feet, 4½ inches,[9] making Bloom notably tall for his era. Joyce intended for Bloom to grow in stature in the reader's mind here at the end of the novel.

### Kitchen

Once in the kitchen, Bloom lights a match, a gas flame, and then a candle. He then takes the candle to the front door and welcomes Stephen into his home. You might consider this moment to be the realization of Stephen's prophetic dream first recalled in "Proteus" (see 3.365–69). Having brought Stephen from Nighttown's "street of harlots" to the "open hallway" of 7 Eccles Street, Bloom is Stephen's "Haroun al Raschid"—an upright man of justice who promotes wisdom and enlightened thinking, a king who walks among commoners. Stephen, no longer the "fearful jesuit" (1.8) of the opening episode, is now "not afraid."

As Bloom lights the fire in his coal stove, Stephen thinks of other parental figures who have previously lit fires for him throughout his life. Bloom begins to fill the kettle with water, and the text provides an overprecise explanation of the water's municipal origins. In the subsequent ode to water, you may detect similarities between the qualities

Bloom admires in water and characteristics we have come to admire in Bloom himself: "independence," "persever[ance]," "solidity," "docility," and "utility" (17.189–222). Bloom washes his hands with his lemon soap and offers Stephen the tap to do likewise. Stephen refuses. We might again wonder if Stephen's hydrophobia goes back to being shouldered into the cold, slimy pond scum at Clongowes, or perhaps it signifies his rejection of his Christian baptism. Regardless, he hasn't had a bath since October (17.239), eight months ago. Pretty gross. Bloom refrains from lecturing Stephen on the virtues of hygiene and good diet, but the text offers Bloom's good advice regarding the "advantages" (17.277) of shaving at night. I challenge anyone to make an equally compelling case for shaving in the morning.

From a kitchen shelf bearing evidence of Boylan's visit this afternoon, Bloom takes a tin of Epps's cocoa powder. Among the other evidence of Boylan that Bloom observes (Molly didn't even bother to tidy up after Boylan left!), he focuses on the betting tickets from the Ascot Gold Cup and notes the race's impact on his day. Out of good hospitality, Bloom uses Molly's fine breakfast cream to make the cocoa, and he refrains from using his favored mustache mug, instead selecting "a cup identical with that of his guest" (17.563). Stephen drinks the "Epps's massproduct" (17.369), which suggests the Eucharist in the Catholic Mass. Stephen has for so long (and as recently as the previous episode) resisted any sort of atonement (eucharistic or otherwise), but he now adopts a posture of openness to Bloom's kindness. Stanley Sultan suggests that by drinking the cocoa, Stephen has finally "accepted the sacrament" and "thus, for the remainder of his presence in the novel, he talks freely, listens attentively, sings, and writes in Gaelic, showing ease, warmth, interest."[10] If you agree with this reading, then Stephen's encounter with Bloom is transformative.

The two men drink their cocoa in silence, Bloom "erroneously" assuming that Stephen is "engaged in mental composition" (17.383–84). Bloom "reflected on the pleasures derived from literature of instruction rather than of amusement as he himself had applied to the works of William Shakespeare more than once for the solution of difficult problems in imaginary or real life" (17.384–87). We can do the same with *Ulysses*. I myself have turned to this novel many times to help sort through a difficult life event, including the miscarriage of our first child and a close friend's father's suicide. This novel can indeed serve as "literature of instruction" of the highest order. Bloom then recalls two of his own poetic works—a limerick and a love poem. We learn that Bloom is thirty-eight years old and Stephen is twenty-two, but, with time, that "disparity diminish[es]" (17.451). The subsequent calculations related to their ages render them eternal, infinite.

We have a reprise of Stephen and Bloom's first meeting, described back in "Oxen" (see 14.1371–78). Five-year-old Stephen, unsure of Bloom, was "reluctant to give his hand in salutation" (17.469–70). Their second encounter, when Stephen was ten, seems to have established a connection between the two; Stephen invited Bloom to have dinner at the Dedalus home. Simon (awkwardly, we might imagine, even if graciously) "seconded" (17.474) his son's invitation. Bloom politely "declined" (17.476) this offer.

Bloom and Stephen compare notes on Mrs. Dante Riordan, a mutual acquaintance from long ago. You may recall that Dante was Stephen's nanny and featured in the Christmas dinner scene in *A Portrait*; she later lived in the same building as the Blooms (the City Arms Hotel) and died eight years ago. Recalling these moments from younger days prompts Bloom to think that maybe he has lost a step, so he considers getting back into the habit of working out, using Sandow's indoor exercise regimen. He's thought of doing so previously in the day, during both the "Calypso" and "Circe" episodes. We learn that he excelled in gymnastics back in high school owing to his "abnormally developed abdominal muscles" (17.523–24). Mr. Bloom had a six pack!

In a funny little riddle, we learn that "[Bloom] thought that [Stephen] thought that [Bloom] was a jew whereas [Bloom] knew that [Stephen] knew that [Bloom] knew that [Stephen] was not" (17.530–31). Or, the reading changes if Stephen knows that Bloom is not a practicing Jew, making it: "[Stephen] knew that [Bloom] knew that [Stephen] knew that [Bloom] was not." You can tinker with this puzzle for a while. We also learn the names of both men's parents and their respective histories pertaining to baptism. They were each baptized by the same man, "the reverend Charles Malone C. C.," and in the same place, "the church of the Three Patrons, Rathgar" (17.545–46). Malone performed Bloom's third and final baptism, marking his conversion to

Catholicism prior to marrying Molly. Bloom's first baptism was into the Irish Church, representing his father's conversion to Protestantism on immigrating to Ireland. His second baptism seems to have been performed by friends (or at least laypeople) using the sacred water from a natural well in Swords, a town just north of Dublin.

The text presents the gulf between their respective academic achievements: Bloom has a high school education, and Stephen has multiple university degrees. In terms of temperament, the text assigns Bloom "the scientific" and Stephen "the artistic" (17.560), although we also know that "there's a touch of the artist about old Bloom" (10.582–83). Along those artistic lines, Bloom's aesthetic principles in "the modern art of advertisement" consist of "maximum visibility," the ability for people to "decipher" meaning, and the "magnetising efficacy to arrest involuntary attention" (17.581–84). Advertising 101. He then compares the relative qualities of a few ads, some of which you might recall from earlier in the novel. For example, Bloom contemplated the Kino's trousers ad posted on a rowboat floating in the Liffey when he crossed O'Connell Bridge back in "Lestrygonians" (see 8.90). He abhors the insensitive placement of the Plumtree's Potted Meat ad beneath the obituaries in the newspaper. The two men share creative thoughts: Bloom explains his idea for a Hely's ad with two women writing in a showcart pulled through town, and Stephen offers a dramatic scene between a young man and a young woman in a firelit hotel lobby. The woman in this scene is writing "Queen's Hotel" over and over again on a sheet of paper, which triggers Bloom to think of his father's suicide in The Queen's Hotel in Ennis, County Clare. Stephen, feeling perhaps more open and at ease than we've ever seen him, then offers his "Parable of the Plums" (the same story he told to the newspaper guys at the end of "Aeolus").

The text then turns to Bloom's relationship with Molly. He contemplates activities they might enjoy together, catalogues examples of Molly's lack of education and knowledge, and presents his various efforts "to remedy this state of comparative ignorance" (17.693). Bloom and Stephen discuss "seeker[s] of pure truth" (17.716), and their Jewish and Aristotelian characters are bridged by Moses Maimonides, who sought to "reconcile Aristotelian reason and Hebraic revelation,"[11] as well as Aristotle himself, who, legend has it, "had been a pupil of a rabbinical philosopher" (17.718). They exchange snippets of songs in Irish and Hebrew and write out alphabetic characters from those languages on a blank second-to-last page in *Sweets of Sin*, the erotic book Bloom procured for Molly back in "Wandering Rocks." Bloom is careful to conceal the title of this lowbrow book from erudite Stephen. They continue to draw connections between the Irish and the Jews. As Hugh Kenner explains, "Each people had a racial identity, Semitic, Celtic; each had a minute homeland boasting sacred sanctions, each a history of being overwhelmed but not disappearing."[12]

After further regarding each other, and after Stephen finishes his cup of cocoa, Bloom encourages Stephen to sing a bit. Stephen does so, but his choice of song is curious. The "Little Harry Hughes" song tells an apocryphal anti-Semitic story of "Hugh of Lincoln, supposedly crucified by Jews c 1255."[13] Stephen's selection of this particularly objectionable song to sing in Bloom's home, especially as the two men seem to be getting along so well, is problematic. Perhaps it conveys a sense of Stephen's rising "suspicion and withdrawal."[14] Hugh Kenner suggests that Bloom's designs on Stephen as a surrogate son present a "danger" to Stephen's freedom and independence. "Bearing the danger in mind, we can understand why Stephen sings the ballad about the imperiled Christian boy in the Jew's habitation."[15] The role of "the jew's daughter" (17.813) in the song prompts Bloom to think about Milly in childhood and, now, in a budding romantic relationship with "a local student" (17.883), Bannon, down in Mullingar. As Bloom ponders Milly's departure into adulthood, he observes the departure of his cat. In light of these departures, and in one of the novel's most anticipated moments, Bloom invites Stephen to stay the night. Stephen "promptly, inexplicably, with amicability, gratefully" (17.955) says no, declining the offer in terms that echo Bloom's own refusal of young Stephen's dinner invitation a dozen years prior (see 17.475–76). Bloom then returns Stephen's money rounded up by a penny in a sort of reverse interest, making Bloom therefore the exact opposite of the archetypal usurious Jew. As Mark Osteen explains, this inverse interest amplifies the net result of the two men's encounter: "Bloom gives Stephen more than he got."[16]

But since Stephen won't stay with Bloom in his home, they negotiate "counterproposals" (17.960), arriving at a series of agreements and exchanges that are "truly reciprocal: each gives and each receives, creating an entirely new phenomenon out of their mutual relationship . . . , a balanced social exchange"[17]—that is, assuming these "counterproposals" are sincere. The questions and answers that follow suggest that this night's encounter between Stephen and Bloom is the end rather than the beginning of a relationship: the coin that Bloom marked never returned to him, and the clown was not Bloom's son. Likewise, Stephen will not return, nor is he Bloom's son. Or so the text implies. I don't want to burst Bloom's bubble.

Bloom reveals that he is often depressed by the failure of his optimism and large-scale ambitions to improve the world, but he finds solace "that as a competent keyless citizen he had proceeded energetically from the unknown to the known through the incertitude of the void" (17.1019–20). Bloomsday itself, then, is the cure for existential crisis.

## Garden

As Bloom leads Stephen out of the kitchen and into the garden/backyard, the text alludes to the biblical exodus of the Jews out of Egypt, the Christian vespers services, and the emergence out of hell into view of heaven's stars at the end of Dante's *Inferno*. The two men "confront" the night sky, and Joyce provides one of his most beautiful sentences: "The heaventree of stars hung with humid nightblue fruit" (17.1039). Prose simply doesn't get much better than that. Reaching that line alone might be enough to make all of your hours of effort and frustration in reading *Ulysses* feel worthwhile.

Meditations on constellations and planets follow. Joyce wrote in a letter that the effect of the "Ithaca" episode's cold, hyperrational style is that "Bloom and Stephen thereby become heavenly bodies, wanderers like the stars at which they gaze" (*Letters* 160). Sublime notions of the universe's vastness and our place within it bring Bloom back to his intention years ago to "square the circle," leading him to encounter ninety-nine to the ninth power, a number that would require "33 closely printed volumes of 1000 pages each of innumerable quires and reams of India paper" (17.1075–76) to represent in integers. In short, this project of Bloom's (like my own little project here in this book) is humbling. Astrological and astronomical ideas continue, and then the men notice a lighted lamp in the house, which reminds us of Molly's looming (no *Odyssey* pun intended) presence upstairs—and in the "Penelope" episode upcoming.

The two men share the intimate male bonding experience of peeing together outside; we learn that Bloom was a champion urinator in high school and remains thusly potent. While they relieve themselves, a shooting star streaks through the night sky. If you are inclined to read prophetic meaning into these sorts of celestial events, the fact that the star moves "towards the zodiacal sign of Leo" (17.1213) augurs well for Bloom. Bloom unlocks the back gate, the two men shake hands, and Stephen departs as the bells of St. George's chime twice, signifying 2:30 a.m. (see the notes to appendixes A and B for further explanation of these bell chimes). The two men mentally translate the sound of the bells just as they did at 8:45 a.m. this morning ("*Liliata rutilantium…*" and "*Heigho, heigho*"), which we might interpret to mean that neither character has been significantly changed from this encounter. Even for a reader trained in Joycean anticlimax, that would be a bummer. More positively, the text describes Stephen's "retreating feet" echoing in the empty street like the sound of a "Jew's harp," so his departure's "double vibration" (17.1243–44) could signify that the impact of these hours will reverberate within both men long after this night.

Any sense of closure or completion, however, is complicated by our curiosity over where, exactly, Stephen goes after leaving Bloom's house. I put this question to the Trinity College professor Terence Brown, who was kind enough to give twenty-three-year-old me an hour of his time when I showed up in his office back in 2006. Professor Brown suggested that, having encountered his subject, Stephen is off to write *Ulysses*. He may finally be prepared to forge in the smithy of his soul the uncreated conscience of his race. Bloom, meanwhile, is left "alone" and feeling "the cold of interstellar space" (17.1245–46). The text informs us that everyone else is either asleep or dead, so we are left alone with Bloom. And he is left, finally, with Molly.

## Parlour

Bloom takes a deep breath, walks through the garden, enters his home through the back door, and uses his candle to light his way through the kitchen, up the stairs, and into the front parlour. As he enters the parlour, he bonks his head on "a projecting angle" of "the walnut sideboard" (17.1285), which has been moved during the day. Indeed, since Bloom left home this morning, much of the furniture in this room has been rearranged, apparently by Boylan and Molly. In the new locations of the two chairs, Bloom finds "circumstantial evidence" (17.1300–1301) of the afternoon's tryst. Molly's infidelity, like the keyboard of the piano, is "exposed" (17.1303).

Like Odysseus, Bloom burns incense to cleanse his home of its impurities. The text notes the presence of three wedding gifts on the mantel: a clock, a dwarf tree, and an embalmed owl. We/Bloom might be heartened by these reminders that he and Molly are bound together by fifteen years of marriage, but we/he might also be disheartened by the fact that the clock hasn't worked since 1896, the tree's growth has been stunted, and the owl is dead. Here, we appreciate that ever since the "Epiphanies," "it was Joyce's unique gift that he could turn the substance of ordinary life into something like myth, not only through the use of 'parallels' and allusions but through direct transformation."[18] These wedding gifts, while merely the stuff of normal life, are infused with elegant meaning by Joyce's art.

Bloom then looks at himself in the mirror. A riddle—"*Brothers and sisters he had none / Yet that man's father was his grandfather's son*" (17.1352–53)—emphasizes that he is patrilineally alone. Seeing his reflection, Bloom notes that he (like most men) increasingly resembles his father as he ages. He also observes his bookshelf in the mirror, and his personal library is catalogued. You might discern from these titles the origins of thoughts and interests that Mr. Bloom has expressed over the course of the day. Bloom undresses, feels his bee sting, and finds in his waistcoat pocket a shilling coin left from his attendance of Mrs. Sinico's funeral back in October (readers of *Dubliners* will remember her death in "A Painful Case"). This coin prompts the text to "compile the budget for 16 June 1904" (17.1455).

In examining this ledger, you may immediately note some inaccuracies: the 11 shillings Bloom spent in Bella Cohen's brothel are entirely omitted, and the 1 shilling cost of a chocolate bar seems massively inflated. The expense of at least one tramfare or train fare also seems to be missing; if we assume that he arrived at the Holles Street Maternity Hospital via tram from Sandymount, then the budget omits the late-night train fare from Westland Row Station to Amiens Street Station en route to Nighttown with Stephen et al. We might be surprised and/or frustrated to find errors within this budget—which should be an objective artifact—within an episode and a novel so exacting in its details. Mark Osteen suggests that Joyce here is prompting the reader to become the bookkeeper (so to speak) as we read and reread *Ulysses*; it is as if Joyce is teasing us, like he's saying, "This isn't quite right, is it? Well, go on, reread the book and fix it for me." But "like Bloom's budget, the reader's [budget] will leave gaps; the book can never be fully balanced or ended, because perfect balance would mark the end of bookkeeping, the end of reading."[19] And I, for one, don't ever want to be finished reading this novel.

There are a few coincidences to be found in the budget. Most notably, Bloom's commission received from the *Freeman's Journal* earlier today is exactly the same as the payment Molly will earn from the upcoming concert tour (a detail we take from a snippet of Boylan's call with his secretary back in "Wandering Rocks" [see 10.392]). "This concealed symmetry again typifies the balancing impulse that pervades 'Ithaca'; more importantly, it suggests an equality of earning power between the Blooms that is manifest in a 'balance of power'" within their marriage.[20]

Bloom takes off his boots, picks off a "protruding part of the great toenail" (17.1489), and takes a whiff. The smell oddly reminds him of his lifelong "ultimate ambition" (17.1497) to own "a thatched bungalowshaped 2 storey dwellinghouse" (17.1504–05) in the countryside. The text describes this dream house, "Bloom Cottage" (17.1580), as well as the idealized Mr. Bloom who might live there in "Flowerville," all in great detail and to humorous effect. One aspect of this vision involves Bloom serving as "justice of the peace" (17.1610) to neighboring "county families and landed gentry" (17.1606–07). This role suits Bloom because of his "innate love of rectitude" (17.163), which the text demonstrates by listing a history of his religious and political affiliations.

The text pivots then to how Bloom might pay for such a home, which prompts the presentation of a series of entrepreneurial ideas, some of which we encountered previously in Bloom's conversations or thoughts over the course of the day. Many of these notions are ingenious, including taking advantage of the time difference between the site of the Ascot Gold Cup in England (Greenwich time) and in Dublin (Dunsink time) to learn the result of the race and place bets accordingly. Other ideas are downright prescient, especially those related to renewable energy, mixed-use real estate development, riverboat tourism, and streamlining the transportation of goods for improved access to a global economy. These are million-dollar ideas. Or, he could always just discover "a goldseam of inexhaustible ore" (17.1753).

Regardless, Bloom has always found it helpful to think about these sorts of big projects prior to getting in bed because doing so "alleviated fatigue and produced as a result sound repose and renovated vitality" (17.1757–58). He appropriately values the quality of his slumber because we spend two-sevenths of our life asleep; he fears sleepwalking his way into suicide or murder. His final thoughts before bed each night often focus on creating the perfect ad. The man is devoted to his craft.

The text then examines the contents of Bloom's drawers. The first drawer contains a hodgepodge of sentimental and ignominious items: Milly's childhood drawing notebook, photos of Queen Alexandra (wife of Edward VII) and Maud Branscombe (actress and beauty), a Christmas card, some office supplies, a sandglass, a sealed note with Bloom's prediction of the effects of an 1886 Home Rule bill (which was never actually passed), a bazaar ticket, a letter from young Milly, heirlooms from each of his parents, the three previous letters from Martha Clifford along with her name and address in code, an article on "corporal chastisement in girls' schools" (17.1802–03), a pink ribbon, two condoms, coins and lottery tickets from the Austro-Hungarian Empire, two pornographic photocards, an article on restoring old boots, a collector's stamp of Queen Victoria, a chart with Bloom's body measurements before and after beginning Sandow's exercises (which would suggest that, while Bloom's workout routine yielded positive results, he is oddly proportioned, or else Joyce didn't get these numbers right), and a prospectus for the Wonderworker, a product claiming to mitigate rectal complaints. Bloom adds today's letter from Martha Clifford to this drawer, and the text nudges us in algebraic terms to discover her identity.[21] Good luck.

Bloom is pleased to think that a few women have found him attractive today: Josie Breen, Nurse Callan, and Gerty McDowell. The second drawer contains official documents, including his birth certificate (his middle name is Paula!), a life insurance policy, a bank statement, a certificate pertaining to his possession of Canadian government bonds, and papers related to his purchase of a burial plot at Glasnevin Cemetery. From these documents, we can discern Bloom's relative wealth. His bank account balance of £18 14s. 6d. (17.1862–63) represents nearly half a year of Stephen's wages as a teacher and is equivalent to around US$5,500 today. Bloom has also invested in Canadian bonds (17.1864), generating annual income of £36—roughly US$10,800 today—more than enough to cover the £28 annual rent for 7 Eccles Street.[22] In short, we learn that Bloom is in pretty good shape financially. Again, his stature grows here at the end of the novel.

The second drawer also contains some family items, such as a public notice of his father's official name change from Virag to Bloom, a daguerreotype of his father and grandfather taken in Hungary in 1852, a Jewish text for the Passover Seder, and his father's suicide note. Phrases from this note pass through Bloom's mind, prompting him to feel some "remorse" (17.1893) for disrespecting Jewish laws and customs in his youth. He also recalls his father telling him at age six the story of the displacement and wandering that took him from Hungary, through Austria and Italy, into England, and finally to Ireland; however, the text tells us that years and distraction have "obliterated the memory of these migrations" (17.1916) in Bloom's mind, which raises some questions about the voice and intelligence behind this episode's questions and answers. In some passages, the interrogator as well as the respondent seem to have access to Bloom's mind, but it seems here that at least the respondent has some measure of omniscience that transcends what Bloom knows or remembers. Elsewhere, the respondent is limited to Bloom's perspective and knowledge.

Some of Bloom's father's "idiosyncrasies" (17.1921) pertaining to forgetfulness are listed, including neglecting to take off his hat at the table, lifting and tilting his plate to drink his melted ice cream, and using torn bits of paper as a napkin. Since we are aware of Bloom's own "idiosyncrasies," we might feel like those listed here are small potatoes. Examples of Mr. Bloom Sr. showing his age include nearsightedly counting coins by hand and by belching after a meal. Regardless, Bloom feels consoled by the evidence of his own financial solvency:

"the endowment policy, the bank passbook, the certificate of the possession of scrip" (17.1931–32).

The text catalogues various impoverished sorts of people, beginning with his own first job as a "hawker of imitation jewelry" (17.1937) and progressing through various other unfortunate figures we have encountered over the course of the day. The "indignities" (17.1948) suffered by these people include being ignored by women and former friends, being barked at by stray dogs, and having rotten vegetables thrown at them. If Bloom were to find himself in this sort of destitution, he would prefer to leave rather than commit suicide. As the text goes on to consider the possibility of Bloom's "departure" (17.1958), we might acknowledge here that the style and voice of this episode frustrate our desire for understanding; clearly, we have lots of questions we'd like answered by this point in the novel, but the interrogator of "Ithaca" doesn't often ask the right questions, nor does the answerer always respond directly or satisfactorily. Hey, but if Bloom were to disappear, somebody could earn £5 by supplying "information leading to his discovery" (17.2005). Good to know.

If Bloom were to leave, he would represent the trope of the Wandering Jew to an extreme by eternally traversing the cosmos. For now, Bloom decides against departure because it is impractical (too dark and dangerous at this hour of night) and because he would rather get into bed with Molly. Prior to Bloom's getting up and going to the bedroom, Bloomsday is thoroughly but briefly "recapitulate[d]" (17.2043) in biblical terms and in chronological order. In an allusion to *The Odyssey*, when Zeus offers a thunderclap to signal his approval of Odysseus stringing his bow and thereby revealing his return home, Bloom's wooden table emits a "loud lone crack" (17.2061). The universe approves of Bloom's return and decision to stay.

The mystery of the man in the brown macintosh makes its final appearance (sorry, no resolution), and Bloom lists the day's other loose ends, failures, and unfinished business: the Keyes ad renewal hasn't been finalized, he was hoping to get some free tea from Tom Kernan, he was unable to determine the anatomical realism of the Greek goddess statues in the National Museum, and he did not see the performance of *Leah*.

## Bedroom

Bloom quietly enters his bedroom carrying his clothes, and the face of his late father-in-law pops into his mind. The next passage is fascinating but a bit tricky to decipher: "what recurrent impression of the same were possible by hypothesis?" (17.2084). If we understand "the same" to refer to Major Tweedy, then this answer implies that Bloom has watched his father-in-law leave and return via train. If we understand "the same" to refer simply to "an absent face," then perhaps Bloom is still thinking about Stephen. Details from the rest of this passage contribute to this reading: the Amiens Street train station is where Bloom began following Stephen "along parallel lines" (17.2086) to Nighttown, and you'll remember that the first line of this episode described Bloom and Stephen's "parallel courses" (17.1). So, the "hypothesis" of *Ulysses*: what would happen if someone like Stephen Dedalus met someone like Leopold Bloom? The examination of Joyce's hypothesis (i.e., the study of this novel) will go on to "infinity" (17.2086).

Bloom notices Molly's clothes discarded on the trunk at the foot of their bed and glances around the room at other objects, including a wobbly commode. He finishes undressing, puts on his "long white nightshirt" (17.2111), and, finally, gets into bed with simultaneous caution and reverence. He notices that Molly changed the sheets prior to Boylan's visit, but she did not clean the bed afterwards, leaving "some crumbs, some flakes of potted meat, recooked, which he removed" (17.2124–25). In the mattress, he feels "the imprint of a human form, male, not his" (17.2124), and he is amused to think that Boylan "imagines himself to be the first to enter whereas he is always the last term of a preceding series" (17.2127–28). The text then supplies a list of men included in this "preceding series" (17.2132), but the criteria of this list is unclear: perhaps these men are all of Molly's former lovers? Suitors? Men who have at one time or another been sexually attracted to Molly? Hugh Kenner describes it as "a list of past occasions for twinges of Bloomian jealousy, and there is no ground for supposing that the hospitality of Molly's bed has been extended to anyone but her husband and Boylan."[23] This list of twenty-five men indicates that Bloom is aware of much of Molly's romantic life, but, as "Penelope" will reveal, he doesn't know everything.

Concerning Boylan, Bloom efficiently labels him as "a bounder," a "billsticker," "a bester," and "a boaster" (17.2145–46); he then reflects on his "antagonistic sentiments" (17.2154) toward this usurper. He feels "envy" over Molly and Boylan's sexual intercourse and "jealousy" over the fresh attraction Molly feels toward this other man. More nuanced, Bloom is affected by "abnegation" or self-denial, implying that he will refuse to confront Boylan for a few reasons: their "acquaintance" (17.2170) and interactions around town, an awareness of racial tension, and a reluctance to disrupt Molly's music tour (in part because of its prospective financial success). Most Bloomian, he feels "equanimity" (mental calm) in accepting extramarital sex as a "natural act of a na-ture expressed" (17.2178), no worse than any number of other illicit behaviors. In terms of "retribution" (17.2200), he will not take violent action, but he leaves open the future possibility of divorce, exposure, lawsuit, and blackmail. Bloom may seek to build his own advertising agency to rival Boylan's shop, and he may introduce Stephen to Molly as a "rival agent of intimacy" (17.2207–08). He justifies these feelings to himself in terms of biology and the grammatical flexibility of the word "fucked." He possesses elevated views pertaining to "the futility of triumph" (17.2224) given "the apathy of the stars" (17.2226) toward infinitely small human dramas. If we are holding Bloom's return home in correspondence to Odysseus's gruesome slaughter of his rivals, this section demonstrates Joyce's recasting of the hero as a figure of empa-thy, enlightened thinking, and endurance.

As a reward for these progressive attitudes, Bloom's "antagonistic sentiments" are "reduced" and "converge" into a feeling of "satisfaction" (17.2227–29). After all, isn't that simply a better way to feel? As Bloom said back in the "Cyclops" episode, "Force, hatred, history, all that. That's not life for men and women, insult and hatred. And everybody knows that it's the very opposite of that that is really life.... Love" (12.1481–85). When he kisses Molly's bottom, itself described as a promised land "red-olent of milk and honey" (17.2232–33), Bloom chooses love.

Molly rouses from sleep and asks Bloom about his day. He tells her about everything except his correspondence with Martha Clifford, his confrontation with the Citizen, his encounter with Gerty MacDow-ell, and (we assume) his visit to Nighttown. He lies and tells her that he saw *Leah* and that he ate supper after the performance at Wynn's

Hotel, where he met Stephen Dedalus, who "emerged as the salient point of his narration" (17.2269). As Bloom and Molly speak, both are aware of the fact that they have not had "complete carnal intercourse" (17.2278) since five weeks prior to Rudy's birth; it has therefore been more than ten years since Bloom has ejaculated inside Molly. Adding to the distance within their marriage, Bloom and Molly have not had "complete mental intercourse" (17.2285) since nine months ago, when Milly had her first period, which bonded Milly to Molly. Since that time, Bloom has felt limitations on his "liberty of action" (17.2291–92) and has been "interrogated" (17.2294) each time he left the house; in short, his wife and daughter have been pestering him.

The text zooms out again to a sublime, elevated perspective as Mr. Bloom and Molly are positioned on the planet and moving through the cosmos. Bloom is "weary" (17.2319) from his travels—justifiably so! It has been a really long day. In a fun, final flourish, the text alludes to Sinbad the Sailor, an Odysseus-styled hero in *One Thousand and One Nights* (as well as in a popular Dublin pantomime) who returns home at the end of each of his adventurous voyages. Stanley Sultan identifies the rhymed companions with whom Bloom/Sinbad has traveled as "the sailor, W. B. Murphy; the tailor, his friend George Mesias, in whose shop he met Boylan; the jailer, Alf Bergan, the court clerk; the nailer, Corny Kelleher, the undertaker; the failer, Simon Dedalus; the bailer, Martin Cunningham, who twice during the day saved him from predicaments; the hailer, Lenehan; the railer, the Citizen; the 'phthailer,' a friend who died from 'phthisis.'"[24] The allusion continues with the roc, an enormous mythical bird; in one story, Sinbad finds a huge roc's egg with a circumference of fifty paces.[25]

The answer to the episode's final question, a large dot, might not appear as Joyce intended in your edition of the novel. This is how it should look:

Where?

•

There are many interpretations of this dot. Maybe it is the roc's egg. Perhaps it is a massive period, indicating the endstop to Bloomsday and serving as a counterpoint (literally) to the absence of punctuation in "Penelope." A. Walton Litz suggests that the dot is Bloom, "the manchild in the womb" (17.2317–18), "from which he shall emerge the next day with all the fresh potentialities of Everyman," making this "final moment of 'Ithaca' both an end and a beginning."[26] The dot could also be Molly's anus, near which Bloom's head rests.

Or, in keeping with Joyce's project, the • is the Earth viewed from space: tiny and unimportant despite the massive effort this novel has exerted toward convincing its readers that every day is a universe all its own. In the end, the paradoxical "square round" (17.2328) *Ulysses* is the novel's demonstration of Mr. Bloom's simultaneous significance and insignificance—Joyce's mystical fusion of the eternal and transient qualities of human life.

## Further Reading

Crispi, Luca. "The Genesis of Leopold Bloom: Writing the Lives of Rudolph Virag and Ellen Higgins in *Ulysses*." *Journal of Modern Literature* 35, no. 4 (2012): 13–31.

 Crispi uses a genetic approach (examining Joyce's writing process across different manuscripts) to trace the development of Bloom's parents as characters through a network of details added throughout the text that accumulate to the understanding presented in this essay.

Norris, Margot. "Stephen Dedalus's Anti-Semitic Ballad: A Sabotaged Climax in Joyce's *Ulysses*." *European Joyce Studies* 18 (2009): 65–86.

 This essay questions the reliability of the narrative voice in "Ithaca" and examines the ethical and narrative effects of Stephen's singing of the "Little Harry Hughes" song in Mr. Bloom's kitchen.

Plock, Vike Martina. "'Object Lessons': Bloom and His Things." *James Joyce Quarterly* 49, no. 3/4 (Summer 2012): 557–72.

 This essay discusses Bloom's participation in the exchange and movement of objects in *Ulysses* as a function of the world defining him. By contrast, analysis of the objects catalogued in "Ithaca" reveals Bloom's attempts to define the world and his means of mediating his emotions.

Rubenstein, Michael D. "'The Waters of Civic Finance': Moneyed States in Joyce's *Ulysses*." *NOVEL: A Forum on Fiction* 36, no. 3 (Summer 2003): 289–306.

 This essay examines in postcolonial and economic terms the "water hymn" and the coin Bloom releases into circulation for possible return.

# Chapter 18

# "PENELOPE" GUIDE

Our odyssey through Bloomsday has always been journeying toward Molly's perspective, delivered in "Penelope" unfiltered and with minimal interruption. The promise of hearing from her in the final episode has been a motivating interest, pulling us through the novel; she seems certain to provide the last piece of the puzzle. Joyce referred to Molly and her monologue as "the indispensable countersign to Bloom's passport to eternity" (*Letters* 160). Sure enough, we can spend an eternity reading this novel and this episode in particular, experiencing the text differently each time. In typical Joycean fashion, "Penelope" will confound our desires for closure and satisfaction, but it guarantees a life's worth of interesting moments to scrutinize.

Some readers of "Penelope" will find Molly offensive. D. H. Lawrence described the episode as "the dirtiest, most indecent, obscene thing ever written."[1] Its obscenity contributed to *Ulysses* being banned for more than a decade after its initial publication in 1922. Mary Colum, a friend of Joyce's, denounced "Penelope" as "an exhibition of the mind of a female gorilla."[2] While that description seems harsh toward Molly, the audacity of a man attempting to represent Woman (much less any individual woman) was roundly rejected in early feminist reactions to the text. Many thought that Joyce had misunderstood and misrepresented the female mind and perspective. Indeed, Molly Bloom herself visited Joyce in dreams, castigating him for "meddling" in her business.[3]

Or, maybe Joyce was a protofeminist, presenting Molly as a sexually liberated woman with freely expressed desires and the agency to speak and do as she wishes. In later criticism, scholars began to recognize a shared purpose between feminism and Joyce's literary efforts to expose and disrupt the patriarchal conventions of literature and representation,[4] and some even considered Molly's soliloquy the paragon of *écriture féminine*, a style whereby language "is fluidly organized and freely associative. Thus, it has the capacity to both reflect and create human experience beyond the control of patriarchy."[5] In this view, "Penelope" opens the door to new postpatriarchal literary forms.

Outside of feminism, scholars have shifted their reading of Molly in each generation. In the 1920s, she was deemed obscene. In the 1930s, scholars seeking to canonize *Ulysses* refrained from criticizing her vulgarity "for fear that in impugning Molly's reputation, they would tarnish Joyce's."[6] Instead, they described her as an idealized force of Nature, a Gaia earth-mother-goddess, and avoided her sexuality. Once Joyce had been safely canonized, it became possible for critics in the 1950s and 1960s to attack Molly's sensuality and label her a "whore," reflecting a larger post-WWII antifeminist reaction.[7] Then, in the 1970s and 1980s, poststructuralists couched her "language, desire, and even her very subjectivity" as products of "her historical formation."[8] To be sure, you can take a deep dive into the scholarly efforts to define Molly Bloom.[9] I myself got a bit lost in this rabbit hole while preparing to write this Episode Guide, and I could have happily spent much longer weighing opinions about this fascinating character. But my project here is to support you as you complete your reading of *Ulysses*. I will reference various scholars' ideas where relevant in this guide, but I intend to focus primarily on the text itself.

So, let's review what we, as readers of *Ulysses*, know about this woman. A thirty-three-year-old soprano of local fame, Molly Bloom has been married for fifteen years to Leopold Bloom, with whom she has had two children: a daughter, Milly, who just turned fifteen yesterday, and a son, Rudy, who died in infancy a decade ago. Marion "Molly" Tweedy was born and raised in Gibraltar because her father, Major Brian Tweedy, was stationed there as a soldier in the Royal Dublin Fusiliers unit of the British military. On this day, June 16, 1904, she received breakfast in bed from her husband and tossed a coin to a beggar. She has been a frequent topic of conversation among various men around town. In the late afternoon, Molly engaged in extramarital sex with Hugh "Blazes" Boylan, the man who is managing her upcoming concert tour of Belfast and Liverpool.

In *The Odyssey*, Penelope has waited faithfully for twenty years for her husband's return from the Trojan War, spending the last four years or so rebuffing more than one hundred suitors seeking her hand in remarriage. Under this pressure, she devises an ingenious plan to delay her selection of a new husband: she claims, citing tradition and decency, that she must weave a funeral shroud for her father-in-law prior to remarrying. She works at her loom all day, and then each night secretly unweaves her work from the previous day. Just as Penelope, in her cleverness, is a perfect match for Odysseus, we might consider Molly and Leopold Bloom well-suited to each other in their shared characteristics of sensuality, sensitivity, and charity.

The "Penelope" episode consists of eight "sentences" separated by paragraph breaks. There is no punctuation in the final version of the text, although "much of the punctuation was deleted only in the proofs, after most of her well-formed sentences had been constructed."[10] In many ways, Molly's flowing stream of consciousness is unique in all of literature. Joyce wrote that "Penelope has no beginning, middle or end" (*Letters* 172), and he listed in the schema ∞ as the hour for this episode. This symbol has a variety of possible meanings: first, it represents infinity; it is also an "8" lying on its side, indicating the eight sentences that make up the "Penelope" episode. The symbol could also depict the image of Molly, a curvy woman, lying in bed.

There's an anecdote pertaining to the composition of "Penelope" that might support the notion of the episode lacking a beginning, middle, or end. Robert McAlmon, an American poet and socially popular member of the 1920s expatriate community in Paris, was out drinking with Joyce one night and casually volunteered to type fifty pages of the "Penelope" episode. In his memoir *Being Geniuses Together*, McAlmon explains the ordeal:

> The next day [Joyce] gave me the handwritten script, and his handwriting is minute and hen-scrawly; very difficult to decipher. With the script he gave me four notebooks, and throughout the

script were marks in red, yellow, blue, purple, and green, referring to phrases which must be inserted from one of the notebooks. For about three pages I was painstaking, and actually retyped one page to get the insertions in the right place. After that I thought, "Molly might just as well think this or that a page or two later, or not at all," and made the insertions wherever I happened to be typing. Years later I asked Joyce if he had noticed that I'd altered the mystic arrangement of Molly's thought, and he said that he had, but agreed with my viewpoint.[11]

Funny, subversive, and revealing, McAlmon's account suggests the absence of order and arbitrary design of Molly's soliloquy.[12] On this point, Maud Ellmann suggests that "'Penelope' is a dangerous supplement in that it undermines the sense of an ending; an opening rather than a closure."[13]

In contrast, Stanley Sultan claims that "Penelope" "has structural integrity and a meaningful development because through it, from beginning to end, Molly *arrives at* her attitude. . . . The chapter is a debate within her mind."[14] She begins with a problem (does she still love Bloom?) and, after engaging this question from innumerable angles, she reaches a resolution (Yes). In this reading, "Penelope" has a clear beginning (question), middle (processing), and end (answer), and this problem/resolution boils down to one paradigmatic question: will Molly satisfy her husband's request for breakfast in bed?

## Sentence 1

This topic (Bloom's breakfast request) is exactly where Molly's thoughts begin in the first sentence. She notes that Poldy "never did a thing like that before as ask to get his breakfast in bed" (18.1–2). Something has changed. Whether Bloom has decided, in the aftermath of Molly's extramarital escapade, that the time has come to assert himself, or whether "his request for breakfast may be just what it appears to be, an expression of fatigue after a late night,"[15] the request demands Molly's attention.

She can only recall Bloom making a similar request years ago when he was milking an illness while they lived in the City Arms Hotel, where Mrs. Riordan (Dante from *A Portrait*) also lived. As suggested earlier in the novel, Bloom sought to ingratiate himself to Mrs. Riordan in hopes of receiving something in her will, but those efforts came to naught. Molly draws a sharp contrast between Mrs. Riordan's sort of woman ("too much old chat in her about politics," "down on bathingsuits and lownecks," and "pious" [18.7–11]) and her own attitude ("let us have a bit of fun" [18.8–9]).

Molly admires a few of Bloom's positive attributes: "polite to old women like that and waiters and beggars too hes not proud" (18.16–17). But she doubles back to roll her eyes at him, imagining that he would flirt with a nurse if he were to get sick and have to spend time in a hospital. You might also note Molly's generalizations about men as she says that "theyre so weak and puling when theyre sick they want a woman to get well" (18.23); this tendency to lump all men together will persist throughout her monologue, causing some confusion because we can't always easily discern to whom she refers when she says "he." She accuses Bloom specifically of being a bit dramatic: "if his nose bleeds youd think it was O tragic" (18.24).

She also reveals that she is aware of more than Bloom knows, including his porn stash and the fact that "he came somewhere" (18.34). Noting his appetite as evidence, she correctly deduces that her husband is not in love with this other woman. She suggests that maybe he had sex with a prostitute in Nighttown and discredits Bloom's report of the day as "a pack of lies" (18.37). She's more than half right in these suppositions.

As we begin to orient ourselves in the prose style that represents Molly's thoughts, we might think of the ∞ symbol listed in the schema as also depicting the pattern of Molly's thinking: her mind circles around a topic; then, after the natural interruption of other thoughts, it twists upon itself and returns to the initial thought. Applying this idea to the previous passage, we note that Molly begins with her assumption that Bloom had sex at some point in his day, turns to considering his story of the day to be a ruse "to hide it" (18.37), and is distracted by Bloom mentioning John Henry Menton, a former suitor of Molly's, whom she remembers unfavorably. Then, she returns to the initial idea that Bloom "came somewhere" (18.34) with "one of those night women" (18.36) "or else if its not that its some little bitch or other he got in with somewhere or picked up on the sly" (18.44–45).

We are able to assemble the complete thought as it circles, twists, and winds back to itself (∞) over the course of these ten lines. That will be the case throughout the episode, and you may find following her thoughts to be circuitous in requiring you to keep going back a few lines and rereading as you piece together the full idea. Sorry.

Molly recalls walking in on Bloom writing a letter and how "he covered it up with the blottingpaper pretending to be thinking about business" (18.48–49). She correctly suspects that Bloom is corresponding with another woman (whom we know to be Martha Clifford), but she is mistaken in assuming that this is the same woman with whom Bloom "came" (whom we know to be Gerty MacDowell). She claims that "1 woman is not enough for them" (18.60) after remembering Bloom's flirtation with Mary Driscoll, the Blooms' former housekeeper, whom Molly dismissed for stealing oysters (and for lying about it). Remember that Ms. Driscoll also appeared in a "Circe" fantasy to accuse Bloom of inappropriate behavior.

Returning her attention to her hypothesis regarding Bloom's sexual activity, Molly notes that "the last time he came on my bottom when was it the night Boylan gave my hand a great squeeze . . . I just pressed the back of his like that with my thumb to squeeze back singing the young May moon shes beaming love" (18.77–80). First, it is important to note that while Molly and Bloom have not had "complete carnal intercourse" (17.2278) together since Rudy died, they still have sex, but Bloom pulls out at the end. They minimize the chances of getting pregnant again for fear of losing another child. Next, the most recent occurrence of their sort of sex was over two weeks ago, the night Boylan and Molly gave each other surreptitious hand squeezes. Bloom observed this exchange and remembered many of the same details back in "Lestrygonians": "She was humming. The young May moon she's beaming, love. He other side of her. Elbow, arm. He. Glowworm's laamp is gleaming, love. Touch. Fingers. Asking. Answer. Yes" (8.589–91). So, Molly knows that Bloom knows and that he stayed away from the house all day because "hes not such a fool" (18.81). Also, Molly reveals that Bloom told her, "I'm dining out and going to the Gaiety" (18.81–82) in their final conversation before he left home this morning.

Molly contemplates seducing a young man, remembers some early encounters with men as a newcomer to Dublin, and thinks of unsatisfactory sex. She seems to minimize her affair with Boylan, saying that "its done now once and for all . . . why can't you kiss a man before going and marrying him first" (18.100–103). Molly reveals how much she enjoys a good kiss. She thinks about confession and briefly fantasizes about embracing a priest.

She turns her curiosity to Boylan. She wonders whether Boylan "was satisfied with [her]" but takes offense at "his slapping [her] behind" (18.122). She wonders if Boylan is awake right now thinking about her, or whether he's asleep dreaming about her (actually, he might still be at Bella Cohen's if that was indeed him entering the brothel at the end of "Circe" . . . which would answer her question regarding his satisfaction). Molly, like the barmaid in "Sirens" (see 11.366), then wonders where Boylan got the red carnation "he said he bought" (18.125)—we saw him *take* the flower flirtatiously from the fruit shop back in "Wandering Rocks" (see 10.328). She wonders about the drink she smelt on him, but we know it was sloe gin (see 11.350). It's fun to have answers to Molly's questions; Joyce here rewards us for our good reading.

She thinks of the exhausting afternoon of lovemaking. We notice the third valence of the "potted meat" (18.132): (1) a food product, (2) a buried corpse, and now (3) sexual intercourse. She and Boylan had multiple rounds of sex—"he must have come 3 or 4 times" (18.143). Boylan is well-endowed "with that tremendous big red brute of a thing" that resembles "some kind of a thick crowbar standing" (18.144–48); indeed, Molly says, "I never in all my life felt anyone had one the size of that to make you feel full up" (18.149–50); some readers use this thought as evidence of Molly's promiscuity.

After hours of vigorous sex and with a belly full of food and port, Molly fell immediately to sleep after Boylan left, but she was startled awake by the loud crack of thunder that boomed around 10:00 p.m., during the "Oxen" episode. Remember that the text there described it "as the god self was angered for his hellprate and paganry" (14.411). It scares Stephen, but the men continue their carousing unabated. Molly, however, responds appropriately: "God be merciful to us I thought the heavens were coming down about us to punish us when I blessed myself and said a Hail Mary" (18.134–36). She is a believer, and she feels guilt, but will she, like the men in the hospital, continue her sinful behavior?

She took measures to prevent Boylan impregnating her, making him pull out each time except the last, and thinks about the unfairness of women having to bear children while men enjoy the fun of sex without the consequences. She considers "risk[ing]" (18.166) having another child (but not with Boylan). She assumes Boylan would produce "a fine strong child" (18.167), but she notes that "Poldy has more spunk in him" (18.168). Point Bloom.

Molly again considers Bloom's assumed sexual activity today and "suppose[s] it was meeting Josie Powell and the funeral and thinking about me and Boylan set him off" (18.169–70). She knows that Josie Powell (now Breen) and Bloom "were spooning a bit when I came on the scene" (18.171), and she wonders if maybe they are now rekindling that old flame behind her back. Molly has confidence, however, that she could easily win Bloom back: a light touch with her gloves on and "1 kiss then would send them all spinning" (18.190–91) out of Bloom's mind.

We get a brief snippet of a political argument they had years ago where it seems Bloom cited Jesus as "the first socialist" (18.178). She remembers the early days of her relationship with Bloom and how "he was very handsome at that time trying to look like Lord Byron . . . though he was too beautiful for a man" (18.208–10). You might again recall Weininger's theory, a popular turn-of-the-century notion regarding gender gradience. She returns to thinking about Josie and how Molly would, under the guise of friendship, "make [Josie's] mouth water" (18.216) with details about Bloom. Josie kept her distance after the Blooms married. She compares Josie's "dotty husband" (18.218), Denis Breen, who "used to go to bed with his muddy boots on" (18.222–23), against Bloom, who "always wipes his feet on the mat" (18.226). She claims she would "rather die 20 times over than marry another of their sex" (18.231–32), which we can read either as a condemnation of all males or a recognition that Bloom is the only man for her. She feels that "hed never find another woman like me to put up with him the way I do" (18.232–33): not exactly gushy, but it is a nicer picture of a happy couple than the stuff about Mrs. Maybrick (a wife who poisoned her husband because she was in love with another man) that concludes this first sentence.

## Sentence 2

Despite Molly's generalizations about men, she begins the second sentence by recognizing that "theyre all so different" (18.246) in their tastes and fixations. Boylan apparently has a foot fetish. She recalls their first encounter at the D. B. C. (Dublin Bread Company), how Boylan stared at her feet, and how her outfit that day made it difficult to use the restroom. She left her suede gloves in the women's room there. She plans to "stick" (18.261) Boylan for a birthstone ring and a gold bracelet. She recalls some of Bloom's "not natural" (18.268) requests involving stockings and boots.

Then, Molly delves into the memory of her fling with Bartell d'Arcy, a tenor who kissed her (and perhaps did more with her . . . it isn't entirely clear). Bloom lists d'Arcy as one of Molly's suitors back in "Ithaca" and thinks of him earlier in the day: "Bartell d'Arcy was the tenor, just coming out then. Seeing her home after practice. Conceited fellow with his waxedup moustache" (8.181–82). Molly suggests that she will tell Bloom about d'Arcy someday and "show him the very place too we did it" (18.280–81); again, we don't know exactly what "it" refers to here, but there's a spiteful tone in this thought. She notes that "he thinks nothing can happen without him knowing" (18.281–82), which we will see is untrue in the case of a man named Gardner, though perhaps not in the case of d'Arcy.

Molly teases that "he hadnt an idea about my mother till we were engaged" (18.282–83), introducing Molly's mom as one of the episode's mysteries; we know a thing or two about Molly's dad, Major Brian Tweedy, but knowledge of her mother, "whoever she was" (18.846), is shadowy. Later in the episode, we learn that her name was Lunita Laredo (18.848) and that Molly got her "eyes and figure" (18.890–91) from her. We also learn that Molly is "jewess looking after [her] mother" (18.1184–85). If Molly's mom was Jewish, that would make Molly more of a Jew than Bloom, based on the Jewish tradition of matrilineal descent.

She thinks about Bloom's fixation on ladies' undergarments and how he can't help himself from looking, as we have seen throughout the day. Molly then recalls an early encounter with suave Bloom "looking slyboots" (18.296–97) in a new raincoat, a brown hat, and a brightly colored scarf "to show off his complexion" (18.296)—she seems to appreciate his sense of style here. While perhaps simultaneously aroused and weirded out as she satisfies Bloom's fetish for underwear early in their courtship, she finds his "splendid set of teeth" (18.307) attractive and was "dying to find out was he circumcised" (18.313–14). She condemns Bloom as a "Deceiver" (18.318) because he suggested she lie to her father in order to stay out later with him, but she then remembers the love letters Bloom wrote her, and she "liked the way he made love" (18.328); her attitude toward Bloom is mercurial. Clearly, she is processing what she currently thinks of him and how she wants to proceed with the relationship.

She appreciates Bloom's talent for kissing, but she compares him unfavorably to the way a man named Gardner embraced her. Gardner does not appear in Bloom's list of suitors, and Molly seems to have had a serious relationship with him relatively recently. Gardner will appear in her thoughts again later, where we learn that he left to fight in the Boer War, meaning that this affair occurred sometime between 1899 and 1902. Gardner is a secret about which Bloom seems totally unaware. As Robert Boyle suggests, "Joyce here deliberately introduces a theme of mystery, faintly analogous to his use of the man in the macintosh, to keep us uncertain about Molly's sexual background."[16]

She shifts her focus back to Boylan, hoping "hell come on Monday" (18.332). She admits that she was nervous that Boylan was going to stand her up. She clarifies that it was indeed her arm back in "Wandering Rocks" that threw a coin down to the one-legged sailor. She thinks ahead a week to the trip to Belfast and is grateful that Bloom can't come along (because he is going to Ennis to honor the anniversary of his father's death). She is also glad not to travel with Bloom because he does awkward stuff, like the time he ordered soup at a train station and then sloshed it while eating it as he walked down the platform and made a scene refusing to pay the waiter until he finished it. She wonders if Boylan will pay for them to travel in first class and whether he will want to have sex on the train. She ponders "elop[ing]" (18.373) with Boylan.

After thinking about Bloom's problematic associations with the Freemasons and Sinn Fein, Molly thinks again about her lover Stanley Gardner and their "hot" (18.393) kiss goodbye as he left for South Africa, where he died of fever.

Her thoughts return to Boylan, whose "father made his money over selling the horses for the cavalry" (18.403), a rumor we also heard back in the "Cyclops" episode. She anticipates that Boylan "could buy me a nice present up in Belfast after what I gave him" (18.404), which at least hints of prostitution. She plans to remove her wedding ring for the trip in order to avoid trouble from the press or the police. She contemplates the ergonomics of intercourse with Boylan and appreciates his expensive sense of style. She recalls Boylan's angry fit over losing £20 in the Gold Cup because he followed the tip given by Lenehan, who Molly remembers "making free with [her] after the Glencree dinner" (18.427) in starkly different terms than Lenehan himself recalled the encounter back in "Wandering Rocks" (see 10.551–77). She notes another of her suitors, Val Dillon.

But back to the Gold Cup for a moment. We might read the race as an analogy for Bloom (the dark horse outsider, Throwaway) competing against Boylan (the phallic favorite, Sceptre).[17] Boylan/Sceptre never had a chance of winning the race for Molly because cuckolding Bloom has only pricked the side of the rightful husband to change the dynamics of the relationship, giving Bloom license to abandon his passivity and his craving for forgiveness over the death of Rudy. In other words, having been cuckolded, Bloom now paradoxically feels empowered to assert himself as Molly's husband in a way that she will find attractive, and Molly will again choose Bloom over any number of other suitors, including Blazes Boylan.

Still, she begins her mental packing list for the trip with Boylan, which apparently won't need to include many pairs of underwear (per Boylan's preference). She plans to buy a new corset and considers cutting out "the stout at dinner" because her "belly is a bit too big" (18.450) but doesn't want to "overdo it the thin ones are not so much the fashion" (18.456). She thinks about soft skin and wonders if Bloom got her lotion made up at Sweny's (we know he did but forgot to pick it up). She complains that she has "no clothes at all" (18.470).

She mistakes her age, saying she will "be 33 in September" (18.475) when she will in fact turn thirty-four. She weighs examples of age and beauty and recalls an apocryphal story involving a chastity belt and an oyster knife. She thinks censorship is bullshit, and the size of baby Jesus in nativity scenes is out of scale. She's not wrong.

Molly turns her focus to Bloom's career, taking a dim view of his work as an advertising agent and wishing he'd take an office job "where hed get regular pay" (18.505). She again questions his masculinity, "wish[ing] hed even smoke a pipe like father to get the smell of a man" (18.508–09) and thinks about women's fashion in clothing and hats. She laments that Bloom lost his job with Cuffe's cattle traders and recounts her efforts to get him reinstated, which were unsuccessful despite Mr. Cuffe "looking very hard at [her] chest" (18.529).

## Sentence 3

Molly's breasts remain her focus as she begins the third sentence of the soliloquy, describing their featured role in the tryst with Boylan. She compares the beauty of the female form to a man's "two bags full and his other thing hanging down" (18.542–43)—hard to argue with her here. She reveals that Bloom suggested that she "could pose for a picture naked" (18.560) when he was unemployed and they were strapped for cash.

She recaps the morning, including Bloom's unsuccessful teaching of "met something with hoses" (18.665) (metempsychosis) and his burning of the pan before turning attention back to her breasts, their ample provision of milk, and Bloom's desire to "milk [her] into the tea" (18.578). Pretty weird, even for Bloom.

Molly thinks about the sex she had with Boylan, and it seems like she enjoyed his roughness at least as a novelty. That said, she ultimately seems not to prefer Boylan's style of lovemaking, saying "theyre not all like him thank God" (18.591); however, she does tick off the days until their next planned encounter, silently exclaiming, "O Lord I cant wait till Monday" (18.595). Her attitude is difficult to decipher, even for Molly herself. She is processing.

## Sentence 4

The fourth sentence begins with an onomatopoeia of a train whistle in the distance (one of very few intrusions of the physical world into Molly's thoughts). She intends to continue decluttering the house and thinks the rain that fell around 10:30 p.m. "was lovely and refreshing" (18.606).

Her thoughts turn to Gibraltar, where she spent her childhood, and recalls the heat, sun, and dramatic geography of the rock. She considers the Spanish bullfights to be brutal and notes the impracticality of women's clothing. Central to this sentence, Molly fondly remembers her close childhood friendship with Hester Stanhope. With the exception of Hester and the Dillon sisters, Molly seems to have had very few female friends in her life. Hester taught her how to do her hair and comforted her in a storm. Molly mentally reproduces the text of a postcard she received from Hester after she left Gibraltar with her husband, whom Hester calls the pet name "wogger" (18.624). Molly notes that Mr. Stanhope "was awfully fond of me" (18.624) and "was attractive to a girl in spite of his being a little bald intelligent looking disappointed and gay at the same time" (18.648–49). She recalls an occasion when their "eyes met [she] felt something go through [her] like all needles" (18.646); while she lost sleep over the excitement of this experience of sexual awakening, she refrained from participating in this love triangle because "it wouldnt have been nice on account of her" (18.651–52). Molly's loyalty to Hester reveals a side of her character that throws the events of this afternoon into relief.

The physical world intrudes as she adjusts the heavy blanket and remembers her shift getting "drenched with the sweat stuck in the cheeks of my bottom on the chair" (18.662–63) and how muggy and buggy the air was in Gibraltar. Molly then recalls Hester's emotional farewell and how her life in Gibraltar "got as dull as the devil after they went" (18.676) with only cannons, guns, and soldiers. She was so lonely and bored that she resorted to sending herself letters "with bits of paper in them" (18.699), which she compares to her boredom now. Molly questions the alleged superior intelligence of men and then returns to the topic of letters, noting that Milly sent a letter to Bloom but only a card to her. The last letter she received was from her old friend Floey Dillon (now Mrs. Dwenn), who was writing from Canada to ask for a recipe and to boast of her marriage to a "very rich architect . . . with a villa and eight rooms" (18.721). Molly remembers Floey's father, Mat Dillon, as "an awfully nice man" (18.722); he is listed in "Ithaca" as one of Molly's suitors. In an honest appraisal of her own lack of sympathy, Molly dislikes hearing other people's "poor story" (18.725); indeed, she has always struggled even to spell the word "sympathy" correctly ("symphathy" [18.730]).

She returns to the topic of letters, hoping Boylan will write "a longer letter the next time" because the one he sent this morning "wasnt much" (18.731, 735). She is clearly affected by textual correspondence, asserting that a good letter "fills up your whole day and life always something to think about every moment and see it all round you like a new world" (18.738–39). She has a literary inclination despite her lack of access to formal education. In a statement that reveals her loneliness, Molly "wish[es] somebody would write [her] a loveletter" (18.731), and she ends this sentence with a fairly dark opinion that "as for being a woman as soon as youre old they might as well throw you out in the bottom of the ashpit" (18.746–47).

Notice that Molly doesn't think about Bloom in the entirety of the fourth sentence.

## Sentence 5

The fifth sentence continues the focus on letters and returns to memories of Gibraltar, recalling that "Mulveys was the first" (18.748) love letter she received; she treasured this secret admirer note, keeping it "inside [her] petticoat bodice all day reading it up in every hole and corner" (18.765–66). This man, Lieutenant Mulvey, was also Molly's first kiss and perhaps her first love. She teased him, telling him that she was engaged to "the son of a Spanish nobleman named Don Miguel de la Flora" (18.773–74), and she appreciates the coincidence of her eventual marriage to a man named Bloom (like flora). She also bashes her Spanish housekeeper, Mrs. Rubio.

Molly vividly remembers these first sexual experiences with Mulvey. While they came close to having intercourse, she refrained for fear that he would "leave [her] with a child" (18.801–02); she gave him a hand job instead. She thinks about the vagina. She also thinks about the penis. She wonders whether Mulvey is "dead or killed or a captain or admiral . . . perhaps hes married" (18.823, 826). She zigzags through gender tropes, first affirming women's superior consistency of character, then taking pleasure that Mulvey's hypothetical wife "little knows what I did with her beloved husband before he ever dreamt of her" (18.827–28). She dismisses a bishop's sermon on "womans higher functions" (18.838). Molly pivots from Mulvey to Bloom, expressing her preference for the name Bloom over a variety of other names. That positivity toward Bloom is short-lived, though, as she thinks, "or suppose I divorced him Mrs Boylan" (18.846).

She returns to memories of Mulvey and the gold/opal/pearl ring he gave her before departing for India. She, in turn, gave this ring to Gardner as he left for the Boer War, where he died. She notes that Mulvey was clean-shaven whereas Gardner had a mustache and then hears the train again in the distance.

Molly dismisses Kathleen Kearney (from the *Dubliners* story "A Mother") and other women as a "lot of sparrowfarts skitting around" (18.879). We might again note that she doesn't currently seem to have many (if any) female friends. She is proud of being an army brat; she is confident in her physical appearance; she asserts that she "knew more about men and life when [she] was 15 than theyll all know at 50" (18.886–87); and she is, after all, a talented singer. In evidence of these boasts, she thinks of her English paramour Gardner's fixation on "her mouth and teeth smiling" (18.888) and her "lips" (18.892). Her competitive attitude toward other women reaches its pinnacle: "let them get a husband first thats fit to be looked at and a daughter like mine or see if they can excite a swell with money that can pick and choose whoever he wants like Boylan to do it 4 or 5 times locked in each others arms or the voice either" (18.892–96). In other words, she is proud of Bloom, Milly, and Boylan as monuments to her superiority over other Dublin women.

She thinks of the program and her attire/accessories for the upcoming concert tour, feels an itchiness down below, and then eases out a fart slowly so as not to wake Bloom (whose head, remember, is by her bottom). The fifth sentence ends with the negative thought that she "wish[es] hed sleep in some bed by himself with his cold feet on me give us room even to let a fart God" (18.905–06). If you are charting her attitude toward Bloom, we are in a downslope.

## Sentence 6

The sixth sentence opens with a few concerns: was the pork chop she ate spoiled? Is the lamp smoking? She also expresses recurrent anxiety about leaving the gas on. She remembers a particularly cold winter back in Gibraltar. Realizing that she's not going to fall back to sleep, Molly expresses some measure of loving concern for her husband, hoping "hes not going to get in with those medicals leading him astray," yet her derisive next phrase, "to imagine hes young again," complicates that concern (18.925–26). In this same way, Molly appreciates Bloom's "manners" (18.927) in not waking her when he came in, but she shakes her head at men staying out late drinking. As you've surely figured out by now, Joyce is never going to make anything straightforward.

For the first time since the very beginning of her monologue, Molly returns to Bloom's request for breakfast in bed, and, by characterizing it as Bloom "giving us his orders . . . like the king of the country" (18.930–31), she seems resentful. As previously mentioned, we can track her thoughts about serving Bloom his breakfast in bed as indicative of her attitude toward Bloom and the future of the marriage overall. When her flush of irritation recedes, she thinks of Bloom first with bemusement over him "pumping the wrong end of the spoon up and down in his egg wherever he learned that from" (18.932–33) and then in terms of endearment, thinking "I love to hear him falling up the stairs of a morning with the cups rattling on the tray" (18.933–34). Notwithstanding the initial negative tone of the thought, these relatively quick shifts in attitude lead eventually to "love," which is promising.

Molly expresses curiosity about their cat, echoing Bloom's thoughts at the outset of the "Calypso" episode. She considers buying some fish today (now Friday) and then imagines a picnic with Boylan and Bloom and "some other woman for him who Mrs Fleming" (18.947). Mrs. Fleming is the old woman who helps around the house; she cleans, darns socks, and so forth, and she isn't particularly good at her job. Assuming Molly intends Boylan for herself and Mrs. Fleming for Bloom, the positivity from the previous thought has faded. She thinks about Bloom's bee sting on Whit Monday (May 23, 1904) and then expresses her annoyance over Poldy posing as a competent boatman, nearly causing them to capsize. A wife fussing at a clumsy husband in a rowboat strikes a funny image. Less funny, she thinks that she should "flagellate [Bloom] till he was black and blue do him all the good in the world" (18.963); little does she know how much Bloom might agree (if we accept his fantasies in "Circe" as genuine).

She thinks poorly of Pisser Burke (the source of gossip cited by the Nameless One in "Cyclops") and wonders about *Sweets of Sin*, the book Bloom brought home for her. She doesn't like tall men, she forgot to bring salt for good luck into 7 Eccles when they moved, and she expresses some fear of "being alone in this big barracks of a place at night" (18.978). This thought continues, worrying over Bloom leaving her home alone all day and a beggar/tramp "put[ting] his foot in the way to prevent" Molly from shutting the door (18.989–92). She supports capital punishment. She has low confidence in Bloom's ability to protect her against a burglar or assailant, but he's "still better than nothing" (18.999). Interrupting this thought, she expresses little faith in Bloom's various grand plans. She first rejects his idea to turn their spare room into "Blooms private hotel" (18.981), especially since Bloom's father undertook a similar venture down in Ennis. She calls B.S. on all the promises Bloom made to her and her father during their courtship regarding livelihood and international travel.

Molly turns her focus to Milly, contending that Bloom sent her to learn the photography business in Mullingar to get her out of the house "on account of me and Boylan thats why he did it Im certain the way he plots and plans everything out" (18.1007–09). Milly was thriving academically and socially in Dublin, but she was getting in Molly's space a bit before she left. Molly takes a cynical view of Milly's close relationship with Bloom, assuming Milly is only "pretending" and being "sly" (18.1018–19). Molly asserts that Milly would come to her for help rather than Bloom "if there was anything wrong with her" (18.1021). Molly comments on Milly's popularity and conveys some mother-daughter tension over attire and posture. She thinks about sex, claiming that she "never came properly till [she] was what 22 or so it went into the wrong place" (18.1051). Note that she married Bloom when she was 18 years old. She considers the rarity of "real love" (18.1056) and attributes Bloom's father's suicide to the widower feeling lost after the death of his wife. Molly notes that Milly knows "shes pretty with her lips so red" (18.1065–66), but Molly gave her daughter "2 damn fine cracks across the ear" (18.1070–71) for ignoring her and Bloom at a major Dublin social event. Superstitious, Molly also got angry with Milly for "leav[ing] knives crossed" (18.1075). She blames Bloom for not being more firm with Milly and for not hiring a "proper servant" (18.1080).

She links Bloom bringing home a stray dog to him bringing home Stephen Dedalus last night. She mocks Simon Dedalus's pretension: he wears a "tall hat" but has a "great big hole in his sock" (18.1089). She scoffs at Bloom climbing over the railing because he didn't have the key and thinks about him and Stephen in "the dirty old kitchen" (18.1094). She sighs that "shes going such as she was on account of her paralysed husband getting worse" (18.1099–1100) — I think this refers to Mrs. Fleming leaving the housekeeping position, but I'm not entirely sure.

For those readers wishing the prose of "Penelope" had periods, Molly has hers. She is annoyed, especially since it will likely disrupt her plans with Boylan on Monday afternoon. Scholars have different readings of the onset of Molly's period. Practically, it "makes it impossible that her intercourse with Boylan will have any consequences [and] significantly alters the tone of her discourse and modifies her relationship first to Boylan and then to Bloom."[18] Metaphorically, "in allowing Molly to menstruate at the end Joyce consecrates the blood in the chamberpot rather than the blood in the chalice. . . . [Joyce] produces living human characters, not ethereal ones. It is human blood, not divine."[19] In addition to confirming that Boylan did not impregnate Molly, the arrival of her period "symbolizes as well the end of a cycle of much greater duration,"[20] meaning the cycle of Bloom's desire for forgiveness over the death of Rudy and Molly's desire for a more assertive husband.

She recalls having her period begin one night while in a box at the Gaiety Theater with a "gentleman of fashion staring down at me with his glasses" (18.1113–14); this guy appeared in Bloom's list of suitors (see 17.2132–42). She counts menstruation among other problems of womanhood, including "clothes and cooking and children" (18.1130).

Molly's final thoughts of the sixth sentence refocus on the afternoon with Boylan. The word "jingling," which in "Sirens" signified Boylan's traveling to 7 Eccles in a jaunting car, here describes the noise made by the loose quoits of the bed as they had sex. She prefers having sex in the afternoon, thinking, "Is it nicer in the day I think it is" (18.1133). Molly worries if she was "too heavy sitting on his knee" (18.1138) and whether her "breath was sweet after those kissing comfits" (18.1140–41), but she is confident "he never saw a better pair of thighs" (18.1144–45). She expresses that she "wouldnt mind being a man and get up on a lovely woman" (18.1146–47).

## Sentence 7

The seventh sentence opens with Molly's past and present gynecological concerns and reviews of various doctors. She remembers the "mad crazy letters" Bloom wrote her early in their relationship, saying that they aroused her to the point that "he had me always at myself 4 and 5 times a day sometimes" (18.1176, 1179). She remembers "the first night ever we met . . . we stood staring at one another for about 10 minutes as if we met somewhere" (18.1182–84). Sounds like love at first sight.

She recalls Bloom's politics in favor of home rule; it seems he was eloquent and presentable enough for some people to suggest "he was going to stand for a member of parliament" (18.1186–87). She notes Bloom's various odd habits, including him "sleeping at the foot of the bed" (18.1199), and recalls them visiting the National Museum together to see a statue of a Hindu god. Noticing that Bloom is "sleeping hard" (18.1208), Molly again assumes that he visited a prostitute. She doesn't initially seem particularly bothered by this thought, but she later determines to "knock him off that little habit" (18.1234).

She counts their many addresses over the course of their marriage and seems frustrated that Bloom is unbothered by being repeatedly "on the run" (18.1218). She also lists his jumpy employment history, as well as various reasons for his trouble: selling Hungarian "old lottery tickets" and associations with "Sinner Fein or the freemasons" (18.1225, 1227).

The peal of St. George's church bells signifies that it's 2:45 a.m., "a nice hour of the night for him to be coming home at" (18.1232–33). She condemns all men as "deceitful" (18.1236) and thinks "they ought to get slow poison the half of them" (18.1243). On this negative thought, her mind returns to Bloom's request for breakfast: "tea and toast for him buttered on both sides and newlaid eggs I suppose Im nothing any more" (18.1243–44). If breakfast is the bellwether for the marriage, it doesn't look good at the moment.

She rebuffed Bloom's desire to perform oral sex on her because "he does it all wrong" (18.1249), causing Bloom to pout. She wonders if, rather than seeing a prostitute, maybe Bloom had sex with Josie: "no hed never have the courage with a married woman" (18.1253–54). Instead, she decides "yes its some little bitch hes got in with" (18.1256) and recalls catching Bloom "throwing his sheeps eyes" (18.1259) flirtatiously at two young attractive women.

She thinks about Dignam's funeral, offering brief, scathing commentary on each attendee. Just as we felt protective of Bloom when he was among this cohort of men earlier in the novel, Molly states "theyre not going to get my husband again into their clutches if I can help it making fun of him then behind his back" (18.1275–77). Setting Bloom apart from these "goodfornothings" (18.1279), she commends Bloom for his moderation and responsibility. Along these lines, she worries about the Dignams.

She recalls the night Ben Dollard borrowed a too-tight tux from the Blooms' secondhand clothing and costume shop—remember that this same event was recalled twice in "Sirens." She knocks Simon Dedalus for being often drunk and singing the wrong verse, but she affirms that he had "a delicious glorious voice" (18.1294). She remembers performing with Simon, notes that he is now a widower, and wonders about his son, Stephen, from whom she is apparently slated to receive Italian lessons.

She remembers previous encounters with Stephen. First, ten years ago, while she was mourning the death of Rudy, Molly saw preteen Stephen with his parents; so, like Bloom, she initially links Stephen to Rudy. She also remembers seeing young Stephen at Mat Dillon's, where Bloom also met him (see 17.467). The difference, of course, is that Stephen shyly refused to shake Bloom's hand, whereas Molly claims that young Stephen "liked me" . . . but, then again, "they all do" (18.1313).

Molly then realizes that Stephen appeared in her tarot cards this morning: "union with young stranger neither dark nor fair you met before" (18.1315). She had initially misinterpreted this stranger to be Boylan, but now she realizes that the cards meant Stephen; Stephen is replacing Boylan in her mind, just as Bloom had designed. She also had a dream involving poetry. Wondering whether she is "too old for him" (13.1328), she tries to figure out Stephen's age (and comes within a year or two). She imagines becoming Stephen's muse. She prefers the idea of conversing with Stephen over hearing Bloom talk about ads. She conflates Stephen with a nude statue and contemplates fellatio, idealizing Stephen as "so clean compared with those pigs of men" (18.1356). Of course, we know from "Ithaca" that Stephen hasn't bathed in eight months (not so clean). She is attracted to the idea of seducing Stephen and plans to use her tarot cards again in the morning to see if he appears again. She intends to learn enough poetry to impress Stephen and plans to expand his horizons sexually. The seventh sentence concludes with her imagining an affair with Stephen and the scandal it would cause.

## Sentence 8

In a signal that Molly's mental processing has led finally to a rejection of Boylan, the eighth and final sentence opens with her using the word "no" (18.1368) five times. Not only is Boylan an "ignoramus that doesnt know poetry from a cabbage" (18.1370–71) (and is therefore inferior to Stephen), but he also has "no manners" (18.1368) (and is therefore inferior to Bloom). Molly also amplifies the umbrage she expressed in the first sentence at Boylan "slapping us behind" (18.122, 1369). In short, Boylan is "vulgar" (13.1373). As Molly has exhaustively weighed Bloom's many failings and virtues, she is realizing that "as compared with Boylan, her husband is the more complete man."[21] She reprises her attraction to the female figure and her jealousy over "the amount of pleasure [men] get off a womans body" (18.1380). In a Weiningerian moment, she says, "I wished I was [a man] myself for a change" (18.1381). She attacks double standards, decides "theyre not going to be chaining [her] up" (18.1391), and claims that her desires are natural and she "cant help it if [she's] young still" (18.1398–99).

She expresses frustration that Bloom doesn't embrace her often enough, and she doesn't like him kissing her bottom. In a wonderfully ambivalent line, she calls Bloom "a madman nobody understands his cracked ideas but me" (18.1406–07); the depth of their connection outweighs her annoyance by his quirks. But then she goes back to her desire to be embraced and fantasizes that she might "pick up a sailor off the sea" (18.1411–12), although she does worry about being assaulted or picking up an STD. She recalls catching a man just leaving a "filthy prostitute" (18.1424). She thinks again of her tarot cards from this morning and how Bloom appeared "in some perplexity" and "in prison" (18.1429–30), which feels accurate to the day we spent with him. She circles back indignantly to the prospect of "slooching around down in the kitchen to get his lordship his breakfast" (18.1431–32) and scoffs "will I indeed" (18.1432). That's the big question. Indeed, will she?

She aligns herself with difference feminism in the vein of Mary Daly, arguing that "itd be much better for the world to be governed by the women in it" (18.1434–35), highlighting the importance of motherhood (and suggesting, rather insightfully, that the death of Stephen's mother is the reason "hes running wild now" [18.1442]). Thoughts of Stephen bring her back to their own lack of a son, the death of Rudy, and the impact of that loss on the marriage. Echoing Bloom's thoughts back in "Lestrygonians" (see 8.608–12), she thinks "we were never the same since" (18.1450). She sandwiches these thoughts about Rudy between thoughts about Stephen, reframing the young man as an object of maternal instincts rather than of sexual desire.

She envies Bloom's ability as a man to go out and "have friends" (which we know is a bit of a mischaracterization of Bloom's social life). She attributes her own lack of friendships to her thought that women generally are "a dreadful lot of bitches" (18.1456, 1459), which complicates a reading of Molly as a feminist. She thinks about the Spanish language, Gibraltar, and the idea of Stephen living in Milly's now vacant room. She considers getting "red slippers like those Turks" (18.1495), corresponding coincidentally with Bloom's dream remembered back at the end of "Nausicaa": "Dreamt last night? Wait. Something confused. She had red slippers on. Turkish" (13.1240–41). This unwitting willingness to fulfill Bloom's dream leads to her final decision regarding Bloom's request for breakfast: "Ill get up early in the morning . . . I might go over to the markets . . . Ill throw him up his eggs and tea in the moustachecup . . . I suppose he'd like my nice cream too" (18.1498–1506). Not only will she accede to Bloom's request; she'll run errands for him and give him something special of her own. "Furthermore, she accepts the implications of her compliance, that getting his breakfast is giving him 'one more chance' to be her proper husband."[22] Hooray! All's well!

Not so fast. She will leave "the mark of [Boylan's] spunk on the clean sheet" (18.1512); she claims, "Its all [Bloom's] own fault if I am an adulteress" (18.1516), and she threatens to "bulge [her bottom] right out in his face" (18.1521). No. All is not well.

Forgetting her period for a moment, she imagines having sex with Bloom. She plans for Stephen coming by and imagines singing and playing piano with him. Then, flowers and nature fill her mind.

She vividly recalls Bloom's marriage proposal on Howth Head, echoing so many of the details in Bloom's own recollection back in "Lestrygonians" (see 8.900–916) with the addition of Bloom's lovely wooing words. Complicated as ever, Molly "liked him because [she] saw he understood or felt what a woman is and [she] knew she could always get round him" (18.1578–80). She thinks of other men and Gibraltar in the midst of recalling Bloom's proposal. She thinks of her first kiss with Mulvey and then transfers the passion of that young love to Bloom as she focuses entirely on her husband in these closing thoughts. All the way back in "Calypso," Molly's first spoken word in *Ulysses* is an obscure "no," but, in a shower of nineteen yesses in the final thirty-five lines, she gets the final word on Bloomsday: a wholehearted, unequivocal, capital "Y" "Yes."

Whether you feel uplifted or downcast at the conclusion of Molly's soliloquy, you can take solace in the notion that if you don't like the ending, all you have to do is read the book again and it'll be different. I've completed at least fifteen readings of this novel, and the ending elicits a different emotional response each time. Reading "Penelope" and writing about it for you now, I feel joy and fulfillment in the remote hope that you have come to share my love for this book and its representation of the beautiful complexity of human life.

Congratulations. You've read *Ulysses*.

PH

## Further Reading

Attridge, Derek. "Molly's Flow: The Writing of 'Penelope' and the Question of Women's Language." *Modern Fiction Studies* 35, no. 3 (Fall 1989): 543–65.

Attridge interrogates the persistent use of the word "flow" to describe the style of Molly's monologue in terms of syntax, typography, momentum, and gender stereotypes.

Crispi, Luca. "Molly, Mr. Stanhope, and Hester: A Genetic Reading of a Love Triangle in *Ulysses*." *James Joyce Quarterly* 51, no. 1 (Fall 2013): 97–117.

This article reveals the gradual amplification of Molly's relationships with Hester and Mr. Stanhope through Joyce's addition of connecting details in successive drafts of "Penelope." These embellishments reveal more about Molly's adolescent sexual awakening than they do about the Stanhopes as characters themselves. Crispi also examines the source for Hester's character in Nora Barnacle's biography.

Ellmann, Maud. "'Penelope' without the Body." *European Joyce Studies* 17 (2006): 97–108.

Ellmann suggests that Joyce's own comments on the fleshiness of "Penelope" are misleading, and she focuses instead on the groundbreaking orthography of the episode and Molly's fixation on language.

Herr, Cheryl. "'Penelope' as Period Piece." *NOVEL: A Forum on Fiction* 22, no. 2 (1989): 130–42.

Herr presents an understanding of the "Penelope" episode as the grand finale of a variety show, an operatic, scripted monologue delivered with gusto by a star performer.

Kenner, Hugh. "Molly's Masterstroke." *James Joyce Quarterly* 10, no. 1 (1972): 19–28.

Although the scenes Kenner imagines have been scrutinized and largely rejected by other scholars, this essay offers a useful framework for the kind of retrospective assembly of details readers can now entertain at the end of the novel.

McCormick, Kathleen. "Reproducing Molly Bloom: A Revisionist History of the Reception of 'Penelope', 1922–1970." In *Molly Blooms: A Polylogue on "Penelope" and Cultural Studies*, edited by Richard Pearce, 17–39. Madison: University of Wisconsin Press, 1994.

McCormick historicizes the various critical responses to Molly's monologue, providing a socio-literary context for the discourses that have engaged with this episode.

# ACKNOWLEDGMENTS

This book would not have been possible without Martha, whose love and support center me, whose advice I value and trust, and who inspires me daily with her grace, selflessness, and dedication to our family and her work. Her patience for listening to me blather on about *Ulysses* has been nearly inexhaustible. My life is blessed by Pierce, Bradley, and Renwick, whose joyful energy has suffused the years I spent working on this project. I am thankful for my mom, whose support I've always felt and who models for me the careful discipline of artistic creation; for my dad, whose loving-kindness shines brightly wherever he goes and who showed me the gratification of diving deeply into a project; and for my sister, whose generosity and humor have always enriched my life.

I owe a debt of gratitude to Gilman School for supporting this project from its outset in 2016 as UlyssesGuide.com and for trusting its faculty to teach courses rooted in our passions and interests. Crucially, I want to thank my students for helping me find my voice in this work and for their willingness to engage so thoughtfully in our shared reading and conversations about this novel. I am perpetually grateful for the pleasure of working alongside my extraordinary colleagues on the faculty at Gilman.

To George and Sylvia Whitman, thank you for your friendship, for planting the seeds of this project with your hospitality in the summer of 2003, and for providing humanity with the gift and wonder of Shakespeare and Company Bookstore.

I am grateful to Marc Conner for guiding my first reading of *Ulysses* as part of my honors thesis at Washington and Lee University and for being a lifelong role model in teaching, scholarship, and fatherhood.

I am thankful to the Bread Loaf School of English for shaping me into the reader, writer, and person who wrote this book. Specifically, I thank Victor Luftig for embodying the sort of insightful curiosity that makes lifelong inquiry a source of fulfillment, Jeri Johnson for introducing me to the body of scholarship that has become foundational to my critical understanding of *Ulysses*, and John Elder for his modest brilliance and immaculate kindness.

I am grateful to Hugh Atkins and the rest of the English Department at Tower Hill School for taking a risk on a twenty-two-year-old kid and for demonstrating the immersive academic passion that leads to good teaching and that led ultimately to this project. I thank Mary Beth Zibilich at Marist School for introducing me to the excitement of reading closely. I appreciate Angus Burgin, Iva Turner, the Stuzins, and Stephanie Shea for their friendship and for their roles in bringing this book to fruition.

I am humbled by the expertise of Joe Abbott, whose copyediting improved my writing, and the full team of professionals at Johns Hopkins University Press. Particularly, I wish to express my profound appreciation for Matt McAdam, whose steadfast belief in the spirit and intentions of this project helped me to revise and enhance with confidence.

# Appendix A

# A CHRONOLOGY OF STEPHEN'S DAY

| | |
|---|---|
| 8:00 a.m. | Wakes up at the Martello tower in Sandycove, has breakfast with Buck Mulligan and Haines.[1] |
| 8:45 a.m. | Walks to Mr. Deasy's school in Dalkey, arriving around 9:05.[2] |
| 9:30 a.m. | Teaches a lesson.[3] |
| 9:50 a.m. | Tutors Cyril Sargent in math, then meets with Mr. Deasy.[4] |
| 10:05 a.m. | Finishes meeting with Mr. Deasy. |
| 10:11 a.m. | Takes a train north from Dalkey.[5] |
| 10:40 a.m. | Walks along Sandymount Strand.[6] |
| 11:00 a.m. | Leaves the strand and walks toward Dublin's City Center.[7] |
| 11:10 a.m. | Seen walking toward town by Mr. Bloom as he passes in the funeral carriage.[8] |
| 12:00 p.m. | Sends a telegram from College Green to Buck Mulligan at The Ship, canceling their 12:30 appointment for drinks.[9] |
| 12:30 p.m. | Visits the *Irish Telegraph* newspaper offices.[10] |
| 1:00 p.m. | Drinks at Mooney's pub.[11] |
| 1:30 p.m. | Drinks at a different pub called Mooney's.[12] |
| 2:00 p.m. | Delivers lecture on *Hamlet* at the National Library.[13] |

| 3:22 p.m. | Stephen speaks with his old voice teacher, Almidano Artifoni.[14] |
|---|---|
| 3:35 p.m. | Shops for books at a kiosk by the river and sees his sister, Dilly.[15] |
| 4:00 p.m. | Drinks at The Moira.[16] |
| 5:00 p.m. | Drinks at Larchet's. |
| 10:00 p.m. | Drinks at Holles Street Maternity Hospital with medical students and others, including Mr. Bloom. |
| 10:50 p.m. | Drinks at Burke's.[17] |
| 11:10 p.m. | Arrives at Westland Row Station and has an altercation with Buck Mulligan; Buck and Haines take the last train toward Sandycove without Stephen.[18] |
| 11:25 p.m. | Takes a train with Lynch from Westland Row Station to Amiens Street Station; walks through Nighttown, Dublin's brothel district.[19] |
| 11:45 p.m. | Visits Mrs. Cohen's brothel with Lynch.[20] |
| 12:40 a.m. | Has an altercation with British soldiers on the streets of Nighttown.[21] |
| 1:00 a.m. | Visits cabman's shelter with Mr. Bloom.[22] |
| 1:40 a.m. | Walks with Mr. Bloom to 7 Eccles Street.[23] |
| 2:00 a.m. | Arrives at 7 Eccles Street; partakes of cocoa and conversation with Mr. Bloom.[24] |
| 2:30 a.m. | Stephen departs (destination unknown).[25] |

## Notes

1. Joyce's schema lists 8 a.m. as the start of the novel (see appendix D).
2. The "Liliata rutilantium" prayer is broken into three lines at the conclusion of "Telemachus" (1.736–38), signifying the three chimes of a nearby clocktower or church bell. These three chimes signify three-quarters past the hour, or 8:45 a.m. Based on my own attempts to recreate Stephen's day on-site in Dublin, the walk to Mr. Deasy's school in Dalkey takes twenty minutes. Assuming Stephen is supposed to be at work by 9:00, he arrives slightly late.

3. We join the "Nestor" episode *in medias res*, perhaps around 9:45 a.m. See Robert Nicholson, *The "Ulysses" Guide: Tours through Joyce's Dublin* (New York: Routledge, 1989), 9.

4. Stephen's class is dismissed with enough time for the students to prepare for "hockey at ten" (2.92), but Cyril Sargent remains behind for extra help with his math.

5. The text does not detail Stephen's journey north from Dalkey to Sandymount, but Danis Rose suggests that Stephen walked four to five minutes from the school to the Dalkey train station in time to catch "the train from Bray which stopped at Dalkey at 10:11." Danis Rose, "The Best Recent Scholarship in Joyce," *James Joyce Quarterly* 23, no. 3 (Spring 1986): 328. Arriving at the Lansdowne Station at 10:32, Stephen then "walked across the bridge at the Dodder River, took a left onto Newbridge Avenue, crossed Tritonville Road and went down Leahy's Terrace to the beach." Jack McCarthy and Danis Rose, *Joyce's Dublin: A Walking Guide to "Ulysses"* (New York: St. Martin's, 1988), 16. Stephen arrives at the strand at 10:40 a.m. See Rose, "Recent Scholarship," 329.

6. Robert Nicholson and Danis Rose both identify 10:40 a.m. as the start time for "Proteus." Gunn and Hart offer a competing theory of Stephen's movements between the end of "Nestor" and the start of "Proteus," suggesting that Stephen takes the train all the way to Westland Row Station in town. They claim that Stephen then takes a 1.5 mile (thirty-minute) walk back to Sandymount Strand, during which Bloom notices him in Irishtown as the funeral carriage passes him on its way from the Dignams' home in Sandymount to the cemetery in Glasnevin. See Ian Gunn and Clive Hart, *James Joyce's Dublin: A Topographical Guide to the Dublin of "Ulysses"* (New York: Thames and Hudson, 2004), 28–30. While Gunn and Hart offer compelling reasons, including the train timetables, I don't see why someone would walk thirty minutes from town in order to walk thirty minutes on the beach before walking thirty minutes back into town. It seems much more likely that Stephen would get off the train at Lansdowne in order to have a thoughtful twenty-minute walk before heading into town. Plus, giving Stephen a northwesterly route would echo Bloom's simultaneous movements in the carriage (just as Stephen's southerly walk from the tower to the school correlates to Bloom's southerly walk from Eccles Street to Sweny's at the same time).

7. At the conclusion of "Proteus," Stephen sees the *Rosevean*, "a threemaster, her sails brailed up on the crosstrees, homing, upstream, silently moving, a silent ship" (3.504–05). In "Eumaeus," Murphy claims that he arrived "this morning elevenoclock [on] the threemaster *Rosevean*" (16.450). While acknowledging that Murphy is an unreliable narrator, we might as well use this corroborating detail.

8. "Mr Bloom at gaze saw a lithe young man, clad in mourning, a wide hat," Simon Dedalus's "son and heir" (6.39–40, 43). Stephen is seen on Watery Lane, which would be about a ten-minute walk from where he left the strand at Poolbeg/Pigeonhouse Road. Martin Cunningham notes that the carriage is "ten minutes" late (6.86).

9. See 9.550–55.

10. The schemas and scholars all list "Aeolus" as taking place between 12:00 p.m. and 1:00 p.m., and Stephen arrives at the newspaper offices almost exactly halfway through the episode (7.506), so 12:30 p.m. seems right.

11. Stephen proposes drinks at Mooney's (7.892), which is located at 1 Lower Abbey Street, right across Sackville/O'Connell Street from his location at the end of "Aeolus."

12. The "Circe" episode reveals the details of Stephen's pubhopping, beginning with "Mooney's en ville, Mooney's sur mer" (15.2518–19). Gunn and Hart suppose that Stephen visited the two Mooney's between the end of "Aeolus" and the start of "Scylla and Charybdis." See Gunn and Hart, *James Joyce's Dublin*, 79.

13. The National Library is a fifteen-minute walk from Mooney's, and "Scylla and Charybdis" opens around 2:00 p.m. *in medias res*, with Stephen already present in the Librarian's Room.

14. As depicted in section 6 of "Wandering Rocks" (10.338–66); the specific time is according to Gunn and Hart, *James Joyce's Dublin*, 58.

15. As depicted in section 13 of "Wandering Rocks" (10.800–880); the specific time is according to Gunn and Hart, *James Joyce's Dublin*, 59.

16. After the two Mooney's pubs, Philip Sober in "Circe" lists "the Moira, Larchet's" (15.2519) as the next two pubs Stephen visits this afternoon. I am assuming that the list is chronological because the novel confirms that the other four locations are listed in the order of Stephen's day. That said, we know neither when Stephen arrives at either pub nor how long he spends there; his whereabouts between his encounter with Dilly and his carousing in the Holles Street hospital are uncertain.

17. Stephen and the other men from the hospital arrive at Burke's at "ten to" (14.1471) the pub's "closing time" (14.1534) at 11:00 p.m.

18. Haines tells Buck to "meet me at Westland Row station at ten past eleven" (14.1027).

19. From the train station, Stephen and Lynch walk in something of a square through the red-light district via "the Mabbot street entrance of nighttown" (15.1) to Bella Cohen's, which would take around ten minutes (per Google Maps).

20. We know that Stephen is already in Mrs. Cohen's brothel when "midnight chimes" (15.1362).

21. The text tells us that "God's time is 12.25" (15.2191) about midway through the "Circe" episode, so 12:40 seems like a fair estimate for the altercation with Private Carr. As corroboration, Nicholson and Gunn and Hart all identify 12:40 a.m. as the conclusion of "Circe." See Nicholson, *"Ulysses" Guide*, 137; and Gunn and Hart, *James Joyce's Dublin*, 66.

22. Assuming Stephen requires a few minutes to rouse himself from being knocked out, he and Bloom would then have a ten-minute walk (per Google Maps) to the cabman's shelter from Beaver Street in Nighttown (15.4365). These details confirm the 1:00 a.m. time listed for "Eumaeus" in the Gilbert schema.

23. The text does not offer evidence pertaining to the time Stephen and Bloom spend in the cabman's shelter, but Gunn and Hart, as well as Nicholson, suggest that the events of the entire "Eumaeus" episode occur in twenty minutes, which seems far too short. See Gunn and Hart, *James Joyce's Dublin*, 71; Nicholson, *"Ulysses" Guide*, 137. Given that the walk to the cabman's shelter alone would take at least ten minutes (not even accounting for the delay of Stephen's conversation with Corley on the way), their chronologies would leave only ten minutes for the remainder of "Eumaeus" (the events in the shelter, as well as the beginning of Stephen and Bloom's walk north). Nicholson's and Gunn and Hart's timelines from this point on seem implausible for trying to fit too many events into the space between 12:40 and 1:30 a.m.; I believe they misinterpret the bells heard in "Ithaca" (17.1226–34) and "Penelope" (18.1231–32, 18.1540), as I will explain in the notes to my chronology of Bloom's day (see appendix B).

24. The walk from the cabman's shelter to 7 Eccles Street takes twenty minutes (per Google Maps), and the Gilbert schema lists 2:00 a.m. as the hour for "Ithaca."

25. As Stephen and Bloom shake hands in farewell, they hear two chimes, "the sound of the peal of the hour" (17.1226). Gunn and Hart claim that these bells signify 1:30 a.m., which means that only fifty minutes pass between Stephen getting knocked out by Private Carr at 12:40 a.m. and his departure from Bloom's house. The two walks (from Nighttown to the cabman's shelter and then from the shelter to Bloom's house) require a total of at least thirty minutes, leaving only twenty minutes for the events depicted in the shelter and at Bloom's home combined. Impossible. Rather, I agree with William York Tindall, who claims these two bells signify 2:30 a.m. See William York Tindall, *A Reader's Guide to James Joyce* (Syracuse, NY: Syracuse University Press, 1979), 220. This chronology allows Stephen and Bloom to spend about half an hour together in Bloom's kitchen and garden. For further justification of this chronology, see notes 33 and 34 in my chronology of Bloom's day.

## Appendix B

# A CHRONOLOGY OF BLOOM'S DAY

| | |
|---|---|
| 8:00 a.m. | Makes breakfast, visits butcher shop, speaks with Molly about the day ahead. |
| 8:45 a.m. | Emerges from his outhouse after his morning bowel movement.[1] |
| 9:00 a.m. | Leaves home and walks south from Eccles Street to Sir Rogerson's Quay.[2] |
| 9:40 a.m. | Visits Post Office.[3] |
| 9:45 a.m. | Speaks with M'Coy. |
| 9:50 a.m. | Reads letter from Martha Clifford.[4] |
| 10:00 a.m. | Visits All Hallows Church. |
| 10:15 a.m. | Heads to Sweny's pharmacist to buy lemon soap and order Molly's lotion.[5] |
| 10:30 a.m. | Takes a bath.[6] |
| 10:45 a.m. | Takes tram toward the Dignam home in Sandymount. |
| 11:05 a.m. | Joins Dignam's funeral cortege to Prospect Cemetery in Glasnevin.[7] |
| 11:35 a.m. | Attends Paddy Dignam's funeral service in the mortuary chapel.[8] |
| 11:55 a.m. | Carriage departs Glasnevin for Dunphy's pub, then back to town.[9] |

| 12:30 p.m. | Attends to business at the *Freeman's Journal* offices.[10] |
| 12:45 p.m. | Finds Mr. Keyes at Dillon's Auction Rooms. |
| 12:55 p.m. | Attempts to negotiate Keyes ad with Mr. Crawford on the street. |
| 1:00 p.m. | Walks through downtown, meets Josie Breen on the street, and heads through Grafton Street to the Burton restaurant on Duke Street.[11] |
| 1:55 p.m. | Eats a light lunch at Davy Byrne's pub.[12] |
| 2:15 p.m. | Enters National Museum to escape Boylan; examines goddess statues.[13] |
| 2:25 p.m. | Visits National Library to see the art he intends to use for the Keyes ad.[14] |
| 2:55 p.m. | Leaves National Library.[15] |
| 3:18 p.m. | Purchases *Sweets of Sin* book for Molly.[16] |
| 3:50 p.m. | Meets Ritchie Goulding and heads to the Ormond Hotel Bar and Restaurant for an early dinner.[17] |
| 4:20 p.m. | Leaves Ormond Hotel.[18] |
| 5:00 p.m. | Goes to Barney Kiernan's pub to meet Martin Cunningham; gets into an argument with the Citizen.[19] |
| 5:45 p.m. | Departs Barney Kiernan's pub in a jaunting car with Martin Cunningham, Jack Power, and Crofton.[20] |
| 6:00 p.m. | Visits the Dignam family to discuss insurance policy and family finances.[21] |
| 8:00 p.m. | Walks from the Dignam home to Sandymount Strand. |
| 8:15 p.m. | Enjoys the sunset, evening fireworks, and his encounter with Gerty MacDowell.[22] |
| 9:10 p.m. | Bloom leaves the strand.[23] |
| 9:30 p.m. | Takes a tram from Sandymount back into town.[24] |
| 10:00 p.m. | Visits Holles Street Maternity Hospital to check on Mina Purefoy; links up with Stephen.[25] |

| | |
|---|---|
| 10:50 p.m. | Follows Stephen to Burke's pub.[26] |
| 11:20 p.m. | Train from Westland Row Station to Amiens Station (eventually).[27] |
| 11:45 p.m. | Enters Nighttown, buys snacks, seeks Stephen. |
| 12:00 a.m. | Finds Stephen at Mrs. Cohen's brothel.[28] |
| 12:30 a.m. | Meets Bella Cohen.[29] |
| 12:40 a.m. | Intervenes on Stephen's behalf in conflict with British soldiers.[30] |
| 1:00 a.m. | Takes Stephen to get food and coffee at cabman's shelter.[31] |
| 1:40 a.m. | Walks with Stephen from cabman's shelter to 7 Eccles Street. |
| 2:00 a.m. | Hosts Stephen for cocoa and conversation at home, 7 Eccles Street.[32] |
| 2:30 a.m. | Stephen departs Bloom's home.[33] |
| 2:40 a.m. | Bloom gets into bed, tells Molly about his day, and falls asleep.[34] |

## Notes

1. As Bloom hears three bell chimes from nearby St. George's Church, he thinks "quarter to" (4.549), meaning fifteen minutes to 9:00.
2. Bloom walks thirty minutes (per Google Maps) from 7 Eccles Street to 4 Sir John Rogerson's Quay (the address for Leask's, the first place noted by Bloom at the outset of the "Lotus-Eaters" episode).
3. Jack McCarthy and Danis Rose, *Joyce's Dublin: A Walking Guide to Ulysses* (New York: St. Martin's, 1988), 24.
4. As the funeral procession passes "National school. Meade's yard" (6.171), Bloom thinks, "An hour ago I was passing there" (6.174). Meade's yard was located at 153–59 Great Brunswick Street, and Bloom opens his letter from Martha near there in "Lotus-Eaters" (see 5.230). Assuming that Bloom is rounding a bit, we can infer the times indicated for events in the "Lotus-Eaters" episode.
5. As Bloom leaves All Hallows Church, he notes that it is "quarter past" (5.462), meaning 10:15 a.m.
6. Although Bloom thinks he might "combine business with pleasure" (5.504–05) in the bath, the tight schedule requires that he must bathe quickly. All business. No time for pleasure.

7. Paddy Dignam's funeral is at "eleven" (4.320), and "Hades" begins as the men are entering the funeral carriage. Roughly five minutes after the cortege leaves the Dignams' home (9 Newbridge Ave.) and soon after passing Stephen Dedalus in Irishtown, Mr. Power asks Martin Cunningham, "Are we late?" and Cunningham replies "ten minutes" (6.85–86). So, I put the *in medias res* start of "Hades" at 11:05 a.m.

8. Bloom notes the time as "twenty past eleven" (6.237) just before the carriage passes "under the hugecloaked Liberator's form" (6.249) of the Daniel O'Connell statue near O'Connell Bridge in the heart of downtown; the cemetery is about fifteen minutes away, so they might arrive around 11:35 a.m.

9. If the funeral service lasts twenty minutes, the carriages leave just before noon to head back to town.

10. If the funeral coaches make the customary stop at Dunphy's pub on the way back to town as Bloom anticipates ("Expect we'll pull up here [at Dunphy's] on the way back to drink his health" [6.429–30]), and if they spend ten to fifteen minutes there before heading back downtown, Bloom might arrive to the newspaper offices around 12:30 p.m.

11. Mr. Bloom initially makes a mistake in thinking, "After one. Timeball on the ballastoffice is down. Dunsink time" (8.109). Gifford explains that the clock he would have seen was keyed to Greenwich Mean Time, which was twenty-five minutes ahead of Dunsink time (the standard time used in Dublin). Bloom realizes his Dunsink/Greenwich time error and corrects himself later in the episode (see 8.571). So, the ball drops at 1:00 p.m. GMT, which means that we can only say for sure that Bloom is crossing O'Connell Bridge sometime after 12:35 p.m. Dunsink/Dublin time, which isn't very helpful to pinning down Bloom's chronology. See Don Gifford, *"Ulysses" Annotated*, with Robert J. Seidman, 2nd ed. (Berkeley: University of California Press, 1988), 160. Hugh Kenner provides further explanation: "The timeball fell at 12.35 by the dial, so when Bloom deduced 'after one' from the fact that it had already fallen his correct conclusion, as so often, was drawn from false premises and correct by luck." Hugh Kenner, *"Ulysses,"* rev. ed. (Baltimore: Johns Hopkins University Press, 1987), 75. In any event, Bloom's walk in "Lestrygonians" would take around ten minutes without interruption, but he stops to chat with Josie Breen for a few minutes and pops into the Burton before doubling back to Davy Byrne's pub. I suggest that the action of "Lestrygonians" prior to Bloom's arrival at Davy Byrne's would span about twenty-five minutes.

12. Soon after settling in Davy Byrne's pub, Mr. Bloom "raised his eyes and met the stare of a bilious clock. Two. Pub clock five minutes fast" (8.790–91).

13. As Gunn and Hart explain, "At perhaps 2.20 Mulligan joins the discussion after having come through the Museum (9.515) where he catches sight of Bloom attempting in vain to examine the backsides of the stone goddesses (9.609–17)." Ian Gunn and Clive Hart, *James Joyce's Dublin: A Topographical Guide to the Dublin of "Ulysses"* (New York: Thames and Hudson, 2004), 44.

14. A few minutes after Buck enters the library, Bloom arrives (see 9.585–603).

15. Bloom departs the library at the end of "Scylla and Charybdis" (see 9.1203). See also Gunn and Hart, *James Joyce's Dublin*, 45.

16. Gunn and Hart, *James Joyce's Dublin*, 58.
17. Inside the Ormond, Boylan hears the "clock clack" and asks, "What time is that? . . . Four?" (11.381, 385) as Bloom and Goulding are being shown to their table in the restaurant. Gunn and Hart, *James Joyce's Dublin*, 58.
18. As Gunn and Hart explain, "The timing of the pianotuner's return to the Ormond, deduced from his movements in Wandering Rocks, suggests that he reenters the hotel to retrieve his tuning fork at about 4:25 p.m., by which time Bloom has already left." Gunn and Hart, *James Joyce's Dublin*, 61.
19. As the text of "Cyclops" reports, "It was exactly seventeen o'clock" (12.604).
20. Bloom's departure is depicted at the conclusion of "Cyclops" (see 12.1768–70).
21. "After arriving at Newbridge Avenue shortly before six o'clock, Bloom . . . spends about two hours in the company of the bereaved family." Gunn and Hart, *James Joyce's Dublin*, 63.
22. The "Nausicaa" episode begins as "the sun was setting" (13.2), and we know from "Ithaca" that the sun would set at 8:29 p.m. on the upcoming summer solstice, Tuesday, June 21, 1904 (see 17.654–56). So, the narrative of "Nausicaa" begins around 8:20 p.m., at which time Bloom is already on the beach. Later, when Cissy Caffrey asks Bloom the time, he replies, "It must be after eight because the sun was set" (13.547–48).
23. Toward the end of "Nausicaa," Bloom thinks that it "must be getting on for nine by the light" (13.1212) and "must be near nine" (13.1274). Then, as he seems to drift off for a "short snooze" (13.1274), the episode concludes with a bell chiming nine times "cuckoo" (13.1288–1306). Let's say he takes a ten-minute power nap before heading back into town.
24. "If we accept the budget at face value ("Tramfare 0.01," [17.1469]), Bloom returns to the city by the Sandymount (Bath Avenue) tram, which would drop him very close to the main entrance of the maternity hospital." Gunn and Hart, *James Joyce's Dublin*, 63.
25. The schema lists 10:00 p.m. as the start time for the "Oxen of the Sun" episode.
26. The men arrive at Burke's at "ten to . . . closingtime" (14.1471, 1534), or 10:50 p.m.
27. Bloom seems to have missed his stop at the Amiens Street Station and therefore has to get off at the next stop (Killester) and catch the next incoming train. Gunn and Hart note that the last train for Howth left Amiens Street at 11:30 p.m., and the train from Amiens Street to Killester takes seven minutes each way (per Google Maps), so Bloom is at least fifteen minutes behind Stephen and Lynch. See Gunn and Hart, *James Joyce's Dublin*, 66.
28. As Bloom arrives at Bella Cohen's in search of Stephen, "Midnight chimes from distant steeples" (15.1362).
29. Shortly before Bloom's fourth sustained fantasy in the "Circe" episode, we learn that the "time is 12.25" (15.2191). A few minutes pass between that fantasy and Bella's entrance.
30. For details and explanation of these late-night happenings, see the notes to these corresponding chronological events of Stephen's day (appendix A).
31. While Bloom and Stephen are together in the cabman's shelter, the narrator approximates that it is "getting on for one" (16.1603).

32. The Gilbert schema lists 2:00 a.m. as the hour for the "Ithaca" episode. (Side note: In his kitchen, Bloom washes his hands with the bar of lemon soap "bought thirteen hours previously" [17.232–33]). Since we know Bloom bought the lemon soap at Sweny's around 10:20 a.m., thirteen hours after that purchase would be 11:20 p.m., which is an impossible timestamp for the events of "Ithaca" given the timestamps provided in both "Circe" and "Eumaeus." I therefore believe that this chronological detail is Joyce's error.)

33. As Bloom shakes Stephen's hand in departure, the two bell chimes of Saint George's Church "sound of the peal of the hour of the night" (17.1226). I have already explained in note 25 of my chronology of Stephen's day (appendix A) why these two chimes cannot signify 1:30 a.m., but they could possibly signify 2:00 a.m. But similar to the issues addressed in notes 22–25 of appendix A, if Stephen departs at 2:00 a.m. that would mean Stephen and Bloom spent only an hour and twenty minutes together after Stephen's collapse at the end of "Circe." If thirty to forty minutes of this time are occupied by the two walks, that leaves only forty to fifty minutes for the events in the cabman's shelter and at Bloom's home combined (say, roughly twenty-five minutes in each location). Possible, but tight given the widely ranging conversation the two men share. I prefer the chronology as listed above for its more natural pacing. Plus, if the bells at Stephen's departure signify 2:00 a.m., then Molly's reference in "Penelope" to "quarter after" (18.1540) would mean Bloom and Stephen arrived and woke her at 1:15 a.m., which is impossible as previously explained in note 25 of appendix A. See my reading of Molly's "quarter after" in the note below.

34. After Mr. Bloom has already gotten into bed, Molly hears "Georges church bells wait 3 quarters the hour 1 wait 2 oclock" (18.1231–32). I understand Molly to have heard three chimes ("3 quarters the hour") and then she figures out the hour, thinking 1 and correcting herself to "2 oclock." So, she interprets the bells to signify "3 quarters the hour" past "2 oclock"; the time is 2:45 a.m. In scholarly corroboration, "Jones, Kain, and Sultan set episode eighteen at 2:45 a.m." Harriet Blodgett, "Joyce's Time Mind in *Ulysses*: A New Emphasis," *James Joyce Quarterly* 5, no. 1 (Fall 1967): 26. Bloom got into bed about ten minutes after saying goodbye to Stephen in the garden, allowing just enough time for him to come back into his house, walk upstairs, get undressed in the parlour (17.1479), hide the letter from Martha in his drawer (17.1840–42), walk into his bedroom, place his clothes on a chair (17.2109), put on his nightshirt (17.2111), get into bed, kiss his wife's bottom (17.2241), provide her with a brief, censored account of his day (17.2250–70), and fall asleep. Aside from these routine events, the rest of "Ithaca" after Stephen's departure catalogues static information and ideas rather than depicting physical action in time or space.

As Molly builds toward the final crescendo of "Penelope," she is thinking of Bloom and notes "a quarter after what an unearthly hour" (18.1540). Gunn and Hart, as well as Rose, read "quarter after" to indicate that the novel is ending just after 2:15 a.m. My previous note regarding Molly hearing the bells for 2:45 makes that reading impossible. If Molly has in fact heard a bell chime to indicate "a quarter after" the hour, my understanding of the chronology would require this final timestamp to signify 3:15 a.m., meaning three hundred lines of Molly's thoughts must span the thirty minutes between 2:45 and 3:15, which feels like a stretch. Rather, I posit that Molly here is not reacting to a bell chime or the present time at all. The text does not indicate that she's heard a bell. Instead, I believe that Molly is simply thinking in her characteristically fragmented stream of consciousness about Bloom coming home so late and waking her up at 2:15 a.m., and she's not pleased: "a quarter after what an unearthly hour." We know from "Ithaca" that Molly has turned on the lamp in her room (see 17.1171–74) by the time Bloom and Stephen go out into the garden around 2:25 a.m., so she likely woke up a few minutes earlier at hearing Bloom and Stephen in the kitchen downstairs.

# Appendix C

# MONEY IN *ULYSSES*

J oyce felt that any writer worth his salt knows how much money is in the pocket of each character. We can discern that Mr. Bloom has 4 shillings, 9 pence when he leaves home on the morning of June 16, 1904, but what does that mean in today's currency? I assume most contemporary readers of Joyce's work (especially those in the United States) are not familiar with the old British system of currency, its terminology, or its value relative to today's money.

The British system of currency featured in *Ulysses* had three units of value, ascending from pennies/pence (d.), to shillings (s.), to pounds (£), as follows:

- 12 pennies = 1 shilling
- 20 shillings = 1 pound

So, there were 240 pence in a pound (because a pound of sterling silver measured 240 pennyweights).

Further complicating things for today's reader, there were names for specific coins and slang terms for amounts of money, as follows:

- Guinea = £1 1s. (considered a more gentlemanly sum than a pound)
- Bob = 1 shilling
- Florin = coin worth 2 shillings
- Tanner = coin worth 6 pence
- Crown = coin worth 5 shillings
- Sovereign = coin worth £1
- Quid = paper note worth £1

Frank Delaney suggests in one installment of his podcast series *Re: Joyce* that 4 pence in *Ulysses* is roughly equivalent to £3 or US$5 today, a conversion rate that jibes with purchases made in the text of the novel: Bloom's sandwich and wine in Davy Byrne's pub would today cost around $9, his purchase of lotion and soap would be roughly $45 today, the coffee and bun in the cabman's shelter would cost $5, and a copy of the *Freeman's Journal* newspaper would cost $1.25. That seems about right. So, adopting the Delaney rate:

- A penny in *Ulysses* is worth approximately US$1.25 (or £0.90) today;
- A shilling in *Ulysses* is worth approximately US$15 (or £10) today;
- A pound in *Ulysses* would be approximately US$300 (or £215) today.

Gifford uses the cost of food staples listed in *Thom's* to equate a 1904 penny to the buying power of $0.45 in 1985, meaning a pound would be worth $108 in 1985, or roughly $260 today (adjusted for inflation). This scale of conversion feels close enough to the Delaney rate to serve as corroboration.

But to answer the question posed at the outset: Bloom leaves his home on June 16, 1904, with roughly $70 cash in his pocket.

# Appendix D
# *ULYSSES* SCHEMA

In a 1920 letter to Carlo Linati (a friend and early reader of *Ulysses*), Joyce wrote, "In view of the enormous bulk and the more than enormous complexity of my . . . novel it would be better to send you a sort of summary-key-skeleton-scheme (for your personal use only). Perhaps my idea will appear clearer to you when you have the text" (*Letters* 146). So, even before having finished writing the novel, Joyce recognized that readers would need some support in grasping the nuanced allusions and intricate structures he had put into *Ulysses*. He later sent similar "schemas" to other friends and early scholars of his work, including Stuart Gilbert. Joyce gave Gilbert permission to publish the contents of the schema in the scholarly study of the novel he published in 1930. The Gilbert and Linati schemas have some differences, but I have collated and condensed their information in this table.

# ULYSSES SCHEMA

| EPISODE | TIME | SCENE | COLOR | TECHNIQUE |
|---------|------|-------|-------|-----------|
| *Part I: Telemachiad* | | | | |
| "Telemachus" | 8:00 a.m. | Tower | Gold, White | Narrative (young) |
| "Nestor" | 10:00 a.m. | School | Brown | Catechism (personal) |
| "Proteus" | 11:00 a.m. | Strand | Blue, Green | Monologue (male) |
| *Part II: Odyssey* | | | | |
| "Calypso" | 8:00 a.m. | House | Orange | Narrative (mature) |
| "Lotus-Eaters" | 10:00 a.m. | Bath | Brown | Narcissism |
| "Hades" | 11:00 a.m. | Graveyard | Black, White | Incubism |
| "Aeolus" | 12:00 p.m. | Newspaper | Red | Enthymemic |

| CORRESPONDENCES | SCIENCE/ ART | MEANING | ORGAN | SYMBOLS |
|---|---|---|---|---|
| Stephen = Telemachus<br>Buck = Antinous<br>Milkwoman = Mentor | Theology | Dispossessed son in struggle | — | Hamlet, Ireland, Heir |
| Deasy = Nestor<br>Sargent = Pisistratus<br>Mrs. O'Shea = Helen | History | Wisdom of the Old World | — | Horse, Ulster, Woman, Common Sense |
| Primal Matter = Proteus<br>Kevin Egan = Menelaus<br>Cocklepickers = Magapenthes | Philology | Prima materia | — | Word, Tide, Evolution, Metamorphosis |
| Mr. Bloom = Ulysses<br>Molly Bloom = Calypso, Penelope<br>The Nymph = Calypso<br>Zion = Ithaca | Economics | Exile, Moon, Family, Vagina, Israel in bondage | Kidneys | Exile, Family, Nymph, Israel |
| Ulysses, Eurylochus | Chemistry, Botany | Seduction of the faith | Skin, Genitals | Host, Flower, Drugs |
| Dignam = Elpenor<br>Menton = Ajax<br>Parnell = Agamemnon<br>Cunningham = Sisyphus<br>Caretaker = Hades<br>O'Connell = Hercules, The 4 rivers | Religion | Descent to nothing | Heart | Cemetery, Caretaker, the Past, the Unknown Man, Heart Trouble |
| Crawford = Aeolus<br>Journalism = Incest<br>Press = Floating Island | Rhetoric | Mockery of victory | Lungs | Machines, Wind, Fame, Kite, Failed Destinies, Press, Editor, Mutability |

| EPISODE | TIME | SCENE | COLOR | TECHNIQUE |
|---------|------|-------|-------|-----------|
| "Lestrygonians" | 1:00 p.m. | Lunch | Blood Color | Peristaltic Prose |
| "Scylla and Charybdis" | 2:00 p.m. | Library | None | Dialectic |
| "Wandering Rocks" | 3:00 p.m. | Streets | Rainbow | Labyrinth |
| "Sirens" | 4:00 p.m. | Concert Room | Coral | Fuga per Canonem |
| "Cyclops" | 5:00 p.m. | Tavern | Green | Gigantism |
| "Nausicaa" | 8:00 p.m. | Rocks | Grey | Tumescence/ Detumescence |

| CORRESPONDENCES | SCIENCE/ ART | MEANING | ORGAN | SYMBOLS |
|---|---|---|---|---|
| Hunger = Antiphates<br>Food = The Decoy<br>Teeth = Lestrygonians | Architecture | Dejection | Esophagus | Bloody Sacrifice, Foods, Shame, Constables |
| The rock = Aristotle, Dogma, Stratford<br>The whirlpool = Plato, Mysticism, London | Literature | Two-edged dilemma | Brain | Hamlet, Shakespeare, Christ, Socrates, Scholasticism and Mysticism, Plato and Aristotle, Youth and Maturity |
| Liffey = Bosporus<br>Viceroy = European Bank [of the sea]<br>Conmee = Asiatic Bank [of the sea]<br>Groups of Citizens = Symplegades | Mechanics | Hostile environment | Blood | Christ and Caesar, Errors, Homonyms, Synchronization, Resemblances, Citizens |
| Barmaids = Sirens<br>Bar = Isle | Music | Sweet cheat | Ear | Promises, Woman, Sounds, Embellishments |
| I = Noman<br>Cigar = Stake<br>Apotheosis = Challenge | Politics | The egocidal terror | Muscles | Nation, Religion, Gymnastics, Idealism, Exaggeration, Fanaticism, Collectivity |
| Star of the Sea = Phaeacia<br>Gerty = Nausicaa | Painting | The projected mirage | Eye, Nose | Onanism, Female, Virgin, Hypocrisy |

| EPISODE | TIME | SCENE | COLOR | TECHNIQUE |
|---------|------|-------|-------|-----------|
| "Oxen of the Sun" | 10:00 p.m. | Hospital | White | Embryonic Development |
| "Circe" | 12:00 a.m. | Brothel | Violet | Hallucination |

| *Part III: Nostos* | | | | |
|---------|------|-------|-------|-----------|
| "Eumaeus" | 1:00 a.m. | Shelter | — | Narrative (old) |
| "Ithaca" | 2:00 a.m. | House | Starry, Milky | Catechism (impersonal) |
| "Penelope" | ∞ | Bed | Starry, Milky, Dawn | Monologue (female) |

*Note:* Ulysses and Eurylochus were listed in the "Lotus-Eaters" episode without specified correspondence.

| CORRESPONDENCES | SCIENCE/ ART | MEANING | ORGAN | SYMBOLS |
|---|---|---|---|---|
| Hospital = Thrinacia<br>Nurses = Lampetie<br>Horne = Helios<br>Fertility = Oxen<br>Fraud = Crime | Medicine | The eternal flocks | Uterus | Fecundation,<br>Frauds,<br>Mothers |
| Bella = Circe | Magic | The man-hating orc | Locomotor Apparatus | Zoology,<br>Personification,<br>Pantheism,<br>Poison,<br>Antidote |
| Skin-the-goat =<br>    Eumaeus<br>Sailor = Ulysses<br>Corley = Melanthius | Navigation | The ambush at home | Nerves | Sailors |
| Boylan = Eurymachus<br>Scruples = Suitors<br>Reason = Bow | Science | The armed hope | Skeleton | Comets |
| Earth = Penelope<br>Movement = Web | — | The past sleeps | Fat | Earth |

# NOTES

## Preface

1. Kevin Birmingham, *The Most Dangerous Book* (New York: Penguin, 2014), 304–06.

## Introduction

1. Hugh Kenner, *Joyce's Voices* (Berkeley: University of California Press, 1978), 17.
2. David Hayman, *"Ulysses": The Mechanics of Meaning* (Madison: University of Wisconsin Press, 1982), 93–94.
3. For further explanation of the arranger, see Hayman, *"Ulysses,"* 88–104; and Hugh Kenner, *"Ulysses,"* rev. ed. (Baltimore: Johns Hopkins University Press, 1987), 61–71.
4. Louis Menand, "Silence, Exile, Punning: James Joyce's Chance Encounters," *New Yorker*, June 24, 2012, www.newyorker.com/magazine/2012/07/02/silence-exile-punning.
5. Sylvia Beach, *Shakespeare and Company* (Lincoln: University of Nebraska Press, 1991), 58.

## 1. "Telemachus" Guide

1. Stanislaus Joyce, *My Brother's Keeper: James Joyce's Early Years*, ed. Richard Ellmann (Cambridge: Da Capo, 2003), 103–04.
2. Bernard Benstock, "Telemachus," in *James Joyce's "Ulysses": Critical Essays*, ed. Clive Hart and David Hayman (Berkeley: University of California Press, 1974), 3.
3. Don Gifford, *"Ulysses" Annotated: Notes for James Joyce's "Ulysses,"* with Robert J. Seidman, 2nd ed. (Berkeley: University of California Press, 1988), 14.
4. Frank Delaney, "Episode 340: Parodies & Pints," *Re: Joyce* (podcast), Sept. 7, 2016, https://blog.frankdelaney.com/2016/09/index.html.
5. Stanley Sultan, *The Argument of "Ulysses"* (Middletown, CT: Wesleyan University Press, 1987), 40.
6. An early draft of the "Telemachus" episode was originally intended as the sixth and final chapter of *A Portrait* rather than the first episode of *Ulysses*. In that version, Stephen departs for Paris after falling out with Buck's prototype.

7. Karen Lawrence, *The Odyssey of Style in "Ulysses"* (Princeton, NJ: Princeton University Press, 1981), 44.

8. You can add "stately" to the list if you elect to read the first word of the novel as modifying the verb "came" rather than "Buck Mulligan."

9. See Sultan, *The Argument of "Ulysses,"* 35: "Stephen is brooding not only about his mother, but also about his 'mother country' and his 'Mother Church'; for not just one but all three bore him and nurtured him, and he has been an unfaithful son to all three."

10. See Kevin Birmingham, "On Joyce and Syphilis," *Harper's Magazine*, July 31, 2014, https://harpers.org/2014/07/on-joyce-and-syphilis/. Birmingham has convincingly demonstrated that Joyce himself was treated for syphilis.

11. Stuart Gilbert, *James Joyce's "Ulysses": A Study* (New York: Vintage, 1958), 53.

12. Sam Slote, *Joyce's Nietzschean Ethics* (New York: Palgrave Macmillan, 2013), 40.

13. Gifford, *"Ulysses" Annotated*, 22.

14. See David Hayman, *"Ulysses": The Mechanics of Meaning* (Madison: University of Wisconsin Press, 1982), 27. Hayman draws an explicit parallel between Stephen and Hamlet: "Perhaps the circumstances of his mother's death, perhaps the failure of his art, perhaps the cool reception given him by the Dublin literary establishment, perhaps his sense of being dragged back into the Irish quagmire he thought he had flown above, perhaps all of these things together have confused and paralyzed him. . . . In this he resembles an Irish Hamlet."

15. Sultan, *The Argument of "Ulysses,"* 38.

16. Gifford, *"Ulysses" Annotated*, 19.

## 2. "Nestor" Guide

1. Cranly's speech: "Whatever else is unsure in this stinking dunghill of a world a mother's love is not. Your mother brings you into the world, carries you first in her body. What do we know about what she feels? But whatever she feels, it, at least, must be real. It must be. What are our ideas or ambitions? Play. Ideas! Why, that bloody bleating goat Temple has ideas. MacCann has ideas too. Every jackass going the roads thinks he has ideas" (*P* 224).

2. Don Gifford, *"Ulysses" Annotated: Notes for James Joyce's "Ulysses,"* with Robert J. Seidman, 2nd ed. (Berkeley: University of California Press, 1988), 33.

3. See Richard Ellmann, *"Ulysses" on the Liffey* (New York: Oxford University Press, 1972), 21. Ellmann suggests that Stephen's debts "testify to his attempt to live in the present" (21). See also Mark Osteen, *The Economy of "Ulysses": Making Both Ends Meet* (Syracuse, NY: Syracuse University Press, 1995), 54. Osteen points out that "a more defiant act would be to forgo IOUs altogether." Rather than living freely in the present, Stephen's conscientiousness of his debts binds him to the past while impacting his future.

4. Robert Martin Adams, *Surface and Symbol: The Consistency of James Joyce's "Ulysses"* (New York: Oxford University Press, 1967), 21.

5. E. L. Epstein, "Nestor," in *James Joyce's "Ulysses": Critical Essays*, ed. Clive Hart and David Hayman (Berkeley: University of California Press, 1974), 23.

6. See Robert E. Spoo, "'Nestor' and the Nightmare: The Presence of the Great

War in *Ulysses*," *Twentieth Century Literature* 32, no. 2 (Summer 1986): 138. Along these lines, Robert Spoo finds "an inscribing of the nightmare of the war within the ostensible neutrality of the 1904 narrative, so that the actualities of 1917 reverberate weirdly, almost allegorically, within the fictive time."

7. Ellmann, *"Ulysses" on the Liffey*, 21.

8. Epstein, "Nestor," 22

## 3. "Proteus" Guide

1. There is some debate over Stephen's movements between the end of "Nestor" and the beginning of "Proteus." Ian Gunn and Clive Hart posit that he takes the train to Westland Row Station in town and then walks 1.5 miles (thirty minutes) southeast to Sandymount, which puts the start of "Proteus" around 11:10 a.m. See Ian Gunn and Clive Hart, *James Joyce's Dublin: A Topographical Guide to the Dublin of "Ulysses"* (New York: Thames and Hudson, 2004), 28–30. Danis Rose suggests that Stephen got off at Lansdowne Station and that the events of this episode begin around 10:40 a.m. See Jack McCarthy and Danis Rose, *Joyce's Dublin: A Walking Guide to "Ulysses"* (New York: St. Martin's, 1988), 16. I agree with Rose, as explained in my chronology for Stephen's day in appendix A.

2. J. Mitchell Morse, "Proteus," in *James Joyce's "Ulysses": Critical Essays*, ed. Clive Hart and David Hayman (Berkeley: University of California Press, 1974), 48.

3. Morse, 37.

4. Eric Bulson, *"Ulysses" by Numbers* (New York: Columbia University Press, 2020), 85.

5. James Joyce, "The Day of the Rabblement," *Ricorso*, Jan. 23, 2021, www.ricorso. net/rx/library/authors/classic/Joyce_J/Criticism/Rabblement.htm.

6. Frank Budgen, *James Joyce and the Making of "Ulysses"* (Bloomington: Indiana University Press, 1967), 54.

7. See Richard J. Finneran, "'That Word Known to All Men' in *Ulysses*: A Reconsideration." *James Joyce Quarterly* 33, no. 4 (Summer 1996): 569–82.

8. Stanley Sultan, *The Argument of "Ulysses"* (Middletown, CT: Wesleyan University Press, 1987), 60.

9. Richard Ellmann, *"Ulysses" on the Liffey* (New York: Oxford University Press, 1972), 26.

## 4. "Calypso" Guide

1. Frank Budgen, *James Joyce and the Making of "Ulysses"* (Bloomington: Indiana University Press, 1967), 91.

2. "Calypso" is the first episode to have an "organ" (the kidney) listed in the schema. Joyce left blank spots in the "organ" column (see appendix D) for the first three episodes, emphasizing Stephen's disconnect from the bodily world.

3. Richard Ellmann, *"Ulysses" on the Liffey* (New York: Oxford University Press, 1972), 36.

4. Erwin R. Steinberg, "Author! Author!" *James Joyce Quarterly* 22, no. 4 (Summer 1985): 422.

5. Hugh Kenner, *"Ulysses,"* rev. ed. (Baltimore: Johns Hopkins University Press, 1987), 48.

## 5. "Lotus-Eaters" Guide

1. We don't know exactly when Mr. Bloom left his home, but he heard the bells chime 8:45 while he was still in the outhouse. See Hugh Kenner, *"Ulysses,"* rev. ed. (Baltimore: Johns Hopkins University Press, 1987), 48. Kenner assembles snippets of information revealed elsewhere in the novel to explain that Bloom must have then gone back upstairs to say goodbye to Molly; in this off-page conversation, Molly tells him "that Boylan is coming at four, and Bloom says that he will not be home early, will dine out, and perhaps go the Gaiety [Theater]." Bloom then departs 7 Eccles Street for a thirty-minute walk to Sir John Rogerson's quay. If we allow fifteen minutes for him to go inside, speak with Molly, and leave his home, the action of "Lotus-Eaters" begins around 9:30 a.m. The chronologies in appendixes A and B offer further notes along these lines.

2. Further bloomisms on this page: Bloom is wrong both times he tries to recall the name of the man who informed against the Invincibles for committing the Phoenix Park murders: not Peter Carey, not Denis Carey, but James Carey.

3. Robert Martin Adams, *Surface and Symbol: The Consistency of James Joyce's "Ulysses"* (New York: Oxford University Press, 1967), 99.

4. Kenner, *"Ulysses,"* 43. Kenner notes that the average height of a soldier in the British army in Bloom's time measured only 5 feet, 4½ inches.

## 6. "Hades" Guide

1. David Hayman, *"Ulysses": The Mechanics of Meaning* (Madison: University of Wisconsin Press, 1982), 93–94.

2. Robert Martin Adams, "Hades," in *James Joyce's "Ulysses": Critical Essays*, ed. Clive Hart and David Hayman (Berkeley: University of California Press, 1974), 114.

3. Don Gifford, *"Ulysses" Annotated*, with Robert J. Seidman, 2nd ed. (Berkeley: University of California Press, 1988), 107.

4. S. L. Goldberg, *The Classical Temper: A Study of James Joyce's "Ulysses"* (London: Chatto and Windus, 1961), 276.

5. Goldberg, 276.

6. Stuart Gilbert, *James Joyce's "Ulysses": A Study* (New York: Vintage, 1958), 173.

7. Adams, "Hades," 102.

8. Marilyn French, *The Book as World: James Joyce's "Ulysses"* (New York: Paragon House, 1993), 85.

## 7. "Aeolus" Guide

1. T. S. Eliot, "*Ulysses*, Order, and Myth," *The Dial* 75 (1923): 480–83.

2. Eliot, 483.

3. Michael Groden, *"Ulysses" in Progress* (Princeton, NJ: Princeton University Press, 1977), 65.

4. Blanche B. Elliott, *A History of English Advertising* (London: Business Publications, 1962), 165. As Elliott explains, advertisement existed prior to the era of Bloom's career, but its most common form was bill-sticking, the practice of displaying advertisement posters in public spaces. Bill-sticking was a violent territorial trade, wherein one agent "established the rights of priority and if

challenged by a subsequent arrival, any ensuing argument was often settled by fisticuffs" (165). This primitive practice seems well-suited to the animalistic impulses of "Boylan, the billsticker" (16.199); appropriately, Bloom's job represents a more evolved form of Boylan's.

5. Elliott, xv.

6. Franco Moretti, *Signs Taken for Wonders: Essays in the Sociology of Literary Forms* (London: Verso, 1988), 193.

7. William Stead, *The Art of Advertising: Its Theory and Practice Fully Described* (London: Browne, 1899), 42, 45.

8. Don Gifford, *"Ulysses" Annotated*, with Robert J. Seidman, 2nd ed. (Berkeley: University of California Press, 1988), 131.

9. Robert Martin Adams, *Surface and Symbol: The Consistency of James Joyce's "Ulysses"* (New York: Oxford University Press, 1967), 163.

10. Frank Delaney, "Episode 300: Falling Winds," *Re: Joyce* (podcast), Jan. 27, 2016, https://blog.frankdelaney.com/2016/01/index.html.

## 8. "Lestrygonians" Guide

1. Eric Bulson, *"Ulysses" by Numbers* (New York: Columbia University Press, 2020), 85.

2. Erwin R. Steinberg, "'Lestrygonians,' a Pale 'Proteus'?," *Modern Fiction Studies* 15, no. 1 (Spring 1969), 73–86; James H. Maddox Jr., *Joyce's "Ulysses" and the Assault upon Character* (New Brunswick, NJ: Rutgers University Press, 1978), 62.

3. For a full recreation of Mr. Bloom's employment history, see Patrick Hastings, "Leopold Bloom's *Curriculum Vitae*," *James Joyce Quarterly* 50, no. 3 (Spring 2013): 823–27.

4. Richard Ellmann, *"Ulysses" on the Liffey* (New York: Oxford University Press, 1972), 75.

5. Hugh Kenner, *"Ulysses,"* rev. ed. (Baltimore: Johns Hopkins University Press, 1987), 75.

6. Frank Budgen, *James Joyce and the Making of "Ulysses"* (Bloomington: Indiana University Press, 1967), 19–20.

7. Budgen, 20.

8. Erwin R. Steinberg, "Author! Author!" *James Joyce Quarterly* 22, no. 4 (Summer 1985): 423.

## 9. "Scylla and Charybdis" Guide

1. Hugh Kenner, *Dublin's Joyce* (New York: Columbia University Press, 1987), 209.

2. Marilyn French, *The Book as World: James Joyce's "Ulysses"* (New York: Paragon House, 1993), 110.

3. Cf. Erwin R. Steinberg, "Author! Author!" *James Joyce Quarterly* 22, no. 4 (Summer 1985): 423. Steinberg, skeptical of the notion of the arranger, simply attributes this creative wordplay to the author, James Joyce, who "comes cavorting onto the stage to the tune, appropriately enough, of an Elizabethan dance."

4. Karen Lawrence, *The Odyssey of Style in "Ulysses"* (Princeton, NJ: Princeton University Press, 1981), 81.

5. I have read or heard somewhere that, in those days, a person wealthy enough to own two beds would reserve the house's best bed for guests, so the second-best bed would have been the only one Anne would have ever slept in, which would render this gift to her more a matter of practicality and less of a slight.

6. Stanley Sultan, *The Argument of "Ulysses"* (Middletown, CT: Wesleyan University Press, 1987), 169.

## 10. "Wandering Rocks" Guide

1. Stuart Gilbert, *James Joyce's "Ulysses": A Study* (New York: Vintage, 1958), 227.

2. Frank Budgen, *James Joyce and the Making of "Ulysses"* (Bloomington: Indiana University Press, 1967), 67–68.

3. Budgen, 122–23. If you are interested in delving deeper into the astounding arrangement, mapping, and minute-by-minute events of "Wandering Rocks," see Ian Gunn and Clive Hart, *James Joyce's Dublin: A Topographical Guide to the Dublin of "Ulysses"* (New York: Thames and Hudson, 2004), 58–59.

4. Hugh Kenner, *Dublin's Joyce* (New York: Columbia University Press, 1987), 253.

5. Gunn and Hart, *James Joyce's Dublin*, 58.

6. Clive Hart, "Wandering Rocks," in *James Joyce's "Ulysses": Critical Essays*, ed. Clive Hart and David Hayman (Berkeley: University of California Press, 1974), 197.

7. Richard Ellmann, *"Ulysses" on the Liffey* (New York: Oxford University Press, 1972), 98.

8. Jack McCarthy and Danis Rose, *Joyce's Dublin: A Walking Guide to "Ulysses"* (New York: St. Martin's, 1988), 40.

## 11. "Sirens" Guide

1. Ian Gunn and Clive Hart, *James Joyce's Dublin: A Topographical Guide to the Dublin of "Ulysses"* (New York: Thames and Hudson, 2004), 58–59.

2. Jackson I. Cope, "Sirens," in *James Joyce's "Ulysses": Critical Essays*, ed. Clive Hart and David Hayman (Berkeley: University of California Press, 1974), 220.

3. Jeri Johnson, ed., notes to *Ulysses: The 1922 Text* (Oxford: Oxford University Press, 2008), 876.

4. See Stanley Sultan, *The Argument of "Ulysses"* (Middletown, CT: Wesleyan University Press, 1987), 220.

5. See Harald Beck, "Joyce's Ormond Hotel," *James Joyce Online Notes*, www.jjon.org/joyce-s-environs/ormond. This page provides the layout of the Ormond Hotel Bar and Restaurant and explains how Bloom and Goulding could remain unseen by the other men.

6. See Sultan, *The Argument of "Ulysses,"* 221–22. As Sultan explains, this song comes from *Martha*, an opera about a noblewoman, Lady Harriet, who gets bored with courtly life and escapes to the country, disguising herself as a commoner called Martha. She enjoys a day of romantic dalliance with a man, Lionel, at a fair, before returning to her aristocratic life. Lionel misses her terribly and sings a song, "M'appari," longing for Martha's return. Lionel later sees Martha

in her actual, noble persona of Lady Harriet; he approaches her, and she rejects him for being an unworthy commoner, but she feels bad about it because she actually liked Lionel. It turns out that Lionel is actually heir to an earldom, so Lady Harriet changes her tune, but Lionel has gone insane because of his broken heart. They find a way to snap him back to normal, and the two lovers end up together happily ever after.

7. Kevin McDermott and Ralph Richey, "M'appari," *Music from the Works of James Joyce* (Sunphone Records, 2004), https://youtu.be/MoQ1pY1vCzg.

8. Hugh Kenner, *"Ulysses,"* rev. ed. (Baltimore: Johns Hopkins University Press, 1987), 65.

## 12. "Cyclops" Guide

1. David Hayman, "Cyclops," in *James Joyce's "Ulysses": Critical Essays*, ed. Clive Hart and David Hayman (Berkeley: University of California Press, 1974), 243. Hayman argues that the Nameless One tells the story later, but other scholars poke holes in this idea and offer other explanations, such as that the narrator is mentally rehearsing his telling of this story as the events unfold in real time; see Herbert Schneidau, "One Eye and Two Levels: On Joyce's 'Cyclops,'" *James Joyce Quarterly* 16, no. 1/2 (Fall 1978–Winter 1979): 95–103.

2. Jeri Johnson, notes to *Ulysses: The 1922 Text* (Oxford: Oxford University Press, 2008), 884.

3. Sean Latham, "Interruption: 'Cyclops' and 'Nausicaa,'" in *The Cambridge Companion to "Ulysses,"* ed. Sean Latham (New York: Cambridge University Press, 2014), 142.

4. Frank Budgen, *James Joyce and the Making of "Ulysses"* (Bloomington: Indiana University Press, 1967), 153. Scholars have developed various and sometimes conflicting interpretations of this device. For example, Fritz Senn explains that the interruptions are emblems of Irish home rule because they abide their own rules and function independently from the dominant text; see Fritz Senn, "Arguing about Law: Cyclopean Language," *James Joyce Quarterly* 37, no. 3–4 (Spring-Summer 2000): 441. By contrast, Robert Colson suggests that they are something like immigrants who don't really belong in the Citizen's conception of an Irish nation; see Robert Colson, "Narrative Arrangements in Superposition and the Critique of Nationalism in 'Cyclops,'" *James Joyce Quarterly* 53, no. 1–2 (Fall 2015–Winter 2016): 82–84.

5. Latham, "Interruption," 142.

6. Marilyn French, *The Book as World: James Joyce's "Ulysses"* (New York: Paragon House, 1993), 151.

7. Mark Osteen, *The Economy of "Ulysses": Making Both Ends Meet* (Syracuse NY: Syracuse University Press, 1995), 262–63.

8. Robert Martin Adams, *Surface and Symbol: The Consistency of James Joyce's "Ulysses"* (New York: Oxford University Press, 1967), 100–101. Adams reports that the Hungarian lottery incident "was picked out of a single paragraph in the *Irish Independent* of June 16, 1904, p. 4. The episode in question took place in London; a printer was summoned into court by the Treasury, on charges of

having published announcements describing the 'Privileged Royal Hungarian Lottery.' Joyce simply moved the episode to Dublin, placed it some years in the past, and attributed the experience to Bloom."

9. David Hayman, *"Ulysses": The Mechanics of Meaning* (Madison: University of Wisconsin Press, 1983), 126.

10. Enda Duffy, "Setting," in *The Cambridge Companion to "Ulysses,"* ed. Sean Latham (New York: Cambridge University Press, 2014), 82–83. In 1904, the Irish nationalist Arthur Griffith "published *The Resurrection of Hungary* in which he advocated that Irish members of parliament, following the Hungarian example, should unilaterally withdraw from the British Parliament and set up their own government in Dublin." In an interweaving of fact and fiction, "Griffin had gotten his revolutionary idea from none other than Leopold Bloom, whose father had emigrated from Hungary to Ireland."

## 13. "Nausicaa" Guide

1. Karen Lawrence, *Who's Afraid of James Joyce?* (Gainesville: University Press of Florida, 2010), 86.

2. Heather Cook Callow, "Joyce's Female Voices in *Ulysses,*" *Journal of Narrative Technique* 22, no. 3 (Fall 1992): 157.

3. Arthur Power, *Conversations with James Joyce* (Dublin: Dalkey Archive Press, 2020), 24. If we take Joyce's statement seriously, the implications are profound, making Bloom's behavior on the beach even more problematic if indeed the mutual attraction with Gerty is imagined. Power admits, however, that he had "irritated Joyce" prior to Joyce's statement that "nothing happened between [Gerty and Bloom]," which leads me to think that Joyce's explanation is a red herring. The encounter on the beach, in my reading, unfolds more or less as narrated.

4. David Hayman, *"Ulysses": The Mechanics of Meaning* (Madison: University of Wisconsin Press, 1983), 99.

5. Sean Latham, "Interruption: 'Cyclops' and 'Nausicaa,'" in *The Cambridge Companion to "Ulysses,"* ed. Sean Latham (New York: Cambridge University Press, 2014), 146.

6. Fritz Senn, "Nausicaa," in *James Joyce's "Ulysses": Critical Essays,* ed. Clive Hart and David Hayman (Berkeley: University of California Press, 1974), 285–86.

7. Vicki Mahaffey, "*Ulysses* and the End of Gender," in *A Companion to James Joyce's "Ulysses,"* ed. Margot Norris (Boston: Bedford, 1998), 158.

8. Michael Groden, *"Ulysses" in Progress* (Princeton, NJ: Princeton University Press, 1977), 169.

## 14. "Oxen of the Sun" Guide

1. James H. Maddox Jr., *Joyce's "Ulysses" and the Assault upon Character* (New Brunswick, NJ: Rutgers University Press, 1978), 173.

2. William York Tindall, *A Reader's Guide to James Joyce* (Syracuse, NY: Syracuse University Press, 1979), 199.

3. Karen Lawrence, *The Odyssey of Style in "Ulysses"* (Princeton, NJ: Princeton University Press, 1981), 136, 131.

4. John Gordon, "The Multiple Journeys of 'Oxen of the Sun,'" *ELH* 46, no. 1 (Spring 1979), 158.

5. Marilyn French, *The Book as World: James Joyce's "Ulysses"* (New York: Paragon House, 1993), 171.

6. See James Joyce, "'Ulysses': 'Oxen of the Sun' and 'Circe,' Drafts and TSS," in *The James Joyce Archive* 14, ed. Michael Groden (New York: Garland, 1977), 61, 69, 73, 82, 89, 99, 115; and Jeri Johnson, notes to *Ulysses: The 1922 Text* (Oxford: Oxford University Press, 2008), 907–18.

7. Hugh Kenner, *Dublin's Joyce* (New York: Columbia University Press, 1987), 14.

8. Richard Ellmann, *"Ulysses" on the Liffey* (New York: Oxford University Press, 1972), 136.

9. Tindall, *A Reader's Guide*, 200.

10. David Hayman, *"Ulysses": The Mechanics of Meaning* (Madison: University of Wisconsin Press, 1983), 74.

11. Jeff McClung, "The Physical Fitness of Leopold Bloom," *International Journal of Humanities and Social Science* 2, no. 2 (January 2012): 18.

12. Stanley Sultan, *The Argument of "Ulysses"* (Middletown, CT: Wesleyan University Press, 1987), 288.

13. John Somer, "The Self-Reflexive Arranger in the Initial Style of Joyce's *Ulysses*," *James Joyce Quarterly* 31, no. 2 (Winter 1994): 69.

14. Ian Gunn and Clive Hart, *James Joyce's Dublin: A Topographical Guide to the Dublin of "Ulysses"* (New York: Thames and Hudson, 2004), 64.

15. John Noel Turner, "A Commentary on the Closing of 'Oxen of the Sun,'" *James Joyce Quarterly* 35, no. 1 (Fall 1997): 96.

## 15. "Circe" Guide

1. Sylvia Beach, *Shakespeare and Company* (Lincoln: University of Nebraska Press, 1991), 58.

2. Michael Groden, *"Ulysses" in Progress* (Princeton, NJ: Princeton University Press, 1977), 175.

3. David Hayman, *"Ulysses": The Mechanics of Meaning* (Madison: University of Wisconsin Press, 1983), 102.

4. Karen Lawrence, *The Odyssey of Style in "Ulysses"* (Princeton, NJ: Princeton University Press, 1981), 150–51.

5. Hugh Kenner, "Circe," in *James Joyce's "Ulysses": Critical Essays*, ed. Clive Hart and David Hayman (Berkeley: University of California Press, 1974), 347.

6. Hayman, *"Ulysses,"* 102.

7. Lawrence, *Odyssey of Style*, 161.

8. Hugh Kenner, *Joyce's Voices* (Berkeley: University of California Press, 1978), 92.

9. After much consideration, Joyce decided that "presence of mind" would be one of the correspondences for moly (*Letters* 147).

10. Kevin Dettmar, "The Politicians Who Love *Ulysses*," *New Yorker*, April 23, 2019, www.newyorker.com/culture/cultural-comment/the-politicians-who-love-Ulysses.

11. Don Gifford, *"Ulysses" Annotated*, with Robert J. Seidman, 2nd ed. (Berkeley: University of California Press, 1988), 466.

12. Robert Byrnes, "Weiningerian Sex Comedy: Jewish Sexual Types behind Molly and Leopold Bloom," *James Joyce Quarterly* 34, no. 3 (Summer 1997): 268.

13. Gifford, *"Ulysses" Annotated*, 496.

14. Richard Ellmann, *"Ulysses" on the Liffey* (New York: Oxford University Press, 1972), 146.

15. Ellmann, 149.

16. Kenner, *Joyce's Voices*, 93.

17. Lawrence, *Odyssey of Style*, 160–61.

## 16. "Eumaeus" Guide

1. Marilyn French, *The Book as World: James Joyce's "Ulysses"* (New York: Paragon House, 1993), 212.

2. Richard Ellmann, *"Ulysses" on the Liffey* (New York: Oxford University Press, 1972), 151.

3. Stanley Sultan, *The Argument of "Ulysses"* (Middletown, CT: Wesleyan University Press, 1987), 364.

4. David Hayman, *"Ulysses": The Mechanics of Meaning* (Madison: University of Wisconsin Press, 1983), 102–03.

5. Hugh Kenner, *Joyce's Voices* (Berkeley: University of California Press, 1978), 21.

6. Kenner, 38.

7. The events that occurred in Westland Row Station are unclear, but we know from the end of "Oxen" that Stephen and Lynch had already planned to head into Nighttown, so Buck and Haines wouldn't have had to "give Stephen the slip" (16.266–67).

8. Sultan, *The Argument of "Ulysses,"* 374.

9. Ellmann, *"Ulysses" on the Liffey*, 155.

10. Don Gifford, *"Ulysses" Annotated*, with Robert J. Seidman, 2nd ed. (Berkeley: University of California Press, 1988), 544.

11. Ellmann, *"Ulysses" on the Liffey*, 154.

12. Ellmann, 150.

## 17. "Ithaca" Guide

1. A. Walton Litz, "Ithaca," in *James Joyce's "Ulysses": Critical Essays*, ed. Clive Hart and David Hayman (Berkeley: University of California Press, 1974), 394.

2. Hugh Kenner, *"Ulysses,"* rev. ed. (Baltimore: Johns Hopkins University Press, 1987), 145.

3. Litz, "Ithaca," 396.

4. Frank Budgen, *James Joyce and the Making of "Ulysses"* (Bloomington: Indiana University Press, 1967), 258.

5. Litz, "Ithaca," 393.

6. Karen Lawrence, *The Odyssey of Style in "Ulysses"* (Princeton, NJ: Princeton University Press, 1981), 154.

7. Litz, "Ithaca," 398.

8. Stanley Sultan, *The Argument of "Ulysses"* (Middletown, CT: Wesleyan University Press, 1987), 384.

9. Kenner, *"Ulysses,"* 44.

10. Sultan, *The Argument of "Ulysses,"* 389.
11. Don Gifford, *"Ulysses" Annotated*, with Robert J. Seidman, 2nd ed. (Berkeley: University of California Press, 1988), 576.
12. Kenner, *"Ulysses,"* 137.
13. Gifford, *"Ulysses" Annotated*, 579.
14. Mark Osteen, *The Economy of "Ulysses": Making Both Ends Meet* (Syracuse, NY: Syracuse University Press, 1995), 401.
15. Kenner, *"Ulysses,"* 139.
16. Osteen, *The Economy of "Ulysses,"* 404.
17. Osteen, 403.
18. Litz, "Ithaca," 403.
19. Osteen, *The Economy of "Ulysses,"* 413.
20. Osteen, 412.
21. See Andrew G. Christensen, *"Ulysses*'s Martha Clifford: The Foreigner Hypothesis," *James Joyce Quarterly* 54, no. 3–4 (Spring-Summer 2017): 335–52.
22. Gifford, *"Ulysses" Annotated*, 597.
23. Kenner, *"Ulysses,"* 143.
24. Sultan, *The Argument of "Ulysses,"* 413.
25. Gifford, *"Ulysses" Annotated*, 606.
26. Litz, "Ithaca," 404.

## 18. "Penelope" Guide

1. Quoted in Michael Chabon, *"Ulysses* on Trial," *New York Review of Books*, Sept. 26, 2019, 4.
2. Quoted in Phillip F. Herring, "The Bedsteadfastness of Molly Bloom," *Modern Fiction Studies* 15, no. 1 (Spring 1969): 57.
3. Karen Lawrence, *Who's Afraid of James Joyce?* (Gainesville: University Press of Florida, 2010), 72.
4. Lawrence, 74.
5. Lois Tyson, *Critical Theory Today* (New York: Garland, 1999), 93.
6. Kathleen McCormick, "Reproducing Molly Bloom: A Revisionist History of the Reception of 'Penelope,' 1922–1970," in *Molly Blooms: A Polylogue on "Penelope" and Cultural Studies*, ed. Richard Pearce (Madison: University of Wisconsin Press, 1994), 29.
7. McCormick, 29.
8. McCormick, 33.
9. See Heather Cook Callow, "Joyce's Female Voices in *Ulysses*," *Journal of Narrative Technique* 22, no. 3 (Fall 1992): 151–63.
10. Maud Ellmann, "'Penelope' without the Body," *European Joyce Studies* 17 (2006): 102.
11. Robert McAlmon, *Being Geniuses Together*, rev. ed. (Baltimore: Johns Hopkins University Press, 1997), 119.
12. Richard Ellmann claims that McAlmon exaggerates his alterations to the text (*JJ* 514).
13. M. Ellmann, "'Penelope' without the Body," 98.

14. Stanley Sultan, *The Argument of "Ulysses"* (Middletown, CT: Wesleyan University Press, 1987), 419.

15. Richard Ellmann, *"Ulysses" on the Liffey* (New York: Oxford University Press, 1972), 161.

16. Fr. Robert Boyle, "Penelope," in *James Joyce's "Ulysses": Critical Essays*, ed. Clive Hart and David Hayman (Berkeley: University of California Press, 1974), 414–15.

17. Sultan, *The Argument of "Ulysses,"* 434.

18. David Hayman, *"Ulysses": The Mechanics of Meaning* (Madison: University of Wisconsin Press, 1983), 127.

19. R. Ellmann, *"Ulysses" on the Liffey*, 171.

20. Sultan, *The Argument of "Ulysses,"* 439.

21. R. Ellmann, *"Ulysses" on the Liffey*, 166–67.

22. Sultan, *The Argument of "Ulysses,"* 443.

# SELECTED AND ANNOTATED BIBLIOGRAPHY

As this project has grown, I've realized with each phase of the writing process that I've barely scratched the surface of understanding *Ulysses*. In particular, I recognize that my reading in the enormous body of scholarly criticism is only just beginning, so I humbly apologize for the absence from this list of the many great books and essays that I haven't yet read. I genuinely look forward to discovering them and to expanding my appreciation for the novel by their insight.

That said, certain scholarly works have influenced my reading of *Ulysses*, and I'm glad to provide this list of texts with brief annotations in support of readers interested in delving deeper into the various topics specified below.

## Major Critical Studies and Collections

Adams, Robert Martin. *Surface and Symbol: The Consistency of James Joyce's "Ulysses."* New York: Oxford University Press, 1967.

Adams dives deeply into many of the novel's puzzles, providing factual and historical context that illuminates many of the subtle ironies at work beneath the surface of the text.

Bulson, Eric. *"Ulysses" by Numbers*. New York: Columbia University Press, 2020.

Bulson applies mathematical modeling techniques to chart elements of style and to map relationships between characters as they appear across the novel.

Ellmann, Richard. *"Ulysses" on the Liffey*. New York: Oxford University Press, 1972.

A canonical work of scholarly interpretation that offers commentary on each episode of the novel and provides a useful conceptual framework for understanding the structures and intratextual resonances in *Ulysses*.

French, Marilyn. *The Book as World: James Joyce's "Ulysses."* New York: Paragon House, 1993.

French presents an insightful and comprehensive study of Joyce's shifting styles and points of view in the novel.

Hart, Clive, and David Hayman, eds. *James Joyce's "Ulysses": Critical Essays.* Berkeley: University of California Press, 1974.

This seminal collection offers an essay on each of the eighteen episodes of the novel, offering the influential arguments of a golden generation of Joyceans.

Hayman, David. *"Ulysses": The Mechanics of Meaning.* Madison: University of Wisconsin Press, 1982.

Hayman examines the novel's structure, narrative techniques, and plot and introduces the concept of the arranger.

Kenner, Hugh. *Joyce's Voices.* Berkeley: University of California Press, 1978.

This slim volume presents Kenner's exposition of Joyce's style, including chapters devoted to the Uncle Charles Principle and the notion of the arranger.

———. *"Ulysses."* Rev. ed. Baltimore: Johns Hopkins University Press, 1987.

Kenner tracks the development of Joyce's methods and concepts across the episodes of *Ulysses* while also offering factual insights and careful reading.

Latham, Sean, ed. *The Cambridge Companion to "Ulysses."* New York: Cambridge University Press, 2014.

This collection offers a comprehensive and thought-provoking engagement of the novel, featuring the insights and compelling arguments of contemporary Joyceans.

Lawrence, Karen. *The Odyssey of Style in "Ulysses."* Princeton, NJ: Princeton University Press, 1981.

Lawrence presents a lucid exposition of the way Joyce's style shifts in ways that inform and enhance the experience of the plot, demonstrating style's gradual emergence as the central focus of *Ulysses*.

———. *Who's Afraid of James Joyce?* Gainesville: University Press of Florida, 2010.

Lawrence reprises her argument on Joyce's style and adds further chapters on gender and other topics.

Osteen, Mark. *The Economy of "Ulysses": Making Both Ends Meet.* Syracuse, NY: Syracuse University Press, 1995.

Highly detailed and deeply researched, Osteen's book makes meaning of the money matters in *Ulysses*.

Pearce, Richard, ed. *Molly Blooms: A Polylogue on "Penelope" and Cultural Studies.* Madison: University of Wisconsin Press, 1994.

A collection of essays that engage Molly Bloom and the "Penelope" episode through a variety of critical lenses.

Sultan, Stanley. *The Argument of "Ulysses."* Middletown, CT: Wesleyan University Press, 1987.

In chapters devoted to each episode, Sultan presents a cogent understanding of the novel's progression toward reconciliation. Intervening chapters engage prominent themes and literary elements in *Ulysses*.

## James Joyce's Biography and the Publication of *Ulysses*

Beach, Sylvia. *Shakespeare and Company*. Lincoln: University of Nebraska Press, 1991.

Sylvia Beach's memoir depicts her bookshop as the hub of the Left Bank community of Lost Generation artists and writers. Beach focuses on her relationship with Joyce and Shakespeare and Company's storied publication of the first edition of *Ulysses* in 1922.

Birmingham, Kevin. *The Most Dangerous Book: The Battle for James Joyce's "Ulysses."* New York: Penguin, 2014.

An engrossing narrative of Joyce's development as a writer; his relationship with his partner, Nora Barnacle; his battles with censorship; and Random House's victory in the trial that finally lifted the ban on *Ulysses*.

Budgen, Frank. *James Joyce and the Making of "Ulysses."* Bloomington: Indiana University Press, 1967.

Budgen was a friend of Joyce's and provides a lively blend of episode summaries, critical insight, and depictions of conversations that he shared with Joyce himself about the composition of *Ulysses*.

Ellmann, Richard. *James Joyce*. Rev. ed. New York: Oxford University Press, 1983.

In this seminal biography of James Joyce, Ellmann builds a comprehensive and vivid narrative of Joyce's life while incorporating critical analysis of his works.

Fitch, Noel Riley. *Sylvia Beach and the Lost Generation: A History of Literary Paris in the Twenties and Thirties*. New York: Norton, 1983.

Fitch provides a deeply researched examination of Sylvia Beach's central role in the Left Bank community of writers and artists, paying particular attention to Shakespeare and Company's 1922 publication of the first edition of *Ulysses*.

Groden, Michael. *"Ulysses" in Progress*. Princeton, NJ: Princeton University Press, 1977.

A study of the three principal phases of Joyce's composition of *Ulysses*, revealing the radical revisions that transformed the novel's scope and style.

Joyce, Stanislaus. *My Brother's Keeper: James Joyce's Early Years*, edited by Richard Ellmann. Cambridge: Da Capo, 2003.

Joyce's younger brother's memoir of growing up with James Joyce.

McAlmon, Robert, and Kay Boyle. *Being Geniuses Together, 1920–1930*. Baltimore: Johns Hopkins University Press, 1997.

McAlmon's memoir narrates his experiences within the expatriate community of artists and writers in Paris during the 1920s. He offers a raw and humorous portrait of Joyce that is notable for not idealizing him.

Power, Arthur. *Conversations with James Joyce*. Dublin: Dalkey Archive Press, 2020.

A slim volume depicting recreations of conversations shared between James Joyce and Arthur Power, an Irish painter and critic.

Schloss, Carol Loeb. *Lucia Joyce: To Dance in the Wake*. New York: Picador, 2003.

A biography of Joyce's daughter, Lucia, who earned renown as an avant-garde dancer and suffered from mental illness.

## Other Guides and References

Blamires, Harry. *The New Bloomsday Book: A Guide through "Ulysses."* New York: Routledge, 1996.

A detailed paraphrase of *Ulysses* that serves as a useful resource for understanding confusing passages and summarizing the plot.

Delaney, Frank. *Re: Joyce*. Podcast audio. 2010–17. https://blog.frank delaney.com/re-joyce.

With delightful humor, Delaney explicates *Ulysses* a few sentences or paragraphs at a time. Sadly, Delaney passed in February of 2017, leaving his project unfinished.

Gifford, Don. *"Ulysses" Annotated: Notes for James Joyce's "Ulysses."* With Robert J. Seidman. 2nd ed. Berkeley: University of California Press, 1988.

An indispensable resource for any reader seeking explanation for the thousands of allusions and references contained in *Ulysses*.

Gilbert, Stuart. *James Joyce's "Ulysses": A Study*. New York: Vintage, 1958.

A contemporary of Joyce's, Gilbert establishes many of the critical approaches that have influenced generations of Joyceans since.

Tindall, William York. *A Reader's Guide to James Joyce*. Syracuse, NY: Syracuse University Press, 1979.

A clear and pointed engagement of Joyce's full body of work, including a few pages devoted to each episode of *Ulysses*.

## Topography and Chronology of *Ulysses*

Blodgett, Harriet. "Joyce's Time Mind in *Ulysses*: A New Emphasis." *James Joyce Quarterly* 5, no. 1 (Fall 1967): 22–29.

An early essay exploring the chronology for the events that occur in *Ulysses*.

Gunn, Ian, and Clive Hart. *James Joyce's Dublin: A Topographical Guide to the Dublin of "Ulysses."* New York: Thames and Hudson, 2004.

A treasure trove of maps, timetables, diagrams, and factual information for readers interested in the wheres and whens of *Ulysses*.

McCarthy, Jack, and Danis Rose. *Joyce's Dublin: A Walking Guide to "Ulysses."* New York: St. Martin's, 1988.

This book includes helpful maps and offers detailed explanations of where and how characters travel through Dublin in the text (and between the lines) of *Ulysses*.

Nicholson, Robert. *The "Ulysses" Guide: Tours through Joyce's Dublin.* New York: Routledge, 1989.

Ostensibly, this book guides literary tourists on walking tours through Joyce's Dublin, but it offers considerable insight and compelling conjectures regarding the characters' movements on June 16, 1904.

Rose, Danis. "The Best Recent Scholarship in Joyce." *James Joyce Quarterly* 23, no. 3 (Spring 1986): 325–36.

An essay that makes strident claims regarding routes and chronologies, making particularly strong arguments about how Stephen travels to Sandymount strand between "Nestor" and "Proteus."

# INDEX

Page numbers in *italics* refer to maps and images

258; and Stephen Dedalus, 16, 18, 27, 38, 198, 221

drinking and alcoholism: in "Aeolus," 77, 80, 81; of Bob Doran, 54, 89; in "Circe," 193; as curse of Ireland, 140; in "Cyclops," 137, 138, 139, 140, 142, 143, 144, 145; in *Dubliners,* 54; in "Hades," 61, 65; of Joyce, 203; in "Lestrygonians," 85, 89, 92; in "Lotus-Eaters," 51–53, 54, 56; of MacDowell, 151; in "Oxen of the Sun," 160, 165, 166; of Paddy Dignam, 61, 65, 119, 151; paying for drinks, 138–39; in "Proteus," 35, 39; in "Scylla and Charybdis," 100, 103; in "Telemachus," 18, 20; and temperance retreat in "Nausicaa," 149, 150–51, 152, 153

Driscoll, Mary, 170, 187, 242

drowning imagery, 23, 27, 37–38, 39, 70, 116

*Dubliners*: Bob Doran in, 54, 141; and "Parable of the Plums," 80; reflections of in "Wandering Rocks," 105; use of characters in *Ulysses,* 5, 54, 63, 77, 79, 207, 228, 251; writing of, 7, 118

Dunne, Miss, *106,* 112

Eglinton, John, 97, 98, 100, 102, 103

Eliot, T. S., 72

Elpenor in *The Odyssey,* 61

English imperialism: in "Aeolus," 77–78; and Boylan, 142; in "Circe," 200; in "Cyclops," 142, 143; and Deasy, 28; in "Eumaeus," 211–12; and Haines, 11, 17, 20, 22; and Kernan, 116; in "Nestor," 28, 30; and "The Parable of the Bulls," 169; in "Telemachus," 20, 22; in "Wandering Rocks," 109, 119–20

"Epiphanies" (Joyce), 6

Eucharist, 36, 56, 166, 209, 222

"Eumaeus," 204–16; map, *205*; schema for, 204, 282–83

Eumaeus in *The Odyssey,* 206, 217

evangelical flyer, 83–84, 85, 110, 116, 118, 192

exile: of Joyce, 6–7; of Leopold Bloom,

60; of Stephen Dedalus, 7, 11, 15, 24, 37, 44, 60, 178, 219

Farrell, Cashel Boyle O'Connor Fitzmaurice Tisdall, 87, *106,* 118–19

father, Leopold Bloom as: as failed, 58, 131–32, 167, 191; and Milly, 62, 63; in plot overview, 3. *See also* father-son connection between Bloom and Dedalus

fathers: Artifoni as, 111, 193; Crawford as failed, 79; Deasy as failed, 30, 79, 193; father-son imagery, 5, 21, 22–23, 35, 99, 102; Hamlet as fatherless, 12–13, 21, 99, 102; MacDowell as failed, 151; in plot overview, 3; Simon Dedalus as failed, 23, 35, 62, 110, 115, 194; Stephen Dedalus as fatherless, 20, 23, 38; Telemachus as fatherless, 12, 23

father-son connection between Bloom and Dedalus: in "Circe," 184, 189, 197, 198–203; and disconnection, 210–11, 212, 214, 225; in "Eumaeus," 204–16; first meeting, 173, 223; and homoeroticism, 101, 104, 216; in "Ithaca," 219–20, 222–27; in "Nausicaa," 152–53; in "Oxen of the Sun," 163, 173; in "Scylla and Charybdis," 101, 104

fertility, 160, 163–70, 171, 173, 174

Fitzharris, James. *See* Skin-the-goat

Flower, Henry: in "Circe," 187, 191, 193, 194; in "Lestrygonians," 87; in "Lotus-Eaters," 53, 55–56, 58; as writer of "Eumaeus," 216

Flynn, Nosey, 90–91, 92, 113

foot-and-mouth disease, 29, 78, 80, 100, 141, 168–69, 213

free indirect discourse, 7, 15–16, 147–48

Freemasonry, 54, 92, 139, 190, 246, 255

funeral of Paddy Dignam: in "Aeolus," 75, 77; in "Calypso," 44; in "Circe," 188; in "Eumaeus," 213; in "Hades," 60–71; in "Lotus-Eaters," 57; map, *61*; in "Nausicaa," 151; in "Penelope," 256; in "Wandering Rocks," 119